SAN MATEO CITY PUBLIC LIBRARY

3 9047 02478650 7

D0871799

MAY - 7 1996

FEB 12 1998

MAY - 1 1998

San Mateo Public Library
San Mateo, CA 94402-1592
Questions Answered

V. S. PRITCHETT

At Home
and
Abroad

1989

NORTH POINT PRESS

San Francisco

Public Library San Mateo, CA

910.4
PRICHETT

Copyright © 1989 by V. S. Pritchett
Printed in the United States of America

LIBRARY OF CONGRESS CATALOGING-IN-PUBLICATION DATA
Pritchett, V. S. (Victor Sawdon), 1900-
    V. S. Pritchett: at home and abroad.
    1. Pritchett, V. S. (Victor Sawdon), 1900-
    —Journeys.   2. Authors, English—20th
century—Journeys.   3. Voyages and travels.   I. Title.
PR6031.R7Z528   1989   910.4   88-32958
ISBN 0-86547-385-4

Jacket photograph, "The Bowler" by Evelyn Hofer, originally
appeared in *London Perceived* by V. S. Pritchett, published in
1962 by Harcourt, Brace & World, Inc.

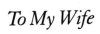

To My Wife

Contents

Acknowledgments

The author wishes to thank the editors of *Holiday Magazine*, who sent him on these journeys, and the editors of the *Christian Science Monitor*, in which the essays on the Appalachians appeared. They have never appeared in book form.

The essays on Czechoslovakia, Poland, Hungary, Romania, Bulgaria, Madrid, Seville, Turkey and Iran appeared in *Holiday Magazine* and also in a book published in the United States as *The Offensive Traveller* (Knopf) and as *Foreign Faces* (Chatto & Windus) in England in 1964.

The long essay on South America published by *Holiday Magazine* has not previously been published in book form.

Introduction

When I look back on my life as a writer I see how much I owe to a sound pair of walking legs. My hopes of the freedom these would give me were almost extinguished at fifteen when I had to leave my decent London grammar school during the First World War and was dumped into the warehouse of the leather trade. I stuck it out for five years until I was caught by the postwar flu epidemic. My one talent was that I was good at French. I craved for France, and with twenty pounds in my pocket I went to Paris, got an office boy's job in a photographic firm and then became a traveler in the glue and shellac trade. My legs took me all over Paris and at one supreme moment one Easter I made a vow—walkers in those days made heroic vows—to walk from Paris to Orléans and to cross the Loire. I was on "the open road." I wrote an account of my trip and the *Christian Science Monitor* published it. I was a travel writer at last.

The editor asked for more travel sketches and then had a reckless idea. He was in trouble with his Irish readers at the time of the Anglo-Irish Treaty. Civil war had broken out. He sent me, a green Englishman, to green Ireland to write not about politics but about how the Irish managed to live while the factions were fighting it out. I was paid twenty-five pounds for six articles. They succeeded. I became their Irish correspondent. For myself the reward was that I met the excellent short story writers O'Flaherty and Frank O'Connor, and even W. B. Yeats.

But news fades. Suddenly I was switched to the troubles in the Spain of Primo de Rivera. The censorship cut down the news, so I was left with time to travel through Spain for a year and a half. Spain changed my life and educated me at last. There I wrote my first book of travel, *Marching Spain*, somewhat in the heroic Bellocian style. I "marched" through the poorest and least-known region of the country, the one that runs along the Portuguese frontier to Vigo. Thirty years later I wrote a far more informative book about Spain, *The Spanish Temper*. The odd thing is that when I was a school-boy I had written a preposterous prose poem on the Spanish Conquest of the Moors in Granada. I had cribbed the story from Washington Irving's *Life of Columbus*.

Now I was a seasoned foot-slogger. I went briefly, for the first time, to the United States and there I was drawn by chance to walk among the "lost" poor whites of the Appalachians, long before it became a national park. Once more I was among the poor—people as "backward" but as noble as the lost people of the Portuguese-Spanish frontier. Incidentally, among them I came across a ninety-year-old man called Pritchett who said he had "fit" in the Civil War.

I settled down at last in London to become a short story writer, novelist and literary critic on *The New Statesman*—in short, a literary gent of the thirties. My most successful novel, *Dead Man Leading*, is the tale of a disastrous expedition up the Amazon. I had never seen the Amazon. I simply made a small model of the river, with string and matchsticks, on the lawn of my house. The ants in the grass served as my explorers. I had studied the diaries of a number of missionaries in that region in the British Museum. One or two real explorers praised the book when it appeared, and indeed when, after World War II, I did go to South America and "up the Amazon" to write a very long piece on that continent for the excellent American periodical *Holiday Magazine*, I was astonished by the accuracy of my invention. After my Spanish experience and my knowledge of Spanish exploration I was excited by the sight of those lands that had made the Spaniards rich, by the tale of their glories and their disasters. And I saw the supreme sights of the Pacific and the Andes. At any rate, I had graduated as a literary globe-trotter.

At Home
and
Abroad

1

South America

"If I were a young man," a famous editor said to me in London years ago, "I would pack up and go to South America for life. That is the continent of the future." Years later, the splendid chance came. Last October I packed up and flew off, not indeed for life, but on a trip several months long which took me from Panama down the Pacific coast of the continent, over the Andes into the Argentine and up through Buenos Aires, Montevideo and into Rio de Janeiro and those lovely coastal towns of old Portuguese Brazil to the Amazon.

The impressions I have set down here are those of the rapid traveler who cannot "stay for an answer." But years of living in Spain and Portugal had had a profound effect upon me: I was eager to see how their superb, nation-creating civilizations had transplanted. I wanted to see what the Spaniards and the Portuguese had done; how America and the Indian and Negro races they had mixed with had changed them. I believe in differences, and I have tried to set out how the Colombian differs from the Peruvian, the Chilean from the Argentine, the Argentine from the Uruguayan, and the remarkable Brazilians from all. I already knew a good deal of their history: I went to see its natural setting. That alone is stupendous. For anyone who lives by eye and ear, as I do, to use them in the exotic South American scene is a major pleasure of life. In the months I was there I flew a good ten thousand miles, saw men and women at their most primitive and most civilized, crossed from sea to sea, from mountain to jungle. Mine was, quite literally, a flying visit; but the impressions of the flying visit are sharp and indelible.

Colombia

By half past six it was dark and the red light at the tip of the plane's wing began to wink. There was a great ragged continent of black cloud and across the sea there were mountains mixing with it. Then we saw a feeble pan of lights spread out and we were being tipped into Cartagena, Colombia. The moment of arrival in a new continent is momentous. I put away the brochures, the maps and the books—the inevitable Prescott, the indispensable Robert Herring—and, in full ignorance, prepared for the body blow of South America.

Like some hot black body, the tropical night flops down on the northerner. There were black faces, white suits, Negro voices that whispered hoarsely or Indians speaking in the Caribbean twitter, and every human being shamelessly scratching or swatting as the squadrons of insects flew in. Luggage arrived in the customhouse. Officials and porters gazed at it meltingly, reluctant to touch it, as if every suitcase were a private poem. One nervous traveler shouted, and the whole customhouse stopped whispering and scratching to stare at the loud man, as if they were seeing some new kind of bird. There were one or two pretty girls and they parted their very red lips. They had lost many of their front teeth. (In all the tropical part of South America, east and west, in the months ahead, I was to dread the moment when a girl opened her mouth.)

And then we were driving on a road full of potholes and flood water, outside the walls of Cartagena—the only walled port on the continent. The houses looked like painted bird cages at night with black birds in them, and the sea crashed under the lunatic coconut palms of the beach. That night in Cartagena we were given haddock, coconut and rice to eat. The heat turned

4

to steam, the rain came down like bullets and ran in lilac lakes down the flooded streets. "I get restless when it rains," the barman said. "I feel I want something and I don't know what it is." The people of Cartagena looked like that the next day, even the macaws in the garden of the hotel; until the sun suddenly came through and on the boil.

Cartagena sizzles at the top of the South American leg of mutton. The town is unique in the continent; it is more Caribbean than South American and more Mediterranean than Caribbean; it is an Algeciras towed out into the tropics. And there is a similar history of piracy, for here you are at the beginning of South American history and Spanish rule and in that corner where the Spanish stain is deepest. From here, through Colombia and Ecuador down to Peru, you are on the treasure route of Pizarro. No other part of South America is so Spanish. Cartagena was one of the best harbors in the north and it was one of the points from which the treasure ships sailed under convoy. Drake and all the pirates knew this. Drake captured the town and exacted a huge ransom. The French got something like five million dollars in one raid. So Cartagena built its wall forty feet thick, a pleasant promenade now for the Sunday parade, but not until the middle of the eighteenth century, when a last grand assault by the British was stingingly repelled, was Cartagena safe.

Now it is a gay and decent little town. "Not like Barranquilla down the coast," the loyal waiter said—and on subjects like this, waiters are infallible. Barranquilla is the new modern port where Colombians ship their coffee. "The police make the people wear numbers on their clothes at the masked fiesta of Barranquilla, so they can pick out anyone who draws a knife or fires a revolver. Never trouble in Cartagena, but at Barranquilla and"—raising his eyes to the furry mountains—"in the interior *mucho cuchillo*," plenty of knife work. The worst thing that happened to me in Cartagena was that a monkey stole my pipe.

And so, preserved in the sun's tropical amber, Cartagena is as Spanish as Quito in Ecuador and Cuzco in Peru. You see the same stone arcades in the squares, the same overhanging balconies of carved and prettily painted wood, the same low roofs with the wide eaves covered with red tiles, the same windows barred with wood. Even the bars of the windows of the fine Palace of the Inquisition are made of hardwood painted white. There are

5

the same patios the Spaniards learned to build from the Moors, the same narrow streets to shut out the overwhelming sun.

The dome of the cathedral is checkered in white and cinnamon, the belfries of the churches are as white as starch; and inside, you meet the golden rococo altars and the fine neglected Spanish cloisters with their palms. Yet Cartagena is not Spain, for it is an Indian and mulatto town. All shops and offices and doorways open to the street to let the sticky air flow through. The fans spin on the ceilings. Men are asleep in the chairs of innumerable barbers, or, in their white shirts and trousers, sit drinking their twenty or thirty cups of black coffee a day in the cafés. There are fruit-juice stalls every few yards and there is every kind of tropical fruit in the market. Rows of mulatto girls sit at their sewing machines in the shops, black babies play naked round the shacks, and from the shrine on the burning green hill that dominates Cartagena you watch the vultures wheeling down and alighting with their strange double bounce upon the refuse. Taxi drivers talk Hemingway.

These tropical towns are all alike. The power of concentration has melted away in timeless distraction. At every door and window a figure stands in gentle lassitude. Nearly every woman, you would say, was pregnant and had a needle and cotton in her hand. She will not be in the act of sewing yet, but sometime in the next ten minutes, and not taking her eyes from the sight she is looking at, she will slowly begin to put the needle into the cloth. There it will remain a long time before she remembers to draw it through.

Groups of half-dressed men lounge in tropical desuetude over the balconies of the broken-down inn, gazing at the market, as if they were rags hung up to dry on a line. Three half-naked men, with a drum, a tambourine and a long whistle like a cane, tootle and knuckle their monotonous tune, hour after hour, and a listening crowd will close round as if hypnotized. In the booths of the market, if one person is buying, he leans on the counter and half a dozen lean with him in a silent, helpless gregariousness.

You can trace the centuries easily in Cartagena. There are the citadel and the churches, not as rich as those in Spain, simply because the treasure was sent home. There is the eighteenth-century fort; there is the desolate statuary of the shoddy nineteenth-century square commemorating the liberation from Spain, when all the South American republics fell into anarchy for two or three generations, lost Spanish craftsmanship and order and split up into family factions. There is the terrible shack town, half under water, a place of misery where the women are always sweeping and washing, but where there are always flowers and an oil lamp on the table. I thought of the poem of Neruda, the Chilean poet; in all their wretchedness, he observed, the poor of South America have their flowers. There is the Californian suburb, the new architecture and the luxury hotel where you can swim in the pool, listen to the Argentine and Mexican singers in the air-conditioned restaurant and go to the casino and, with proper South American passion, gamble until dawn. And you will meet the temperamental engineers of the foreign company that is finding what every South American republic prays for more than all the gold of Pizarro: oil. Oil wins half the battle for solvency. Colombia, like Venezuela and Peru, can stand on its own feet because it has oil.

The only way to get out of Cartagena, unless you have weeks on your hands, is to fly. This is true of almost all South American cities. Until the airplane came they lived in extraordinary isolation. Cartagena is a good place from which to survey the continent that lies before us. We shall have to form new ideas about size and population.

The republic of Colombia is the size of Texas and California combined, but two thirds of it lies in the wilderness and jungle of the upper Orinoco and Amazon and is scarcely inhabited. The population of 12 million lives on the tableland between the Andes or in the narrow tropical plain on the coast. Only 2.5 million of these people are "white"; most of the rest are mixed white and Indian.

If we look beyond Colombia, from this beginning, we have to imagine a continent which is more than twice the size of the United States and nearly twice the size of Europe. Brazil alone is larger than the United States. To the European, all the Americas, north, south and central, seem empty lands; even in Uruguay, where it is most thickly populated. South America has only thirty-five persons to the square mile, seventeen is nearer the average; and in Bolivia, the South American Tibet, the density is only eight. In the United States the density is fifty-three; in underpopulated France two hundred two! We shall have the impression of traveling to a string of distant cities, with little but geography between them. There are a few motor roads, but it is rather startling if they connect one place with another. There are few railways. Before I left London I heard a British manufacturer scheming to send machinery overland from Belém, up the Amazon to La Paz. "The country hasn't even been explored," said the scornful Bolivian consul. Those machines would have just sunk into the forest.

So, we shall be flying in all kinds of aircraft, from the superb international planes, the "mixed"—goods and passengers—and the scores of little private and company planes that hop out of some twentieth-century capital into the camps of primitive man. Up the Amazon there will be more danger from poisoned arrows than from engine trouble; in the Andes we could simply be lost altogether. We shall look out of the windows of our luxury hotel at a president's palace or a mulatto shack town, at a handsome park or Indians trotting barefoot to market.

But, more than anything else, more than life or a collection of civilizations, we shall be flying over Nature in its most primitive masses. Where else can we fly, day after day, for almost four thousand miles if we like, down one of the highest, longest and most turbulent mountain chains in the world—the cordillera of the Andes—with their unnumbered volcanoes and always, somewhere, an earthquake? And, beside them, observe a desert like the two-thousand-odd miles of withered and glaring sand dune that runs from Peru south into Chile? There is the great billiard table of the Argentine pampas; there are the thousands of miles of wilderness and scrub, and then the unbelievable jungle of the Amazon water system, more than thirty-three hundred miles across the country and immensely deep.

In that flight we shall be in a green mid-Atlantic—a limitless pan of crinkled green, stewing like kale beneath us, featureless except where the palm top stars it or where there is a steamlike puff from a tree in silver leaf. And, as we move from mass to mass, we shall be caught like flies in molasses at the tropical sea level; then, suddenly, shot on to a tableland where the ground floor is ten thousand feet up. We shall cross peaks at twenty thousand and come down short of breath and with hammers going in our heads. In the morning it will be summer; in the afternoon midwinter. We shall know all the world's climates from day to day. After sweltering in Cartagena, I was soon shuddering in the cold drizzle of Bogotá.

And the people? It is too early for us to say yet, but we ought to be clear about what to call them. It is dangerous to call them Latin Americans, for they come from Spanish, Portuguese and Indian or Negro stock, in many but not all of the republics; and the Spanish and Portuguese are not pure Latins. Their culture is a modification of the Latin by the African—Africa of the Arab in Spain, Africa of Arab and Negro in Portugal; and in both those countries, for many centuries, the Arab was the conqueror, the ruler and man of learning, the superior of the white southern European. And phrases like Latin America or Ibero-America leave out the American Indian who in Mexico and Peru created the only Indian urban civilization in the Americas. The South American Indian was massacred but not exterminated; he exists in his millions. He is not dying off in reservations. Bolivia is over 80 percent Indian or mestizo and there the politically conscious Indian miner has marched armed into La Paz and claimed his country.

To the American from the United States—the North American, as these people call him, for they regard themselves as the only true Americans—South America is at a stage comparable to the United States of frontier days. To Europeans, it is a crude Europe—imitated, parodied, transposed. They see only two unifying forces: the Roman Catholic faith, and language—the Spanish or the Portuguese.

And we recognize at once the intense differences separating republics which—according to the North American ethos—ought to be united. Differences of stock and history, of work and climate, have been stamped all the more firmly upon these peoples by absence of communications. Uruguay is the first modern welfare state; Ecuador is remote in a feudal order; the Argentine is half modern Italian, Chile half central European; in Brazil alone the melting pot has really melted. Impossible to run the twentieth-century machine over these republics and make them all alike, even impossible to make them homogeneous within their own borders; the men of Cartagena or Barranquilla in Colombia, for example, are utterly different from the people who inhabit the highlands in the same country.

It is true that the European atmosphere of South America is intensified by the vitality and conservative individualism of southern Europe, by immigration and the dominance, in the nineteenth century, of European capital; in the twentieth century the economic power is passing rapidly into the hands of the United States, and where Europe once educated the upper classes, this role is passing to North America also. We cannot foretell yet the personality of South America when it emerges. The profoundly American

9

things are the dispersal of the intense European man into greater space; the melting pot; the tearing up of the old European political and social roots. Only the cultural roots are still markedly European. In this last respect Brazil is the exception; it is creating a new race with a pure Brazilian culture.

What is the Colombian variation on the South American theme? The tourist with time on his hands takes the paddle steamer up the Magdalena River to the railhead for Bogotá, learns patience as it sticks on the sandbanks and he stares into the water for the snakes that lie among the roots of the water lilies, and for his first sight of the obscene anaconda. Bogotá is the least accessible of the South American capitals, nearly nine thousand feet up in the cold drizzle of the plateau where the Andes gather for the great snowy procession southward. Bogotá used to regard itself as a kind of Athens—a place of high-minded intellectual and political discussion in the best-spoken Spanish of a continent which has murdered the mother tongue, the place where "even the bootblacks have read Proust." It is, or was, a fine colonial Spanish city with a steady tradition of decent behavior in politics. And then, after the war, the ideas of Franco and Hitler entered Colombia; assassination, civil war degenerating into murderous anarchy, spread over the whole country. In Bogotá there are machine guns outside the president's palace, the free press is muzzled. Just now a General rules. His task was to stop wholesale murder and village burning. He succeeded for a time, but rather than have the traditional parliamentary parties back, he tried to found a new party on the Peronista model; the villages in the backlands have once more joined the guerrillas and there has been fighting. Colombia's still far from the relaxing, free and dignified way of political life that was once its pride.

There was a politico sitting in a newspaper office. I won't give his name or the town where I met him. Gentle, cultivated, a figure typical of those who have been educated in Europe, he had survived the violent rioting and burning at the time of the International Conference of American States in 1948, the shooting in the Chamber of Representatives in 1949, the machine-gunning in the streets, the horrible massacres in public halls, and his talk recalled the shame of the liberals who had failed to stop Hitler. The fact is, as he explained, that Colombia, Peru and Ecuador have the violence in the Spanish inheritance. The other fact, which he did not explain, is that the highly developed Europeanized group in these countries is the flower of a small "white" minority. The mysterious, upheaving force around them is the mass of the mestizo population who have never been allowed beyond a certain point in political and economic power.

Meanwhile the traveler flies with delight from one valley in Colombia to the next: to Medellín, to exquisite Popayán, and the lovely warm Cauca Valley, to the boom town of Cali, half of it white and modern among the flowering tulip trees of its romantic ravine, the other half low, pink-walled, barred and shuttered colonial Spain. The women of Cali are lovely; the town appears full of beautiful, educated girls. The people are ecstatic about each new building, each new suburb, its magnificent club, its immense hospital, its colleges and schools. Last year the electricity came on full and now the narrow Spanish streets are jazzed up with neon lighting; the cars speed along the river drive and the new roads. I was driven by a psychiatrist. "Next year," he said, as we charged a few rival cars—"we hope to have our first traffic lights"—and next year, his profession seemed to imply, he hoped for the first crop of twentieth-century nervous breakdowns. For there is another side to this agreeable picture. I counted twenty murders in the province that weekend. "These people do not dream," the psychiatrist complained. "If there is anything in the unconscious it comes out in action at once."

On the mountainside outside Cali are the immense shack villages, waterless, evil, infected. Meat and bread are beyond the purses of the wretched. They work in the cane fields and on the farms; on Friday they carry their branch of bananas home to feed the family for the week. They are industrious, intelligent, imaginative people; but once the *aguardiente* which is made from molasses gets inside the idle, smiling man in jeans who is fingering the blade of his machete, he will use the weapon on his neighbor instead of on the sugar cane.

Green, fertile, flowering, rich in all fruits and crops, the Cauca Valley is lovely under its mountains. The mulatto women stand knee-deep in the streams washing their linen. In the streets of Cali there is always someone sweeping the dust off the pavement with a broom. At night you see the twinkle of altars through the open doors of the churches. You see the signals of lovers from doorway to window or the couples under the jasmine-scented trees of the park by the rushing water of the ravine. The air is warm and fragrant and heavy and the villas of the rich look like wedding cakes. It is idyllic.

And there is the pleasure of knowing this is a place growing carelessly. In the restaurant the saxophone player did not play to us but went out to tootle on the balcony because he hoped to see a friend; and when the couple at the next table got up primly to dance, they had to do so with circumspection; a rat was running round the tables.

Ecuador

I got up at six and left Cali on a damp morning for Quito in Ecuador. The clouds were low on the mountains but after a few hours we saw the green forests give way to the bare, brown, terraced mountains of Ecuador. We were entering the valley where Quito stands at one end of its famous avenue of volcanoes.

Ecuador is a small country and, like the others of the Spanish corner, it is divided into three parts: the tropics, the tableland and the peaks. Between 10 and 15 percent of its people are white, of Spanish blood, with some central European refugees; the remaining two million odd (they guess) are Indian, mestizo, Negro or mulatto. There are also a few Asiatics. In Ecuador you stand in soundless and breathless leagues of acacia scrub, among the volcanoes and, for the first time, among Indians. From Quito to Cuzco and on to La Paz, in the Tibet of South America, you are always at ten thousand feet or more, breathing thin air, deafened by the hammers in the head, and a little mad. The skin cracks, the voice goes husky. You stare back at the expressionless stare of Mongolians who seem to have been cut out of mahogany by an imperceptible dry wind that is as fine as a knife. These men and women, sexually distinguishable only because the woman has a little mahogany baby sticking its head out of the blanket on her back, are the dispossessed heirs and slaves of the Inca empire, and now the bond servants of the feudal estates of Ecuador and Peru. (The Inca empire lasted four hundred years and stretched from Quito down to Chile, where the Araucanian Indians fought it off.)

The Indians squat, still as stone, against the walls under the arcades of Quito, motionless in their ponchos, oddly sophisticated in their brown trilby (fedora) hats. They seem to possess the city by force of peaceable but perhaps meaningful vigil. They camp in the markets, they cry "Oh, Father" or "Oh, Mother" as they kneel before the altars in the churches.

I went late one night to the congress and, in that little parliament like a shabby and romantic nineteenth-century ballroom, with its chocolate pillars, its gold cornices and its oil paintings of generals and presidents, the Indians had turned the visitors' gallery into a camp. The men in ponchos and hats stood in a row looking down at the black-coated politicians; the women, squatting on the floor behind them, fed their babies in a mess of sugary drinks and nutshells. Some were drunk. One drunken soldier, with only one leg, was propped against the wall, snoring louder than any oratory from below.

"The captain," someone said. "The hero of the revolution." Which revolution?

A man from Uruguay said that such homely and feudal behavior would never be allowed in Montevideo. An Ecuadorian apologized. To me it was moving.

Occasionally the men standing at the edge of the balcony cheered and applauded. A second later, the women behind clapped their hands too. Was it the new democratic feeling for freedom and free speech for all, established by Galo Plaza, that distinguished and genial president and landowner, educated in the United States? Or was it the old feudal life of the hacienda where the servants gather with familiarity about the masters, the old human democracy? I do not know. I suppose some Ecuadorians will be annoyed when I mention the youth in jeans who yawned on the steps of the president's dais and scratched his armpits, but I hope not. The sight of the working parliament in Ecuador was, for me, one of the most hopeful sights in South America.

The Indians are in the streets, the Indians are in the art. There is a cult of the Indians. But they are still serfs on the huge estates where the Friesian-Holsteins graze in the lovely Andean valleys.

Quito is the most Spanish-looking city in South America and architecturally the richest. The fine things of all this Pacific coast are survivals. Earthquakes have destroyed city after city. Travelers complain of the lack of Gothic architecture but—who knows?—there may have been Gothic brought down in a cloud of rubble three or four hundred years ago. The wonderful churches of Quito are now drenched in the Inca gold of the baroque. The Spanish artists came out here at the beginning of the sixteenth century and (it is evident) there must have been Moorish converts among the conquerors. You look up at magnificent ceilings of cedar conceived in the Moorish geometry and honeycomb. The noble doorway of the Compañía is in the full flourish of Spanish baroque; San Francisco echoes the Escorial outside Madrid; the tiled domes of churches and cathedral recall Valencia and Saragossa, and as the day ends, you hear the rancorous Spanish bells. The riches of Quito in Ecuador and of Cuzco in Peru show us that if the Spaniards were destroyers they were also builders. Pizarro, the swineherd from the tableland of Castile who became the great conquistador, the discoverer of Peru, the destroyer of the Inca Empire on the tableland of the Andes, led his men on a staggering enterprise that began as a search for gold and plunder, but the imperial and religious impulse was behind it. The Spaniards brought their fighting powers and religious fanaticism from hundreds of years of warfare against the Moorish invaders in Spain; and some of that fighting was in living memory of Pizarro's men. The bells of Quito ought to suggest to the imaginative ear the bells of a resurgent civilization.

In Quito there was gold for coloring the decorative orgy and there were hardwoods for carvers of pulpits and chapel rails, choirs and organ lofts; for the sculpturing of angels' wings and climbing flowers and peeping cherubs and saints that seem to waltz like people in a painted enchantment. Fancifully they carved the nipples of fertile women or the faces of demons upon the choir stalls; with naïve terror they cut the wing and eye and claw of the condor or of some mythical bird; under the severe thumb of the classical master, his Indian craftsmen copied the classical Spanish austerity. In Mexico, where the Spaniards were extirpating a bloody religion and felt themselves more violently challenged, they allowed the Indian craftsmen less freedom. In any case, Mexico felt the first passion of the Spanish impulse; South America felt the second, less exalted wave. Pizarro was not Cortés and the Indians were less bloody. The madonnas have sometimes an Indian look and are, at any rate, less fair than the Mediterranean goddesses; the Christs bleed at the knees for, no less than the Spaniards, these people delight in the sight of blood or at least do not show the usual northern aversion to it.

A great many of the Indians in Ecuador are the tied serfs on the great estates. They live in clay-colored adobe huts which shake to dust in their earthquakes. You see the Indians at a country market like Otavalo, stirring their stewpans or eating some yellow mess, one or two eating, one or two against the wall brooding, one or two stretched out dead-drunk. They have been at the market since the hard cold dawn. They stand before their sacks of beans, their yellow and speckled corn, their heaps of newly sheared wool, the wool they have dyed and woven into ponchos, blankets and scarves, before their trays of golden-looking glass beads. These, coiled many times round the neck or dangling in great loads, indicate the wealth of the woman who wears them. The women, in their heavy, white, basinlike hats, sit and stare across their earthenware, their carven bulls, their heaps of purple pineapples and tropical fruits. These markets are crowded and silent—though you hear the loudspeaker in the modern market—and there will be no sound but the whisper of bare feet on the ground. Speak to the Indians and few can answer, for they do not speak Spanish, but they will utter an obsequious and bashful twittering.

By midday they will be drunk on *chicha*, the sugared alcohol made from maize, or on the alcohol that has been collected in a hole cut in the stems of the aloes which stand along the roads of the wilderness like swords. A pole with a white rag sticking out of a doorway is the sign of a *chicha* seller; a red flag denotes not the Communist party but the butcher; a bunch of flowers, the seller of coca leaves. There are sacks of these dried leaves in the market. They are bitter-tasting and the Indians add lime leaves to sweeten them. The coca comforts, but the lime dries and draws the mouth. Out comes the flask of *aguardiente* and the marketplace is harmlessly drugged and drunk at once—harmlessly because the Indian, unlike the mulatto, does not get out his knife, but rolls stiffly about with the innocence of an uncoordinated marionette.

There is continual controversy about the evils of coca chewing and the wickedness of the landlords who grow it and the governments that allow it to be grown. The Incas knew the power of the coca leaf. The rulers controlled its use. They reserved it for soldiers; for the wonderful runners who carried news and royal commands along the mountain highway from Quito to Cuzco; and for their priests. To the soldiers and runners the coca leaf gave energy in the thin and exhausting air of the high mountains; in religion, the leaf was used only in those annual ceremonies which required religious ecstasy. The coca leaf was rare and valued. The Spaniards broke the monopoly and allowed it to everyone, and now it has become the general drug that takes the mind of the Indian off his continual hunger.

No one can say whether the passivity of the Indian is the result of life at high altitude—it has obviously affected his voice—or how far the drug has induced it. One can only watch him stagger home, his tarry pigtail wagging, across the plain where the blue and yellow acacia shrub grows on the burial mounds of his great ancestors, to the little hut on the great estate. Cotopaxi and Chimborazo, those two volcanoes with the starch-white peaks; green Coliachi by its cold lake where the flocks of white herons rise and the women beat the clothes with frothing aloe leaves—all the volcanoes of Ecuador stare at him as he tumbles into the ditch or a friend props him desperately against a wall. Will it matter to him that the Fascist party is on the decline, that Galo Plaza has given friendly lessons in Western democracy, or that the rich traders of the tropical plain at Guayaquil are troublesome to the well-educated rulers of Quito? What does he think of the rich dancers and the excellent band at the nightclub outside the city? And does he know that down in tropical Ecuador thrive his red-painted cousins, the Colorados, who paint their bodies with the dye of the *achiote* seed? We cannot tell. He is simply one of the millions of violently disparate human beings in South American life.

The Inca highway ran from Quito down to Cuzco. You can sometimes see it scratched and zigzagging up the flanks of the mountains—miles of it are still paved—and imagine the relays of royal runners who brought the news of the Spaniards' arrival over a thousand miles in a day or two to the emperor Atahualpa, whom Pizarro captured and murdered.

But Cuzco was still to come. I sat eating cold lobster in hot peppery sauce and drinking beer at midday at the airport in Quito, waiting for the international plane to take us down to the tropical port of Guayaquil, where the sea was white in the heat; and then on to Lima in Peru. We would arrive in the evening. It was the first of the superb Pacific flights.

Peru

In Ecuador, even in that valley called the avenue of volcanoes, you know the Andes only by one or two peaks that stand up like white strangers in a sky that is as blue at the zenith as it is at the horizon. Now, flying down the coast over the sea's edge, you can survey at leisure the full splendor of the cordillera, hour after hour. Whether to look at the Peruvian mountain or desert is the difficulty. Between twenty-five and forty miles wide, the desert runs for fourteen hundred miles of bleached, blinding, waterless sand and continues into the chemical-and-copper desert of Chile. Occasionally a short Pacific watercourse brings a stain of vegetation, but, in the main, the desert is picked as white as a skeleton by the ferocious sun. At sunrise, there is the sound of drums: it is the curious music of the sand grains being blown against the dunes. From this flat desert floor the Andes rise abruptly, so that for the first time in our lives we see mountains from top to bottom, from sea level to their peaks.

They are set out, capped by their ice helmets and snow shields, with the flash and the packed shadows of some endless encampment of chivalry standing around its tents; and on clean, blue afternoons, as we fly along them hour after burning hour, we cannot hide the feeling that the wit of man in his roaring dragonfly is triumphantly vying with the majesty of nature. They have mere pedestrian eternity; *we* have been given these immortal moments. There are very few boring flights in South America—the drama of climate and geography, of sea and jungle, sees to that. But this flight down the Andes is one of the superb ones. Ocean, desert and mountain compose themselves into a spectacle which, I think, cannot be surpassed on earth— for the Himalayas have not the sea to set them off—and the sight holds for fifteen hundred miles.

And, if so much of the sublime becomes monotonous, there is the strange bamboozling of the cold Humboldt ocean current to trick the eye. Small balletlike puffs of cloud come over the sea an hour or so off Lima and gradually curdle and thicken until they are a solid floor beneath us. It covers the desert, moves in among the lower hills until a whole new fantastic region of false milky harbors, misleading bays and lagoons without reality is created as the sun sinks. We are gradually deceived by the new, untrue version of the coast, and when the plane suddenly turns and takes a steep dive into the cloud over Lima, we get the fright of our lives. We have forgotten the cloud floor; we think we are diving into the sea, and come through low over the sunless roofs of Lima to a landing that is just this side of hysteria.

Under its pan of gray cloud Lima is Londonish. Its pavements are always wet and greasy in the small hours at which, inevitably, you set out on all South American journeys. Lima ought to be an oven, but the cloud from the Humboldt current has made it livable. You sweat in the sun, but there is a deadly cold and continual flutter of air in the ears; you shiver in the heat. It is really a pleasant climate made for civilization, like the climate of Chile or the Mediterranean, but you have to get used to it and use the Peruvian cunning. I was ill in Lima. The Peruvian doctor said, "Don't go to the mountains yet." The maid said, "Don't go out today. There is a cloud."

It is a city of flowers. In the cloisters of the University—the oldest in South America—you might be in one of the ecstatic patios of Seville; in the gardens and avenues that run down to the sea at Miraflores, along the smart corniche and in the gardens of the hotels, the tropical trees blossom heavily and all blooms are brilliant and large. You walk at a saunter, taking peaceful breaths. You are breathing something else. What is it? It ought to be the serenity of the Mediterranean, but here, in Peru, the serenity is what they call "the Pacific sadness," a loneliness in the midst of well-being that comes, perhaps, of looking across a sun-slashed ocean for thousands of miles, into nothing. The Andes lock out the wars and troubles of the world.

The Peruvian quarrels are internal, bursting out in coups d'état, in abortive revolutions, in *pronunciamientos*, ending in the execution against some village wall, in imprisonment on that island of San Lorenzo that floats like a distant liner out at sea, or in the indignant newspaper articles of the exiles; but these are the savageries of what is really family life. "Here," people of the middling sort say, "we can live at peace."

Earthquakes, sudden incursions of new wealth from oil at Talara, from mines, precious stones, wool, tea and cotton, have destroyed a great deal of the old Lima, with its single-story houses with the iron-grilled windows, the high doors, balconies, the painted porches and the inner courts. Round the pretty square of the Pueblo Libre with its remarkable National Museum of Anthropology and Archaeology—it has the richest archaeological collection in Peru, indeed in South America—and in the streets by the bullring, you see the old city. Life here is simple and shuttered. It goes on in courtyards, roofed by matting against the sun, where the smoke of the charcoal fires rises and the flowers grow and the mulattoes and cholos sprawl with their hats over their eyes and the tarry-haired women call out. The old Lima had its fantastics. There is a pagodalike building near the bullring, built (I was told) by a jealous rich man so that his wife could sit at the top of the painted-glass tower and, from this purdah, see the bullfight for nothing.

Of course, the fine, new white schools and popular suburbs, the streets of painted villas, the mixture of architectural styles copied from the Californian and Mexican and the half-timbered Tudor English, are dramatically modern. They indicate that (with Venezuela and Colombia) Peru is solid in the South American boom, and by solid we mean it can deal abroad in foreign exchange and not be on the rocks like Bolivia, shaking like Chile, unbalanced like the Argentine and living breathlessly off its prospects like Brazil. Oil! There is a sigh of relief. And if not oil, there are mines hardly touched, in the mountains.

No South American state speaks well of another. To the rest, Peru is at once privately fantastic, outwardly formal in the Spanish manner, stuck fast in pride and the past. Peru has some of the Spanish pomp, the lazy official pride, the obstinate and moneyed addiction to custom. Pizarro founded Lima; he is buried in the cathedral. The city was the solid administrative capital of Spanish rule.

The struggle between the outlying regions and the center goes on in all South American states. Here, in Peru, where distances are great, local corruption and indifference is the inevitable result of overpowering central government. The Inquisition looked after religious heresy; but Lima had the administrators and the seventeenth-century courtiers, the vested interest in the distribution of trade that Spain imposed, and even the caste system that put the creole (or colonist) under the thumb of the Spaniard. Spain had even the fantastic notion that it could reconquer Peru as late as 1866, after Peru had known independence for a generation.

There is a somnolent weightiness in the Spanish inheritance, the habit of sitting impregnably on wealth, the strengthening of related families into nations within the nation. Brash, pushful, Italianized people from the Argentine come up to Lima and find society impenetrable. They play polo with the rich but never find friendship. As in Spain, casual encounters everywhere; in the home never. The young girls are chaperoned. There is even a fixed day upon which sea bathing begins; it would be solecism, vagrancy, a sin, to bathe a day sooner. Custom, custom! Lima has its tea hour, as elegant as it used to be in Madrid in the '20s. The rich women and their beautiful daughters sit stiffly, speechlessly, dressed by Fath and Dior, manacled in gold, set off by diamonds and emeralds in that silent and most deadly of all warfares of women: the warfare of jewelry. Each diamond is an accurate shot at neighboring diamonds in the room; even more it is brilliant with contempt for the luxury of Buenos Aires, Rio or New York. The flash of a sugar estate answers the challenge of an oil well or a mine, the fortune of a hacienda weighs itself against the emeralds of a fortune cut out of the Andean rock.

Behind the glitter are the ruthless struggles of politics, the suppressed political parties. And as the tea party goes on, the German, American and British engineers and commercial men go boisterously past the tables, having already drunk too much. Foreign capitalism has built the railroads, the factories, drilled the wells and opened up the country. With intelligence and disdain the clever and lethargic Peruvians watch the aliens and then drive off in their Cadillacs to enjoy themselves, or sit playing poker dice and sending out messages by the page boys.

And, being Spanish, Lima has kept the bullfight, where the other countries, except Venezuela, are either bored by it or have forbidden it. The bullring is across the bridge at the top of the city, under the mountain that looks like Vesuvius in the sun-shot haze, that gives a veil of blue heat when the cloud gives way to the sun and the skin begins to burn. I went twice to the bullring, first when it was empty and they were sweeping the sand and cleaning it for the *corrida* on the next day, in the company of an excitable Argentine who, with the push and intensity of his race, wanted to know the points.

"Look now," said the shameless Argentine, a serious man and a polo player, a colonel in the army and an old enemy of Perón—which was why he had left his country—"look now," he said to the mulatto guide. "Explain to me. I know nothing. I am the bull now"—he crouched—"you are the picador. Now you try to get the lance—where? Here? On the shoulder. Right. Then why does the crowd whistle with disapproval? What have you done wrong?" "Gone in too deeply," said the mulatto in his hoarse kind voice. Up and down the alley, the mulatto in his shabby jeans and singlet was playing the sporting colonel, making veronicas and coming in for the moment of truth. "Good, now I understand," the Argentine said. The mulatto looked with dignity and grave irony at the excitable man and winked at his mistakes. "Come and have a bottle of beer," said the colonel.

We saw the bulls arrive in their packing cases. We sat sweating in a bar on a street noisy with grinding trams and a jukebox. It was the day for getting ready for the annual fiesta, the religious procession of the Señor de los Milagros, the image of the Christ that was strangely preserved in one of Lima's disastrous earthquakes. The mulatto, a huge, heavy man in his fifties with a rolling walk, was one of those who would bear the image for his parish, expiating—as he gently said—his sins.

That night the procession shuffled round the streets, the crowds blackened, the booths of the open-air fair were lit up; over the loudspeakers came the voice of a popular priest in the full, angry roar of Spanish imprecation, scarifying the sins of the multitude and making their skin tingle with the dread of eternal punishment. His was a blasting and relentless voice whipping up the lethargy of the passing crowds in the night.

Peruvians, like Spaniards, get the bull fever young. A boy of ten beside me was disputing the finer points of the *corrida* with his father, but both were seized, as the whole ring was seized, by that short, frightening and unanimous gasp of admiration which punctuates the intensely critical calm of the bullfight with short crises of masculine ecstasy. There was a Venezuelan who circled like a heavenly messenger with unfailing banderillas, but who was uncertain in all else and unnerved at the kill. Just before he thrust home the sword, some man bawled out to him, "Do better than last time!" Even the easygoing Peruvians have inherited the Spanish gift for total abuse.

There was a young, plump Portuguese in pale blue who looked as if he lived on sweet cakes and had been trained for the ballet, who swept us all by his courage and his art. He fought like a rocket breaking and blooming into star after star. There was a young Spaniard, new to Lima, wonderfully indifferent as he dominated the bull. When the bulls got bored and the fighting went all over the place, Lima shouted out satirically, as Seville does, "Music! Music!" asking the band to play in contempt. And scarves, coats, purses, handbags went down in showers in the moments of triumph. There is one tall gentleman of great dignity in Lima who sends his straw hat spinning into the ring when he is pleased, and it goes spinning faultlessly back to him, so that it is never off his head for more than twenty seconds. For twenty seconds that man has his public triumph.

After the fight in Lima, the indispensable thing is to go to the open-air stalls outside the ring and eat chopped sheep's hearts, grilled over charcoal on a bamboo skewer, and dipped in three or four tongue-tearing yellow sauces. There is only one that is hotter: the violent Peruvian onion. "What wonderful superstructure these Lima girls have," my shouting Argentine said as we drove away, pointing in two or three directions in a scream of brakes, horns and police whistles. Only one thing, he indicated, was missing: an earthquake.

The narrow streets were packed with people walking up and down in families, the girls looking at the silver and the jewelry in the windows and now and then an Indian running among them. Ignoring the traffic lights, the cars shot over the crossings. Men and women went into the churches, those richly furnished churches of much gold and crowded carving, to sit, to kneel and burn a candle at the favored altar. In the square outside the cathedral and the palace of the president were the scarlet guards caught by the floodlighting against the white stone, while the easy crowds lay on the grass or walked in the spring warmth, ate their sweet cakes and drank their fruit juices. In their faces there were often traces of the hard Indian bone or the narrow slit of the Indian eyes, the hard look of a lost Asia; and sometimes of an Asia left only two generations ago, in the survivors of those Chinese who were brought over to build the Peruvian railways. These new countries devour people and races, but the survivors make their obdurate corner somewhere: the Chinese are now the grocers of Lima.

The main avenues under the perfumed trees were lipsticked with neon lights, the car doors banged all night, the newsboys bawled papers in the streets, the mothers were at home, the demimonde sat, with equal formality, in their appropriate places, the old men rolled their poker dice round their bottle of beer and the foreign snobs drank their whiskey.

Which century is one in: the seventeenth of the courtly Spaniards? Two thousand years back with the Indians? In the twentieth with the international contact? In the twenty-first with the restless cholo or mestizo triumphant at last? In a Cadillac? In some grinding nineteenth-century tram? On a mule?

You sense the violence of a life cut up into frontiers of race, politics and fortune. You go away doped by the narcotic smell of the white bells of the floripondio tree, outstared by the flowers of the tropics and the new buildings, remembering the golden dust of the Andes, daydreaming about the fortunes buried there.

This is an age of building and strung-up nerves. For Lima grows. Attracted by the wealth, depressed by life on the great estates, the mixed and Indian people pour into Lima, pour out and stake their claims in the desert, seep here and there into the new schools and universities, either sink into misery or go to swell the beginnings of a new middle class.*

"The past. The past," people say. "The future. The people." Cry and countercry are in your ears as you fly away.

The visitor to Cuzco flies there in two or three hours from Lima, spends a few days there, takes the light railway to Machu Picchu and then flies back from Cuzco to Lima. You can travel to Cuzco by train—they supply oxygen at the great altitudes—but it takes a long time. I flew there. It is the most exciting short flight in South America.

On this flight the Andes give us one more sensation. We have flown beside them and kept our distance; now it remains for us to fly over them, to exchange voluptuousness for a terror that, at the breaking point, suddenly becomes the sublime. We have looked down upon the patterns of desert or plain and have had the impression of seeing a mind in the earth itself and of reading its hieroglyph. But when we cross the Andes they rise up and assault the flier. When we cross those hundreds of miles of peaks and brown ranges,

---

* For the past eight years Peru has been run by a dictator, the cholo general, Manuel A. Odria, who had outlawed the popular revolutionary party, APRA. This past summer there were free elections, in which the APRA party helped to elect Manuel Prado as president. Dr. Prado has already legalized the APRA party, but whether this decision, and others, will be respected by the army remains to be seen. The important fact is that under free vote, the electoral power is in the hands of the increasingly politically conscious masses—a new, real if unpredictable, factor in South American politics.

the rock wilderness that lies between viceregal Lima and Pizarro's Cuzco, it is like flying over the blades of knives. Shoulders and summits, ravines, whole systems of them by the thousand are spread about us and are not exhausted at the hard horizon. It is a sea of solid iron and almost without feature. There may be a blue-eyed lake, like a single, hard sapphire dropped there; an enameled vein of green in a ravine so deep that it might be a mere snick in the bed of the sea; but these are glints, like malice rather than beauty, in a world that is obdurate, upheaving and unconquerable beyond our conception. The sight hurts the whole body and appalls the mind; we are so high above it that we fear we could be whisked off the curve of the world into outer space.

And then, as we suck at our sweet oxygen tubes like babies—and sag at once if we take them out of our mouths—the gloom lifts and the incredible happens. Suddenly, rising out of the roof, the snow peaks jut up one by one in the higher courts of the sky like cruel kings. There is hierarchy even among rock. We approach them clumsily bumping, we pass slowly between their silence. They stand, withered and distraught, caparisoned with snow. We have been clambering over rock walls for hours, and now, hardly beyond the touch of our wing, we come into these white and royal presences. They look as mad as Lear and as lonely. Slowly they pass—for it is they who seem to move away, not ourselves—with, perhaps, a rag of cloud drawn after them like ermine whipped away with the fretfulness of old kings. And there behind us, they wait. The horrible thing is that they wait: we have got to return. It is not a place, you feel, as the pilot finds his way between them toward the bare and winding stairway into the valley of Cuzco, where you would choose to hear one of those motors stop. These ravines are solitudes and are—in a word whose meaning we had not realized till now—savage. Now we can say we have seen the savage with our eyes, the landscape of the condor.

We landed at Cuzco in the dust and sunlight and, taking the tip of those who know how cautiously one must make the change from sea level to the high altitudes of the Andes, I went straight to bed for a couple of hours. Cuzco looked as if it had been bombed. Five years before there had been an earthquake. Builders were still working on the colonial houses where the Spanish copy has been imposed on the great locked stones of the Incas. In the baroque churches the belfries had crumbled, the walls split and the ceilings brought down. In 1950 two thirds of the buildings in a city of eighty thousand had been made uninhabitable. If the people had not gone in thousands to a football match—football at that altitude!—the casualties would have been far greater.

The Pacific coast is the region of earthquakes, from the tiny quakes that wake you up for a second or two in the small hours of the morning, the sudden rattle in the day that shakes the roofs, the windows and the floors and brings down stones and dust on the mountain roads, to the catastrophe that occurs once or twice in a generation.

After the Romans, the Spaniards have been the world's great builders, but the disaster of Cuzco confirmed again that once Spanish rule ended after the Napoleonic wars, there was a general decadence in craftsmanship and care, just as there was also a relapse into political anarchy. Numbers of families in Cuzco go in for the simple trade of making adobe bricks as a sideline; the material is not really strong enough to support the heavy tiled roofs of the houses; poor softwoods, above all the feeble eucalyptus, have replaced the hard, and the tools and skills of both the adobe makers and the stonemasons have declined.

The aspect of Cuzco is perfectly Castilian, in the austerity of its arid mountain setting and its bare brown tilled fields, which are marked by the poplars the Spaniards brought from the dusty roads of Castile. Pizarro entered Cuzco in 1533. He had marched his paltry army of 177 men up from the coast to conquer an empire and capture Atahualpa, its ruler. The Spanish genius is the gambler's. Pizarro, remembering the boldness of Cortés in Mexico, got his blow in first and took the Inca by bloody stratagem; and then, after a terrible march over the Andes, arrived in Cuzco, the capital of the kingdom. He had fought his way there, but he had murdered Atahualpa by then and arrived a conqueror.

Pizarro came to Cuzco in November, when all is brown and the air is clean and cold under a changeless sky and when a white cloud will stand still like a piece of sculpture; and the landscape must have reminded the conqueror of the land he had known in his youth. Spanish and yet not Spanish. For he saw the heavy, low-standing Inca temples and houses, built of huge blocks of stone, the temples shining with walls of gold and silver inside.

Those implacable walls of the Incas, beautiful in their mortarless, ingenious interlocking, became foundations on which the Spanish manors and cloisters, the Spanish arcades and green and brown balconies, the rich Spanish churches, have been built. Here and there, the religious symbols of the Incas are embossed on a building; the cabalistic sign leaps like a serpent close to the Spanish coat of arms or the richly ornamented doorway.

We climb, losing our breath in that fine air, giddy with the height, up streets cut in steps, looking into courtyards that might be in Spanish Toledo, though here is greater misery. We pass the tailors at their sewing machines or dressmaker's models (for male tailors are as numerous as barbers). But at the top of the street we do not hear the Spanish goat bells; instead there is a group of long-necked llamas heavy with their wool, looking at us *de haut en bas* with a disdain one had never noticed in duchesses. The Inca stone blocks are a timeless and simple geometry, one of the fundamental inventions of the human race. What hands first moved them? We see their silvery bloom in the streets of Cuzco, in the fortress of Sacsahuaman, and in their unanswering mystery at Machu Picchu. Old explorers of the Andes regret that Hiram Bingham's almost impassable mule track from Machu Picchu has now been replaced by a light railway which wanders down the gorges and connects the Indian villages, and that vulgar tourists can get to a lost city that is lost no more. But is Pompeii the worse for being visited?

You journey to Machu Picchu—some fifty miles north of Cuzco—by rail, through high and flowering valleys of broom. Then the mountains close in, the corridors of the gorges begin. You shiver at ten thousand feet and stare at the sky for a sight of the condor that never comes; you drop down into the dripping tropical forest that clots the air. The mountains shut you in. The train whistle sends echoes bounding from wall to wall; outside their huts, the Indians stand, dirty, bedraggled, the last hopeless heirs of the race, or trot in panic on their donkeys along the track in front of the train. You follow the "river with three names," the Urubamba, that storms over its boulders for tens of miles. You see the rope bridges spanning it; and then, when the gorge divides and you are at the bottom of the mountain hole, a furry cone of rock shoots upward for a couple of thousand feet. On the wall opposite, out of sight from below, is the lost city, the condor's nest. There, terraced on the summit, with its altars open to the sky, its ruined windows turned for the rising and setting sun, its worshipers gone, is Machu Picchu.

This is one of the supreme sights of the Andes and one of the unsurpassed archaeological finds and mysteries of South America. Not even a swarm of tourists could take from the height and the surrounding mountain mass their overpowering communication of solitude. The silence belongs to the earth and the rock, and the human voice and person are trivial beside it. We know, in any case, that one step beyond the precincts and we could be lost, starved and infallibly dying. The most insensitive of us is forced to see here that he has come to an end, that a town not only can die but that all memory and knowledge of it can pass out of mind.

Machu Picchu was discovered in 1911 by Hiram Bingham, the American archaeologist. He climbed the precipice and found the ruins buried in undergrowth. At first they were thought to be purely Inca, but then pottery was found which suggested at least part of the town had been built in pre-Inca times. There is no tradition to say how the town came there or why it was abandoned, yet it can have been no more than four hundred years ago that one of the Inca princes fled there with his nobles from Pizarro. A very large number of female skeletons have been found and some have thought the prince fled there with the Virgins of the Sun. The huge stones of the walls, the cells, the temples and the altars and places for observing the rising and setting of the Sun God stand smooth and silvered and perplexing. Did the Spaniards not know of the place? Did they never march up the gorge? And why did the town die? Did the inhabitants perish of some plague? Did they simply die out, from hunger or old age? One pictures, as one stands there, the last aging handful and then the last human being of all among the dead. Yet it may not have been like that. The people may have gone down to the jungle of Peru; they may have been wiped out in war.

Pre-Inca pottery has been found in Machu Picchu. Legend overlaps legend, as one master race with its new propaganda overlays another in Indian history. On the topmost stone of Machu Picchu we see with awe "the stone that measures the sun." First it is the moon who sends her child, the sun, in the form of a jaguar to beget a child with an Indian woman and create the race. Centuries pass and then it is Viracocha, the god who comes out of Lake

27

Titicaca to create heaven, earth and men, but forgets to create light. In darkness men destroy each other and Viracocha turns them to stone. Then, trying again, he creates Manco and Ocllo, son and mother or brother and sister, to redeem the fallen world and to create a civilization of which perhaps the triumphant Incas before Pizarro were the descendants. The scholars dispute, the archaeologists dig, there is no written tradition. We can only know that the Indians of today, living on a little maize and sometimes a bit of dried guinea-pig meat, are worse off than the Indians of those times who discovered and grew the potato and made maize flour, bread, drink and honey. They used the seed, the leaves and the roots of the aloe. From the roots they made soap and, even now, you see the Indian women beating their washing with the aloe leaves so that the soapy pulp froths out. Even now you find the hole in the root where the sap gathers and ferments and from which comes the liquid they boil or used to boil for treating their black hair. Their dyes come from plants, their wool from the llamas. A constant sight on these roads is of women trotting along with their distaffs, frantically spinning their wool as they go.

Death is familiar to the Indian: the Incas—as you can see in the wonderful museum at Lima—mummified their dead and buried them in a sitting posture, binding the bodies in graveclothes that are now spidery with age. From its cobweb of clothing the shrunken face, oddly Hindu in appearance, gazes back at us with cynical intensity. The dead person's spirit placated by being buried with his favorite things does no ill to survivors. The Jívaro Indians of the Amazon shrink heads. In the fields you sometimes see a ring of men and women squatting in the evening outside some village. It is a wake. They are eating the dead person's favorite dishes and soon they will sing and, as the *chicha* works on them, they will dance and get drunk. In a year's time they will mark the anniversary of the dead person to fend off any ill intent of his spirit.

I saw the priest—a hearty Irish-American from Chicago—rapidly baptizing the newborn babies in the church on the plain outside Lake Titicaca. The mothers knelt on the floor afterward, took their babies that looked like little skinned rabbits, bound them into their shawls, slung them onto their backs with the swift skill of a lifetime, and trotted off to the market.

28

"Most of them die very soon," said the priest, "but if the babies are not baptized before they die the parents think their spirits will return in the form of hail and destroy the crops. And now," he said, "I've got to bless all those clothes, the clothes of the dead, so as to free them from evil spirits until the next anniversary."

"As far as I can figure it out," said the man from Chicago, "their life is a system of elaborate insurance policies."

The next day I was flying from Cuzco, over the desert toward La Paz and the Bolivian mines; I was done with the old Spanish corner of the continent.

Bolivia

The most dramatic and frightening of all South American experiences is Bolivia. It is hardly a country; it exists for scarcely any reason except the world demand for tin. But it is an unforgettable spectacle; a close-up of the crust of the moon, a visitation from Tibet, yet as marshy as the wastes of Ireland's Connemara with its decaying thatched huts. The whirlwinds travel like specters over unbroken tableland and the jagged snow peaks stand up all round. Not all Bolivia is like this; there is jungle beyond the Andes and there are those distant, lower towns where life is kind and the Indians smile and laugh at last. There is sport: hunting and skiing.

For myself Brazil and Bolivia are the two major experiences of the continent: in the former you are sane; in the latter, the hair stands on end and you are mad. The floor level is fourteen thousand feet and in that thin air it takes a two-mile runway to get an airplane off the ground. A stoical llama, scratching his belly with his hind leg, greets you at the highest commercial airport in the world and you drive over a rough flint road into the cold inferno of La Paz; an inferno because you descend by the terraces of a Dantesque hell which is fifteen hundred feet deep, with the snow peaks standing pitilessly round it as tawny and blue as iron.

You come at last to the main square where two Mongolian sentries stand with fixed bayonets guarding a lamppost. It is the sacred lamppost where the previous president was hanged. There are bullet marks spattered up the walls of the Ministry of War. The Bolivian revolution was serious. We are in an active Indo-America, over 80 percent Indian or mestizo, armed, taciturn, ruthless, cunning, starved.

You cannot say that Bolivia really lives: say rather it survives as stone survives, as rock splits but still, fantastically, stands. Bolivia is pure geology. The inhuman jungle poisons but entrances; the tableland and the mountain passes frighten but have an inhuman spell of their own. The roads vanish into wilderness tracks of whitened rocks that have been withered like ghosts, for even rocks can die and turn into whorled specters in their mindless cemeteries. At this height much of what you call yourself dies out with a snap, like that; but what survives becomes intensed and overexcited.

Something (the least observant person can see at once) has happened lately in La Paz—even if he did not see the anti-Communist posters on the walls, hear the countercry for the release of Communist prisoners, or the blare of the radio of the national revolution. You can tell it at night by the homeless dogs that gather on the main avenue and in other streets; large watchdogs, most of them, from the large new villas of the expropriated landowners and mine owners who have fled. For in 1952 there was revolution—not the short, usual South American coup d'état—but the real thing coming up grimly from the mines. Three thousand people were killed in La Paz. The new government armed the miners as a militia—the arms were said to have come from Perón. Communists? No. Nazis? No. Though German Nazism was strong in Bolivia. Nationalism is the strongest popular force in South America, and the first emergence of the masses is starting a new long reign of demands; but, of course, it pays to frighten advanced countries by pretending to be Communist.

Foreign experts tell Bolivians to move the scanty population off the highlands, or altiplano, to the tropical regions where they can develop farming. But the people will not go down. The terrible Chaco war with Paraguay in the 1930s frightened the people of the tableland. They died in thousands in the tropics. So the villas of the millionaire mine owners are rented, the hunting prints hang in the empty houses of the haciendas; and in La Paz the Point Four official and the United Nations research workers, the economists and martyred diplomats of all the nations scream with claustrophobia. And the homeless dogs camp at night in the avenues.

The exchange makes tourists rich and if they cannot buy as good silver in La Paz as in Peru, it is far cheaper. The best company in La Paz are the travelers, gamblers and those adventurers who have found a mine. Here are the mad Nazi Germans, the mad English, the mad Americans; the mad Spaniard from Franco's Russian Brigade arguing his head off with the liberal Spaniard from Córdoba, and the Italian chess player pleading for peace and civilization. The trigger-happy Bolivians get rowdy on whiskey at the nightclubs, while the Indians crawl on their hands and knees outside, peeping in at the people who have the energy to dance and the money to spend for girls.

In La Paz the Indians dress in brilliant clothes. The women stride in gay petticoats—orange and pink and green—and wear hard derby hats, and carry their babies on their backs. The shops are packed with their woven blankets, their mule bags and purses, their ponchos and huge piles of gaudy dresses. In the market of La Paz you see that they have a passion for clothes and fine things. The women are as gay as parrots in their plumage. The Aymara—the Indians of Bolivia—are a genial race, reveling in their fiestas and their jokes. Here, in La Paz, for the first time, I saw an Indian laugh: saw a woman bent double carrying a bed on her back; she passed a man bent double under a load of boards and, as she passed, she gave him a push that sent him twirling helplessly round under his top-heavy load until, as he spun back, he managed to give her a push too. Tottering helplessly, these two cheerful pack animals reeled with laughter.

There are shops where the Indians make the white top hats and the stiff glass-embroidered waistcoats of linen which they wear for the wild, long-legged glide of the dances at the fiesta of Cochabamba; the hats make these short people suddenly tall and witchlike. The dancers rent the green and purple horned heads of the devil dancers with glass set in the cheeks. There is glass, too, in the donkey mask with its red lips salivating, and in the satirical image of the Spanish don that goes back to the Conquest—the absurd, dandyish little head with silver mustaches and a smug little mirror in the chin.

The Indian of La Paz is gorgeous. He is only a few hours from Lake Titicaca, the cradle of his race. Out of that wide stretch of water came the god who created the children of the sun. Their descendants sail their long canoes made of rushes, with straw sails. (The trout of Titicaca is the best food in Bolivia; they are the largest I have seen. The imported food is terrible.)

To what extent are the Andean Indians Christians and Catholics? They are baptized by the priest; they send for him when they are dying. They are completely Catholic, for they were forcibly but easily converted by the Spaniards. Their own religion had been authoritarian, there were doctrinal similarities. The Inca priests maintained a confessional. The Indian is a passive character and the breaking up of his communal life destroyed the only organized force that could have kept his pagan faith alive. The Church stood between the Spanish adventurers and the Indians; the Church abhorred the Indians' destruction, yet dreaded his heresy and miscegenation. The Jesuits segregated the Indians in communities run by the Order. The system broke down; human nature, released for new freedoms and new evils in this new world, was too strong for priest and Church.

By the time the traveler has got to Chile, least Spanish of the republics, the churches are less interesting, the sense of religion is less pervasive; and except for the Araucanians in southern Chile, there are no Indians.

Chile

You take off from La Paz for the thousand-mile flight south to Santiago, the capital of Chile. The moment you have flown off the tableland of Bolivia—over the Chilean nitrate desert, over the largest copper mine in the world, lost in its vast pitiless amphitheater of rock and sand—the plane turns toward the kinder sun of the subtropics and you are in a different world.

Once again you see how irreconcilably the South American states differ. Peru is courtly; Bolivia is barbaric. In Chile the Spanish spirit has been diluted: central Chile has the classical grace of the Mediterranean; southern Chile of the lakes, with its cool and rainy climate and its blossoms hung against the snow mountains, suggests a Japanese print, or again, because of its plantations of firs, some part of Germany or Scandinavia; in the extreme south the cold and harshness of the uninhabitable country are Antarctic.

I have heard the Chileans called the English of South America. There is a long tradition of English settlement there, and a strong link with the British navy. I have also heard the Chilean described as frank, uncouth, masterful, ill-mannered and efficient. He has no equal in South America as a soldier and is, in the sense that the Northern races understand this, a strong character. That is, a man of action, more honest, less sensitive than is general among Latins; less subtle, and with less of that "delicacy" which is one of the fundamental qualities of the South American, and that marks him off from the Northerner in the New World or the Old. In Peru and Bolivia, and even in Ecuador, the Spanish stock is being Indianized; but in Chile, the Araucanian Indian is being Europeanized. But if we left the primitive in Bolivia for something that is nearer the modern world in spirit, the modern world of Chile is, to be frank, circa 1900. The Chilean has the island temperament. He looks out from the pretty harbor restaurants of Valparaíso—the food in Chile is the best in South America—and sees the Japanese merchant vessels lying there. This long narrow country, shut off in a narrow strip 2600 miles long and, on the average, 110 miles wide between the Andes and the South Pacific, is far away from the rest of the world.

And there are economic reasons for Chile's isolation. The opening of the Panama Canal cut down the voyages round the Horn. This took away the trade of Valparaíso, where every sailor in the world once called. The manufacture of synthetic nitrates has eaten into the wealth of the nitrate deserts, the copper market has dropped. Less than a quarter of the land in Chile is arable. There are fine horses and cattle but the country cannot keep itself in beef.

So far, on the journey down the coast, you have been speaking to people of a basically alien civilization. Here, in Santiago, as soon as you arrive, you note how people speak closer to your mind. They do not stimulate the imagination by dramatic gulfs, but talk in the same way, read the same books, believe in the same things, enjoy the same jokes. An odd thing is the Chilean voice: it is musical. It is strange to hear Spanish spoken musically, without harshness, almost in singsong. In Chilean women, this vivacity is delightful. The formal señorita has given place to *la femme*; the secluded madonna to the married woman of active mind. She is often fair-haired, a vivid mixture of Northern and Spanish types, with quick nerves and freedom of manners. The women do not dress as well as in Peru—indeed the crowd in the street dresses in the shabby fashion of provincial British; but they excel in the choice of pretty hats. "*Ola, hijita,*" the gay Chilean mother greets her daughter at the airport. They love the affectionate diminutives. The airport at San-

33

tiago is the gayest in the continent, crowded with laughing and waving people.

In Santiago the Andes seem to come down into the top of the main avenue. A foreground of wild, yellow poppies, a bruise-colored haze that darkens in the sunlight, and then those sudden helmets of the peaks and the flashing snow. Aconcagua, the highest (22,835 feet) mountain in the Americas, lies in its glaciers beyond, in the pass that leads over to the Argentine. Here, in all central Chile, the light swims and shimmers.

"I don't feel safe away from the mountains," says a young Chilean, and that is how you feel about this land. There is no jungle. You are safe. Chile is shut in between its mountain wall and the sea.

In the spring heat, the scent of carnations and roses blows along the roads, the long tresses of the white acacia are in bloom, the broom is in flower; in the pastures, there are the dark orange flowers of the espino tree and those large, broad, drooping willows that stand like green crinolines in the meadows and flow and float in the soft breezes. From the green-painted valleys the mountains rise gracefully. The cactus is cultivated and also the vine. Between Valparaíso and Santiago is the Pan-American highway, no longer a dream or a surface of grit, but a concrete road. Long avenues of poplars or eucalyptus go up straight to the *fondas*—the small manorlike farms—and brown streams lie under the womanish tresses of the willows. Oxen are plowing fields. Vines are trellised between the adobe cottages; there are fields of carnations in the market gardens, of snapdragons and white roses, beds of arum lilies and geraniums. The chestnuts are heavily in flower and the hydrangea in its electric colors. It is November—the Chilean spring— and the wheat is on the turn from green to gold. There is an annual spring show of flowers in Santiago, an affair of great elegance, with an art and care equaled only in England and Luxembourg.

The walls of the *fondas* are tiled in blue, in the Spanish fashion. There are oak beams, open fireplaces and fine polished iron such as you see in rich men's houses in Spain. The furniture and the pottery have the formal style of modern Spanish. The designs came from the famous patterns of Talavera in Spain. The young owner will seem like a gay, horse-riding Andalusian, grave but always with a candid smile and the impulsive gesture. He is, it is clear, a gentleman. He wants immigrants, but from northern Europe. He prays at night, you may be sure, for an oil refinery to be built, for Chilean air-craft, for something to raise the rather faded economy of this beautiful coun-try. He is a parliamentary democrat who fears the miners' unions. He is like—and yet he is not like—his opposite number in Spain, for he is less for-mal, less extravagant and fantastic. The New World, by giving people space, has lowered their intensity.

He watches your face inquiringly, divided in the American fashion be-tween uncertainty of himself and a deliberate, warm moving forward to dis-claimer and assertion. He laughs at the Old World because he has a sense of his own land and his soil; he feels everything is possible, but he also feels in-secure. The geographical and economic madness of Chile gives him a cer-tain defensive irony, but it gives him energy, too, and a quizzical tenacity. In his gaiety, he looks handsome, practical, but lost. He is lost perhaps because the mixture of Scandinavian, English, German, Spaniard and Jew has not quite been made. Or perhaps it is I who was lost.

I thought of the brilliant professor from the University of Concepción who burst out one night in a Santiago café, over his glass of "gin *con* gin," with these words: "South America is backward and lost. There was nothing we could bring from eighteenth-century Spain. We turned to French ro-manticism in the nineteenth century after the Wars of Independence—to Hugo, Chateaubriand, a culture of rhetoric. We have found no culture of our own strong enough to replace it." Yet in Neruda and Gabriela Mistral his country has two world-famous poets.

I will say this for the young landowner: his family is rich. He could have had a good time. Instead he is a practical farmer, getting down to work on the land and in his community. He rounds up the cattle with his brilliant cowboys—the rodeo is the great sport of Chile. For gaiety he has the rather solemn "boîtes" of Santiago, the packed cinemas. On Sundays he can go down to Viña del Mar, the Rapallo of the southern Pacific. The tea dance starts, the couples sit on the terraces and listen to the sea roll in. The ladies are heavy, voluptuous, lively. Tea—it is the great Chilean extravagance and el-egance. With the best food, the most enjoyable fruits, and the only drinkable wine, he has an agreeable life. He can forget how much his country depends on grim copper mines like El Teniente up in the Andes or on Anaconda in the desert.

Argentina

We have reached the halfway mark in our journey. Suddenly, as we leave Santiago and turn to the east—toward Buenos Aires and the Atlantic—after that long journey down the Pacific coast, we feel a change of mood. People on the west coast, in Lima and Santiago, have warned us, "Don't be taken in by the flashy modernity of the East; the future is here."

It may be; but, as the plane takes you eastward, you wake up; you feel the unmistakable and irresistible electric shock of the twentieth century. In Buenos Aires you are very near to what you know in London, Paris or New York. Once more you are in contact with the great cities, the million windows built into severe walls; by day impersonal as print, by night a brilliant geometry of light standing still high in the sky or moving in endless traffic along the ground. Every light represents a human being like yourself, the electric man. By instruments the pilot lands you in a city of instruments and tensions. The nerves tighten. You are caught between the artificial screams of the modern world—fire engine, police and ambulance—and a hygienic quiet that is not exactly silence; simply a current that has been switched off.

You feel the tension sixty miles out of Buenos Aires when the lights of this continually spreading urban area begin to form in a countryside that one hundred years ago was a pampas of thistles and clover. The cattle have yielded to the wheat, the wheat has yielded to the market garden, the market garden to the factory and the extravagantly spaced suburbs and their electric railways. The tension increases. It was no great surprise when the pilot came alongside and said: "There's political trouble in Buenos Aires. We got it over the radio. I would advise you to see about your reservations before leaving the airport." It was the classical twentieth-century remark of a technician: "Keep moving. Organize." He did not want his plane grounded. Not to move was his idea of a tragedy. We city people are machines; we break down if the machine stops, or at least so it appears in these new countries which have never known modern war. But we are not so easily rattled; what sane man would miss a revolution?

There is a splendid airport at Buenos Aires, an excellent fleet of motor coaches meets the planes. "The man who built that place is in prison now," laughs a man in the bus. It was probably true; the airport was built under Perón and a good many Peronistas are in jail. The modern world again. In Buenos Aires itself there are police cars in the street. There are arguments between groups of men along one of the main avenues; in the innumerable coffee bars, long rows of white cups wait on the counters as innocent as choirboys, untouched. No hiss from the espresso machines; the cash registers are still. The crowds stand outside the newspaper offices waiting with religious, upturned eyes for the news flashes from the upper floors. Yet the cinemas are packed.

Like the other cities of the east coast of South America—São Paulo and Rio de Janeiro—Buenos Aires is a Babylon shot up suddenly out of the prairie, plantation and jungle. It shouts money and progress from its skyscraper tops. It is almost impolite to mention that it was established toward the end of the sixteenth century. The people like to regard themselves as no older than their sudden tremendous wealth and expansion, no older than the furs and diamonds in the street called, with classical Spanish lettering and economy, Florida; they are the latest edition of Bond Street, Fifth Avenue, the Rue de la Paix or the Avenue Hoche. Latin conservatism and sensibility are their weapons against the Anglo-Saxon. If the sense of time is to be valued, for them it is the future. It belongs to them, they feel, yet they cling to the illusion that money can keep the old Faubourg St.-Germain alive. Upon the future they act aggressively and without apology; they have the aggression and arrogance of the Americas mitigated by sensations of loneliness and insecurity.

Argentine writers say that the Argentine is a lonely man not only because behind him is the loneliness of the pampas where he once made all his wealth, but because he has built a city that might be a lovely importation of Paris, Genoa, Madrid or Milan and yet is inconsolably far away from the great centers of power in the United States and Western Europe. The Grands Boulevards glitter with traffic uncontrolled, under the thick plane trees. The Argentine flatters Paris by imitating it, like the newly rich; but he hates it because, in making money out of Europe and America, shaping his life and economy to theirs, he feels he has made nothing that is his own. Or perhaps he has lost what he had in the cattle-raising days.

His blood is Spanish, scarcely touched by Indian. Italian stock has been

37

grafted onto him to redouble the dramatic sense of the virile and masculine sensibility and the ethos of southern Europe. His culture is French and profoundly so. In the nineteenth century the British bankers were his servants; in the twentieth he looks toward New York. A chauvinist and proud, he rails against foreign capital. Yet he will build himself an English Tudor house and racing stables, play polo like a Virginian, re-create Longchamps and throw up a skyscraper or two. Is not the Argentine the most powerful, the most advanced of the South American states, the one chosen to lead, unify and even to conquer? The dilemma has been how to allow the indigenous to grow amid so much assertion of the will and so much copying. Among Spanish Americans, it is he who has the publishing houses, the bookshops, the writers, the newspapers and reviews that have an international standing. He wishes for foreign cultures, as the Mexican and Brazilian seek strength in their own.

What I have just written is taken from the talk of Argentines, but it is important to understand the tone of the talk. It was the talk of people with strong personalities and ambitions. The anti-Peronistas were the more vocal; the others had much to fear. A man in a travel agency, who was also a journalist in his spare time, said he was ill from worry and overwork. "I now have to write my articles; under Perón we just printed the official handouts; it was easier." A Peronista, he took my notebook and wrote: "Four revolutions. 1930, 17 deaths; 1943, 32 deaths; June 16, 1955, 4000 deaths; Sept. 16 to 23, 1955, 30,000 deaths." And handed the book back without a word. He feared arrest.

I dined with anti-Peronistas in what might have been the Paris of the Avenue Hoche, among French books and paintings and the best conversation. Three of the guests had been in prison—a lawyer, a professor, a landowner. They showed me indignantly the blasphemous schoolbooks, done on Nazi lines, that had been issued by Perón to schoolchildren. That week one of the strange sights of Buenos Aires was the daily queue before one of the palaces where Eva Perón's diamonds and fur coats were on show. Every day there was a new announcement of embezzlement, sexual vice and political terror. The relief at Perón's downfall was enormous. It amounted to a real liberation but it was tempered by the knowledge of the vacuum he had left. It was infected by uneasiness. There was a strike in the *frigoríficos* out of which one generation of Argentines had made their fortunes, troops were posted along the miles of empty dockyards, and the red mud-colored water of the Río de la Plata had no moving ships on it. This quarter is a little Marseilles of dockside bars and fish restaurants, rough but good, where you could come at night and eat octopus cooked in its ink. They were empty.

The Argentines are sufficiently serious-minded to realize they cannot go back to pre-Perón Argentina. They now understand there is an uncomfortable popular movement in South America and in the world at large. One hostile but sensible *interventor* said: "Perón gave to the working classes with one hand and took with the other, in the Nazi fashion, but he undoubtedly gave them new rights before the law, and those they will never lose." There was the spring glitter, the sensuous, perfumed Parisian air. The revolutionary situation quieted after a couple of days. The packed gray trams made you jump back against the shop windows in the narrow streets. In the parks the acacias hung their blossoms. "Look," said a woman as we sat under the flowering creepers on the terrace of her house: a butterfly as big as my hand was on my shoe, opening its huge wings as if yawning in the heat. The voices of people had the dramatic Italian intonation. In the cake shops, mothers and children were eating ice cream; in the coffee bars rows of men stood before the rows of cups; in the cafés they sat drinking beer and eating plates of hors d'oeuvres: the black olives, the slices of salami, the nuggets of hot tripe.

In the streets and the beautiful parks walked the brown-eyed women, with their strong Roman noses and that carriage of body and limb which is meant to display sexual attractiveness to the utmost for admiration only and for its own sake. The men gazed and were provoked by the sight of sexual arrogance and were left staring the Argentine stare, alone, to consider its fatality. You sense in the men and women a mingling of Italian virility and violence with that alternation of passivity and compulsion which is the Spanish inheritance. Buenos Aires is a city of lovely flowers. You may see a girl carrying a bouquet of fifty roses as she walks between two men; and when a private celebration takes place, say a cocktail party for the opening of a new dress shop, scores of superb bouquets of flowers, fit for opera singers, are sent by friends.

Six in the evening is the hour of the *paseo*, when the street called Florida is closed to traffic and the women, who have spent hours preparing for this moment, walk in groups. This *paseo* is less militant than the *paseos* of Spain; the sexes are not segregated, and the exhausting Spanish eye-warfare has been softened by Italian gaiety. The Italians have improved rich, bourgeois Buenos Aires. Diamonds, emeralds, sapphires, pearls are in the shop windows. Inside, the jewelers sit formally at their velvet-topped tables, like croupiers waiting for the rich gambler. For the true inhabitants, Buenos Aires is the delightful city. They have the American gregariousness, the easy feeling for the surface of life. They live in sets and groups that are always in and out of each other's houses, always giving parties with energetic gaiety, always amusing themselves. They bubble along, hating to be alone. The elegance and liveliness of the rich in the smart bars is diverting; the gaiety is not noisy and it is free of the boring Anglo-American drunkenness. I have never liked the look of the rich so much, the young above all.

In shops, they prefer long transactions. Four assistants will hang about a man buying a hat; it will not be a matter of a hat for hat's sake, as in London; or a sale for sale's sake, as in New York; it will be a hat for life's sake, an opportunity for the buyer to talk about his life, his friends, his family, and a pretense at bargaining which will interest everyone completely. They sigh to see a customer go; a life has gone, they gossip about him afterward. The personal is everything for them. They inherit from Spain the wish to preserve the sense of personal favor, that one is buying a hat there through the influence of a friend of a friend of a friend. The dictator, in the personal politics of South America, is simply the dominating personality, the man himself with all his anecdotes, interests, deals, habits, passions, friends, whims. He is not the father of his country, but perhaps, the uncle on the make. To the general American alacrity is added refinement; the cardinal thing in manners is not candor or directness but indirection and the importance of not wounding susceptibility.

There is often a damp haze or a dust haze over Buenos Aires. Its parks and open spaces are gracious, planted with lovely flowering trees of the subtropics, and they sweep in little hills and drives to the reddened waters of the estuary which stains the sea for miles outside. The river is too wide for us to see the farther shore; its mouth is an ocean in itself, but only an hour's flight away is Montevideo, and on the far windy beaches of Uruguay the sea becomes fresh and blue again. Up the great river Plata, for tens of miles, Buenos Aires has spread its low white-walled houses with their heavy carrot-colored tiles, with all the space of the pampas to use up. Along the modern highways and the cobbled avenues, no police or traffic lights control the traffic, which has its own skin-of-the-teeth methods of cutting across. Occasionally, you see an empty pagoda where the white-helmeted policeman is supposed to stand. He is rarely there.

The light in the Argentine is strong; the sky seems higher and steeper, a vertical wall at the plain's edge. Trees and buildings stare like cutouts. Clouds are hard. If ever a landscape was made for horse racing, it is this one. The eucalyptus trees and the poplars are planted in platoons around the farms. These trees are immigrants. The characteristic tree of the pampas, where, in its fertility, nature has hardly troubled to make a tree, is the low and spongy ombú. It does not burn, it cannot be used for anything except its rich shade, and, under it, when the land was not wired off and the cattle were wild, the gaucho rested with his horse, his knife and his guitar.

Little trellised restaurants are outside Buenos Aires, dancing places where men take their girls. At the home of the rich landowner, whose family may have built an English country house, you are back in the society of the Edwardian rich. The English house has been copied almost too perfectly: the oak beams, the open fireplaces, the English prints and the grim manorial bedrooms. His English lawn has fine grass, not the coarse grass of Europe, and is religiously watered. In the meandering *jardín anglais*, you stand under the comical rain tree that spits water from its leaves. You see the slap-up flower beds, the swimming pool, the stallions and racehorses in the stables, the grooms and the gig to trot the visitor round the orchards and the fields where the sheep or the beef cattle graze. A butler of fifty years ago will bring an English tea and, by some touch of excess, a bottle of whiskey too. Where is "the family"? In England? No; in Biarritz, Paris, Monte Carlo. The pony trots round, we hear for the first time since childhood the delicious lick of a whip, feel the rumble of hard wheels in our spines, the scented dust rises; some burned-up peasant from Spanish Galicia, lisping his *c*'s or his *z*'s with snobbish contempt for his Argentine masters, gossips away to the jaunty foreman and calls him señor. "Before Perón went," laughs the foreman, "he was the head of the local Peronista delegation and was going to shoot us all. We've done with all that nonsense now. He's an innocent." But no Galician is an innocent. It is country life, lazy-voiced, drawling, merry, shrewd.

You have flown over this scene, over the green watery-looking billiard table of the pampas. This is far, far from being the whole of the Argentine. There is the scrub forest of the Chaco, from which (when I was young and worked in the leather trade in London) we used to get our quebracho wood—the "ax breaker"—there is the flood plain that lies between the Paraná and Paraguay rivers; there is wild Patagonia, where the English shepherds emigrated last century and the Welsh colonists still sing their hymns and speak to no strangers, as clannish as the Basques. Along the Paraguay River they grow the *yerba maté*, which the Jesuits were the first to cultivate in this meat-eating country. The maté supplies the ordinary man the vitamins he would get from green vegetables. And up on the frontier, where the Argentine and Brazil and Paraguay meet, the water of the Iguazú Falls comes crashing in broad beards out of the tropical forest. It is an irony that this rich country disappointed the early travelers. They called it Argentina in despair, for there was no silver. The wealth came first from the clover and the grass, from the horses that sprang from the seventy-two which the Spaniards let go wild four hundred years ago; and from the cattle. Then when the Italians came, bringing the energy of Europe, crops were planted: grain and the *frigoríficos*, those vast freezing plants and slaughterhouses that stand by the waterside in Buenos Aires, created a nation. At the turn of the century began that industrialization which has enormously enlarged Buenos Aires, drained people into the towns. A new urban middle class appeared. Behind all South American cities lies the empty land where no new immigrant wants to settle.

The cities of that coast from south of Capricorn to the Equator—how violent is their difference! European in one respect: they are not standardized. Little in Rio recalls Buenos Aires, except a phalanx of tall buildings; and Montevideo has nothing in common with its neighbor over the estuary of the Río de la Plata, except the *frigoríficos* and the meat ships waiting in the harbor. Across the continent in Chile the people have one official meatless day a week, apart from any religious fast; in Uruguay it is reckoned that everyone, rich and poor, eats one pound of meat daily; in Buenos Aires they eat more. Good meat on the east coast, poor on the west; so the gourmand might divide the continent.

Uruguay

From Buenos Aires to Montevideo is scarcely an hour's flight. You take the flying boat from the dock close to the center of the city and fly across the estuary whose opposite bank you cannot see. Some travelers prefer the night journey by the ferry steamer, to see the lights of Buenos Aires drop away and Montevideo come up. I took the plane. Like any weekend Argentine tripper or escaping politician, I arrived in South America's little Sweden. Sweden (they call Uruguay) for cultural and political reasons. It is, for a large part, a very flat country and bears no physical resemblance to Sweden at all. Uruguay acts as a buffer between the ambitious Argentines and the imperial Brazilians. Pure Reason (assisted by the independent Spanish spirit in the Uruguayans and by the commercial British who found family wars damaging to their trade monopoly) made Uruguay strong. Which was to be Paris—Rio or Buenos Aires? Montevideo keeps the quarreling prima donnas apart. Buenos Aires is a tour de force (Waldo Frank has said) imposing itself on the pampas; Montevideo is an ordinary city with the provincial air blowing in from its pines, its dunes, its flat plains and little hills. Uruguay is a mild place, so well behaved that foreigners smile: all the schoolchildren in neat aprons and carrying their notebooks, hardly any illiteracy, higher education free and generally available; retirement on full pay at sixty; no income tax, no president, but rule by a sacred committee of nine—their nine Cadillacs stand outside the Presidential Palace. Uruguay is the one unmistakable, working democracy and the world's first pocket Welfare State. One could imagine Ibsen rewriting his plays there. "Prudent, distrustful, sterling, efficient, realistic," Count Keyserling wrote of the Uruguayans.

Montevideo is the least American of modern South American cities. It is very Germanic. It even goes in for small British and German motorcars. The Italians have brought it gaiety; from central Europe has come something

43

very serious, the latest books and the best music. And Uruguay *is* provincial; it is so democratic that even its handsome parks and streets are littered with wastepaper, its people wear standardized clothes, its nightclubs are dim and decorous. They call them *boîtes* as in Chile, or—horrible word—*whiskerías*. But conversation is good here; learning is considerable; books are read. There is no dread of "dangerous thoughts." In José E. Rodó, Uruguay has produced the only great South American thinker. There is intellectual liberty, liberal civilization without the horrors of mass society. Life is like a long weekend with the like-minded. Montevideo is the one place in South America where you see people of all classes enjoying family weekends on the beaches. Acres of bodies brown in the sun. Out they drive in thousands along the miles of Atlantic sands and bathe, sit in the little restaurants and bars, and indulge the national passion for picnicking in the thoughtfully planted pine woods or by the sea. It was once a treeless country, but the good Uruguayans saw *that* defect was put right. The wealthy can drive out beyond the miles of hotels and villas to the fashionable resort of Punta del Este and look out on that island where nature, with an eye for our education, has placed one of the world's largest colonies of sea lions. And do not say that the lovely harbor of Montevideo is dull: the Antarctic whaling fleets put in there for the winter. Mr. Onassis had an office there before he moved to Monte Carlo.

Those beaches were the holiday grounds of the Argentines until Perón stopped his people going to this corrupting liberal land. Some of the hotels closed down. One became a nunnery. But now the weekend parties of Argentines return. There are vociferous reunions in restaurants. People make speeches of welcome and take a semipolitical delight in private parties. Freedom has returned. "Argentines!" say the Uruguayans with amusement and with natural self-congratulation. It is nice to be admired for your sea bathing and political enlightenment. I walked out of the hotel and saw a group of young Argentines putting wreaths of flowers against the statue of Artigas, the Uruguayan national hero, in the main square of Montevideo. The poetic sensibility of the Latins comes out not only in boiling rhetoric but in many gracious private gestures, with flowers.

Montevideo is a capital bemused with the magic of the number nine. A Committee of Nine, representing the political groups, runs the country. So well regulated are the Uruguayans, so caught by the prosaic magic of fair shares, that even the jobs in the many state organizations are distributed proportionately to the numbers of their political group. If nine stevedores are required on the docks, they must be in the correct party proportions. This making everything go by nines is a religion.

And how do the Uruguayans raise money for the government without an income tax? By direct taxation on property, pensions, sales, reserves, profits, banks, and so on, and a good deal by the manipulation of a sliding scale of exchange rates and price regulations in certain areas. This leads to little comedies; on the way to the airport you notice a group of new bungalows and huts. They are really butchers' shops. Anyone with a car can drive out here and buy meat at half price—on Sundays only. He is avoiding the city sales tax by buying in the country. A day on the beach and then a drive into the pines to buy meat; there are many ways of contentment in Uruguay. There is one alarming thought: why should so much happiness have led to inflation?

Brazil

You leave Montevideo, fly up the Atlantic coast of Brazil to Rio de Janeiro. The arrival over Rio at night is a magnificent experience. Flying has not stolen the drama of the most fantastic harbor in the world. At night all capitals are the *ville lumière*, but Rio displays an unexampled intricacy in the hard and ingenious magic of light. You never knew that electricity could be so fantastic simply in the course of fringing hills and water. Those brooches high in the sky as we turn, are golden ships; those long insectile shapes like centipedes, devils' coach horses and sacred beetles fixed in their jeweled battle pieces, are the quays, the peninsulas, the promontories, the sugarloaves. There are the pearl strings that go from bay to bay, from mountain to mountain, with a recklessness that turns you into a child exclaiming with wonder. Nature has gone the limit of its possibilities in South America—in mountain, snow and glacier, in prairie, desert and jungle, in the huge red-river systems like the Río de la Plata, the Amazon and the Orinoco. But in Rio, a sort of theatrical folly has been added to the natural fecundity. For here are harbors in colonies, mountains upended in collections of furry cones and shaggy pyramids. The jungle curtains the ends of streets, hangs over the roofs of the low, pink-walled colonial homes, or sets off modern buildings that shoot up in stacks of steel and shuttered glass. Even the sea is rich as it breaks along the splendid curve of Copacabana and sends up a soft smoke of hot foam over the high buildings. At night Midas changes Rio to gold.

By day, when the gold has gone, if we climb a few hundred yards from the sea's edge, we are looking into the pulpy green, underwater world of the tropical forest. It hangs heavily down upon us, entices from shade to shade. Flowers are as big as faces, leaves are like bodies, stems are like human legs. You half expect to hear the sap pumping and the strange plants speak. Those leaves like swords, like scissored cardboard, like fire, like feathers, like the lolling tongues of huge animals; those trunks so bulbous; those flowering creepers like bursts of colored smoke—all combine to give the tropical hot-house the look of an overpowering court. A court which suddenly becomes silent and motionless the moment your step is heard. We stand only a yard or two off the road, in one of these tropical gardens, and have the baffling sensation that someone or something has, in that very instant, slipped away to tell someone else. We are left with the impudent sexual stare of flowers (they have none of the innocence we imagine in the flowers of our milder climates)—the jacaranda, the flame drip, the yellow cassia and silver imbauba, the hibiscus, the banana and the little red flower like a traffic light, called "the shameless Mary."

Cities that are crushed between mountains and sea commonly spread up the mountains, if only for air. Not so Rio. Its originality is that the rich keep to the flat and drive the slums into the hills of the city. So there is not only twentieth-century Rio fitted between the hills, but the hill villages, the shack villages, or *favelas*, which crop up just above the roofs of the offices, the rich apartment houses and even the brilliant tunnel that takes the speedway out of Flamengo into Copacabana. It is as if slums of native huts, made of old timber, corrugated iron, flattened petrol cans, bamboo, palm leaves and sacking were built on the skyline of the Rue de la Paix or were dotted about Manhattan in the 50's at the twentieth-floor level. There is old nineteenth-century Rio, three stories high, a refuge from the blinding light, where the houses lie in the shade of large trees and the rooms have the relief of air and semidarkness. And there is Rio of the mid-twentieth century, built at an as-tonishing speed, a place of tall steel-and-glass boxes where people fry in the summer, are blinded by light, catch chills from the air conditioning or are driven quietly mad by its relentless buzz. It is not quite like that, of course; but the Brazilians inherit the Portuguese weakness for leaving nothing alone. They bulldoze the hills away, tunnel under them, fill in large areas of the central bays—so that some people fear the lovely colony of anchorages will one day be solid concrete. So the wretched are driven up to the *favelas*. There are dangerous *favelas*, perilous at night, hardly policed. At least one of them is better off and has television sets and nightclubs. But most have no light except the candle or the oil lamp on the table; and the life of the women is the perpetual journey for water. You look out of the office windows and watch the women carrying their empty petrol cans down and their full ones up the steep red mud paths. When the tropical rains come the red soil dis-solves, the hillside slips, the shacks are crushed.

Brazil, more than any other of the republics, is a country that absorbs the alien life. It is the one major melting pot of South America, the one place of positive ferment. Our only chance of judging it is by its cities and it would of course be true to say that only the cities are modern, that the rest is backward, often wretched and isolated; but we can make certain guesses from the cities and above all from their architecture. The sudden awakening from long co-lonial sleep came first with the late abolition of slavery in 1888, later than anywhere else, but (most important) without bloodshed or deadening race segregation; and then with the late arrival of industrialization. Lúcio Costa (who, with Niemeyer, Serrador, Baumgart, Rino Levi, Warchavchik, Burle Marx and others, is a leading figure in Brazil's architectural revolution) puts these two facts first in explaining it.

The abolition of slavery had shown that the traditional style of building was no longer efficient. Brazil's first modern building to be mounted on pil-lars—*pilotis*—was designed in 1931, and since then Brazil has been exuber-ant in its bold modern designs. A final stimulus—as so often happens in art—was a fundamental difficulty, the lack of steel. The architects had to do what they could with reinforced concrete—on this coast there are no earth-quakes. Sun, concrete, vegetation—"these," Costa said, "are the *données*." Sometimes originality has been extravagant, as in Niemeyer's famous church of Saint Francis at Pampulha outside the astonishing new city of Belo Horizonte. The church, a series of parabolas of glass and concrete and tiles, decorated by the painter Portinari, looks like a fantastic phosphorescent snail on the march. (The bishops refused to consecrate it.) In the same town Niemeyer built the lake casino, a minor masterpiece which follows the shoreline of the lake, and which combines a theater, cinema, restaurants, cafés and swimming pools. Some of the luxury hotels, like the hotel at Petrópolis, said to be the largest in the world, are built on a casino plan.

What must strike the connoisseur of Brazilian architecture is its élan, its variety and its freedom from those boring surfaces to which the cult of shape and function too commonly leads. In the new villas of Belo Horizonte the sharp, boxlike lines have been ingeniously broken, the impersonal stare has gone; graceful snakelike ramps, cagelike galleries all light and air, verandas shaded by grille and Venetian shutter, and outer walls in beautiful patterns of color as if they were textiles or even wallpapers—which is, incidentally, an extension of the old Portuguese tradition—relieve and divert the ennui of the eye. The *brise-soleil* (or outer shutter), which brings shade to these tall buildings in the tropics, is a Brazilian device though it was Le Corbusier who suggested the movable shades which project from the walls of the Ministry of Education. These interest the eye and, like the honeycomb grilles in the walls of schools, hospitals and apartment houses, make fascinating patterns of light and shade in the rooms.

Personal privacy is as strongly desired by the Brazilians as by the British, and modern architecture—so obviously designed for the collective life—hardly seems to offer this intimacy. There are, however, many examples of private building. Above all, gardens and trees have been drawn into the setting. You can see examples in São Paulo created by Rino Levi, the distinguished Italian in that very Italian city. The apartment house built by Lúcio Costa at the Parque Guinle is delightful.

It is typical of the present generation of Brazilians to want the new, rich thing, whatever it is. São Paulo, as sudden as Chicago in its growth, was ambitious to possess famous French pictures and has bought a collection which, however, has not yet been housed in that city. Insofar as they inherit from the Portuguese, the genius is decorative and exotic, even indiscriminate. "The Spanish-speaking republics," an old diplomat said to me, "are pyramids tottering on their apexes. Brazil is a pyramid standing on its base. It is as well founded as Mexico and is the one country that is really creating an indigenous and original culture."

That sense of the loss of loved, hated and continually imitated Europe is absent. There was no violent break with Europe. The relationship between Brazil and Portugal is close. The Spanish-speaking countries were separated from Spain by wars of independence. Brazil separated peacefully with a lawyer's sigh, and some writers have said that to the practical virtues of the Portuguese the Brazilians have added an aristocratic sense which the Portuguese have lacked. For until 1889, Brazil was a monarchy, the only monarchy on the American continent. The Emperor's palace—now the National Museum—may be seen in Rio, and up in the mountains at Petrópolis is a summer resort that recalls Cintra or Saint-Germain-en-Laye. You can visit the houses of old families in Rio who once belonged to the nobility of the Brazilian court. They speak French like the old White Russians did, but they have no tradition of hostility to the republic.

Just as, after visiting Spain, you are struck by the gentleness and sensibility of the Portuguese, so you are struck by these qualities in the Brazilians when you come here from the other republics. They have added great wit and a taste for wild comedy. The dislike of violence, the apparent passivity of the Brazilians, has been despised by Northerners and has been laid to the tropical climate and to a disintegration and decadence of character which, it is argued, comes from the tolerance of mixed blood. The latter argument, however, finds no support from science, and sociology shows it to be nonsense. Climate has its influence, but it is only oppressively tropical along the Amazon, where the white race does indeed degenerate rapidly.

We drove out one night, after a meal of *feijoada* and palm-tip salad, with a Brazilian playwright and editor, and one of his knowing Negro reporters, a cheerful expert on the popular life in Rio and a connoisseur of the samba. We drove into the collection of pimplelike hills behind the mountains, past those lightless shack towns along little-known roads that skirted strung-out townships. Negro gentlemen in pajama jackets did what they could to guide us, but they had to be gently held up while we asked directions, because they were amiably drunk. We were looking for a samba club but ran into a fiesta on the way. Brazil often offers these gay night scenes. There was a pretty sev-

49

enteenth-century church standing like a doll's house on a little hill in the wasteland, one of those churches that have a small graveyard attached in which the ornate funeral monuments look like squads of ghosts in the moonlight. Close by was a bandstand, where a band was thumping its drums and playing its whining and bleating instruments, while someone sang and the women and children stood listening and laughing or wandered about or sat against the church wall. In all Brazil the pretty cotton frocks of the girls give grace to any scene. Their carefully done black hair, the dignity of their carriage and their slenderness are a delight. Only when they speak do they disappoint, for at an early age many lose their front teeth. (A doctor told me there is no chalk in Rio's water, and the diet of all the tropical parts of South America is deficient in vegetables.)

At night these noisy, simple little fiestas, without booths and held together by the unending throb and chuckle of the drums, are very gay to look at. There was a stone cross here, its steps covered with candle grease and, inevitably, those offerings which indicated that adepts of *macumba* were in the crowd. *Macumba*—it has other names in the old slave-owning regions of Bahia and Pernambuco and is found even along the Amazon, which is Indian country—is an African magical religion. It is very active, despite the hostility of the Church, and has many Christian figures in its mythology. St. Michael and St. George find a place among the traditional good and evil spirits from the African jungle. Crowds of people slip off to see a *macumba*. Some hotels stage *macumbas* for tourists, but the adepts regard these as faked.

It is a religion of incantation, with songs invoking the angels and the demons, sung in a mixture of Portuguese and African, and it has serious, if grotesque, rituals. Evils are cast out by mediums. There is dancing and drunkenness, there is the continual beating of drums which have the power of inducing frenzies, convulsions and trance; these, too, rid the body of disease and the mind of the evils that choke it. The adepts wear the white clothes with the white-fringed trousers of slave days; there is a symbolism of colors in their scarves and in their offerings, grotesque as these sometimes are: a beer bottle, a cigar, a heap of dust, a box of matches.

Some of the *macumba* dancing rites take place in beautiful surroundings; I heard of one held by a candlelit waterfall with rock platforms. The "priests" smoke cigars as they dance to smoke out the evil spirits and throw clouds of dust to dispel them too; they strike colored matches to produce the red smoke which is the sign of the Fallen Angel. The people dance until they are exhausted. Some fall into insensibility, and then the priest tests them by giving each a hard blow on the back of the neck to see that insensibility— and therefore purgation—has been achieved. Once it has, a rocket is sent up. A successful *macumba* can eventually be mistaken for a fireworks display.

Macumba is a pervasive form of African spiritism with a serious ethical side. The believers think that by the end of this century the world may be destroyed and that Satan will have been redeemed; many describe it as a "White" or healing magic. Its ethic of the war against sin, its cheerful borrowing of Christian saints, its ceremonies of baptism have alarmed the Church, for the strength of African tradition is immensely powerful. We are only beginning to learn about the African imagination from native African artists. Against the White Magic must be set the Black that works evil against enemies. Rich people in Copacabana are convinced that their Negro servants place beer bottles—as a *macumba* offering—at the street corners to puncture their masters' tires and that *macumba*, in its way, has a political as well as a religious magic character.

The popular movement in Brazil exists in an emotional fashion. Vargas, the late president who committed suicide, represented it in the manner of a benevolent demagogue, manipulating it gently rather than dramatically leading it. He was the god of the poor in Rio; but the true wretchedness of Brazil is in the interior, in the dejected villages and towns. The extraordinary thing about masses is their power to turn everything into popular song and wit and, of course, the samba.

One of the first things I heard that night at the samba club, which was organized by a committee of Negro dockworkers, was the famous and mournful samba recording the suicide of Vargas. The words are the complete letter he left to his followers at his death. It was like listening to a newspaper article set to music. It made a strange death dance for the Negro crowd in the open hall under the moon. We sat bemused by the deafening yet subtle manipulation of the drums, in which new clicks, new thumps of doom come in, step by step, against the rhythm and presently grow in power until they dominate it. The timing of these players—young laborers all of them—and their relaxed demeanor, as if they were passively waiting for the inner voice and listening with an inner ear, is a wonder; they awaken the same expectation in yourself until presently this curious, impersonal, sexual poetry captivates you. But it is the squeaking and peculiar sounds, hostile to our ears, that come from the small three-leaved metal instrument, the tambourine and the seed of the shaken gourd, that catch the nerves. They are slyly soothed by that slow sob of the deep drum; it beats like a heart.

The band we listened to was one of the scores that march for days in uproar round the streets in the Carnival, the saturnalia in February or March, banging in an orgy of noise and reviving themselves, as they totter along, by icy whiffs of ether.

We sat all night drinking beer and strong spirits, watching the footwork and the entranced goggling of the dancing couples. Beside us sat a tremendous old lady covered in gold—gold spectacles, gold rings, bracelets—sitting before a large three-tiered cake covered with green-and-pink icing. She was with her exquisite daughter, whose ancestors must have come from ancient Assyria. It was a gentle evening. One after the other the members of the committee put their arms round our shoulders and leaned on us, as they gazed with delight at the heat of the dance and then smiled affectionately at us. Outside, the lovers sat on the dangerous steps in the rocks that lead up from the shacks, and the whites of large eyes looked like flowers among the scented bushes. We drove back to Rio at dawn. The fantastic bays were like quiet opal, creaming on the sand in whispers as the yellow sun came up. The earth, for a moment or two, was new.

The most dramatic transition from new to old, from present to past, is the journey from the new city of Belo Horizonte—250 miles north of Rio—to the old gold-mining town of Ouro Prêto, not far off. It was from this town, the greatest producer of gold in the world in the eighteenth century until the mines gave out, that the Portuguese kings and the Church gathered the enormous riches of the Portuguese abbeys and churches. The glory of Ouro Prêto is in its lovely and fantastic baroque churches, each different in design, in its use of tower and scrolls of masonry and color, in its sixteen famous fountains, but most of all in the works of the greatest of all Brazilian masters, the crippled mulatto sculptor, Aleijadinho. He has been called the El Greco of Brazilian sculptors, because of the audacity of his religious carvings.

Their distortions are imaginative; Brazilian art and literature have a strong feeling for exaggeration, distortion and satirical caricature and wit. The huge figures at the church in Congonhas do Campo are his.

Traditionally, mining is an industry that is violent in its human relationships, whereas the slave life on the adjacent plantations of old Portuguese Brazil was patriarchal and, within restrictions, self-indulgent and benevolent. I flew in a number of small hops through this region. First up the coast from Rio to Salvador in Bahia; then to Aracaju, Macao (Maceió); afterward to Recife in Pernambuco and on to Fortaleza and Belém. These were charming journeys. You are never far from the sea; you are going round the hot bulge of the sizzling South American leg of mutton. You find yourself in the Brazil of the seventeenth and eighteenth centuries, among lovely churches and monastic establishments, pretty streets and fine houses, and all the painted grace of the *ancien régime* where life is modern enough but retains the old idle things of more leisured times.

There was an open-air exhibition of modern art in the main square of Salvador, on the tremendous cliff on which the town is built—there is a strong vogue for art sculpture in all important Brazilian towns. Down the street are the old warehouses of the plantations. The churches are splendid. The Jesuit church of São Francisco in Salvador is one of the loveliest in the country. As you walk under the superb paneled roof the late-afternoon sun turns the golden altar and all the gold in the church to chaotic fire. The white pillars are bound in golden tropical leaves from which the naïve and pink human figures look out like little dolls, and tropical birds perch among them with nuts in their beaks. The harsh, nasal sound of the Latin chant rises in this riot of luxury; its formal monotonous discipline puts order on a mind disordered by the fantasy of art. For most of us, aliens to this flamboyant art, the beauty of these churches is external; at São Francisco, it is in the flowering scrolls of the façade. The church of Nossa Senhora do Pilar in Salvador is reckoned one of the most delicate and lovely exteriors in Brazil. It is surpassed, travelers tell us, only by the Churrigueresque art of Mexico.

Salvador is a town of churches and old doorways, of gramophone shops that blare out sambas and tangos all day while the crowd hangs round the doorways listening. The population is chiefly Negro or mulatto. It is a place of cotton frocks, beauty parlors, barbershops. White trousers, white shirts, white frocks, everywhere, give these places a littered appearance. In the superb blue and steaming bay, the steep-prowed fishing boats in the Portuguese style come in with their lateen sails; and the purple pineapples, the bananas, the mangoes and the innumerable other fruits are heaped in the market and carried in baskets on yokes in the street. We never, in the north, eat pineapples like these, without acid or stringiness, as soft as scented water ices to the mouth. The Brazilian picks out his mango and smells it first, as if he were pausing to accept or reject the bouquet of a wine, making sure it has just the right, faint exhalation of the curious turpentinelike fragrance. In tropical countries, the scents and savors of the fruits are a refined pleasure of the senses. They are like wines in their vintages; indeed the fruit of South America is really the wine of the country, and the juices offered at the stalls belong to a world of natural soft drinks that is closed to palates hardened by alcohol. For myself, though I cannot drink the sweet Guaranà which is consumed all over Brazil, I find the dry Guaranà sold in the Amazon delicious. Most of the whiskey in South America, by the way, is a swindle, the gin deserves only to be drowned, the lager beer is excellent and the various vodkalike fire waters are for desperation.

North of Salvador is a foaming coast of white china clay, scrub and coconut palms. The country scene is made delightful by the sight—made so well-known to us by painters—of Negro women washing their linen and spreading out the sheets on grass that is as green as parrots. I watched a team of expert, nearly naked men play football at midday and some sweatless Negro athletes running through the town in training. At noon, on some little plane, a "mixed" of goods and passengers, you bump over the estuaries of the copra trade, tip giddily over the palms and come grating down on a blazing strip in the low jungle oven.

The company in these planes is familylike: a nun meeting relations, a couple of sailors, a Swiss trader, mothers and children. A car picks them up at the airport and takes them off into the trees. You step out into flame, crawl to the shade of a shed, where some silent man with a wheelbarrow of large green coconuts hacks the top off with one frightening slash of his machete, sticks a straw in it and hands it to you without a word. He knows what you want: a drink of that cold, refreshing milk; the knowing scrape out the yoghurtlike pulp afterward.

This is copra- and cotton-growing country. The plane comes down in Recife, which is called Pernambuco by sailors. It is on the most easterly hump of the South American leg of mutton, halfway between Rio and the mouth of the Amazon on the coastal route. Recife is the direct Atlantic airport for Africa and Europe. You land among the mango trees and a car bumps you over the bad roads into that flat Venetian city. The families, the young men and girls sit, silently, on the low walls of the serene, lagoonlike rivers in the hot night that is unendurable indoors. In your hotel you like listening to people talking all night long in the street below. When do they sleep in these places? Not in the morning. They are up at seven. Most journeys begin before dawn, when you pull yourself together with three or four cups of strong black coffee, before getting down to the real bouts of coffee drinking in the daylight hours. In this climate you are always drinking, sitting, mopping until—acclimatized at last—you watch without interest the flies sticking to your shirt. Recife has some of the oppression and desuetude of the tropics; a gray day there will be like lead. The trousers of the dockworkers are dirty and torn, coconut shells litter the gutters, beggars are numerous. You see the mulatto women asleep over their babies against the walls, or whining for alms, and others crying lottery tickets. Quite a portion of the population seems to be peddling ties and belts on the streets. It is a packed and dusty, swarming little town. There are sores and scars on the mahogany and malarial faces. To the mixture of races you saw at Salvador there is the addition of the old Dutch stock at Recife. There are pictures of the Portuguese victory over the Dutch in one of the churches. There is a superb golden sacristy here which has the beautiful blue Portuguese tiles; and in all the churches the decorations, the little pillared and petticoated balconies, are made of hardwood painted chalk-white or in clever imitation of marble. There was wood here, but not much stone, except the gray soapstone; much of the granite and stone and tiles, even the cobbles and bricks, were originally brought from Portugal in ballast.

All these coastal towns, where scrub and jungle and palm grove are not far off and sometimes come in to engulf, are interesting chiefly for the people. At the barber's in Recife, the fat man cutting your hair is almost asleep as he leans against you; some of his customers are fast asleep at eleven in the morning. On the blue river at Recife, with its brown Venetian shadows from quays, bridges and buildings, the crabcatchers go out on their curious plank boats, poling what seems no more than a board across the water; later, they will carry dozens of these electric blue crabs on strings through the streets. The suburbs of Recife are enchanting, the pretty houses are under the deep shade of the trees: the mangoes holding their fruit like large solid green tears, the palm, and the banana, that joyous and giant vegetation which is itself a kind of light masonry. In the gardens grow the millions of empty, vivid flowers and among them the golden and silver birds fly. At a street corner I remember the bamboo cages of a bird market where the birds gave their piercing tropical whistles and the blue macaws screeched like temperamental opera singers who have lapsed into vulgarity.

Amazonia

In South America there are two major experiences which humble and dwarf the traveler, which could easily exhaust a lifetime, which make him feel like an irrelevant insect: I have written of one of them—the Andes. There remains the Amazon, not only the greatest river in the world but the immense, almost untouched tropical forest which extends for nearly three thousand miles from the Andes to the mouth. Amazonia is a country in itself, totally without roads—for you cannot count the few miles of road that run out of Belém at the mouth, or from towns like Santarém, Manaus in Brazil and Iquitos in Peru—knowable only by the numberless waterways that spread like veins from the gross red arteries of the main rivers. Not always red; at Manaus, the great Río Negro comes in gray and silver, and for miles the two unmixing waters—the Amazon and the Negro—flow side by side. It is hard to know which of these seas of water—they will rise more than forty feet when the rains come—is the main one. You are looking down on a huge brown drainage system of innumerable lakes and tributaries and there is no feature in the unchanging landscape by which you can pick them out and name them with certainty. From the paddle steamers that go up to Manaus—those flat-bottomed, wood-burning houseboats, several stories high, with their scores of hammocks slung on the lower decks so that they look like floating laundries—the continuous jungle is a low wall standing back from a vivid green verge of reeds and grass and sand. I flew a thousand miles up the Amazon from Belém to Manaus; and, once there, up the Río Negro by boat.

From the air, the jungle is a close-packed carpet of what might be kale, starred by the palm trees or by puffs of silver. It is unchanging for thousands of miles, without hills or mountains, at any rate in the first fifteen hundred miles or more, and it is apparently uninhabited. Yet in a day's travel you come across numerous small riverside towns. The palm-thatched houses are propped on thin tall poles on the shore, against the seasonal floods, and there the river boats of all sizes, thatched or boarded against the sun, come with their fruit, their mandioca flour, their beans, their snakeskins, their cloth, to tie up or go phutting off on their daylong journeys up the blinding road of light. The alligator gazes at them from the bank, the angelfish cloud round them at the quays, the bloody piranha wait to attack in the streams and the pools.

In the boat the Indian family lives. The babies crawl about, the woman cooks or hangs out her washing, or calls to her neighbors—for these boats string along in tows, with the family parrot riding at the stern. These journeys start in the cool of dawn; by nine o'clock it is dangerous to expose your skin to the sun: in an hour you are blistered and in a fever of sunburn, deceived by the river breeze or the black, electric cloud-mountains of the coming tropical storm. When the rain comes, sky, forest and river turn to dirt and the spirits sink low, for the heat of the day is close and animal.

At first the jungle wall looks innocent and familiar like any stretch of creepered woodland we know, and there are places, above Manaus, where you would not be greatly surprised to see some well-known church spire rising. Then you notice the sudden flaunting of the fleshier trees, the liana curtains and the metallic leaves of the giant ferns, the immense bamboos and the scores of packed-in growths you may never know the names of, spreading their spell. You breathe the hot rot of the primeval forest floor. And there *is* a spell. This region acts like a drug. Men settle at Belém and then, once curiosity gets them up the river, they cannot rest until they have gone "further." I know a Brazilian engineer who took his wife and newborn baby up the river for months. "She knows that I am married also to the jungle," he said. Traders do well in Manaus and then sell out in order to get away to the upper, more savage reaches of the river. The climate reduces them to skin and bones, the bad diet ruins them, their will is eaten up by the lethargy of the forest, but they are held entranced by it. It is, they say, like a congenial poison and though sickness or exhaustion may make them glad to get out, they are just as likely to go back, as sailors go back to the sea on a bad ship they claim to hate.

The Amazon matches central Africa, but it is an Indian, not a Negro, region. Its soil is leached by rain and flood and can grow little in the way of crops and, of course, there are no cattle. Fresh meat, milk and vegetables must be flown in for those who cannot dispense with these luxuries. Those who live off the land live on nuts, fruits, beans, mandioca flour spread over tasteless dried meat, a little game and, when they can be had, turtles. The people of the Amazon are thin. The figures of the women are as straight as thin-armed boys. The people are all bone and have the Indian sharpness; yet they seem strong. They split the huge *bolas* of rubber with a blow of the machete; they load the boats, drive the trucks; they can hold the jaws of the alligators shut as they lever them out of the mud; they can hunt the puma, the peccary; they work in the rubber and jute factories. Near Manaus, oil men have found petroleum and are building a refinery. Along the river-banks you see the tall sticks of the prospectors and engineers. There is a strong river trade in snakeskins, indeed in all animals. A boy of fourteen caught a black puma on a fishing line last year. His father, an Austrian collector from Bolivia, had to play it as you play a salmon. A hunter's story? Down at pretty Belém, at the delta, you pass the little shops where the jaguar and the alligator skins are cured.

We stand high up in the Opera House at Manaus and look down on what for forty years has been a dying city. We see the Negro and the Amazon rivers divide, immense melancholy highways through forest that surrounds us for thousands of miles. We are in a kind of midocean. It looks innocent. Hard to believe all the tales of the poison trees, the stinking and the narcotic blossoms, the pools solid with giant toads and heaped with alligators, the terrible processions of ants, the hourly battles between mantis and beetle, the fantastic and disgusting lives of the parasites, the awful breeding and killing that goes on every minute. The hummingbirds rape the passion flowers and when the birds have gone, the huge butterflies—biding their time—follow in flocks to the scene the birds have betrayed to them. Yet, if nature is incredible here, man, too, has been astonishing. He found the secret of the rubber tree and when we see these half-naked men splitting the balls of rubber in some city warehouse, we see an industry that once made millions, now reduced almost to its primitive state once more. He built Manaus in the boom. He imported the city mainly from Portugal, all the cobblestones and black-and-white marble of the pavements, almost all the bricks and tiles. Some marble, especially in the Opera House, came from Italy and England. In a few years he created a spectacular capital; in a few years the boom ended, and now the city rots, the steel rusts, the walls crack.

Yet Manaus is not dead. The Indians trade on the river, the big ships sometimes come up in the nut season, or the jute season. If the town has decayed, it is nonetheless full of life. The airplanes land at the handsome airport. There is a luxury hotel. The modern world has not given up here, even if most of the food has to be flown in at heavy expense to sustain the impudence of modern man. And when we go back to Belém at the Amazon's mouth and see the shipping there, we once more have that sense of dramatic awakening we feel everywhere in Brazil.

We wait at night at the airport of Belém, listening to the deafening noise of the crickets, for the plane to take us back to New York. We have flown over ten thousand miles in South America. We are standing only a mile or two from the huge red maw of the greatest river in the world. It has been a journey through superlatives of size, through all that Nature is capable of in mountain heights, river, jungle, desert and plain. What can we compare with those thousands of miles over the Peruvian desert or the Andes, or over the jungle of Brazil? What was mere romance to us has now become real memory. We have seen the unparalleled lights of Rio like brooches pinned and pearls strung over the sea. We have seen Cotopaxi in its shirt of snow, the cobbles of the Inca highways, the Cyclopean stone of their temples; we have stood under the rain tree and the ombú and have gazed over harbors sailors have told us of: Valparaíso and Callao, Macao and Pernambuco. We have eaten the mango, drunk the Chilean wine, kicked avocado pears in the streets. We have seen the alligator in his river and seen butterflies the size of handkerchiefs. We have been frozen and breathless at Titicaca and have eaten its wonderful giant trout; we have had the night sit on us like a hot elephant in the tropics. We have talked with Indians, Negroes, mestizos and mulattoes, with all the Spanish and Portuguese mixtures, with great men, with ordinary men and the poor. We have seen the Indian woman trotting down the street shuttling her llama wool; we have seen the wives and daughters of the millionaires of Lima, Buenos Aires and Rio, in their diamonds and emeralds. In Colombia, Ecuador, Peru, Chile, in the Argentine, Uruguay and Brazil, we have seen seven versions of Iberian civilization transplanted, some feudal, some ultra-modern, all violently different and continuing that tradition of explosive individuality which they brought from Europe. We have been plunged into a life whose values are often basically distinct from our own, and which is awake and creative. What, we must ask, will this continent become when it is fully opened up and its huge natural resources used? All travelers in South America are staggered by its wealth and its prospects. They are overcome by its beauty. We have had the incredible luck to see a continent at the moment of its awakening.

[1956]

2

Portugal

The first things one must understand about Portugal are that Portugal is not Spain and the Portuguese language may look like Spanish in print, but sounds impenetrably unlike it.

There was, for example, the shouting man in the chief café of the Portuguese town of Évora. Évora is a small place of twenty-two thousand people, with a square of white arcades, standing like a pile of hot white china on a bluff in the brown and melancholy plateau of the region they call the Alentejo, which spreads south of the Tagus to the Spanish frontier. The shouting man was tall, gaunt and black haired, with agitated and flashing eyes; he was making gestures two yards wide with his fingers spread apart and talking with all his body. Adventures, tales, people, opinions poured out of him, though one could not hear exactly what, because Portugal is the land of tiles. The houses, the churches, the banks, the cafés are tiled inside and often outside, too, and the tiles echo so that one or two men in a room sound like a crowd in a bathroom.

The man was surrounded by a respectful group of short, stoutish listeners who said nothing. "Who is that man who talks so much?" we asked the waiter. The waiter said, "He is a Spaniard." He was. He was the gay caballero in person, the stage Spaniard as the Portuguese see him—the man of emphasis, theater, fantasy, distraction, explosion, words.

The group of small Portuguese listened in the obliging and acquiescent manner of their nation. They do not like Spaniards much: from Spain, says the Portuguese proverb, no good wind blows. "We do not take them too seriously," they say. "They are fantastics. We are a small nation. We have to work. You will perhaps find our country lacking in drama." They say this wistfully but with a good deal of irony; and perhaps they will tell the old tale of the Portuguese and the Spanish student: At the university, the Spaniard proclaimed that one day he would be Archbishop of Salamanca; the Portuguese modestly said he was content to be the parish priest of his village. Years later the two friends met in a Spanish village. The Portuguese had indeed become the parish priest, the Spaniard was a mere ragged sacristan. "What has become of your great ambition?" the Portuguese asked. The Spaniard replied with pride, "Had it not been for my great ambition I should never have risen as high as this."

Spain is hermetic. It turns a mere shoulder to the Atlantic, and where it faces the sea, that sea is the Mediterranean. But Portugal faces the long roll of the great ocean. It has been called five hundred miles of Atlantic beach. There are no Spanish extremes of climate. Here everything is warm and mild; the Atlantic moistens the air, the rainclouds come and go over a fair and delicate sky.

One can see from an aircraft that the great tableland of Spain breaks at the Portuguese frontier into lower hills and small wooded mountains. There are scarcely any peaks as high or as wolfish as those that put their black ears through the cloud when the aircraft is passing from the Bay of Biscay to the northwest of the Iberian Peninsula. The lionlike tableland and dry rock, the clear air, give way to smaller country; and a haze, no more than a puff of tobacco smoke, gives a tenderness to the brilliant light of Portugal. The great river Douro which, like the Tagus, has come hundreds of miles out of Spain, lies as green as oil between the terraced ravines where the vines of the north are growing, and everywhere there are woods of pine and oak, chestnut and birch and eucalyptus, and in the marshes by the coast, the rice fields and the long pyramids of white salt. We are in a country altogether gentler than Spain. We are flying over a garden, and the sun, though very hot, boils rather than flames.

When the plane wheels over the heat haze of sea and sand and comes down at Lisbon airport, the buildings there indeed have the Iberian stare, but the gay colors in which they are painted—the saffrons, the greens, the pale blues and pinks and lilacs—soften the blinding effect. One smells an air that moves among flowers, hangs under fat palms and has honey in it. There is sweetness. One is going to be living in a sort of *gâteau* laced by some sweet liqueur. Consideration, quiet, a domestic simplicity, make the fine buildings of the airport a place of ease. The very language of the people, with its closing vowels, cooing *o*'s, its slow shuffling *sh*'s, diphthongs which strike like guitar notes and sobs in the middle of a word, and its habit of cutting off syllables and running words together, as if the speaker had awakened too briskly from sleep, suggests a Spanish blunted and softened by the crunch and shishing of the Atlantic on the shores.

Why are Spain and Portugal separate? It is a question which puzzles Spaniards but the Portuguese not at all. They have (they say) been able "to imagine themselves as a people," in spite of their similarities of history. Before the twelfth century they were not separate, and for a short time they were ruled by Philip II—a Spanish royal coach can be seen in the fantastic museum of royal coaches at Belém, outside Lisbon.

The seaboard formed and aided the Portuguese; they were seamen and traders. Spanish power stood between them and Western Europe, and in the struggle of Britain and France against Spanish totalitarianism, the Portuguese became their natural allies in sea warfare. The westward-looking Portuguese turned by need to the sea and the foreigner; the Spaniard turned against him.

That is the huge difference. In every century the Portuguese has admired the foreigner; he will go to astonishing lengths of hospitality, friendship and even humility in order to oblige him. The man in the garage or office will leave his work at once to show the visitor his town, pointing out the carvings in a library or the sculpture in a cathedral, and the traveler in Portugal finds everywhere people who are, with almost artless courtesy, his friends. The educated are good linguists; they prefer to speak French rather than Spanish. Since the middle of the eighteenth century the most favored foreigners have been first the French—whom the Spaniards detest—and then the British. Foreign electric signs are mounted on the roofs of the squares and avenues of Lisbon; foreign domestic goods pack the Lisbon shops; a British company owns the tramway system in the capital. Foreign fleets anchor in the splendid estuary of the Tagus; foreign sailors have given famous nicknames to the squares. And when the Spaniard tells the Portuguese that they, too, are Iberians, and that they have enslaved themselves to the foreigners, the industrious Portuguese, a grave and patient man, points to his contacts with the world at large and says he is placidly free from that violent love-hate toward Europe which has been the dramatic but often destructive conflict in Spanish life. Tact, sensibility, a regard for the sentiments rather than the passions—this comes out at once in the Portuguese. This does not mean that he lacks the hard core of Iberian pride; foreigners who have employed servants in Portugal and Spain say that the Portuguese is not to be casually treated and requires a regard for his private feelings, interests and life which the Spaniard is indifferent to as long as he can amuse himself.

Portugal is one of the two surviving corporate states in Europe, designed on the Italian-Fascist model but very different from the excitable government of General Franco. Salazar, the Portuguese dictator, did not rise to power after conducting a civil war against his own countrymen. He is not a general, nor even, in his early career, a politician. He is a professor of economics and a bachelor from the old University of Coimbra, and he was put into power by the army a couple of years after the military coup of 1926. He has ruled undisturbed ever since.

Salazar's portrait can be seen in many offices in Lisbon. It is the picture of a shy, wistful, rather sly, shrewd and sad-looking man, even cruel, in an ascetic way, in the mouth. He is not Big Brother. One is more inclined to call him Big Sister. He is reputed to be a fanatical worker, relentless to his assistants, deeply and ironically cunning in his political moves. He appears very little in public. He is a pious Catholic. The power of the Church is far less in Portugal than in Spain, for the country has retained a good deal of the liberalism of its constitutions of the 1820s, which Spain never did. The Church has never recovered from the dissolution of the monasteries in 1834, when they were turned into barracks. That power increased under Salazar, but his aim has been to create something in the nature of the peasant Catholic state—certainly not Fascism.

There are of course secret police, and people are noticeably cautious about talking politics, but occasionally one hears a public outburst. On the tram coming in from Belém one day the conductor said to me, "There's no freedom here. The government is corrupt. We are silenced. We have the lowest standard of life in Europe and we are in chains." I have seen lower standards of life. No one took any notice of the conductor, perhaps out of Portuguese politeness to foreigners: they did not wish to involve me; perhaps out of fear of being concerned with politics; perhaps they were not interested. The taxi driver to whom you say, "Everyone seems happy here," replies quizzically, "Anyone who says he's happy is not Portuguese." And if one says to a doctor, a professor or a businessman that Salazar has obviously modernized the country to an enormous extent—for the difference between Portugal twenty-five years ago and Portugal today is immense; in housing alone the advance is remarkable—and has put Portugal economically on its feet, he becomes touchy and says, "Yes, but it is frustrating and destroying to be ruled by an accountant."

Portugal has not lost all its liberal spirit. There is opposition to Salazar, and it is hard to know what goes on underground; but when trial elections were held a year or two back, the opposition came from the older generation. The suspicion was that the young, apparently, had lost interest in politics, a tendency to be noted all over Europe. As for the corporate state, that is one more of the political blueprints which the Iberian nations excel in producing—and never really put into effect. Cynics point out that the final organization to cap the pyramid of corporations has never been created. The government is simply a "strong government," based on army support, which is tiding the country over the change from backwardness into modern techniques; it has made, for example, notable inroads on illiteracy. The pro-Nazi phase of Spain never spread to Portugal, which is inevitably the ally of those who control the sea and, like maritime nations generally, little subject to fanaticism.

There are only two cities in Portugal: Lisbon with nearly a million inhabitants and growing every year, like all southern European cities; and

Oporto, the wine and textile city in the north, where the revolutions have traditionally started, with 300,000 people. Lisbon is the most splendidly situated capital in Europe. Something of the sparkle of Venice and the pleasure of Naples is in its character. The great river Tagus, cutting its way through Castile, widens in the softer Portuguese landscape and opens into sealike lagoons as it comes toward the estuary where Lisbon glitters, so that far inland one can see the tall russet sails of the luggers moving, as if they were some magical landcraft, between the prairies and the vines. At Lisbon itself the estuary is widening fast and is marked all along by the chalky flush of pretty villages and little towns. A nation seems to be gathering itself jubilantly to look at the sea.

At first sight Lisbon looks like a sedate Oriental arrangement of clean-colored plaster boxes, cut sharply into the sky. It is built on a great many short hills, nobly crowned here by a castle, there by a palace or by the dome or tower of a church; but the center of the city has the dignity and order of all creations of the eighteenth century. It was rebuilt after the great catastrophe which shook the Age of Reason everywhere in Europe and was indeed used in Voltaire's *Candide*—the earthquake of the 1750s. To this Lisbon owes its eighteenth-century squares, above all the elegant Black Horse Square, on the waterfront, which is often compared to Saint Mark's in Venice. The crowds who cross by ferry from the opposite bank of the Tagus, a mile or more away, step off the boat to stand at once before this palatial entrance. From here the city rises into breakneck hills paved in skiddy black-and-white marble mosaic. (One might exaggerate and say half of Portugal is paved in marble and walled in tiles.) Up these steep streets the yellow trams are always groaning, the cars changing gear, the crowds climbing or mounting by short funicular or by the astonishing street lift in the center of the city. One looks down over red roofs and gardens upon the Rossio, where the crowds stand about on the pavement and sit in the cafés. Descending to the middle of the square, one can see a small section of that waved puzzle-paving of marble which once covered the whole space and got the name of Rolling Stone Square from every British sailor who tried to cross it in his cups; it has never puzzled the abstemious, coffee-drinking Portuguese.

Above the Rossio is the Avenida—a wide imitation Champs-Élysées with flowering trees—and beyond are the fine modern quarters of a city beautifully planned to please the eye with its colored walls. Always the tactful adapters of foreign things, the Portuguese have taken the violence and megalomania out of modern architecture. They have colored it, calmed it and set it in trees and flowers, for Portugal is a subtropical garden. The flowers hang from the balconies, the long parades of scarlet and yellow canna from the West Indies civilize the avenues; bougainvillea and the blue-trumpeted convolvulus hang like colored foam from the iron-gated villas, creepers flower on the walls and, in the wide walks under the trees, acacia and mimosa sweeten the air. Capital cities tend to public display and monumental magnificence, but the public things in Lisbon have a familiarity and grace, as though public splendor were tempered by private fantasy.

And that is what one finds all over Portugal. It is above all a country of family life closely connected with the farms and the land. Victorian in its domestic living but, as in Spain, with some passive, torpid inheritance from the Orient in it. Lisbon is masculine, not feminine like Paris; nor do the sexes seem to challenge each other, as they do in Spain, in formal battles of eye-warfare and display. There are more homely women than there are alarming beauties. Men and women pursue their lives separately and, in the middle classes, women rule their lives by the strictest appearance of propriety: "I could not be seen at such and such an hour in such and such a street." They rarely go out alone; or if they do, they provide their families, their aunts and cousins with proper explanations. They delight demurely in an elaborate web of conventional intrigue.

In the working classes and among the peasantry, there is a marked difference of custom, for here the women work in the fields, wash clothes in the rivers, spin wool, mend the nets. Women are the great carriers of the country. They walk like queens, with a basket of wash, a pumpkin, a water jar, a load of sticks on their heads. I have seen a pair of them loaded up by men with a heavy glass door or a spring mattress—talking and gesticulating as they go without concern. And, since everything in Portugal is sooner or later turned into a fiesta, the women carriers of the country can be said to have their formal celebration in the procession of the Tabuleiros by the river and gardens of Tomar. The girls, each accompanied by a young man, carry on their heads new loaves of bread skewered by canes into a high pyramid and decorated with flowers. It is the stateliest of all the Portuguese processions.

The fishwives of Lisbon are the most famous community of head carriers. It is sometimes believed that they are descendants of the Phoenicians, as are also the curiously costumed, silent fishermen at Nazaré up the coast, where the wives sit mending the nets on the shingle, side by side with the teams of oxen who drag the moonlike fishing boats up the beach. Whether they are Phoenicians or not, the Lisbon fishwives are a strong-hipped, strong-armed race, with iron calves and iron voices. In their bunched cotton petticoats and colored scarves they come shouting out of the market by the Tagus, carrying heavy trays of fish on their heads, swinging both arms free as they stride or half trot along, the trays turning without tipping as they glance at the traffic. The feet of these women are large and broad and scarred, sometimes bandaged, and the law has lately obliged them to wear slippers. They race in pairs up the narrow side streets and there start bawling, take their slippers off and put them on the fish until they catch sight of a policeman. Then on they go again. The fishwives of Lisbon are the powerful matriarchy of the port.

You sit in the early evening in a café under the trees of the Avenida, where the cars are racing in the rush hour. The bootblack, the youth with his tray of ties, the pencil sketcher who draws your portrait and leaves it lying about if you don't want it, come to the table. They do not pester. Almost shyly they go away. There are no Portuguese apéritifs; one or two men drink iced beer, but most are drinking the small cups of strong black Brazilian or Angolan coffee. The especially sober add a little water to it. In the bar a man here or there drinks *vinho verde*, the young heady acid wine from the north, out of a china mug.

The restaurants fill up with solemn family parties—father and mother, son-in-law and daughter—who eat heavily. There is a habit of serving a spoonful of rice, a piece of lettuce or raw tomato with nearly everything, even fish and sucking pig. The most powerful dish is *bacalhau*, the stew of dried cod served in a bed of sliced potatoes, and the ways of cooking it are noted by connoisseurs in every town. It is the national dish and an acquired taste, for it is preferred strong. The oil on the salad will be strong, too, for the Portuguese like it on the rancid side and let their olives rot a little before the oil is made. The portions are huge and the light wines are good, though often thick to the palate. No one drinks port; that is an English or a French aberration.

Toward eleven o'clock one goes to the Bairro Alto or to the Alfama, the warren on the hill where first the Jews and then the Negro slaves lived and listened to the street songs of the city.

What *cante flamenco* is to Spain, the *fado* is to Portugal, though the only thing they have in common is the popular, even vulgar nature of their origin. In some tavern of the Alfama or in a simple nightclub of the Bairro Alto one can hear these popular songs, sometimes (it is true) in a debased jingling song-hit form, but quite often in their true melodious, insidious manner.

The genuine *fado* is melancholy and melting. Three guitarists come; two playing small, round Portuguese guitars, a tinkling and sweet instrument which runs on like a woman's voice, the third touching the rhythm with the deeper-toned Spanish instrument. Presently the singer gets up—either a woman in black, wearing the long black woollen shawl of the people, or a man in his most sober suit. The singer's face becomes trancelike; he clasps his hands before him, leans his head back so that he is all throat, closes his eyes in an expression of surrender and pain. And then out comes the little song, some ballad of parted lovers, of loss, despair, longing or resignation, perhaps of prostitutes and criminals or of popular religion. The tune runs and falls to an undulating rhythm—some have suggested the *fado* was the song of the fishermen as they came home on the Atlantic swell—it has lilting pauses on suspended notes which break suddenly like sobs and create a new mood, and then it either fades away to a hesitating murmur or skirls out in a melo-dramatic climax. The diphthongs, the nasals, the narrow and manipulated vowels of Portuguese, in themselves give a delicacy to the simple words.

The *fado* catches something of the Portuguese proneness to mood rather than to passion. Two key words occur over and over again: *sentimental* and the famous, untranslatable *saudade*, to which these untrained voices bring a melting power. *Saudade* is sometimes called nostalgia, but it is not quite that. It is a longing for something that can never be defined; or, perhaps, a mixture of the vague longings of the Celt (for the Celtic strain is strong in Portugal) corrected by Latin realism: but the longings are unattainable. The result is a mood of stoicism in despair which, from the days of the early terrible sea voyages to India, has been fundamental in Portuguese character.

Some writers say the *fado* was taken to Brazil by Negro slaves and given back to Lisbon when the Negroes were brought here, and there is indeed a blurred, plaintive, African softness in the song. A classical *fado* of a more polished and lyrical kind is sung in Coimbra, the university city. It is composed and sung by parties of students in their black cloaks as they walk under the poplars and cypresses and acacias of the romantic Mondego River. In Coimbra, the *fado* is aristocratic; it is a street song no longer.

Portugal is a small country, but it has those intense differences of regional life that astonish the traveler in both countries of the Iberian Peninsula. The Tagus cuts the country in two. In Estremadura one is in country of high rolling hills, with pine and eucalyptus that break into rice fields, maize plots and olive groves in the steep yellow places. There are small colored villages each with its white church, framed in gray stone and embossed with the seignorial flourishes of baroque ornament, its beds of brilliant flowers. Hills of vines break the woodlands. There is the strong smell of pine; the yellow irises grow near the watercourses, there are cyclamen and jonquils; bougainvillea and convolvulus hang in purple and blue cascades on the walls of the houses; hydrangeas bush by the roadside, with the cactus and the aloe. A land of kind climate, without frost, for a simple, dreaming, yet hardworking, people.

At Coimbra, the elegant university crowns the steep hills of the old town (which, alas, the Portuguese with their mania for modernity and restoration are beginning to pull down) looking over the long gracious valley of its river. There are superb libraries in Portugal, and Coimbra's library, with its lacquered stepladders and its profuse, painted ceilings, surpasses the elegant library of Mafra. In Coimbra no first-year student is allowed out in the street after six in the evening, and if he is caught by the "bulldogs" they have the right to shave his hair off then and there. They do. (I notice in the last twenty years the students are giving up their fine black cloaks.)

In all that is decorative the Portuguese have delighted and excelled. This happy region is fertile, but it is never far to the mountains, to a tougher mountain people, to the rock villages of Beira, and to the wild places of Trasos-Montes, the forgotten province on the Spanish frontier. At Oporto, in the north, we enter the most Celtic part of Portugal, the gayest and (as they quickly tell you) the hardest working. This region is the Minho, with its wool towns, its textile towns, its small felt factories, its timber, its wine. In the vineyards the grape gatherers and treaders wander from *quinta* to *quinta* to the music of accordion and guitar, and tread the grapes to their sparkling tunes until the treading is itself a dance. For miles and miles in the Minho the vines grow on trellises and are trained to the poplars so that the whole country is garlanded, festooned and boxed in vine. The wide-horned oxen draw the carts on the road and the plows in the fields between the silvery veiling of birch trees and solid chestnuts and pines. As the infinitely slow train bumps along there is the twang of a guitar at the stations of small towns, the cries of the bread sellers and water sellers; the black-suited, wooden-faced peasant walks with his umbrella against the sun or the rain, or with his long crook-like stick; a girl will walk with a pumpkin or a washing bundle on her head. Under the shade of her vines, where an ox is turning the waterwheel, an old lady will be working her spinning wheel, passing the pink wool through her hands. Wool hangs bleaching in the gardens and barefooted women tread the maize or scutch the flax.

Small charcoal fires are lit everywhere for the cooking; mechanics, plow-men, farmers buy their tools for the year; and in the autumn the chestnuts are stacked. The chestnut roaster sits up in the alleys of the fair, and placid ladies sit before their little tables with clean white cloths spread on them, two or three glasses, cakes and a bottle of syrup, almost like a doll's tea party, for those who want a drink. Rarely does one see a drunken man at these cele-brations. The Portuguese wines are light, and drunkenness and violence are frowned on. Even to raise the voice is not liked; the imperative is never used; orders are framed as questions.

Oporto stands on a steep ravine crossed by spectacular hooplike bridges. It is a city of granite and gray—severe, rather slummy, rimed by fogs and struck by rain in the autumn and winter. On the south bank of the river are the port-wine lodges. The wine is brought down the river on the strange sail-ing barges with their galleylike prows and their long, curved tillers, and the black casks in the lodges stand in rows like some solemn and full bellied priesthood. There the blenders work, the coopers hammer at the casks and pairs of men seesaw the barrels as they wash them out. In a room like a dis-pensary the tasters sit, working out their formulas; they consider the rows of labeled glasses, take a mouthful on their valuable palates and then give the ritual spit of their profession. They must be born with the palate; no voca-tional training center or university course can give it to them. They are the high priests, and some have a look of rubicund sanctity and of exquisite mar-tyrdom to the vine.

South of the Tagus is a different Portugal, something at once more Spanish and, eventually, more African. The country of the cork forests has begun, the bare hilly lands of scrub and olive, where goats are herded and pigs fatten on acorns. The prairies of the horse breeders and the bull breeders are in the upper valley of the Tagus near Vila Franca de Xira, where the bunched-up country women kilt their skirts and tie them round their legs like trousers, and the men carry their day's food to their work in pots made of cork, which act like vacuum flasks and keep the food hot.

If one travels first of all toward the perfect little town of Évora, the country loses its garden aspect and opens into a rising and tawny plateau. As in the wildernesses of eastern Spain, the air here seems drier and more limpid, the sky takes on an extra height; at night the brilliant hard stars are close to the soil. Here are large estates, and mournful songs are sung by the brushwood fires in the evenings. The men walk into the arcaded square of the white town of Évora wearing jackets of sheepskin and the long, green stocking hats. They spread the colored saddlebags on their donkeys, or carry striped blankets over their shoulders. There is a thin garlic soup to eat, stewed tripe with bits of sausage to follow, boiled potatoes and sliced tomato and the rancid olive oil. On gray days, as in Spain, the sky is fixed like some thundery and motionless sculpture over the scrubby, silent, monotonous land. One passes chalk-white villages, each house framed in a border of blue wash, and they are as startlingly clean inside as they look outside. A town like Évora is a museum piece of the baroque. Every house has its seventeenth-century flourish, every church its extravagance. The barley-sugar columns of the altar may be in indigo or blue. Like all Portuguese towns Évora seems to be populated only by men. Male voices echo in the tiled walls of the cafés, men in the billiard rooms above, in the market square, in the buses, in the shops. I counted only thirty women coming out of the cinema there in the evening, and at least three hundred men.

On the south side of the Tagus one drives through cork forests, where the tree trunks, stripped every nine years, seem to be wearing dark ginger-colored nylons. Here the gypsies are camped; slender and smoky-skinned, beautiful in carriage, there is no gypsy like the Iberian, but, unlike the Spanish, the Portuguese gypsy is not a dancer. One moves on to the Arrabida, the southward-facing mountain range, where there is an almost Mediterranean stretch of coast to Setúbal, the delightful sardine town, one of the great packing places of the country. The wide, clean avenues of palms and flowering trees, the acacia and the jacaranda, the pretty, colored houses, the candid sky, give this place of fishing boats an air of well-being and gaiety. There is a graceful, odd church with columns which seem to be of three loosely twisted hanks of stone, like yarn or rope. This is the work of Boytac, often called the inventor of Manoeline architecture—that form of baroque which draws so many of its motifs from nautical themes.

One is traveling now over open brown hills, with windmills set in threes or fours for corn grinding on their summits—the windmill is one of the common sights of Portugal and commoner than Don Quixote's windmills in La Mancha. The country becomes lonelier, emptier, the villages farther apart, until after a day's driving or a night in the slow-moving train one is in—Africa. The air is strongly scented, and hot with that soft and total heat that takes the strength out of the bones. The locust flutters on the canes, the flies bite, the cricket trills at night as people sit half asleep in the cafés. The houses are low and white and have religious pictures done in light tiles on their walls. Along the roadside geraniums grow like trees. Here in the huddled Moroccan villages one sees the small, pierced, nearly conical chimneys of Africa. The fig trees droop their long branches and, in October, when the leaves have fallen, look like the gray skeletons of huge crabs crawling across the ground in the moonlight.

Just as the Lisbon *fado* differs in spirit from *cante flamenco* as it is sung in Seville, so the Portuguese bullfight differs from the Spanish. In Spain, the bullfight is tragedy: in Portugal, comedy. In Spain, ritual; in Portugal, chivalry, a real survival from the original bullfights of the sixteenth century, when the bull was fought on fine horses by the aristocracy. If Spain is the country of the bull, Portugal is the country of the horse; in their bullfights the Portuguese desire most to bring out the superiority of the graceful horse and the stupid violence of the bull. And, unlike the Spanish, these gentle people do not allow the bull to be killed. The reasons for this are historical but they are also in the Portuguese character, which is noted for its care of animals and its dislike of violence—in passing it may be noted that capital punishment has long ago been abolished in the country.

There are not many bullrings in Portugal, and there is no hierarchy of famous bullfighters. The most important ring is the strange, Russian-looking place in Lisbon with its onion-turrets. When the opening parade marches into the ring, the chief figures are not the *toureiros* but the horsemen, who come in on perfectly trained animals with the step of the *haute école*. The horsemen wear the traditional costume of the old court, the horses are often plumed and beribboned.

The opening move in the fight is a pursuit, so that the bull may show his fury; at the barrier, the pursued horseman skillfully turns and plants a small dart from his lance in the bull's neck; he then rides back to the middle of the ring and makes the dramatic "call to the bull," shouting to him to come on. From that moment the fight becomes a series of exciting skirmishes, sudden turns and evasions, thrilling in its grace. The bull's horns have been shortened and are capped by leather knobs so that the horse cannot be injured; but an expert rider will ride close to the bull and avoid even a graze from the bull. The whole art lies in taking the charge and yet, by a flick of the reins, cheating the bull of his collision. There are no wild careers or clumsy scuffles. After a number of darts have been planted, a *toureiro* may work on foot with the bull, making the Spanish passes and simulating the death stroke.

After this comes the most curious act of the spectacle. A file of men, wearing the dress of the peasants on the bull-raising farms and called *moços de forcado*, advances upon the bull. The bull charges at the leader, who flings himself between the horns and weighs down on the bull's head, while the rest of the team scramble on his back or hug him by the tail until he rolls over. If the first man is tossed, the next takes the charge, but once the bull is down he is officially dead; there is the pleasant deep clang of cowbells, twenty or thirty bulls are driven in and the defeated bull goes out with them.

The evening is milky over the Tagus, the red sun goes down in a fume of lilac haze over the sea. The waves roar under the most westerly cape in Europe, and from the little fishing town of Cascais one hears the evening bugle call at the fort and sees the barefoot fishermen on the shore and the bright blue floats among their nets. The estuary is rimmed by lights for mile after mile. At Estoril, the little Monte Carlo, the flower gardens are drawn up like a military review for the consolation of the exiled kings, heirs and pretenders to European thrones who preserve here their waning protocols, their large cars, their tennis, their stamp collections and their surviving scandals. It is a little Ruritania in Riviera dress, with beach guards to supervise the propriety of the bathing costumes.

Estoril's last high moment was the war; for Lisbon was the gateway in and out of occupied Europe. Inland at Cintra, the moon—indispensable to the romantic scene—sails up over the Moorish castle on the "horrid crag" and the grotesque Germanic castle which was the home of Manoel II, the last Portuguese king, who left the country in 1910. The view from the castle is stupendous and the gardens of the park that hangs down the hill are enchanting at the time of the camellias. Cintra is cool after the heat of Lisbon. The fountains tinkle in its still and wooded gardens; cascades and cisterns make their birdlike water music among the trees. Cintra is a cool and shaded Capri; there are villas like fantastic wedding cakes, and a gazebo to every wall. The horse carriages trot, the donkeys come clipping in from the outlying farms, the barking of dogs echoes back over the lemon groves in the ravine. Time has stopped since the decorous days of the Romantic poets; Byron or Southey might be walking there.

From its terrace high over the plain Cintra looks to the site of Mafra, sticking up like a wisdom tooth miles away on the horizon, a royal palace and monastery built to surpass the Escorial in Spain. The marble of Mafra chills one to the bone. This is the last and most despotic monument to the royal wealth that Portugal lost in Brazil, and it declaims, on its bleak site, that it was one of the most costly buildings in the world. Once more the bugle call. From some side door the slack sentries come shuffling up grinning to a change of guard: the monastery is part barracks.

There are three Portugals for the traveler: Portugal of the garden and the peasant's plot; the historic and living Portugal of the sea; and sometimes oddly allied to it, the Portugal of architecture. In painting there is little to see. On the crag at Cintra the Moorish castle stands like a falling crown; the Portuguese drove the Moors out of Portugal. The Portuguese stared at the sea and went to Madeira and the Azores and the African coast. They traded in ivory and slaves. Under their half-English king, Henry the Navigator, their energies came to a head in the great age of discovery. Spain and Portugal shared the world. There were great captains like Vasco da Gama and Albuquerque; Magellan was Portuguese. To Spain went the Americas, but not

75

Brazil; to Portugal the African coast, India and the East Indies. There was a tremendous and, as it turned out, mortal upprush of energy and the reward of enormous and sudden wealth. The Portuguese genius was dominant, like the Spanish, in the fifteenth and sixteenth centuries, and it declined as rapidly. The great discoveries in India and Malacca and Africa meant setting up trading stations; stations meant forts; the drain of life in shipwreck, fighting and, above all, sickness was enormous. There was a heavy loss by intermarriage and desertion. Slaves, Negro and Indian, were brought back to Portugal to replace the declining population. The Portuguese of today is of a very different racial strain from his forebears in the sixteenth century. One historian writes that the Spanish discoveries were dramatic but that the Portuguese were tragic. The Spanish ended in the bitter smile of Cervantes; the Portuguese, less emphatic and better balanced than the Spaniard, ended in the stoical sadness of measured people.

Not only slaves came back—to be freed in the eighteenth century—but gold, silver and precious stones. The palaces and altars of Portugal are dark with gold leaf. This wealth went mainly to the court and the Church, and the great captains who went out from Belém quay, committing themselves to God, were to awaken an appetite for fantastic luxury, for ornament and the grandiose, which is one of the paradoxes of the frugal Iberian temperament. In Lisbon, in all the small towns, in the great convents and palaces, the traveler finds himself moving from one golden room to another. None reveled in the baroque or elaborated the rococo like the Portuguese, none enjoyed so much—for love of fine work and detail is in their nature—the inlaying of fine woods; ebony and walnut, mahogany and cedar.

Portugal has always been the country of the tile maker and the potter and so, in the churches, the walls are glazed by profuse murals in blue and white ceramic telling the story of the Fall of Man or the Crucifixion. And in this bold, blue setting are placed the painted sculptures of the time. The saints and the angels stare rosily and with ardor, and there is all the grace of living expectancy and movement in the carved robes of the beckoning and turning bodies. At churches like São Roque in Lisbon, the luxury may surfeit the northern eye, which wonders, too, at the scores of relics encased in glass boxes held in some painted arm or metaled hand; but presently, as one abandons oneself to it, one feels the sensuous spirit of the makers of the country itself. The barley-sugar columns of rococo art are golden; all that is not rare marble, or rare wood, is gold; for golden vine leaves wind round the columns bearing their golden grapes and (as if this were not enough in an orgy which suggests the gaieties of the wine harvest), cherubs appear like pink rosebuds among the vines.

In Lisbon, in Oporto, in Braga and the little textile town of Guimarães, there are silver altars. The dream of precious metals has never died, though the mines of India and Brazil are gone. At Oporto is the most bizarre of all the golden-leaf churches of Portugal, for here not only the altars but the pillars and the vaulting are covered with fantastic golden leafage, and one seems to be walking in a hanging subtropical forest, where vines climb the columns and the pampas waves among golden angels and cherubs. Even hosts of golden birds are flying among the chaotic foliage.

The discoverers of India and Malacca awakened this appetite for wealth and excess, and though it gluts the eye, its heaviness is relieved by the artlessness of the things used. The Portuguese architects and sculptors did not think it incongruous to use motifs from the tackle of ships or the grotesque sights of the sea. Textures and shapes suggested by cork—for Portugal is an important supplier of cork to the world from the woods of the Alentejo—frame the windows. In the magnificent convent of the Templars at Tomar is the well-known chapter window, a window that Vasco da Gama or some fisherman might have dragged up in his net from the bottom of the tropical sea. The framing pillars are fashioned to look like coral, and the buttresses appear to grow out of sea anemones; rope and sails appear, and below is the figure of a sailor drowning or riding with the gale. This is not one of the aberrations of art nouveau but something cut daringly out of the riotous confidence of Portuguese life in its time. The articles of the mariner's life, his fears and fantasies, have been subdued into an astonishing work of art.

It is one of the strange contrasts of this peasant country, where the people are seen always in their gardens, that it is also the country of the ocean and all that it makes men imagine. The traveler who spends a few days at the little fashionable resort of Praia da Rocha, where the Atlantic comes in warm, its spray smoking in the sunlight, can drive out across empty country, marked here and there by little villages which look purely Moroccan, to Cape St. Vincent and catch something of the drama of Portuguese discovery in its beginnings. On this lonely cape one of the most powerful lighthouses in Europe now swings a light that is seen far out into the Atlantic. The time to go is in the evening and to imagine the hiss, which (the Arabs said) the setting sun made when its fireball met the ocean; but what really moves one is the sight of the ruined royal hermitage where Henry the Navigator worked at his nautical sciences, and the rudimentary compass drawn out in small cobblestones on the grass. It stares up like a skeleton on the loneliest, most westerly outcrop of Europe, at what was once the very edge end of the land known to European man. It is a sight as moving as Stonehenge or Avebury, and as one stands there one can hear the ocean crack against the cliffs and suck in the tunnels it has cut under them. It howls up the holes in the scrub of the clifftop where you walk, like the voices of the thousands of Portuguese sailors who left their country for new worlds.

[1956]

3

Down the Seine

The Seine is the life stream of Paris; it is part of the life stream of all of us. So much of us has been left behind with it. There have been very few years of my adult life when I have not walked for days, weeks or even months beside the river, daydreaming with that effervescence of the senses and that leaping and dragging of the heart that the perfect river evokes. It is conducted through the city with great and simple art. The roadways run above it and the trees—the plane, the acacia, the poplar and the linden are continuous. More tall trees grow from the quays below, their long trunks sloping a little toward the river at an angle that breaks the monotony of upright line. The walls in the main are of white stone, not glaring white, but those varying whites shading toward saffron, like the cheese of Brie, and when they are gray, as they are in the Île de la Cité, it is not an implacable prison gray. The stains are not foul. Although Maupassant and others have insulted the water, the Seine is far cleaner in Paris than is the Thames in the middle of London. Fish can live in it. It is far beyond the reach of the tides, it has a calm close rippling movement and never swirls except in the time of winter floods, and it has not that leathery look of rivers near the sea. It is a quivering and marbled water. Its surface is made of millions of light brush strokes of tarnished silver and green-grays, and under the faintly ochered arches of the bridges there are jade pools where the light sometimes catches the waltzing fishes. From the river the eye never winces. It is not mysterious even when the white winter fogs lie on it, and there is always enough mist in the Paris air to soften any hard, urban formality the architects have imposed. At night, because trees parade the banks through the city, the lime-colored and golden lights that pierce the water are not the riotous lights of buildings but come from the lamps which proceed with that measured gaiety found in the movement of the water itself.

In the center of Paris the Seine is a bookish, cultivated and learned river. Religion, politics, the law, the sciences, the arts are close to it—the law even parks its cars on the lower quays—and engrave a sort of reflected Latinity on the water. Except at Passy, wealth and fashion avoid it. There are two huge popular shops—the fabulous Samaritaine and La Belle Jardinière, by the Pont Neuf—but apart from these, the Seine's banks are not for shoppers who are interested in other things than fishing rods, antiques, pictures and books. There are bars and restaurants for a short distance on the Left Bank; but for the rest, the Seine is a river to stroll by or drive by in that screaming wolf pack of fast traffic that is more terrifying, more concentratedly breathless, more egotistical, more ravening after human prey than any other traffic in Europe. Studying the fixed ecstatic expressions of Seineside drivers as they howl by, a crude Anglo-Saxon can think only that this traffic is a direct product of the Latin capacity for abstract thought. He makes for the relative peace of the bridges.

In Paris there are thirty-three of them; a few are beautiful, a few neither here nor there, a few odd and one or two are disasters. It is the variety that strikes the stranger; James Fenimore Cooper, once a considerable name to Parisians, noted it. There is one unlucky little footbridge, the Pont Saint-Louis, a structure that looks like a flytrap, or a bird cage or something the Army engineers have thrown across the river in a hurry. It connects the Île de la Cité and Île St. Louis. Something bad always happens to any bridge on this site. Its predecessor was knocked down by a tanker barge a few years ago.

I am no friend of the vainglorious Pont Alexandre III, splendidly placed to receive the Tsar of Russia at the turn of the century in celebrating the Glories of War and Peace and the Fame of France at different epochs of her history. It is a piece of exhibition rhetoric; couples point and giggle at its comic pomposities—those golden Pegasuses flying off into the sky from the four pedestals, those metal lions coaxed along by fat bronze infants trailing sea plants and flowers, those lamp standards that might have come out of some old Ritz.

A revered Parisian curiosity is the statuary on the Pont de l'Alma. The central arch is guarded by four enormous stone soldiers. One of these, a Zouave, is consulted like an oracle at periods of flood—"The water's up to his gaiters. It's over his belt. It's approaching his chin"—and passengers on the *bateaux-mouches* always give it one of those derisive salutes that Parisians affectionately save for municipal objects.

Of all the Seine bridges the Pont des Arts is the pleasantest to sit or walk on; it is reserved for pedestrians and is really a promenade pitched between sky and water for students, nursemaids, children, old gentlemen and for painters having another go at the classical view of the Pont Neuf and the Île de la Cité, picking out the light on the Tour St. Jacques, struggling to get that flaking-gray shade of the river buildings. Nothing sacred or secular, joyous or macabre escapes the inflection of French irony. I was chatting with a plump and rosy young man who is in charge of the small lifesaving station that is cozily shaded by the trees close to the bridge. Every couple of days, he said, people jump off the Pont des Arts or the quays close by the river. It is the bridge, he said, most esteemed by those wishing to make a show of ending their lives. "But never at night," he added. "No Frenchman ever commits suicide at night. He wants to be seen doing it. *Il veut se faire un drame.*" The stagelike elevation of the bridge, he said, with its fine view of the Louvre on one side and the dome of the Institut on the other, contributing their romantic suggestions of art and poetry, makes the spot appropriate. But between his little boat moored below and the skiffs of the river fire station on the other side of the bridge, he said that the chances of a fatal success were small. The morgue, by the way, so conscientiously visited by the French Naturalist school and the painters of the nineteenth century, has been moved from the Île de la Cité. A garden is there now.

This nest of bridges on the two islands and the upper quays beside them contain much of the dense early history of Paris. Many had houses on them until the late eighteenth century. The Pont Neuf—not, as is often thought, the oldest bridge across the Seine—never had houses, but was notorious for its market stalls, thieves, money changers, prostitutes, goldsmiths—and its famous open-air dentist. Trade long ago moved off the bridges, but the tradition survives in the stalls of the *bouquinistes* along the river walls. Second-hand paperbacks are spoiling the stalls and someone has flooded the market with Baudelaire's *Les Fleurs du Mal*, but the *bouquinistes* are still amusing. And very convenient, I remember from younger days, for selling your books when you had run out of money. All my Molières went that way. One can still have a squint at the Gravures Libertines and the girl dreaming that the bolster is her lover; but a cynical commercialism has come into the trade in books on aphrodisiacs, the lash, Oriental perversion and the erotic manuals. They are packaged in impenetrable cellophane and Peeping Tom can peep no more, while the old lady in charge sits on her stool under the plane trees, slicing her potatoes for the midday meal. The high moment of the *bouquinistes* was at the time of Anatole France, whose father had a bookshop on the quays. One of the *bouquinistes* wrote a book on the trade. I used to call on this old gentleman and his wife in their attic in the Rue Jacob. Their couple of rooms were as musty as their bookstall. Though the market trades have gone from the bridges, they have stuck to the neighborhood. The Quai des Orfèvres still has goldsmiths, the Quai de la Mégisserie has its bird and flower market, and you still buy your fishing rods on the Quai du Louvre.

It is a long time since I have seen a mattress maker at work on the lower quays of the Seine and I never did see the poodle clipper. Perhaps he has gone with the laundry barges that used to be near the Pont Neuf. One or two of these abandoned laundries have been towed down beyond the Bois de Boulogne to become floating restaurants and cafés, for the French are always looking for new settings for their meals. It is a shock to find car parks along some stretches of the lower quays. But there are one or two trees on the Right Bank, close to the water and having large, conveniently shaped boles, that are specially suited to couples who like to be caught dramatically kissing against water and sunset. And, in addition to lovers, fishermen and tramps—the genuine Parisian *clochard*—are still there. In spite of all the old ballads, the true inhabitants of "*sous les ponts de Paris*" are the tramps. In winter the less hardy go up into the city and sleep on the pavement, preferring the metal covers of central-heating pipes; but the morning sun brings them down to the shelter of the arches, where they light their fires of twigs and start cooking breakfast in cans. There are far more fishermen, however, than tramps or lovers. Hundreds of rods can be seen between the Concorde and the Cité. There they stand, males of all ages from ten to eighty, in blue berets and leather jackets, flicking and dipping their rods, like little orchestras. It is a delusion that they catch nothing. Fish leap onto their lines, mainly, I'm afraid, mere cat fodder like the *goujon* and the little perch. But there are small bream too. And I need hardly say that a man near the Pont de Sully "only last Tuesday" had a carp "at least eighty centimeters long" and "which must have weighed four kilos"—but it got away. (The fisherman has the art of making much out of very little and fishing fulfills that profound and frugal French attachment to "*le tranquil*," the word one hears dozens of times a day.) The dream of the Seine fisherman is a large carp or—unrealizable in Paris but possible between Rouen and Le Havre—an enormous *brochet*, the pike, that he can rush off and sell to a restaurant, though the pleasures of eating *quenelles de brochet* are wasted on me. I have even seen a woman fishing in the Seine, and everyone knows there was once a fishing cat, commemorated in that dirty little alley opposite Notre Dame—the Rue du Chat qui Pêche. The last fishing I saw on the Seine was off the Île St. Louis. A crane was doing it. Quite a crowd of us leaned on the wall wondering what would come up. It was a diver in a pink rubber suit with a load of tiles from a sunken barge. He opened his helmet and there was the little frogman's tiny face grinning at the nursemaids and puffing at a cigarette. "*Comme chez soi*," I heard a soldier say. The diver was a perfect example of "*le tranquil*."

Finally, there are the painters. There are two classic views on the Seine: the Pont Neuf with the arms of the river clasping the tall, leaning, crowded seventeenth-century houses of the islands. The other is Notre Dame. Is any other cathedral in the world so often painted, not only by masters, but by every student who ever came to Paris? Is any other cathedral painted *every day*? It is one of the compulsive subjects, one of the great clichés of the river and therefore one of the most excruciating tests. Day after day, imitators and sentimentalists go down to disaster before that foreground of green water between the stone walls, the hollow eye of the white bridge that crosses it and the two gray fretted towers with the mass of the cathedral rising above. And then, suddenly, some genius comes along and snatches one more secret out of the great Gothic platitude—a Matisse, for example, gazes at the cathedral from his studio atop the Quais des Grands Augustins, and floats that solid stone on fire.

There are two kinds of light in France: the tender, subtle light of the Île-de-France and the North, and the strong, unmisted and candid light of the South. They are the light of the Seine and the light of the Mediterranean, the former dappling and dissolving the sights of nature, the latter revealing their volume and density. Expressing this in terms of painters, Monet, Manet, Renoir, Pissarro, Sisley, Berthe Morisot and Seurat reveal the light of the Seine; Cézanne and Van Gogh mainly reveal that of the South. What poetry has been for the Thames, painting has been for this river. The Louvre is on its banks in the middle of Paris; the schools, the studios and galleries are on the Left Bank, in the little streets between the Institut and Saint-Germain-des-Prés; and then there are all those painters—a procession of palettes, easels, brushes and umbrellas—painting their way from Paris to Le Havre.

A minute's walk from the river, there are two little temples in the Tuileries, close to the Place de la Concorde, that commemorate this extraordinary conjunction of genius and the river. In the Orangerie one sees the final expression of Monet's lifelong passion for this water—the two oval rooms that contain simply the murals he worked on year after year in the last quarter of his life: the *Nymphéas*. No other pictures are in these rooms. Generally you are alone in them; it is like being underwater and you think of the eyes of the master, gradually failing but—almost like the eyes of Balzac's fanatic genius of Le Chef-d'Oeuvre Inconnu—tormented by his obsession with the elusive movement of the water. Caught by it when he was young, when Boudin, the pilot's son, had shown Monet, the grocer's son, the seas breaking in the harbor at Le Havre or the changing forms of the Seine estuary; entranced by the suburban river at Argenteuil; held in its grip when he and Renoir painted the floating cabaret, *La Grenouillère*, setting out in his studio boat with its little blue cabin; making his lily pool and Japanese garden at Giverny, Monet is inseparable from the Seine. It is his mistress.

Opposite the Orangerie is the Jeu de Paume, where the other Impressionists are permanently shown. It contains the *Déjeuner sur l'Herbe* which caused one of the earliest scandals. Travel by river steamer out of Paris toward Le Havre and you will see hardly a village or town that has not been touched by the brushes of painters: Bougival, Marly, Saint-Germain, Argenteuil, Pontoise, Mantes, Vétheuil, Vernon, La Roche Guyon and on to Rouen and Honfleur. Every old railway bridge, every picnic, every skiff and rowboat, the gaudy swimming parties, the river cafés, every stretch of poplars and willows, every chalk bluff and every apple orchard in flower in the Normandy spring recall their work. Look at a battle map of World War II; the Allied armies seemed to choose the painters' favorite spots for crossing the river: Mantes, Vétheuil and all that country between the La Roche-Guyon and Rouen. Enclosed in calm green country that rises to hills, the Seine widens and narrows, takes its broad bends and tight loops, leaves its willow-silvered islands, drops through its locks while the wash of scores of barges sucks and gurgles at its banks.

I went down the Seine as far as Rouen recently on one of those little three-hundred-ton seagoing cargo boats of the Compagnie Maritime de la Seine that ply between Paris and London: and though I gave a reverent salute to Argenteuil in honor of Monet—and of Maupassant too, for his weekends of rowdy rowing parties—and to hallowed suburban places, I was glad the painters could not see the changes of time. The factories pour their filth into the bather's stream. The gracious curving of the river cannot be lost—but, oh God! what a terrible slum of ruined shacks the Grande Jatte has become, and where is there grass to picnic on near Asnières? There must be some, but who would dare go into that water? Maupassant of course would have noted for some story that grotesque little Île de Clichy that is occupied entirely by a dog's cemetery and checkered with little tombstones—the last fond absurdity of the bourgeois. It was a Saturday afternoon when we passed it and processions of people were solemnly carrying wreaths and bunches of flowers to the graves of their pets.

There was the ghostly feeling of being on the edge of one of Maupassant's river stories in my journey down the Seine to Rouen. How often he must have gone by river when he went to Flaubert's house at Croisset to learn to write. Were those two rival, derelict-looking restaurants just below the Renault factory—A la Pêche Miraculeuse and A la Pêche Merveilleuse—thriving in his time?

There was a gay little scene aboard our ship, the *Gâtinais*, just before we sailed. The retiring commandant came to say good-bye to his ship, after the best part of a lifetime in her. We drank his health in port and then in champagne and talked about motors and income tax, made salty remarks about the young assistant engineer who had just married and whose bride was making the trip with him, and then, after the commandant had been hugged and kissed by the jolly secretary of the company, the brave man jumped ashore in his best navy-blue suit, with her lipstick on his face, carrying a little case and a couple of coat hangers in the best seamanly fashion. No longer would they swing and tap on his cabin wall.

We saluted the Zouave on the Pont de l'Alma and cursed those huge blocks of flats that have ruined Passy but, save for them, we did not look at Paris. We were too interested in our *andouille*, our *colin mayonnaise*, our *tête de veau* and in sampling cheeses to notice much until we were off the Bois de Boulogne. Also we were dumbstruck by Pico, the ship's boy. This youth, with straight black hair combed forward and the eyes of an astonished doll, had picked up a new bit of slang. This was, I suppose, his first day with the new word. It came out scores of times. The word was *"saignant"*—raw, bleeding, bloody. *"Saignant!"* he would exclaim if we passed a pretty girl, a car, or if he spoke of a film he'd just seen. It was *"Saignant!"* when the light went red against us at the first lock; it was *"Saignant!"* when it turned green. It was *"Saignant!"* when we listened to a quiz on Radio Luxembourg. If he fell asleep for a quarter of an hour he would wake up and shout *"Saignant!"*, as if to remind himself that he was alive. He caught a cold halfway to Rouen; only that stopped him. Pico had worked in one of those smart petrol barges that go between Paris and Rouen in huge fleets and which pay very high wages. He preferred lower wages in a real boat.

Nine members of the crew were solid Bretons from St.-Malo and Brest, but two were Normans: the melancholy, chain-smoking engineer and the pilot ceremoniously referred to as M. le Pilote. The engineer was a sad fellow with loose teeth who had knocked about Africa and who detested the modern world. We often stood on deck smoking a last cigarette, just before going to bed, and blundering through arguments on economics, while the country dogs barked on the banks. The pilot was quite different. Enormous, pink and old, his little blue eyes well bedded-down in pink cheeks, he came of a family who had been pilots for generations. He lived in the little Normandy village of Poses, at the last lock above Rouen, and he loved to talk about food, wine and fishing. He honored us by opening his own bottle of plum *eau de vie* from his village of Poses on the second night, and he gave it the reverence due Napoleon brandy. This courtly old gentleman had had a tragic life. When we got to Poses he pointed out the red roof of his home.

It was a new house. His wife and three of his children had been killed in the Allied bombing, when we were smashing Rommel's armies in the Falaise pocket. With that rational sense of self-definition for which the French have a natural gift, he said to me: "I never remarried. I now live for myself." For his stomach, the Chef said, but with respect.

The charm of these river voyages is their monotony. The only drama was getting into the locks, waiting for the lights to change on the lock towers and hearing the loudspeaker bawl across the water, "*Attention, attention, bateau de mer.*" We had precedence, but there would be as many as five barges with us in some of the locks, with Pico crying "*Saignant!*" and scampering to tie us up. There was a tremendous jam of barges at Conflans at the junction of the Oise, which is one of the great barge stations of the lower Seine. They looked like rows of black, red and blue beetles on the water. (It was here our new commandant told Pico, who hadn't heard an order, that his "Portuguese" had sand in them—real docker's slang, "ears" being "*huîtres portugaises*" or Portuguese oysters.) The sight of the barges at Conflans was astonishing. There were scores of long black hulls with their few inches of freeboard, their steel-gray, blue, red or green decks, and their handsome deck cabins with neat curtains, their pots of flowers and ferns and their shining brasses at the stern, with the children sitting there reading their Sunday books. There were Dutchmen bound for Amsterdam by canal, Belgians for Ostend, Frenchmen for all parts of France. The women were hanging out the enormous family wash, or hauling in buckets of water and mopping the decks. They are the hardest-working women I have ever seen. They and the children have to stop whatever they are doing and jump ashore with the ropes at the locks or to put out the rope fenders. At night they tie up: the law prohibits navigation then because of the impossibility of working in shifts. Many of the crews are made up of families. It is a gypsy life, hard on the children's education. But it seems a happy life too; when they pass friends on the river they shout, wave and call messages across the water. The barge people are a race, a nation in themselves. All watermen are. While waiting at the locks I listened to a lot of argument about the effect the doubling of the Havre-to-Paris pipeline is having on the barges. But the wine barges and those that haul brick, cement and sand have an eternity before them.

These lower reaches of the Seine are placid and sweeping. For tens of miles the willows lean and the poplars stand in their quivering, silvering curtains. The nests of mistletoe in the trees give a touch of folly and lightness to the landscape. In the thirty years I have known this river there have been changes. The old bridges at Poissy, at Mantes and at Triel—that pretty place of regattas—have gone. They were too low. Towns like Poissy, resorts like Villenne and Meulan have grown enormously. The Seine has no dramatic falls or gorges, but the chalk cliffs draw close together in Normandy. At La Roche-Guyon—where Rommel had his headquarters—there are a castle and a château and there are deep caves in the hills. Pissarro painted there. We tied up one night at Les Andelys, a pretty place under steep cliffs on which Richard Coeur de Lion built a castle. It is a reminder that this part of France was once English—that is to say, when the English were much more French than they are today. Learned friends tell me that Henry V must have made his famous speech before Harfleur in French. And when Normandy wasn't English, the English for centuries were fighting there. They built a church in Harfleur and I won't mention what they did in the marketplace of Rouen. The castle at Les Andelys was built to defend Normandy—against France!

It stands at the entrance to a few miles of the nearest thing the Seine can offer to a gorge—a row of high cliffs with droll chalk bluffs sticking out over the river like clowns' faces. They looked strange in the white river fog that held us up outside M. le Pilote's village of Poses. At Elbeuf we entered the smoke of the Rouen neighborhood and the *Gâtinais* men bet me that the cloth of my suit came from this old weaving town. It didn't—but there's nothing like patriotism! This is the region of textiles; Flaubert made a great point of Madame Bovary's taste in clothing and curtains and tablecloths and the amount of money she spent on them when she went into Rouen. After Poses, you feel the first touch of the tide. At Rouen you even feel the *mascaret*, or "bore," the tidal wave that comes in sixteen feet high at Le Havre. It has been tamed now by new breakwaters at the mouth. The big ships come up as far as Rouen—we tied up beside a monster from Africa—and I stared at a city I did not recognize. Nearly all the quayside district of Rouen and much of the rest of the city were destroyed by the Allies when Rommel's transport was trapped there. A new city has sprung up, but a good deal of the old, timbered part of Rouen is left. Le Havre also suffered severely. It is all rich woodland, cliffs, meadows of cattle, Normandy butter, cheese and cider from Rouen to Le Havre. The Seine smiles as it widens to its difficult mouth of shifting sandbanks.

Like the Thames and Tiber, the Seine has gathered more delight and intensity of meaning in its few miles than any other of the monstrous, helpless, swirling drains of the other great continents. Even in France, so far as length and volume go, the Seine is inferior to the Rhône and the Loire; and it can be argued that without the luck of having Paris on its banks, the Seine would be simply one more river to cross. But the argument is feeble. There is no luck in it at all. Paris did not grow out of luck but out of judgment. When the Romans conquered Gaul, they saw in the Seine basin a natural barrier between Latin civilizations and the barbarians of the north; and the little island called Lutetia became the decisive outpost. Centuries later Clovis, the Merovingian king, confirmed their foresight by making Paris the capital.

Four hundred and eighty-two winding water miles from the sea, in the Burgundian hills northwest of Dijon, is a little grotto that was built by the City of Paris in the nineteenth century. (The sins of art in the nineteenth century were always municipal.) In the grotto reclines a plain, stone nymph with stone leaves on her head and her hair parted in the middle, dangling a bunch of grapes from a hand that rests on her raised knee. Below the stone on which she lies water oozes out of the earth. It is one of the half-dozen springs nearby that are the source of the Seine. This ground is almost holy, for we are at the source of those waters that washed the walls of the earliest Western civilization . . . that were drunk by the monks of Cluny . . . in which François Villon occasionally must have washed his face . . . on which Maupassant, centuries later, rowed his boat . . . that Monet painted . . . and that have carried away something of the hearts of hundreds of thousands of us foreigners who have made love or talked our heads off on its banks.

To follow the Seine from its source is to see what uncertainties and little deaths occur at the beginning of great things. The trickle makes a puddle or two under walls and manor gates, it dries up in the summer, and without the reviving water of the pretty Douix River that bursts out of a cavern near Châtillon, the Seine might vanish altogether. It recovers and, sparkling with vigor, runs down the middle of the village street at Mussy where it meets its first laundress scrubbing her washing on the bank. Before reaching Troyes, it is big enough to drive waterwheels; and, now ten yards wide or more, it works the flour mills and stocking factories of the solid little cathedral town. Here it rates a long stone quay in the Flemish manner, but at the end of the quay it dives underground, and I fear that it becomes a sewer, for I saw a woman standing over a grating there talking to her husband who was down below. Beyond Troyes, it winds across lightly wooded and open plains, dusty in summer and bleak in winter—champaign country they call it—until it reaches the woods and watery glades of Moret and the forest walls around Melun and Fontainebleau. The Aube and Yonne give it heart; and near Charenton, where the Marne comes in, some three hundred kilometers from its beginning, Paris is created. The trickle has become more than three hundred yards wide at the Pont Neuf and has established the most important inland port of France.

The fact is surprising. We thought Paris was above mere trade. The explanation springs from the nature of the river. The Seine is slow-flowing water; its descent is gentle, it winds. The English Channel is only 112 miles from Paris as the crow flies but the Seine more than doubles that distance. It is quiet enough to be a link in the extraordinary canal system of Europe, by which a barge can travel from Amsterdam or Le Havre to the Mediterranean. As you look over the bookstalls near Notre Dame, you see Dutch and Belgian barges living below you. Farther up the Seine, toward the Austerlitz railroad station, you spot those small seagoing boats of five hundred tons that trade between Paris and London. From Paris to Rouen, the phutting of barge engines goes on all day—they don't travel at night—and between

Rouen and Le Havre, at the river's mouth, they are joined by the great cargo ships.

All the same, as you walk under the plane trees along the riverbank in the center of Paris and look down at the cobbled quays, you don't get a strong impression of commerce, unless it comes from a steam shovel emptying unending loads of gravel from the quarries of the north. You rarely see a crane; the cargoes are handled by hand. Most of this is done at the canal docks at St. Denis and the new barge docks at Gennevilliers in the Paris suburbs. (This, incidentally, is a hot place for Communist propaganda, as you see by the slogans daubed on the river bridges. These have been astutely obliterated by turning the Latin alphabet into something that looks like Greek lettering.) There also are the timber quays above Notre Dame and at the Pont de Bercy in sight of the cathedral, and there are the wine quays and the acres of wine cellarage with their evocatively labeled "roads" between the casks: Vouvray, Barsac, Chablis. In the last one hundred years the mercantile pandemonium of the central quays has declined, but the barge traffic is greater than ever.

The Seine has flowed, like a life stream, through the heart of Western civilization. It bears on its current all the thoughts of the Sorbonne, all the learning and grace of Latin culture, all the waywardness and simplicity of nature. It is a fortunate river to have on its banks the Cathedral of Rouen and the hundred belfries of that city, to have been gazed at there by Corneille, to have nurtured Paris, the one city in the world whose people have known how to think and please and live and to awaken the minds of all who have been lucky enough to spend a year or two there when they were young. To those of us who were born in foreign lands the Seine is more than a river, it is a gift from France to all who have seen it. It must be the most remembered river in the world.

[1963]

4

Europe's Mediterranean Coast

There are two Mediterraneans: the native Mediterranean of work and living, and the foreigners' playground. The pleasure phase began in the eighteenth century with the Grand Tour, the aristocratic and educative journey to France and Italy by English and Germans; for centuries northern Europeans had had to admit that only the Italians knew how to build cities, palaces and country houses, that only the Italians had manners. And then, in the 1830s, Lord Brougham discovered the climate of Cannes, in Provence. Soon all the comfortably-off families of Europe were establishing themselves for the season in that southern sun-trap, building villas all the way from Hyères to Rapallo; and the French and Italian cartoonists were drawing comic pictures of the whiskered English, always dressed in kilts and gazing with horselike hauteur at the foreign scene. The retired colonelcy and gentry of Europe, the scandals and eccentrics of Victorian society, the spinsters, settled in their pensions: they were there to escape the northern winter and to live cheaply. The painters followed, searching for the picturesque—the wash hanging in the slums of Naples, the peasant on mule or donkey, standing (if possible) under vines at a well, or beside a crumbling church or palace.

This paradise lasted until 1914. There followed a larger crowd: the tourists who always settle around painters. Cézanne and Van Gogh had worked in Provence; Picasso and Matisse were there now. In the cheap 1920s the Mediterranean was deep in post-Impressionism.

The next war finished that. First of all mass tourism, based on mass motoring, came in, bringing the motel, the apartment houses, the campsites. After 1956, the package tour dealt the final blow at the scene of *la douceur de vivre*. The words Eats, Snacks, Fish and Chips, French Fried, Night—and Nite—Club appeared in the streets of the basket makers and the fishermen, and turned quiet, pretty places into circuses. Fishermen who preferred their women to wear four petticoats and to be bloused to the chin found the bars and cafés filled with girls in bikinis and large women in pants that looked like pumped-up inner tubes. The respectable townspeople noted that the social tone of tourism had gone down: the newcomers could not bear the local food and drank the local wine to excess and—most shocking to a Mediterranean—not knowing or caring where it came from.

In short, the flood of sun-seekers from northern Europe and America runs to millions. Spain claims fourteen million a year, France and Italy reckon on equally fantastic figures. I think all exaggerate. But it is true that the city of Venice receives 700,000 people in a year. The outskirts of Málaga have become a fantastic Montmartre. The beaches have become an international rotisserie of naked Anglo-Saxons and French. North of Valencia—a stretch of coast that had been untouched for centuries and was simply a land of juicy market gardens or vines—you now strike a continuous suburb of apartment blocks, hotels and camping sites running through Tarragona, Barcelona, and with one or two breaks (such as the marsh and mosquito country between the frontier and Marseilles) all the way through France to Portofino. The old, touchingly sentimental idea that you went to the Mediterranean not only for the sun but to recover the good life that had been preserved here from the pressures of machine civilization—food grown in the village, fresh, unrefrigerated, tasting of its natural and not chemical flavors; wines from the vines nearby; festivals that had not been contaminated by city culture-forcing—this old idea, and the notion that it was your duty to *know* the people, have been frankly chucked out. The sun-seekers of today come in by automobile and plane, and they demand machine-age life. They have no interest in Mediterranean man or woman, except as a lover, servant or provider of pleasure.

And in this the newcomers are on the winning side. From the eighteenth century onward, Mediterranean society was stagnant, surpassed in power by the Atlantic countries. In the nineteenth century the Industrial Revolution remained, with a few exceptions, in the north. But since the last war, industry has started to move into the sun, especially industries based on oil and electronics. Huge modern constructions have sprung up. The south is becoming more "modern" than the north. And this movement fits perfectly with the worldwide decline of the traditional peasantry, which bore the weight of civilization on its back. The peasant is leaving the land for the big cities. He is beginning to let the stone walls of the Italian mountain terraces go unrepaired. The family is scattering. If there is a traditional Mediterranean way of life, one would have to look for it a few miles inland.

Still, in becoming modern, Mediterranean life cannot possibly cease to be itself. The sun, the wind, the matchless light, the fruitfulness of the soil do not change. It is we northerners who change when we come south. We come down over the Alps, over the rocky hills of Provence or the spurs of the Pyrenees, or the sudden drop from the tableland of Castile, into softer, warmer air that acts at once upon us like a potion. We are changed by the clarity of the light—and this is important to us who live either in mists or in a northern light so hard that it illuminates nothing—because the Mediterranean light makes us see each thing, each stone, wall, house, tree, separately, so that we accept it—as Mediterraneans do, for itself. We cease to live in the future; we start to live in the present hour. We begin to feel, as they do, the satisfaction of small near things. We begin, without knowing it, to contemplate. We feel—it is not entirely an illusion—something ancient stirring in ourselves. What is it? This year I came down from Castile to Valencia and I felt there what in Castile I can never feel. In Castile I was faced by something austere, puritanic, noble, soldierly and saintly—but alien. In Valencia I was reunited with my civilization.

It is the sight of the long milky strip of the Mediterranean, the largest lake in the world, softening this coast of orange groves and almond trees and small farms of the richest *huerta*, or garden, in Spain—where in fact a man can be well off on ten acres of its fertile soil—that starts the change in us. That sea is unlike all others. Its shores contain the foundations of Western civilization. It was for centuries the scene of the greatest creative force in the Western world, and indeed from its works the whole world has had an imprint. Until the Age of Discovery it was the whole known world. The map shows us the fringe of Africa crumbling into outer space. China is a rumor, the Americas not even conceived. We would not be what we are but for Greek genius, for Roman administration and law, for the Renaissance and the discoverers. We are looking at a sea where something was born, grew, matured in the course of violent centuries and became complete. It is moving, in our uncompleted time, to see the Mediterranean completion; indeed innumerable completions of civilizations and cultures. The very ruins commemorate not tragedy but a one-time fullness of life.

Valencia is a dull little city, now made hideous by new building; one hopes it can afford its modernity. Its traditional meaning lies in its orange groves, its farms, its rice fields—a sinister modern meaning lies in the air base not far off—and in its port. The orange carts and the orange lorries drive in dense procession down the road, under the dusty trees, to where the ships are waiting. You have hit upon the basic fact of Mediterranean life: for twenty-five hundred years, its wealth has been that of sea traders. The other thing that strikes you is that the flash of sea and sun and blossom seems to be in the eyes and temperament of the people. Castilian pride, melancholy and classical clarity of speech have given place to a gay, quick, excitable, difficult Spanish that seems to have crumbled. And you notice, when people talk to you, that the fanaticism of central Spain is replaced by tolerance and liberal ideas; as in all seaports, as with all sea traders, the mind is open to the foreign.

Valencia was, and is, a republican city, and its religion, if it happens to be religious at all, is accommodating, good natured, half pagan. Now this is not Spanish. In fact if one redrew the map one would find that Valencia, Barcelona and Marseilles, the regions of the France-Spanish border, are historically one, with a people whose speech is full of Provençal words, with chopped-off endings and squeezed vowels. This was a sort of state with colonies of its own, trading colonies and monopolies, with its own laws and wars, its own piracies; so that behind the petty trade or the bigger commercial interests, there is evidence in stone, in churches, fortresses and great houses, of a past individual greatness, a sense of style fitting to city-states that had a court life. These places have produced great men who lived, fought or worked there. It is not easy in Valencia to forget the Cid.

In Barcelona one has no time to think of the past. This is a rich and thriving city, the center of Spanish textile manufacture; its large port is full of ships and heavy with traffic. Here you meet the Mediterranean boosters—hard-headed, money-minded men who shout their commercial dreams in harsh voice, who like the large and splendacious. The spirit of the place is rhetorical. The wide avenues are like vainglorious public speeches. The evening drive, six deep in showy cars, up the Avenue of the Generalissimo, conveys extravagant luxury. The restaurants are the latest thing. The rich are enormously rich; and the city absorbs the poor peasant who comes up from the south. For generations this Catalan city wanted to be free from Madrid, and it fought against Franco. Now the cult of the Catalan language is dying and the desire for independence has gone. The anarchist movement has gone. All this has been swept away by the growth of Catalan affluence.

All the same, Barcelona has a double character. It is superbly placed under its mountains. With an extravagance that also characterizes Marseilles, an atrocious pseudo-Byzantine church has been put on the top of the hill that dominates the city. It is an aspect of the ghastly Sacré-Coeur complex that has ruined Latin ecclesiastical architecture in this century. More fitting—as an extravagance—is the notorious art nouveau "cathedral," the Sagrada Familia, which is still unfinished and which is having a vogue among architects. But in spite of its gaudy side, Barcelona has its other, indigenous Mediterranean side. Its narrow streets are packed with small trades, small shops, small bars of rabid individuality.

And here you come across another basic thing in Mediterranean life: patience. This feeling is perhaps ancient, some recollection from the early days of the Folk. You are walking under the trees of the Ramblas when you hear the sound of whistle and tambour from one of the eighteenth-century squares. On a platform in the middle, a small orchestra is making a sharp yet wistful piping, and a group of young people are dancing. It is a little folk dance, the *sardana*, that goes on and on without the swirlings and stampings of Spanish dancing, an innocent pastoral thing in the heart of a modern city. It goes on in the evenings in all Catalan towns; children join it, and their mothers too. When you see it being danced in some little town by the sea at six in the afternoon the feet of the dancers seem to be making the small even steps of the Mediterranean waves when the sea is quiet, even but sharp. That evenness, a sort of sweet monotone, is one of the essential Mediterranean elements.

Any Mediterranean knows what he wants, what it should be like, where it comes from. In a restaurant he asks searching questions about each item of the food, how it is cooked, and he will complain on principle if there is the smallest doubt or disappointment, so that often the chef nervously comes up from the kitchen halfway through a meal to see how his customers are taking it. It is a point of honor to complain. In a shop he makes the same demands; patiently the assistant brings out all the cloth, all the shoes, and is not in the least upset if the customer refuses all. On the contrary, the assistant admires the discrimination. For life is not buying or selling; it is getting what you exactly wish for, what you can afford. The wish is everything, and for that, patience is indispensable and life is timeless.

This matter of the wish is of great importance to all Spaniards and even to Catalans, who sometimes claim not to be Spaniards. I had to break my Mediterranean journey and came back later from Paris to Marseilles. In the dining car of the train a huge, fat Catalan was eating, drinking a great deal of wine and shouting to people around. It was very hot. He wanted the window to be opened. This was refused because, at the speed we were traveling, everything would have been blown off the tables. The French are great lawyers when it comes to rules. They lay them down with an abrupt air of intellectual authority. Spaniards do not like the superiority of the French. And so our Catalan is at first dumfounded, then the *furia española* breaks out; he swings his fist and bashes the window. In this he asserts his hairy masculinity, and he shouts for more wine.

The French are used to the eccentricities of foreigners, especially in the *wagon restaurant*. They remark merely that a rather low class of person travels nowadays, but they have other customers to think about, so they bring the Catalan his bill. He studies it, opens a wallet stuffed with notes. He has made

97

a personal estimate of what he thinks the meal was worth, which is very lit-tle. He puts down five francs for a forty-franc lunch—and refuses, in a voice that deafens the whole dining car, to pay a penny more.

An exemplary Mediterranean comedy—or more precisely, a Franco-Spanish one, the clash of two cultures—now takes place. The French wor-ship *le règlement*—the rule, the system—which is like a written constitution in abstract language and which covers all contingencies. Slowly they put it into action. A plain waiter calls for the superior waiter, the superior one calls in a Spanish speaker who calls in the headman who calls in one or two con-trollers. Quite a crowd. But the Spaniard holds out. Then a whisper. Some-one runs off into the next coach to get the State authority. He appears. A neat, terse fellow wearing the red-white-and-blue band of the republic. "I must ask you to pay your bill. What is the objection?"

There is an instant and final answer, the answer by which the Spaniard utters his impenetrable and immovable Spanishness. He shouts, "*¡Porque no me da la gana!*"—not quite "Because I don't wish to," but rather, "The desire or will to do so has not visited me." One can act if one has it; but it is psycho-logically impossible, as if one's will had gone out of one's entrails, if one has not got the *gana*.

"Your passport," says the police officer, for that is what he is.

The Catalan's utterance had come from such depths that it had exhausted him. He handed over his passport like a child. Half an hour later, I saw him standing in the corridor outside his compartment of the train. He was an oldish man and was now melancholy. What had happened I could not bring myself to ask, but inside the compartment sat four or five young Spaniards, all looking gentle and sad. One of them was softly strumming a guitar, and to its note the old man, quietly and in broken voice, was singing a song. I caught just one line, which said, "I am a poor man and you have broken my heart." It was like seeing the funeral of an ego. Resignation, the curious re-lapse, after violence, into apathy: even the earthshaking Catalans of the Mediterranean have this habit. Across the border in France, in Arles, in Mar-seilles, you can pick out the Spaniards at once by their look of resignation, indifference and blank sadness.

The Catalan coast is mountainous and rocky. The sea burns blue in the coves and caves of what is now called the Costa Brava, where the tourists

98

roast. (In lively weather, the Mediterranean waves have that nasty short punch or chop that deceives and almost winds the bather who is used to the longer Atlantic rhythms.) But for a long interval after you have left Spain for France, you are in a plain of salt marshes that spread out from the mouth of the Rhône. Rock will not begin again until you reach the limestone of Marseilles. This marshy Camargue region is one of the strangest along the Mediterranean. In some places it is a stretch of sand that blows under the stilted houses; in others it is a land of large meres where the village houses are roofed with reeds and where the bulls and the famous stocky white horses of the cowboylike warders wade in the summer heat, where the ibis, the avocet and flamingo live. Being horse country, it is gypsy country too; the gypsies come in to Saintes-Maries on their annual pilgrimage. Inland at Arles, Julius Caesar's Roman lull town, you are in the Van Gogh country; there are his torn cypresses that act as windbreaks for the peach orchards, the swirling wheat he painted, and the plantations of sunflowers. Farther inland you are among Cézanne's rocky hills. You are beginning a journey through the Provençal Mediterranean, and it is like passing from one Impressionist painting to another.

You understand why these painters, who set out to paint light itself and who stared straight into the sun, settled in Provence. There is a difference between Spanish and Provençal light, and how to define it is difficult. I would say that the Provençal light has flecks of gold in it; it is clear, but since there is more water than in Spain, the heat hazes are veils of moisture through which the limestone seems to burn. The light has silver in it, too, the silver of the turned leaves when the mistral blows—the wind that tears down the funnel of the Rhône Valley.

The force of that wind is as surprising as the force of the Mediterranean Sea; the sea that looks so peaceable, the wind that seems, until it strikes you, like a breeze that is going to cool the fiery heat. It is an angering wind, clattering the shutters and windows, keeping up its mindless cold whistle for days. It makes the vineyards toss and the trees look mad. It breaks the cypresses, drives in the dust, plays intolerably on the nerves and the eyes. Its particular nastiness is that it comes violently out of a clear sky and leaves the sun naked, wild, without heat.

The mistral is blamed for the violence in the south of France. Avignon is noted through history for its crimes, especially murders. Bodies are thrown into the Rhône. (The body of a murdered English girl was fished out when I was there.) One hears of the driver who shoots a man who keeps him waiting for gasoline. People get "nervous" and quarrel. The waiter announces he is going to shoot his wife. *C'est le mistral.* It was at Saint-Rémy that Van Gogh walked into the asylum after cutting off his ear. Van Gogh saw none of the gaiety of Daudet's novels. He didn't find the girls beautiful. (Henry James admired them; he called them "straight-nosed," and those slender straight noses are indeed very fine.) In the arena, the bulls frequently jump in among the spectators. Zola's violence is associated with the country around Aix. His father brought a lawsuit against the town: here he got his material for his novel about Cézanne, whose friend in youth he had been.

All regions of the Mediterranean are different. In the triangle between Arles, Aix and Marseilles you are at a junction of landscapes—marshland, rocky plateau where the sheep graze, and rich farming country. The traffic beats down the main roads, the lorry drivers strip to the waist in the heat. Arles, you have been told, is a town of beautiful women, and you expect to find that this is a romantic lie, boosted by Daudet and light opera; but in fact the number of beautiful *Arlésiennes* is astonishing. I was there during the summer fete, when they parade in the streets in costume, and the sight takes one's breath. It is all solemn but simple. The comic bugle bands and the drum-and-whistle bands walk by—for no one really marches—and the girls, the children, the elderly men and women follow in their costumes. The grace, the instilled sense of occasion, the lack of showing off are delightful. Compliments are shouted out to some of the beauties, the people sitting in the cafés stand up and clap their hands, especially at the ladies who sit on the white horses behind the men of the Camargue. Occasionally one of those solid, sun-burned horsemen will be unable to resist showing how he can turn his horse full circle in one sudden, acrobatic movement.

Occasionally you will see an alien Spanish touch in the black Cordova hat of one of the women. Next afternoon there will be a bullfight, with local and Spanish *toreros* in the fine Roman arena of the town. And it *is* Roman, not a mere twentieth-century Plaza de Toros; it is the real arena the Romans used for their bloody sports. The evening concert will take place in the Roman theater. Of course the tourists come in, but what strikes you is that this is a real fete. In the morning the farmers stand talking among the tables of the cafés, as if at the market. They do not sit down to drink; they don't drink at all; they have more serious things on hand. And the waiter does not mind, except that he wishes they would not block his way to his few real customers. And as the morning hots up, the sad young Spanish guitarist strums at the street corner, giving a Spanish shrug, full of indifference to this world.

You make for the narrow, shaded streets of Arles to get out of the great heat. You go to the bank, and here you find a scene that drives the northerner mad. It is good to get out of the heat into the cool office where the clerks sit at desks covered with papers and forms that look as though they have been there for years. At once a clerk leaves the customer he is dealing with to ask your business; he cannot bear to think you are waiting. But he at once abandons you for another customer, who may be some gossiping old farmer's wife who chats about her relatives and who will draw you into the conversation. And everyone who comes in shakes hands with half the staff.

Suddenly the clerk, indeed all the clerks, it seems, disappear; not for coffee or anything idle like that, but impelled by some psychic distraction. The manager comes out of his office, a man in an open-necked shirt, leading his little daughter, so we go through compliments again. Then a clerk you have not seen before, a woman who has been typing away in a dark corner, looks up at your desperate face, and in a headlong rush comes over and deals with you. She has to write everything down in triplicate and in her best handwriting—which is very slow, clear and good—and then you wait for the cashier to come back to his glass case and count out your money. You have been there about half an hour. In the street afterward, you have the suspicion that by the standards of Arles and any farmer for miles around, you have done something very eccentric; in Arles you don't go to a bank to take money out, you go to pay it in.

The summer night in Arles, in all the Provençal towns, is what you are waiting for. You walk down the black tunnels of the trees, passing the families sitting out on the benches—a time for old people and for lovers to take the air. You come into a sunken earthen square enclosed by huge planes, four deep, that shut out the sky. The place is almost deserted. You hear the voice of a young man making up to a girl. You pass down the empty avenue of ghostly trees; you cross one of the canals that lead out from the Rhône. You take a towpath under the trees, where the mosquitoes bite and a few late cicadas are scissoring away. Just behind you in the black water, you hear a sudden bark. A bullfrog is barking, and then, in from the old Roman "catacombs" (they are, in fact, above ground)—and what an appropriate place!—you hear the true night sound of Provence, the mass chorus of the bullfrogs. It is as if all the Roman and medieval dead were harshly talking, thousands of them. The manly din of shouting corporals can be heard for miles. All day in the woods, the cicadas; all night the frogs.

In all Provence, as indeed in Spain and Italy, the wise inhabitants keep out of the sun. The famous light is to be avoided. How often you pass a bar where men sit around playing cards or reading papers in darkness, or a dark room where a woman sits sewing or stands at her ironing. In these places they are cool and their eyes are rested. But noise does not afflict them. The din of a motor bicycle in a narrow street distresses only the foreigner. The more noise the better in the south.

Arles was a Caesar's strong point, commanding the roads to Spain and Italy. He sent his boats down the Rhône for the recapture of Marseilles. Now Arles is dead and Marseilles claims to be the second city of France; more than a city, it is an enormous industrial conurbation, a place of soap makers, millers, petrol refineries, heavy industries and docks. The ugly church of Notre Dame de la Garde on its precipice dominates as Sacré-Coeur dominates Paris. One looks down from it at steep limestone hills that are now crowned by high apartment blocks. It is a place of brick and concrete; more and more concrete and long, hilly distances and noise.

Before the war, they used to say vice was more open in Marseilles than in any other seaport of Europe; it is fairly open now, but in general it is probably true that the city has become relatively respectable. This is still a sailor's city, providing at night the eternal comedy of the sailor and the girl. (Conversation in the square by the town hall. Anxious, battered fat lady to swaying sailor: "You love Chuchot. You do not love me." Sailor swears he loves her. Lady asks doubtfully, "Are you sincere?") And by day there is the comedy of sailors not knowing what to do with themselves. One sees groups of them tacking from one side of the street to the other, from one stocking-shop window to another, where they stand dumfounded, nervous and in committee, before the terrible question of what to buy for a lady. The decision is beyond them. You have never seen men so gloomy. They long for the shops to close and the night to come.

The Germans blew up—it is said at French request—the old night town of Marseilles by the Vieux Port, and the cheerful prostitutes moved over to the Opera House district. The Vieux Port is still gay. The yachts and the fishing boats are still there, and so are the cafés and the restaurants, which are either expensive or bad. In spite of the songs about bouillabaisse, Marseilles is not what it was gastronomically. The south of France is always twice as expensive as Paris, for its season lasts only half the year; but the average restaurants are terrible. Still, the taste for bouillabaisse clearly lasts. The jolly girls who stand by their boats, selling the fish and squids and eels that are the basis of it, do a busy trade. Elsewhere fishwives have a bad reputation; something about the popular fish trade calls for a lot of shouting and for slapping the fish over to the customer and daring him to hesitate. Not so in Marseilles; the fish girls of the Vieux Port are merry and even gracious. Again, this is a southern trait in all the markets; they like you to discriminate and take your time. They recognize your innate human right to pick your fish and to consider it carefully.

There has been one big change in the Marseilles crowd around the Canebière district in the center—a street whose drains now stink. There used to be Arabs in burnoose and slippers; now they wear European dress. The change is that there has been a huge increase in the Algerian and Negro population (with that gift for the vivid phrase, the Marseillais calls both *pieds noirs*). Over 200,000 of these people came in from Africa when Algeria became independent and were absorbed by Marseilles and the towns of the Riviera. The oily black hair, the sallow faces, the eyes sharp as needles make them instantly recognizable. Many of them are very poor, but they are enterprising, energetic people. Very quickly large numbers have got into shopkeeping and offices. They have captured important businesses. This has rather shaken the native Marseillais, an exuberant man who works in bursts. You see the poorest of the Algerians or Negroes begging, working as street photographers, selling combs, playing mandolins; and stopping everything to be lost in a long, gazing dream if a beautiful girl goes by.

There are rich meadowy belts of country, stretches of forest and wilderness as you travel eastward out of Toulon to Hyères, Antibes and Nice, but there the mountains come in close with the Alps behind them. The mistral is not supposed to strike here. You are indeed in a coast of pleasure, but one in which two kinds of pleasure run side by side. One is the sheer pleasure of sun and sea and abandon, in which the body comes into a freedom that was lost to it in office and factory; this is a place of wholehearted festivals. The other pleasure, in the inner Riviera, is of a reflective delight, in which the artist and thinking being can work. It is a safe guess that nearly all the distinguished men and women of our civilization have spent some time on this coast. It is dotted mostly with painters and craftsmen—workers in ceramics and glass—but also with writers, actors, even philosophers. The lure is the climate, the sun, the good life. There is, especially in the old towns, the feeling of the intensity of an old civilization with established habits and inherent dignity. Anarchy and publicity break in, of course; Saint-Tropez is now filled with the faces that appear in the international glossies, yet I remember it as a little town with one café and one town drunk—who followed the one town crier through the streets imitating the trumpet with which he called the people together to announce all the market prices of sardines—and with miles of deserted beach not far beyond.

What the millions cannot destroy is the landscape of this coast. There are the fiery-colored mountains of the Maures, that stretch eastward from Marseilles. Then there is the red rock and the encroaching of the Alps above Antibes and Nice and Monte Carlo, giving shelter but also a sort of triumphant, overpowering fantasy to the crowded scene. The unending loops of the rocky bays and promontories will continue far into Italy. The real towns are fragments of rock surrounded by villas. Monaco is the strangest fragment: the smallest state in Europe, only two and a quarter miles long, as narrow as 160 yards and never wider than 1100 yards. There has been gambling there since 1856, but the inhabitants are not allowed at the tables. The state exists as a tolerated protectorate of France and depends upon the millionaires.

But the strength of Monte Carlo is in its legends: the stories of the losers kept off the cliff edge and paid off to commit suicide outside the principality, the cinema scenes at the tables, the robberies, the tales of the man who broke the bank, and the endless stories of successful "systems" with their mathematical fancies. The past memories of princes and dukes, the bejeweled gamblers, the present glamour of Princess Grace leave the tourist open-mouthed as he goes in to make his cautious and humble throw, just to say that he has done it. He has challenged Fortune in its most glittering home and has the illusion of being back in *la belle époque*, when kings were kings and courtesans were Cleopatras. Unreal kingdom, it is really literature or film. Even the Monte Carlo motor race, roaring up those one-in-seven streets, is converted to extravagance. The car crashes of the corniche have a sort of permitted folly. *Le pile-up* is a sort of pleasure.

It is in the evening that the northerner feels the dramatic spell. The mountains and promontories are cut out sharp against the sea. The sunsets are reddened but hard. At Antibes, as at Marseilles, one is transported on some nights into Japanese paintings, into a gaudy Gauguin, a sportive Chagall, into a colored scene that is a scene of theater. It will seem like that again at Ventimiglia, on the Italian border, when they thrust bouquets of carnations at you into the train; at Menton, all down the tormented and tunneled coast to Genoa, and beyond to Rapallo, Portofino and Spezia. Indeed in Italy the sense of theater will become operatic. The roses and flowering creepers pour over the dusty walls. Nature outglares the human being. The flowers live to the full their unrestrained electric lives.

One sees how it must be for these Mediterraneans: they will not, in this hard, rich exuberance of the earth, believe in anything beyond what they can see or touch or smell or taste. Why should they? They accept the cornucopia that overflows; they will also accept it when, by misfortune or the hard seasons of the year, it is empty. The Mediterranean is a realist—a realist about the body, about his feelings, about money, about human nature. The good life is possible only when you accept things as they are.

At Ventimiglia, French gray and white is giving way to the green shutters, the saffron walls of Italy. You notice that the sense the French have of knowing everything and of having settled it, precisely, once and for all, is giving way to something else. The Frenchman does not need to love you. But the Italian does. The Frenchman corrects your mistakes in French. The Italian never corrects your mistakes in Italian. He is too eager to love you to mind a trifle like that. He needs you, clamors for you, to dance around you, dazzle you, please you. He doesn't want to be loved, but he needs to love you. He is an actor, you are his audience. If you happen to entertain him by putting on a play yourself, he will adore it. If both these things happen to fall flat, he will fall into a dignified melancholy. There will be a feeling that you and he are in an empty theater. He falls back on the Mediterranean glumness.

Of course, your impression is superficial. There are other sides to it. There are marked differences in the character of the Italian regions, and especially between the north and the south of Italy. In Genoa you are in the relatively flourishing, money-minded, businesslike north. Here people say, "This is not like the rest of Italy. This is like London or Rotterdam, a place of serious people—bankers, merchants and shippers, steel mills, docks." And indeed the weight of the commercial buildings does suggest the northern gravity. The city, especially in the dock area, was badly damaged in the war, but that has been put right now. The new elevated highways, the armies of cranes over the harbor and the mills, the big ships blowing in the harbor, the banks and shipping offices, establish that commerce comes first here.

The competition with Marseilles is constantly in the port's mind. The Genoese weigh their disadvantages and advantages. The first disadvantage is obvious. Shut in by high mountains, the city is like flights of stairs cut out of rock. It cannot spread far backward; it has been forced to stretch for twenty miles of suburb along the narrow shelf of the coast. It has no great navigable river. It is near the Alps, without a natural route through them. There can be no water traffic with central Europe. Everything has to go by train through the Alpine tunnels. And it is only with great difficulty and huge expense that the harbor can be enlarged. The advantage is the industrial and mineral wealth of the hinterland: behind Genoa are Milan, the most vigorous up-to-the-minute city in southern Europe, a place of millionaire manufacturers, and Turin, with its Detroit just outside, pumping its little Fiat cars into Italy, the rest of Europe, Africa and even across the Atlantic. The density of cars on the road in Italy, at any rate around the cities, must be one of the highest in Europe.

Fortunate Genoa. It is commercially and industrially rich, yet in the nineteenth century industrialism did not destroy its character. The city is piled up into its steep hills, so the ground floor of one street is at roof level of the one below. The colors are gentle, soft saffrons and pinks and pale greens in the old city, and in the new one they are still not garish. The city is pierced by road tunnels—the Italians have had to be the world's great tunnelers—and one seems to be passing from one town to another as one whizzes through them.

Genoa is cooled by arcades. It has gateways that suggest a late-medieval city, and old merchant palaces that remind one that it was one of the great city-states. Historians tell us that when Ferdinand and Isabella of Spain deported the Jews, they called in the Genoese bankers, who were far harder than the Jews in their dealings. Columbus, who was born in this city, was a hard bargainer; he was a trader before he was a seaman.

Great seaports are liberal and independent in spirit. Foreign trade civilizes. Populations mix. People are accessible.

I used to go and call on the editor of a newspaper in Genoa.

"What is the character of the Genoese?" I asked him once.

"Like Londoners," he said. "Except that here everything is run by inter-related families. But if they tell you the Genoese are interested only in money and not in the arts—deny it, I beg you." There is no need to. Genoa has its superb palaces.

"The essence of the Genoese," he went on, "is, first, pride, then independence, liberality and love of work."

The great wooden shutters of the editor's room—he was an old man—were drawn, and in the cool semigloom he sat at a table covered with pamphlets. He had a deep, gentle voice and a sun-cracked skin, and he wore an open-necked casual shirt. "Pride," he repeated. "Mazzini was born here, Garibaldi's father was from Genoa. The Risorgimento, the liberation of Italy, began here."

The good restaurants of Genoa are hidden away down side alleys. They are not infested with musicians. You enter by the kitchen and you see the whole family, maybe three generations, working there, with the oldest woman at the cash desk, with the voice of authority. You are in a large room, without any show, where the businessmen order enormous quantities of food, choosing their fish or their pasta or meat from the dish or spit, saying exactly how they want it done. (But a Genoese won't cook, say, in the Florentine fashion; he will direct you to a Florentine restaurant for that—pityingly.) Italian food has no great art but it relies, as the people do, on the fresh natural taste of things. In fact, if the Italians of the Mediterranean have the art of living, it is because they live openly, simply, immediately, naturally. Whatever may be going on secretly in their lives, they have outwardly the art of appearing smiling and pleasing on the stage of life.

There is a narrow street, a kind of alley, that wanders for a long distance across the city just above the dock quarter. It must have been one of the old main streets. You go steeply down and are suddenly—as you seem so often to be in Italy—in the whole of life. There are the lively little shops, the bars, the churches, and down the street stroll the respectably dressed-up women and their children, walking severely past the prostitutes smoking at the doorways or the priests on their way into the church. The gamblers pitch their little tables on which they do their card tricks. These always fascinate men and children, even those who know each trick inside and out. Patiently they watch, in suddenly acquired naïveté, which they can instantly conceal if a real customer comes along. A pretty girl goes by with her basket and every man turns and studies her body, and she shows it off with pleasure. They shout admiringly at her, they pinch her, they put an arm round her. She is never cross, but she evades neatly, laughing. Who is she? The girl from the cakeshop, no doubt. Nearby men, with no commercial sense, are standing four or five together trying to sell transistor radios. If naval vessels arrive, there is a sudden rush to sell enormous dolls to the sailors. It is far from being an innocent street, but it is well mannered.

And then, rich and poor Genoese have the superb coast to play with. The small and the grand bays of the Gulf of Genoa are at your door. For tens of miles, the buses, cars and motorbikes charge noisily down the winding corniche, twisting around promontories that stick out into the dazing sea, roaring over gorges, looping round deep valleys, banging past the dusty walls that seem to topple under flowers. The hills are made of villas all the way to Rapallo. Dozens of little launches lie at Santa Margherita, to go across the bay to the fantastic little hothouse cove of Portofino, where the yachts of the film stars and the millionaires are gaped at by the factory workers of Manchester, Düsseldorf, Lille and Turin.

The Mediterraneans of Genoa may be southerners to us, but they are northerners to themselves. Severe, hard-headed, hard-working, active, businesslike people—even harsh and puritanic; that is how they see themselves. They deny that they are actors. The actors, they say contemptuously, are in the real south, in Naples, Calabria and Sicily, the Italy that is poor, ignorant and, in religion, childishly superstitious. This is right, up to a point. Naples is a city given over entirely to the histrionic. It is theater in every gesture, in every yard of pavement. It is a very Spanish city, for it was long a Spanish kingdom, and its sense of theater has a lot in common with the theatrical strain in Seville.

The stage setting is notoriously spectacular. The whole world knows the famous view and never tires of beauty that seems ever to renew itself. There is Vesuvius (silent for years now, almost a comic friend to be greeted) at one corner of the bay, and below it the vineyards and orchards and carefully tended market gardens that grow on the rich volcanic soil. The walls, even of the houses, are masses of lava rock. The city rises in terraces over the steep hills between Vesuvius and the massive castle at Santa Lucia, and then sweeps for miles along the boldly balustraded seafront in avenues of palms, to rise to Posilipo, to sink to little sea towns like Pozzuoli, and to rise again, sweetly smelling of herbs and myrtles, to Greek Cumae, the Lake of Avernus, the world of Parthenope and Ulysses. From the city one looks out on the Apennines hanging in the haze above the close orange and lemon groves of Sorrento, and before us Capri is cut out like a blue cardboard stage piece. The heat is moist, the honeyed air hangs on the body, the sea is glazed and almost silky white. Energy seeps away.

Coming in from the airport, one is struck by the steepness of the hills, the scale of the buildings. The famous ones are immense and massive, with high, cool halls; the whine of the air conditioner is rare. In old Naples, the streets are narrow and the houses very tall, and it must be said that the city is brownish, yellowish and ugly in color when you are below; though from above, it is roofed in terra-cotta tiles and broken into livelier yellows and whites. It looks dusty, dry, gritty and wearying. It has some horrible, ugly fountains and an out-of-date bourgeois pretentiousness in its nineteenth-century avenues. The dramatic things are its monasteries on the cliffs in the middle of the city, its well-placed palaces and its barnlike churches, great crumbling and peeling gorgonzolas of baroque and rococo.

But it is the human swarm that is the real sight of the city. When one asks what Naples *does*, one has to say that it makes people. It has certainly exported them to the United States and the Argentine by the hundreds of thousands. And here we come to anti-Neapolitanism. From Victorian times until the end of the war, perhaps still, Naples has been regarded as one of the sinks of Europe. The seat of a kingdom, it has never been governed and it is said to be ungovernable. Its poverty is notorious. The washing that hangs across the poor streets was a favorite subject for painters of picturesque squalor. Its sexual immorality, its beggars, its thieves and pickpockets, its propensity to cheat, and its crimes are famous. Shelley called it "the metropolis of a ruined Paradise." At the end of the last war, after the city had been badly bombed, the spectacle of hunger, of begging children, was terrible. A lump of sugar, a crust, a pomegranate were snatched feverishly from one's table.

But in the last twenty years there have been notable changes. The bombs cleared long stretches of the dock-area slums. Industry has moved down from the north to make up for the losses of a not very flourishing port. NATO has a base there, and this is responsible, alas, for the ruin of Posilipo, once a hill of orchards and gardens but now a terrace of ultramodern apartment houses inhabited by the American colony and the rich property speculators who have made fortunes all over the Mediterranean. The mass of people are obviously just a little better off, and if one were to judge by the tens of thousands of Fiats driving round and round the city like so many beetles, all day and all night, by the swarms of motor bicycles and the noise, one would say that more people shared in the city's wealth than before. I saw only one beggar on my last visit to Naples, and she was a gypsy. There was no begging down in those amusing restaurants by the harbor at Santa Lucia. The farcical collection of violinists and singers there kept up their soulful or roguish antics as usual and seemed even prosperous. I'm afraid Neapolitan food is not very good as a rule, and when it is, it is never hot enough. The waiters are so frantically caught up in private dramas that they dash about, leaving your dish to go tepid.

It is said that thieving on the crowded buses has declined—however, I did have to give a sudden twist one day to get a man's hand out of my jacket pocket. There was nothing in it. His face was superbly blank. They say that matters improved after bus drivers were obliged to drive all their passengers to a police station if anyone cried "pickpocket." At this, the brilliant Neapolitan pickpocket could be relied on to slip your wallet back without your knowing it, so that at the police station the passengers would fall on you for raising a false alarm.

I like to think such tales are true; if they are not, they are perfectly in accord with the Neapolitan temperament, which delights in intrigue and the tit for tat of farce. A foreign dealer in ceramics, to whom I had said that Neapolitans are born rascals, replied, "They go far beyond that. They are criminals. But you mustn't be morally indignant. They love it when you see through them and laugh admiringly, indeed affectionately." This upsets the rigid moralist. An old cab driver once doubled my fare and gave an explanation so farcical that my wife and I burst into laughter. He was delighted. We had caught him. He could hardly stand for laughing, and indeed put his arms around our shoulders to support himself. We rocked together, and for two pins we would all have kissed one another.

The fact is that a Neapolitan cannot resist making little plays. At Santa Lucia the tourist is pestered by peddlers of watches, fountain pens, photographs, tortoise shell and flowers. The tourist becomes exasperated and indignant. He even shouts and waves his arms angrily. But during the lunch hour, when the streets are empty, I have seen two peddlers amusing themselves by acting the tourist-peddler comedy to pass the time: one takes the part of the tourist; the other pesters. They imitate us! The accuracy of observant mockery is brilliant.

In the narrow streets of Naples you see the whole of life with little or no protective veil over it. Sometimes there are terrible primitive scenes, *cose all'italiana*: a madman rushes screaming down the street; children stop their play and run after him, throwing stones at him. Their mothers come excitedly to the doors to watch. At night cripples come out like injured insects to take the air. There may be refuse in the streets, but the houses are clean. The women have a passion for laundering. You learn to look at the cobbles as you walk under the lines of washing, for there you can see which sheets are dripping and so avoid them. A lot of life goes on on the balconies; people talk and shout from one balcony to another.

The family's only room contains decent furniture—a couple of double beds, a dining table and chairs—and is also the workshop of some small trade. First thing in the morning the chairs are put on the table, to make room, and will stay there until mealtime comes. The family is large. Perhaps three generations will live together. All the events of life take place before all eyes: copulation, childbirth, illness and death. As you pass by you will see a sick man in bed, a woman ironing or sewing; or a family eating while, in a bed within reach, the wax-faced, toothless grandmother is drinking her bowl of soup. Once the meal is over, everyone goes out into the street.

In the evening, when the dead heat goes, and late in the night, the doorsteps are crowded. The birds that were twittering in their cages outside almost every window during the day are silent. The candles on the innumerable shrines twinkle. And everyone shouts what he has to say. No one is drunk in the south of Italy. They have more excitement in their blood than alcohol could ever give them.

Naples is Greek, Roman, French and Spanish. Some say the intensity of facial expression is purely Grecian. If you stand in the Galleria, that central arcade near the Opera House, and watch the crowd of men who stand there in a large knot, talking so loudly that one seems to have come to some Bourse at the peak hour of buying and selling, you notice the individuality of the faces and gestures. They are astonishing. I watched two men talking in a café here, and their gestures were so extraordinary—a finger to the eye, the temple, the nose, the palm of a hand, fingers flickering, a hand on the heart, clenched hands, wrung hands, circles made by thumb and finger—that at first I supposed they were dumb and that this was sign language. But they were in fact talking.

What is that crowd of men in the Galleria talking about hour after hour, every day? It is their club. Or, as some say, it's the labor exchange. They are looking for a job. The prostitutes are around the corner. Do you want a girl? Do you want to buy something, see the museum? What do you want? Essentially, they are looking for what is called a "combination." You do not buy a house or a lorry, you do not make a straight deal. You enter innumerable personal intrigues, working from person to person, bribing, obtaining the ear of someone, trying the back door. Dozens of people gather around your enterprise, to be in it or to obstruct. The financial corruption of Naples, the collapse of any kind of government, springs from this "big flea and little flea" system. The failure of government has created a vacuum that has been filled by the church, which, in Naples, is completely identified with the childlike, even playful fantasies of the mass of people. They passionately like to be distracted and amused. Life is bitterly hard. For historical reasons, what northerners call society does not exist. There has been no strong middle class. All but one of the university professors I wanted to see were never there; they spent half their time at other universities. To live they have to "combine."

The fact is that Naples simply exaggerates what has been general in Italy. The state is weak. Law is unreliable, money and justice are hard to come by. Two thousand years of history have been savage. The Italian, therefore, puts all his faith in the family: the interests of the family come first. Nepotism becomes the supreme virtue. Family comes before the police, the courts, even public opinion and private conscience—according to Luigi Barzini in his brilliant book, *The Italians*. On this last point I can cite the case of an English doctor who had a small motor accident in Italy. If he had not had the presence of mind to get out of his car quickly and take several photographs of the two cars, his case would have been lost. For the rival motorist gathered a formidable group of "eyewitnesses": several of them came from twenty miles away, and all of them turned out to be his relatives. The defense is that the family is the only secure thing in an unstable state. The general hostility to divorce is not religious—even the Communists oppose divorce. It is sad that individuals suffer, but we are not in this world for the pleasure of romantic love. We are here to beget children and survive. The family must not be weakened; if it is, money, property, jobs, status, all are jeopardized.

This doctrine gives great power to women in a country where they have little apparent liberty. Yet as the south "organizes itself"—that is to say, as it comes into the late-twentieth-century world—the family tends to break up. Jobs change. Children scatter. People defy the divorce laws. The young assert themselves. In the industrial north the family system has been shaken. The Neapolitan is alarmed. The outward face of Naples itself has changed enormously in the last twenty-five years. How can the inner life not change too?

They say the sun, the curiously corroding climate—which takes away the power of concentration and saps the will, so that one lives for the moment only—will preserve the ancient Mediterranean habit of thought and feeling. I do not want to convey the impression that Naples is picturesque. It is not. It is ugly, harsh and horrifying. Yet such is the expressiveness and vitality of the people, they seem superior in looks, in human dignity and intelligence, to the stunned slum populations of Liverpool or New York.

And there is poverty worse than the Neapolitan farther south, in Calabria and Sicily. Those fly-blown, hungry and dirty little towns; the stare of misery in the eyes. The sun appears to redeem, but Italy has a changeable climate. The rain comes down in sheets; the cold can be harsh. When I was in Sicily recently, the wind was cold, the rain clouds boiled up black and purple over the grandiose mountains of Palermo. One might have been in Kerry; the stone walls, the poor soil, the few sheep and the bent trees evoked Ireland.

The little plane I flew down in was packed with wooden-looking men who, one imagined, belonged to the Mafia. At the airport we were held up by one of those wild Sicilian family meetings. An aunt, large and jeweled, had arrived from Chicago. She charged across the tarmac; a large collection of relatives charged to meet her. They collided and became a howling human knot, weeping, shouting, embracing, clinging. Officials stood by appreciatively. Half an hour later, the family were still at it, in twos and threes. One had seen the Family in all its generations, complete and unrestrained.

In Sicily one sees all that is Italian magnified and exaggerated—all except one thing. The Sicilian is a dour man. He is often violent, morose, harsh and melancholic. He has the art of utterly avoiding the law. The spirit of the Mafia is in the blood. Sicily is Italy's Ireland, a country at odds with the national government. Italian-made law is made to be broken. And then the people are a Mediterranean mixture of Greek, North African, Spanish, Norman French and all the pirates. There is a primitive regard for the presence of death. The mother of Giuliano, the bandit, kneeled down and licked her son's blood in the courtyard where he lay shot dead. Aeschylus wrote in Syracuse: one would say that he might still be at home in Sicily. The mourning notices on the wall are common in Italy and Spain; in Sicily these notices are everywhere. They bring home a fact that northerners shy away from— that the southerner is asserting family status: you have standing, you belong, you know who you are; there is no question of your not having identity.

Palermo astonished me. I remembered it as a small eighteenth-century city, with youths serenading with mandolins in the streets at night, and the pretty, paneled carts painted with scenes of the wars of Charlemagne and the struggles between Christian and Moor. A new and much larger modern city of apartment blocks has now grown up beside the old one.

I had tea with a university professor—he was from the north—in Palermo. He lived in one of these brand-new modern apartments. How prosperous (I said) it looked. "Pure façade," he said. "It is built on the Keynesian principle; if you want to be rich you must first of all appear to be rich. Sicilians—like all Italians—are expert in appearances." Palermo is famous for being the headquarters of the Mafia, and everyone had told me its power had gone. "Not at all," he said. "It is permanent. It rules and rigs everything. Not one of these buildings could have been put up without paying the Mafia. If a builder refused, his scaffolding would mysteriously collapse. The hand of the Mafia lies on everything you touch."

"On the university?" I asked.

"No," he said. "There's no money in education." Nevertheless, one is told, one would never dare fail a Mafia man's son in his exams.

Naturally the foreigner sees no sign of this. The interesting thing is that the Mafia is powerful only in western Sicily, in the region of feudal estates, where there has been little industry and no middle-class movement. In eastern Sicily, with its long history of prosperous commerce and manufacture in Catania, the Mafia is said not to exist. Indeed that pleasant, modern and hospitable city—so absurdly despised by the guidebooks—has nothing but contempt for "aristocratic" Palermo. And in Palermo they do not call the Mafia by its name: they call it "the honored society," "the friends," and refer to its members—in sinister voice—as "qualified" men or "specialists."

It was Easter time in Catania. The cars streamed out to the seaside or north to Victorian Taormina, where the motor bicycles deafen one on the steep cliffside, where cameras click endlessly in the Greek theater; or to the little town of Aci Castello, to see the three sharp rocks that are said to be the rocks that Polyphemus, the Cyclops, threw into the sea. One fascination of the story of Odysseus is its topographical accuracy: Polyphemus, the one-eyed, was clearly Etna; that single eye is the crater, and those rocks were hurled by Etna in eruption.

To the south, on the way to Syracuse, the Easter crowds were out in their thousands; families were picnicking among the flowers and under the trees, and in Syracuse itself there were scarcely any foreigners in the Greek theater. Any small Italian car built to hold four or five people will always carry ten: in a poor country you have to pack everyone in. The driving is terrible. A pile-up of half a dozen cars on these gay holidays is common. The accidents are not usually serious, but to crunch and be crunched appears to be the aim of Sicilian motoring. The number of children that can be hung about a small motor bicycle is remarkable.

I was in Palermo, too, during the Easter season, and there the scene in the back streets was dark, primitive and forbidding. In the butcher shop an Easter lamb was standing on its hind legs and looking over the low door, bleating into the street. Flayed cows' heads stared down. The intricately decorated bars were crowded with men drinking strong wine. Others sat playing cards in the street, always surrounded by a tense small crowd. In the innumerable cakeshops, huge Easter cakes were being made, each shopkeeper's family struggling with the dough and the decorations. Lighting was dim: electricity is too expensive. The lines of washing across the alleys were wretched: the washing of Naples is far superior.

In old Palermo there is a darkness and the dereliction of the last war. Before the war there used to be dozens of puppet theaters where the story of Roland and Oliver was endlessly re-enacted, in squalid dockside show houses where one sat in a sea of peanut shells. Now I saw only one puppet theater. And to see a decent paneled cart you have to go to the museum. Very sad—but there was no clean, modern Palermo then. There were no little planes, full of business people, flipping about from town to town over the enormous mountains and the poverty-stricken wilderness of the interior. The evening view of this splendid mountain island from the sky is momentous and alarming.

Aeschylus wrote in Sicily; but so did Theocritus. People still swear they see Greek-like goatherds on the mountains. The sensation that Sicily is a country blackened by the ferocity of the sun, by the gloom of the rock of Etna's lava towns, and by the darkness of poverty and primitivism is only a part of the story. The flowers wave by the roadside in the spring, the grasses are fresh, the leaves of the olives glitter in silver, and the orange groves are dense in the narrow lucky valleys and coastal strips. The mimosa seems to roll like yellow smoke mile after mile.

There is a fine university in Catania. It is extraordinary to think first of this modern, industrialized region, with its clean, well-housed industry and well-housed workers (it calls itself the "Milan of the south"), and then of the wretched stone villages and towns on the big estates in the harsh heat and bitter cold of the mountains, and of the misery and violence on the side of the island that faces Africa.

The Mediterranean genius is intellectual, realistic and sensual, but before all these things it is individual, and most individual in Italy. And in the matter of cities, it has created one that resembles no other in the world, a place that—however often one goes there—blooms in the water like some miraculous flower: Venice. It is an estuary island or collection of islands—despite the modern causeway that joins it to the mainland now—lying in shallow seas on the edge of malarial marshes, by which it was protected from attack. Its trade and naval power dominated the Mediterranean for centuries. The Venetians were the best gunners in the world. The place was a republic of merchants. It was at the Mediterranean end of the great overland trade route that ran over the Alps and down the Rhine to the marshes of that northern estuary where stands also the only city that can be compared with Venice as a work of engineering: Amsterdam, whose canals echo the canals of Venice, and whose solemn seamen and burghers, in their way, have something in common with the long-headed shippers of Venice. Both cities were founded by refugees driven out to the marshes by northern tyrannies. But in Venice the effect is Oriental; it evokes Istanbul in its extravagance. Yet it also evokes the Gothic north.

Seamen, colonists, carriers, an island people protected by the sea, hard bargainers who put trade first, the Venetians have been compared by some with the English rather than with the Dutch. It is true that the Venetians are not exactly Continentals: they are cut off, self-regarding, self-interested islanders, and it has been held against them sometimes, as it has against the English and other island peoples, that they think they are always right. It is said that even in the museum life the city leads today, the Venetian puts on a morose and withdrawn face behind which lies his conceit in his rightness. He has a certain subtle, malicious wit. Venice was never feudal. Its people were always united, and the sense of equality is strong. Throughout history it has been expensive to deal with the Venetian; invisible subclauses and exceptions have notoriously emerged in his contracts from the days of the Crusades onward. He has, as a citizen of a once great power, become quite indifferent to his old unpopularity, and is complacent in his isolation. The theatricality of Naples is alien to him.

You suppose this is the only silent city on earth simply because it has no road traffic. The silence of Venice is in this sense blessed, a gift from heaven. To wander in the tangle of clean, narrow streets, alleys, lanes and passages, crossing the little bridges that span the scores of little canals—there are 177 of them and their total length is 128 miles, which accounts for your sudden feeling that you are tired out—is an astonishing rest to the mind. The senses awaken, and in the soft, humid air you feel the famous sensuousness of the city, its mysterious gentleness. You have been taken clean out of clock time, into time that is measured by mood and by the trailing, evanescent motions of desire. But when you confide this to a Venetian, his long-nosed face and his malicious eye light up. His liverish look becomes gay. Venice, he says, is built out of water and the purest light of the Mediterranean—and noise! One grants him at once the noise of the *vaporetti* and motorboats of the Grand Canal. In the daytime you can sit outside the Accademia, drinking a Campari, and not hear a word that is being said to you. The Venetian will curse that noise with you, and even more the smell of petrol and diesel fumes, and the smog blowing over the water. The fact is that, like all Italians, he likes noise and that Venice makes you aware of noises you had forgotten: the vague cloudy *rumeur* of cities, the continual slapping of water, the bumping of gondolas, croaking all night long, violently at the turn of the tide; the extraordinary whispering tap and scrape of footsteps—the real surprise of Venice—the words of a conversation a hundred yards away, the shouts and singing of people going home at night, the thumpings and fiddlings of the rival café orchestras in Saint Mark's piazza, the church bells, the hooting of the large ships, the shout of a gondolier. Half the night, if you are sleepless in Venice, and are in some inner street, you will be kept awake by the loud Italian voice, the endless arguments of waiting gondoliers, the straining of ropes against piers. Even the clatter of the pigeons in Saint Mark's is deafening. The voices of four men playing cards in a café late at night, the last customers, can be heard streets away.

Some have found Venice slimy and stinking. In the early morning, a journey through the narrow ways, where the filthy water is eating away the rotting brick, where one glides appalled through orange and potato peelings and broccoli stumps and other garbage, spotting the rats run into the warehouses, is hard to bear. The rubbish barges do not elevate the soul. One thinks of miasma and prays that the tide will be strong and swill the city out; and one concentrates on the skill of the gondolier as he steers to within an inch of the mossy wall on a blind corner and skims you faultlessly around.

Nevertheless, you pass out of the dark and miasmal into the glitter of the sun and the soft blue air, and everything is changed. You live in gold, pearl and enamel. The Doge's Palace and Saint Mark's dazzle you, and if Saint Mark's Square is no longer "the drawing room of Europe," it is still lordly in its stone and princely in its fantasy. It is only you and thousands like you who have deteriorated and are unworthy—one of the terrible punishments to self-esteem that tourism has brought us—and you try, as you go to look at church after church, at Tintorettos and Bellinis, Titians, Guardis and Carpaccios, to redeem the squalid condition of your soul.

What is going to happen to Venice? It is not as fashionable as it was in the nineteenth century. It is no longer a place for the Wagners, the Brownings, the Henry Jameses and Ruskins or the Thomas Manns. It has its Biennale, of course, its many conferences; there was an international conference of lighthouse experts when I was there last, which is, on reflection, fitting. The Venetian channels are tricky. Most of its shipping trade goes to the docks and huge industrial complex of Mestre, on the mainland end of the causeway, but some of it and the passenger lines come to Venice itself. This is, after all, an important port. The business people in Venice complain that it is an empty shell and important businesses and their workers have moved, leaving the innumerable small craftsmen behind—the picture-frame makers, the glassmakers, who work in their dark little shops. Some monsters want to fill in the canals and get cars into the city: they are sick of being dependent on tourism and show transport.

In the meantime, while this dream hovers, one is captivated by a city that has preserved, especially at night, a look of mystery and enchantment. The place is scarcely vulgarized. Even the swarms of tourists cannot ruin it. The lively sea comes sparkling to the street's edge. One is lost in the labyrinth, everyone is lost; it is a maze, and at every little bridge one looks up at tall walls and high windows. They are waiting for the Hoffmann story, for music, for Casanova and for the ghost of some Renaissance crime.

We are near the end of our Mediterranean journey. We are of course in the Adriatic, facing eastward, looking across to the Slavs. But there is one more port of call before we come to the end of Western Europe, and it is one that contradicts half of what we have said. We arrive in Trieste.

Trieste is a hybrid, the city of perplexity. What is it—Italian, Austrian, Slavic? Is it a little Vienna by the sea? Once the entrepôt of central Europe, rich in the grand and spacious manner of the Austro-Hungarian empire, it has been torn between the Italians and Yugoslavs. It has seen its shipping trade decline—Fiume, now in Yugoslavia, rises at Trieste's expense—and has attempted an industrial revival. At the moment Trieste has a new interest—atomic power—and with this in mind a new university has been built. The sadness of Trieste springs from the fact that the Italian frontier lies a mile or so outside the city; and the wild mountain country and beautiful Adriatic seaports of Yugoslavia are closed to the Triestinos. For a long time Italy's relations with Yugoslavia were very bad; in the last few years they have greatly improved. Trieste has a considerable Slav population, mainly in the poorer classes, and the two peoples get along moderately well, though they scarcely meet.

A rich young couple off a yacht, celebrating something with quantities of French brandy, called across from their table asking what I thought of Trieste. I said I found it delightful, and so alive. They said I was talking nonsense. It is, they said, neurotic and dead. It had sunk from eminence to provinciality in a few years. It had lost its style. There is something in this, but the city has not lost its basic character. To the Italian lightness, the Triestinos have added the idiosyncrasy and intelligence of educated Vienna. They are born café people. Half the day one sees them in the large cafés, drinking coffee, reading newspapers and holding long conversations. Their most interesting novelist, Italo Svevo, who had a great vogue in Paris and London in the 1920s and who was quintessentially Triestino, was a café writer in the Viennese manner—the spinner-out of intellectual paradoxes and of inquiries into sentiments. To Italian gaiety there is added the morbid brain of Vienna, the Vienna of the psychologists. An elderly lady of Trieste, living in a vast apartment in old Trieste among the grand old-fashioned furniture of another generation, said sternly that when she first went to Florence and Rome, she was shocked by the superficial education of upper-class girls in Italy; from central Europe, Trieste had imbibed serious education. At parties I was at once struck by a neglect of the Italian passion for the *bella figura*, and by the amusing and instructed talk of the people. There was nothing provincial about the doctors, lawyers, architects and professors who were there. Trieste, in fact, has that nervous intelligence of a city where several cultures spark off one another.

The total brain power in Trieste must be formidable; and I would guess that Trieste is a good place for writers, whereas the south of France is certainly not—well, if one excepts such experienced ancients as Somerset Maugham. Mascherini, a sculptor of European and New York fame, lives in Trieste. In their eagerness to have foreign friends—and in their houses, too—ones sees not only the comfort of their mercantile life but the uneasiness about their isolation. Italy is a place for dazzling acquaintance, but in Trieste there is the assurance of knowing that people are more likely to mean what they say, and that they like the solace of long friendships. I get most polite and pleasantly worded formal letters from Italy, but from Trieste I get witty letters, invitations to parties a year ahead. The northerner finds a handsome Austrian eighteenth-century city, massive and well-ordered, where he is not an alien, where his interests are understood, and where, alas, he sees a look of desperation in the eyes. This must not be entirely attributed to political fear; it is a look one often sees in frontier people who belong and yet do not belong.

In the last forty years there have been great material changes in Mediterranean life. The people hung on longer there than elsewhere in Europe to the conventions of the nineteenth century. The women, for example, were still wearing black until the 1930s or later. There was an air of severe mourning; and manners in all classes followed rigid patterns. Custom ruled absolutely. In commerce, in travel, one was surrounded by unnecessary difficulties; a large, ill-paid bureaucracy hung on to its jobs by evolving a maze of petty regulations. All this has vastly changed as the lessons of the north are now learned by its old teacher. The south—one can't repeat this too often—is organizing itself. It is possible for the Mediterranean now to be an *effective* active man. If he emigrates to the Americas, his rapid and penetrating intelligence brings him, again and again, to the top, especially in the sciences, for his educated men have been exactingly well-educated. An ordinary ill-paid engineer will not only know two or three languages but may be an art historian or a wide reader of serious literature. One continually meets the multiple talent. But whether the man of the Mediterranean succeeds or not, his profound gift for putting personal life and care for the arts of living and pleasure first never leaves him. It is the great benison of that ancient civilizing sea.

[1966]

5

Guideless in the Pyrenees

You wake up in the morning to see the green rump of a mountain slanting from top to bottom of your window, and a corner of a fair blue sky at the side. High up among the rocks are two or three white goats; below them, on the vivid mountain turf, a man is raking down the grass he has scythed; at the end of the day he will put it into a long sack like a bolster and roll it home. The place where he is working can hardly be called a field, but a ragged strip of short grass hanging between the boulders. It is astonishing that he can stand upright there. The mountain plunges among rock, ash trees and beeches to the bed of a noisy torrent, whose green water whitens and boils all day and night, drops under a stone bridge seventy feet high and goes cascading mile after mile down the valley, from gorge to gorge.

You open the window. The mountain air at four or five thousand feet is light and sharp. There is the smell of grass, moss, thyme, ponies, cows—something clean and keen and milky. You are at Gavarnie, a *jasse*, or high valley, of the central Pyrenees on the French side.

Presently the peace is broken. A motor coach comes pah-pahing up the hill and unloads a dozen French families; husbands in shirt sleeves, grandmothers, aunts, mothers and children get out near the hotel opposite, which advertises *"Terrasse et télescope."* That beautifully dates the place sometime before 1914: the telescope is for looking up at the snow peak, a few miles off, and at the fantastic waterfall that hangs like the thin beard of a ghost, from the ledge of a mountain wall that the Romantics could have called horrendous and impenetrable. On the other side of it, the people tell you, is Spain.

The coach passengers despise the telescope. The businesslike villagers have got them all bundled and tied safely onto ponies and donkeys, and the procession trots off through the village. Hour after hour new busloads will arrive, new cavalcades of ponies and donkeys will start off. They climb over the rough paths, round cliffs and precipices, until at last they arrive at one of the most dramatic mountain sights of Europe: the Cirque de Gavarnie, a semicircular "wall" rising in sunless, vertical terraces to a height of fifty-six hundred feet, two miles in diameter, all but enclosing an amphitheater that could hold an army. Last winter's stale snow is still on the higher ledges, down streaks the water—for some reason frightening because it is so thin a streak—into a natural tunnel of snow that has been preserved and frozen hard at the sunless base of the precipice. You crick your neck to look at the line of ten-thousand-foot peaks that top the wall. And as you stare, your French friend reminds you that it is precisely these *cirques*, or semicircular walls, that distinguish the Pyrenees from all the other mountains of Europe.

The Pyrenees are not as lofty or as compact as the Alps, although their passes are high. They are not snow covered all the year. Their valleys are greener. Glaciers scarcely exist, the lakes are small. On the French side the scene is verdant, well watered by the Atlantic winds blowing across the pine-covered Landes, over Bayonne; on the Spanish side the scene is burned up, desolate for large areas, and austere.

As they run, separating France from Spain, for some 240 miles from the Atlantic to the Mediterranean, the Pyrenees do not flash as the Alps do in the north of Italy. They move in wild, waving procession. They mark a single frontier and a very strange one. It is supposed not to exist in any fundamental sense by those who think of Spain as European; but it does exist. On the north side, in populous France, anywhere between Bayonne and Perpignan, you are a Western European; in the scattered villages of Aragon on the Spanish side you are likely to be quite courteously asked arresting questions such as "Are you a Christian?" by a passing peasant or Guardia Civil—a common phrase harking back to the time when it was important, for the future of the world, to know whether you were a Moor and an infidel and intended the conquest of Europe. The hackneyed phrase that "Africa begins at the Pyrenees" is not entirely a metaphor. In the Alps you are at the hub of the European wheel, where its German and Latin strains are jointed, but in the Pyrenees you are on the rim, where Europe grates against something not quite like itself. Travelers in the Pyrenees often say that they feel "freer" there, and indeed the mountains are more open; but they sometimes mean that on the passes they are looking down into another civilization. This has been true from the time of Charlemagne, when Roland fought at Roncesvalles, and when slowly the Saracen was driven, century after century, back over Spain and across the Straits of Gibraltar.

Until not long before World War II there were only two completely finished railroads through the Pyrenees, one at the Atlantic end of the chain, at Hendaye in the French Basque provinces, the other at the Mediterranean or Catalan end, at Port Bou. The central Pyrenees were a real wall between France and Spain for centuries; now four railroads and four motor roads break through, and the Spanish side is a little better known.

The names of the peaks on the Spanish side testify to the hard desperation of the mountain scenery of Spain: the Accursed Mountain, the Peak and Mouth of Hell, the Lost Mountain (above Gavarnie) and the Bewitched. The highest peaks are on the Spanish side and, as so often happens in the Spanish scene, the rock shapes are tortured into fantastic shapes. One understands why there is so much fear and mystery in the legends of the Spanish Pyrenees. The fact is that the French side has always been more accessible because there the valleys travel direct to the backbone of the range, like a flight of stairs at right angles to the main ridge. As you stand twenty or thirty miles away on the famous promenade at Pau you see the Pyrenees as a long, serrated cavalcade of peaks. Change your viewpoint, cross over to Spain, and the sense of a procession vanishes. You are faced by a running tawny tide of parallel ranges; crossing one you are faced by another, so that you are lost like a swimmer in the trough of a wave, in a sea that is sixty miles wide. To fly over the Pyrenees into Spain is to see gay green country torn into the great brown and furrowed shoulders and head of a bull that comes charging up against the lighter body of Europe.

The Pyrenees have cut Spain off for centuries, and the low penetrable eastern and western ends are occupied by alien races: at Port Bou by the Catalans who are more Provençal than Spanish; at Hendaye and Bayonne by the Basques, whose origin is a mystery and who are neither Spanish nor French. Both have sought freedom from Spain in the last 30 years; both have traditionally blocked the gates.

At Bayonne in the Basque country, it is hard to know whether one is in France or Spain. The white stone arcades are Spanish, the cathedral Gothic and French. Almost all churches in the Pyrenees are Romanesque. In the back-street bars of Bayonne there are the smoked farm bacon, the Basque wine and the bullfight posters. There is even a bullring, although bullfighting is not a Basque taste: that is for Spanish visitors. The Basques prefer pelota.

But in the bars under the arcades the talk is either French or Basque, but chiefly French. The old postman and his friend from the chemist's will come in for their glass of port while Madame is dampening the table napkins, and the old sinners will delight her swelling eighteen-year-old daughter with compliments about the white skin of her shoulders and the dip of her breasts. The beauty of a young woman is not a matter for one short compliment. It has to be gone into in as many epigrams, proverbs and amorous jokes as they can think of. This salty gallantry is not Basque; for the Basques are hearty, sporting fellows, fond of larks, horseplay, trade and feats of strength. It is not their idea to waste much time on women. Nor do they talk much. They would sooner be with the Iceland fishing fleet. Their unmusical language sounds like the crunching and banging of boat hulls against the quay, or the clang of a hoe on a stone. And although they are gay enough when it comes to vigorous dancing—for they are dance-mad and on the Spanish side will even be seen dancing under umbrellas in the village squares in the pouring rain—their usual manner is, in the stout ones, stolid, obstinate and silent; and in the thin ones, shrewd, hawklike and watchful. Lyrical is not the word for them. Good-natured, yes—but dry.

A storm of rain came on suddenly one day in Bayonne when I was sitting in a bar, and here I saw how different from these people the true Frenchman is. An old gentleman came in. He was about seventy; he was very distinguished; he had walked down the street in his shirt sleeves, soaked to the skin. With him was his wife, also distinguished, elderly, arthritic, walking with the aid of a stick but as rigid as he in the determination to be unruffled. She was wearing excellent clothes out of date by thirty years.

"Please bring me two glasses of cognac." The old gentleman sparkled at once as he came in. "No, not cognac, this is Armagnac country, it would be more suitable to have two little glasses of Armagnac. A pleasant rain. I am, of course, soaked to the skin, but that has given me the pleasure of ordering an Armagnac and I shall be beautifully warm. I may, in spite of that, catch pneumonia, but that will give me one more pleasure: I shall be nursed by my beautiful wife. I may of course die, but even there I shall be lucky, for she will give me a splendid funeral. Drink up your Armagnac, my dear, the rain is stopping. We must go."

And as they went into the downpour, he was still expatiating on the delights of adversity and she was following with silent elegance: two addicted pursuers of pleasure.

The Basque spirit is at once more formal and more impish. That night in Bayonne, when the shops were closed and those narrow streets that climb to the cathedral were empty, I heard the notes of guitar, whistle and tabor. At a street corner a dozen young men and girls were performing an elaborate dance for their own pleasure. When it was over they went off playing their music round the dark streets, sometimes stopping to give one of their formal dances, sometimes singing a folk song. Occasionally they broke into that comic dance in which the guitar stops and all crouch on their knees except a witch figure with a wand, who tries to catch a defaulter. The guitar starts up again, up they get and on they stroll until the music stops again. I believe this dance represents a crowd of peasants hoeing a field, kept at it by the stick of the master. The delightful thing about this performance was its decorum and its impudence, the gaiety and yet the care with which the steps were correctly done. When they got down to the main road where the traffic streamed by heading for Biarritz, a waiter ran out offering them drinks if they would play in the café.

"One moment," the leader said solemnly. He gave an order. They squatted on their haunches, in a circle in the road, silently. In chorus they rapidly slapped their knees with a sound like a hundred pigeons flying up, and gave that weird Basque cry, something between the yelp of a jackal and a childish cry of wonder. Then they rose to their feet and went to the café. There they were, singing and dancing. The cars pulled in. The French crowd watched. A dozen Spanish Basques had held up the town with laughter for the evening.

The French, of course, disapprove of the Spaniards, but they can never resist them. That is one of the lessons of the Pyrenees. One shout of *"cante flamenco,"* one swirl of the *jota* brought over the mountains from Aragon, and the French forget they have just been calling the Spaniards in the next frontier town quarrelsome drunkards, always fighting among themselves, idle, simple, backward, proud and bloody-minded. And, of course, in the Pyrenees, the French understand that they long ago lost what the Spaniards have retained: the stubborn, regional spirit. The folk cultures of the world are dying out; the Basque language is dying, the Pyrenean dialects are dying, and where the dances and costumes survive in France, it is by conscious desire to please tourists and to foster folklore as part of "culture." In Spain, where such impulses from the central government are fitful or incompetent, things survive only if the people themselves want them to.

And here we come upon that basic difference between France and Spain which has existed since the days of Charlemagne. North of the Pyrenees: civilized Europe, central government, authority, intellectual leadership, the powerful, logical and able Latin spirit. South of the Pyrenees: regionalism, rejection of the leadership of Europe, denial of the Latinity of civilization, the belief in men not Man, the ambiguous attitude to authority. The Spanish leader must be overwhelmingly a person who dominates other persons and yet must not give himself an air of superiority. To quote the old oath of Aragon to the King, "We who are as good as you swear to you who are no better than we, to accept you as our King and sovereign lord, provided you observe all our statutes and laws; and if not, no." *Si no, no*: the famous double "no" of Spain.

So that when you ask travelers about the French and Spanish sides of the Pyrenees, the reply is generally: France for landscape, food, gaiety, instruction and pleasure; but Spain for people.

Down from St.-Jean-Pied-de-Port is Navarre and the road to Pamplona. Navarre is not really Basque, or not purely so. A great deal of it is well-watered country of mountain, wood and wide pasture. It is rich. This is one of the contented regions amid Spanish poverty. It is worked by people who have always owned their farms, and the father has always chosen an heir from among his children to hold the farm for the family. Navarre is patriarchal, aristocratic, isolated and virile, violently conservative. It is the home of absolutism and traditionalism, more papist than the Pope, more royal than the king. The Navarrese took the side of the pretender Don Carlos and the ultramontane priests in the civil wars of the nineteenth century; in the civil war of this century their furiously Catholic troops, called *requetés*, gave a violent medieval color to General Franco's lower-middle-class Falange. The famous fiesta of Pamplona, where the young men of the city tackle the bulls let loose in the street—an orgy of danger, wine drinking and wildness—expresses the spirit of the Navarrese. They are bold and reckless. A few hours of their company is like an injection of strong spirit.

And as one moves eastward into Aragon, into the wide desolate valleys or the tangle of mountains sixty miles deep which are built up against the Pyrenean peaks, one encounters yet another variant of the mountain character. There is nothing more striking than to come over from the beguiling, well-buttered and nourished towns of the Béarn or Roussillon to the austere Aragonese towns. They are poor, they are sternly dilapidated, they are rough yet noble. The food is strong and crude, the wine harsh. Up in the higher mountain towns of Aragon I have frozen all night in my room in some bare *posada*, with oleographs of the Virgin and the Carlist generals on the walls, and have been awakened every hour by a night watchman shouting out the hour when the church bell clanged: *"Ave María Purísima. Son las quatro."* Four o'clock. And strong Spanish oil and wine fighting in your stomach.

I do not confound the Basques with the Spaniards, though for claims to ancient race, great family and the practice of personal equality, the Basques and Spaniards are matched. In Bayonne, the Basque is a peasant subdued by the central power; he is poorer in France than he is in Spain. At the border in Irún, he is an urban industrial worker whose devout and solid Catholicism differs strongly from the fanatical Catholicism and anti-Catholicism of Spain, and who is not only egalitarian in his habits but a natural parliamentarian. His habits have not always been peaceable. The Basques held the gates to Spain. They plundered the pilgrims going to the summit conferences of the medieval Crusaders at Santiago de Compostela in Spanish Galicia. The Basques were converted very late to Christianity and have been, some would say, more tough than Christian. When you stand on the long bridge at Bayonne where two fine rivers meet, and watch the rows of men fishing from the balustrade, your mind may go back to the times when the Counts of Bayonne hung their tortured prisoners over the bridge and watched them drown in the rising tide.

One is, alas, constantly reminded that the Pyrenees are a frontier and that along frontiers there are hairbreadth escapes to freedom and appalling betrayals and trappings of prisoners. It must however be said that, on this frontier, it is usually the Spaniard who is escaping from his own people. Spain has always been a prison for someone. In generation after generation the smuggler, the donkey, the mule, the bus, the train have brought the political exile over the frontier. Tens of thousands of Spaniards must have gazed up at the Pyrenees and cursed a country that cannot tolerate its own people.

At Bayonne you are still on the plain, but after an hour or so's journey you are in St.-Jean-Pied-de-Port at the foot of the pass of Roncesvalles. It is not a high pass, nor is it austere, for it is gracefully wooded; but at the top you stand at what Hilaire Belloc called "one of the sublime heights" of European myth and history. For here, according to *The Song of Roland*, Roland blew his horn so hard that his brains came out of his ears. He was calling for help for the dilapidated rear guard of Charlemagne's army.

All the way from Bayonne the traveler knows he is in the Basque country, not only by the big blue pancakes of the Basque berets, or the walls of the pelota courts in the villages, but also by the names on the houses. With long overhanging roofs to hold off the rain, these houses are not as a rule called by some fanciful name, but each boldly bears the name of the family, by whose joint fortunes it was built. For, before everything else, before every human wish or adventure, the family house, to the millionaire as to the poor farmer, is preeminent. A man is not an individual man, nor a woman an individual woman. A man or a woman is his or her family. The remarrying of widows was, up to a few years ago, an unpopular enterprise; she would get a serenade of catcalls and tin cans. Families require men for the young girls, not for a woman who is already established as a family woman and may have a husband's name on her house.

The plains run up to the gates of the abrupt Pyrenean gorges and passes. The roads run under the shade of the close-packed plane trees, in those long tree tunnels of the French highways, tens of miles at a stretch. In this checkered shade one moves between fields of flowering maize in August, a crop feathery and light. Electric-blue hydrangeas hang over the stone walls of the villages, the vines trail the porches, peaches weigh on the trees and by the roadside bracken grows. Below the road the wide, deep river quietly flows. This is a flat, watery world where the sunlight seems itself to blow like a breeze over fields and trees. It is a quiet, sparkling region, and as you pass out of the Basque preserves into the country of Béarn it suddenly comes to your mind that what has always held you to the French countryside is some nourishing quality of nonchalance and simplicity in the very intensity with which it has been tilled and cared for. No neatness kills it, yet every inch is used. It is careless to look at, yet there is no waste. There is nothing parklike about the French landscape.

It is at Pau that the strategic traveler can most conveniently get an idea of the terrain he has to tackle. The city stands on a long, crowded cliff above its river and from the gardens of the château of Henri IV, or from the famous promenade, you see the Pyrenees parading before you—if you are lucky. The French poet Lamartine is notorious for saying the view is as stupendous as that of the Bay of Naples; but he did not mention that it might be blotted out by rain, fog or the hazes of summer heat. It took me a week to see the view. Pau looks what it is, a fine French-gray spa of the nineteenth century, now in decline. The audience that gathers now round the bandstand in the evening is not fashionable, it comes from the mass public of scooters, motorcycles, little cars and motor buses, and only occasionally does one see some elegant case of arthritis of the Old School, being wheeled by in a Bath chair. The English made Pau fashionable—it has an excellent winter climate. One or two families went to the length of bringing out a pack of foxhounds!

From Pau you begin one more attack upon the mountains. You have seen the wide river, the Gave, and you are going to follow that river back to its source, for that is how the French Pyrenees are penetrated. In three hours the climbing bus will take you into Lourdes. Here you are at the "gate"—that is to say at one of those points where a Pyrenean valley debouches upon the plain; or, you can call it the first step of a flight of stairs that will take you from one green valley–landing to the next, upward until you get to the final high valley, or *jasse*, below the summit. At most of these "gates"—at Lourdes and in Foix, for example—you will find a rising rock and on it a citadel or castle; for these were the towns that guarded the plains in the Middle Ages, the bases for the defenders of the mountains up in the passes. You realize that people on mountain frontiers are by tradition fighters. They live hard. They produce famous generals. Foch was one of them. They know that they have always lived on the routes of invasion. And when there are no invaders, they are on guard against the inhabitants of the next valley. When the Saracens had been driven out, the story of the Pyrenees became the story of the wars of Count against Count, until eventually the central power in France put a stop to it. You can still see fortified churches on both sides of the Pyrenees, and on the Spanish side, loopholes in the farm walls that were used in the Napoleonic wars and the civil wars of the last century.

War never quite dies in the Pyrenees. In the Spanish Civil War of this century the defeated remnants fought on in the passes, the refugees streamed over; and even now, when rumors of a rising against Franco are heard, it is to the hideouts in the mountains that people turn their heads.

But healing as well as war has also been a powerful interest of the Pyrenees, as indeed it is of the Alps. Whatever is claimed for Lourdes in the way of miracles, there is no doubt about the benefits of its mineral springs and of all the springs of the Pyrenees. Their virtues have been known by mountaineers for centuries. Lourdes represents the mysteries of healing at their most extravagant. Lourdes claims to be the most popular place of pilgrimage in Christendom, outside of Rome. A million pilgrims go there every year to see a spectacle that is part sordid, part fantastic, stirring both pity and wonder. The rigorous rejecter of miracles is bowled over by the manifestation of faith and the extraordinary emotional effect of the winding torchlight procession to the Miraculous Grotto at night, when the human crowd appears to have turned into a lashing and flaming serpent. It is strange to reflect that this pretty, medieval town, dramatically divided by its ravine, woke up in 1876—when the appalling Byzantine basilica was created—and became one of the first places in the world to perceive that to do something about

132

pent-up mass emotion was profitable and perhaps necessary. It is impossible to see those packed trains, those loaded lines of motor coaches, the long, patient trailing queues of sick men and women in the procession, the cripples laid out on their stretchers waiting to be immersed in the miraculous water, without being saddened by human agony. A dying little town has become a rich city and, on the whole, a cheerful one.

There is a lively market in Lourdes and a strong whiff of the mountains comes into it. You see dressed chamois skins hanging on the stalls—it is common to see herds of thirty or forty chamois prettily dotted near the higher passes. Wild-looking Spanish gypsies come down to buy. They look like bandits and are raggedly dressed, but the things that delight them on the market stalls are the baby clothes. The men crowd round the little dresses with childish pleasure. "Pretty, pretty!" they shout to one another, holding up a child's dress, and the eyes of their women sparkle keenly. This market goes in for all the finery of the mountaineers—the mule blankets, the bedding, the rope-soled shoes. One often sees an old man sitting on a chair in the street binding the rope into the shape of a foot and stitching on the cotton top. The Sunday heat, the smell of frying and Pernod give a tang to the market. The bistros are packed, the jukeboxes are going full out. The Paras—parachute soldiers—on leave, wander about looking for pretty girls, who are very sharp with their tongues. The traffic gets in a mess at the crossroads and one sees the classic French sight of the motorist jeering at the policeman who tries, in vain, to stop him. A fire engine goes by and that, in France, is regarded for some reason as the most ludicrous sight in the world. A whole café full of men bursts into laughter.

What would shock the tourists of the nineteenth century if they came here now would be that, like Pau, Lourdes has lost its high bourgeois elegance. In the days when Lamartine, Hippolyte Taine, George Sand, Mérimée, all the talent and fashion of France went to Pau and Luchon, the mountains were romantic, ideal and bourgeois; now the rest of us, the millions, swarm over them.

From Lourdes the climb begins. The river is smaller, stonier. It is caught between hot ravines that turn into hotter, deeper, narrow gorges. The little towns are built into the mountainside. You sit outside some little café, breathing the mountain air, your ears full of the sound of water dragging and gushing over stone and boulder. For this is the underlying sound of the mountains, the brawling noise of water somewhere near. You look down at the gorge at Luz and cannot see the bottom of it. You can almost hear the voice of George Sand saying across the generations, like any other French tourist: "*C'est formidable.*"

The gorges are part of the stairway. They take you to a few miles of valley where the mountains open up in what are called *plans*; then the mountains close, you are winding along precipices once more, under ways that are tunneled at the points where avalanches are likely; there comes another "formidable" gorge; you ascend more and more steeply, and now the stream that was a river at Pau is a clatter of waterfalls, tumbling down. You try to sit down by the roadside and cannot find a level piece of grass or rock to sit on; all is tilting and headlong; the mountains shoot up and seem to hang over your shoulders, gang up, crowd in. The peculiar gleam of high country comes into the grass; the leaves shine here with a polish you don't see below. Bridges are suddenly high, villages seem to be perched above. Until at last you are on the top landing but one—the poorest, bleakest of all the settlements—and against the mountain wall.

After this the true climbing begins, rough, bone-shaking footwork to the col and the Pont d'Espagne. Most of the passes of the Pyrenees are bald patches and a dangerous optimism is likely to fill the climber as he stands against the sky and takes in the sight below him. Here the new ranges seem to break against the main wall like a jagged sea, brown in the nearer ranges, fading to unearthly blues, violets and grays; and if there is cloud below in the valleys, the sea seems to foam and the peaks to stick out like tusky rocks.

A schoolmaster and his wife were staying at Gavarnie, a short stout middle-aged couple, who would set out in the morning at a military pace, and return in the evening dusty and scalded by the mountain sun. They were always on the march. Their life was one long epic of energy.

"For the Pyrenees," the schoolmaster said to me, "you must not be too optimistic. You must make your plans precisely. Until you reach the pass you can allow yourself confidence; but at the top—you must reflect. One sees three or four tracks on the descent. Be careful. One can easily be deceived. The obvious is certain to be wrong. You take it and you are lost on some spur. Twice I myself, monsieur," he said, "have nearly lost my life." He turned to his wife for confirmation. "Two nights I spent on that mountain without food. And remember—mountain travel goes by hours, not miles."

"I myself," I boasted in return, "once got trapped into sixteen hours' walking, the last hours in the dark, on the Spanish side. Luckily there was a moon. I slept in a room where goatskins were being cured."

"Ah!" he said, "the Spaniards live like rats."

Most Pyrenean walkers tell you it is wise to reckon on twenty-four hours from one human habitation to the next over the passes, and that it is best to find a hut for the night and be polite to the shepherd if he happens to come in and find you lying on his sack. Occasionally there are formal meetings between Spanish and French shepherds on the cols. In the valleys of Ossau and Assape, the French shepherds go up once a year in feast-day costume to meet the Spanish mayor of Roncal at a spot called La Pierre Saint-Martin, to pay dues for pasturage. The politenesses end with a loud cry of *"Patz Aban!"*— Peace in the future!

Gavarnie is not a difficult crossing and is very well known, but it is hard enough. Above the *cirque* are the far peaks of what is called the Marbore— the Pic, the Epaule, the Tour and the Casque—also the spectacular Brèche de Roland, that sudden split in the ridge, so sharply cut that one can easily believe that Roland's sword had really hacked through it. One can indeed believe anything at these heights, among these upper rocks that look like old teeth, human heads or coldhearted, baleful giants, and it is no wonder that the Spanish side has been populated by legendary demons, warlocks, witches. It has been suggested that the Pyrenean witch legends refer also to isolated people of the old pagan religion, and were encouraged by popular imagination or by Christian propaganda in the Middle Ages.

But nature has required no human aid. For the inside of the Pyrenees is rich in fantastic formations. As the mineral springs show, there is an active inner life going on in the Pyrenees, sulphurous, mineral and icy. There are miles of underground rivers, the range is riddled with caves. Some of them were inhabited by prehistoric man: at Niaux, in the valley of Vicdessos, there are drawings of bison and horses on the cavern walls. At Gargas, near Luchon, there are those astonishing caves whose walls bear the imprint of more than two hundred hands. At first sight they might be thought to be hanging bats. Many have chopped-off fingers and this has been thought by

135

some experts to indicate a ceremonial mutilation. For in many of the caves there is evidence of religious use.

You go back down the French valleys, zigzagging your way to the eastern end of the Pyrenees toward Ax-les-Thermes. It is an up-and-down journey among beechwoods, along little transparent rivers that sparkle against the stone walls of the villages, past towns crowned by the fortified towers of Romanesque churches baked brown in the sun or gleaming in the wet. It is the mixing of steep woods, ravines, rock, water and tree-dappled pasture that is the making of the ever-changing scene. One never knows whether a new valley will open at the next turn of the road. The larger towns are sleepy; at midday when the awnings are out over the cafés and you sit among the flowers, these places are soundless. You sit eating trout, perhaps a *cassoulet* of Toulouse—goose and mutton browned with bacon and hard, strong sausage and haricot beans—or content yourself with *pipérade*, the omelet of sweet spices and tomatoes, or *gargalada* (snails with red pepper), and you drink the wines of Jurançon or Roussillon.

There is Luchon, a ravishing and lively town of fine eighteenth-century houses, avenues of limes and the tinkling of water; above it the mountains become tremendous, and the hot springs bubble in the grottoes. There is St. Bertrand-de-Comminges with its Roman statuary, especially notable to me for the sight of a guest at the hotel struggling down through the woods with an enormous fungus, the size of a small hat. He came in and was soon surrounded by lady admirers. He got the cook to fry the mushroom and ate it.

"I am going to get another," he said. "They do me good." And late that afternoon, as the bus took me away, there he was once more, a fat little man of fifty, in shorts, like some triumphant big-game hunter, with another monstrous kill. "You've got to know them," he had said. "Or else . . ."

He closed his eyes and drew his hand across his throat and did a small death scene very neatly. If it would only rain, he said, he would be out with a bag "collecting my snails." *My* fungus, *my* snails, *my* soup, *my* cassoulet, *my* coffee! The French discuss these matters in detail and go into them all with the waiter before they order, with a pertinacity seen nowhere else in the world. These are the most serious things in life.

From Ax-les-Thermes you go up to Andorra, the little roof-top republic of six thousand people, a miniature nation which has been independent since the thirteenth century and exists under the joint suzerainty of the French government and the Spanish bishop of Urgel. A wooded upland valley, snowed-up in the winter, Andorra is not as poor as might be thought: it has its sheep, it grows tobacco and it is famous for smugglers, although smuggling in the Pyrenees is an arduous trade. It is a subject on which no Pyrenean ever has any knowledge if you ask him! The utter isolation of Andorra has gone because a motor road runs through it now; its little medieval Council and peasant president have been interviewed by journalists from all over the world. Some shrewd businessman installed a radio station there, but a later attempt to turn this severe peasant Arcadia into a little Monaco for gamblers has failed. The Civil War in Spain also interfered, for Franco's police state has sent up gendarmes, fearing that revolutionaries might use Andorra as a jumping-off place. It is, after all, on the edge of Aragon, the hearth of Spanish liberty, and of Catalonia, the center of an ardent movement for independence.

By Ax-les-Thermes one has noticed a change in the country. The mountains are harsher, browner and burned on the heights, and in the lower valleys the Mediterranean pine replaces the beech. The lower plain of Roussillon is rich, a stretch of vineyards in the blinding Mediterranean light and of torrid flats by the sea. Here are the great cities of Toulouse and Perpignan and that peculiar piece of stage scenery called Carcassonne, a complete medieval city artificially preserved and restored like a museum piece by Viollet-le-Duc in the nineteenth century. In the clear Mediterranean air Carcassonne looks startling, unreal and almost deathly. It is, I suppose, the most remarkable fake in the world, or rather the most remarkable architectural fly preserved in amber. Prosper Mérimée, the author of *Carmen*, has the credit for saving Carcassonne and Viollet-le-Duc for restoring it; but when I grew up feeling against that sort of thing was strong and I cannot overcome the prejudice.

For most people Spain spreads into France like a deep, rich wine stain at the Catalonian end of the Pyrenees, and the Catalan tongue is near enough to Spanish, though abrupt and shortened, to keep up this illusion. You smell Spain in Toulouse; in Perpignan the oily odor comes even more strongly out of doorways as you pass. You see the Catalan bonnet on the heads of the girls. In the avenues of Perpignan the people themselves have something that looks like the Spanish gravity. No French sculptor could have carved the dramatic and violent Christ of the cathedral of Perpignan, a figure that transcends any other piece of sculpture from the Atlantic to the Mediterranean. But there is really a subtle deception. Test a Catalan with your proverb that Africa begins at the Pyrenees and wait for his rage. No, he will say, "Africa begins where Catalonia ends and Spain begins, further south, at the Ebro."

There were Spanish exiles in Perpignan, working as waiters or barmen, running restaurants, or living—to all appearance—as Spaniards do, simply by walking up and down. In the evenings you see three or four people sitting in a shop talking; they are Spaniards, they have created, inevitably, a *tertulia*, a little talking club that meets every night. You see a lonely one sitting before a glass of water in a café. If they drink a glass of wine they will put a slice of orange in it. I saw one Spanish couple add Coca-Cola to theirs! Théophile Gautier said Spanish wine was vinegar, but it is not as bad as that. Indeed the wines of French and Spanish Catalonia are sweetish but good.

It was by the harbor of Collioure, where the Pyrenees can be said to end, that I met the quintessential Catalan, "the earth shaker." Tall, heavily built, treble-chinned, laughing, his vast harsh voice boomed over the harbor as we ate our prawns. His thoughts shook him from head to foot. Everything outsized he loved: high mountains, large cars, large business, big long books, huge numbers of shares, enormous women, big families, colossal emotional crises, travel all over the world. He was in textiles. In a minute, I thought, I should be swept into textiles too; or out to sea. It was like talking to an opera.

"We are Romans," he shouted as loud as Nero. "Older than the Romans. More modern than the Americans!"

We had finished our dinner. He became quieter.

"I will show you some conjuring tricks," he said suddenly in a childish voice. "Look at this. This will be stupendous. Waiter, bring me a glass of water."

I sat through an hour of floating pennies, disappearing watches, knives stuck in the ceiling and goodness knows what.

"Ah," he said in a throwaway line when he had done. "The Catalan has the gift of miracles"—and he produced *my* fountain pen from *his* pocket. His hug when we parted made the whole town tilt, to my eye.

All the Spanish regions struggle to get away from the central Spanish axis of Aragon and Castile, but the Catalans—like the Basques though for different reasons—have strong racial and cultural justification for their restiveness. The Pyrenees in fact stretch between two nationalisms—the Catalan and the Basque—and their situation in the lower mountains at either end of the chain and by the sea have given them that intimate contact with the outside world that central Spain has always hated. On the French side, as in the Basque country, the Catalan has been tamed by the powerful logic of the French central government; but on the Spanish side the Catalan character is untamed although racially it is more French than Spanish. The Catalans, as you can tell from their language, are a good deal Provençal; their culture is Greek and Roman; their national dance, the *sardana*, is a purely Mediterranean measure—no wildness of the Spanish dancers here. It is at the foot of the Mediterranean mountains that Picasso—half Catalan, half Malagueño—Braque and Dufy have painted.

Most of all the traveler feels the change in light: he is standing in the luminous, classical clarity where the burning light of the land is indistinguishable from the burning light of the sea. And he notices too the change in the people. He has traveled from the solemn, silent Basque at one end, the proud and goodhearted seaman, to the exuberant, rhetorical fantasticating Catalan, whose geese are all swans; from the canny Basque bankers to the booming, go-getting Catalan manufacturers. And between the two extremes lie the mountain people, who may be tinged with the Spanish habits of Aragon and Navarre, gleam like butter with the contentments of Béarn or turn rosy with the wines of Roussillon, but who are fundamentally of their own separate mountain valleys, handing down their little independent farms from generation to generation, minding their sheep and marked by the acute watchfulness and the independent temper of mountain races. Modern roads, tourists by the million, newly discovered oil wells, new natural-gas plants, have smoothed away the exclusiveness that pleased romantic travelers generations ago; but one has only to look at the sharp faces, the steady yet fast walk of the villagers, to know that a Pyrenean type still exists.

[1962]

139

6

Journey in Greece

It was a hot night in September. I had arrived in Athens a few hours before, and I was sitting in Constitution Square, trying to learn the Greek alphabet from the neon signs. I was also listening to my friend Kosta. Greece is the land of oracles, and Kosta is both a Greek and an oracle, mystifying and loud. His voice silenced the traffic, the cars that went by like glossy schools of fish. There were the neon signs on the roofs, and beyond them we could see the cliff of the Acropolis like lit-up toffee and on top of it the Parthenon dressed up by floodlighting to conceal the tragic brutality of time. I thought it was pretty, and still do. But not for Kosta. He banged his stick on the pavement. "The Acropolis striptease for foreigners. It looks like a whore." And then, suddenly finding the idea in his head and being a Greek uttering it at once, he said: "At night all modern cities are alike. But by day we have light that no other country in the world has. Greece was created by its light."

The Greek light—who has not heard of it? I had seen all Athens and its mountains turn pink as the sun went down and then change again to white for a minute or two, a white as dead and staring as a stick of chalk, when the day abruptly died. The flight from Paris had been a journey into fire—as Kosta said, into light, pure and elemental. He knew and I knew the hard and, to us, empty light of North America; we knew the painted light of the European Atlantic done with the charged brush, sweeping the greens, the blues, the purples on and off, emotionally, every quarter of an hour.

We knew the subtle light of France, the light refracted in curved flashes from the Alps, the tender cloud operas of Italy. But, as the plane passes from the heel of Italy to Corfu and the Gulf of Corinth, you enter the pure Greek flame. It has burned the mountains white. It has burned all moisture from the air. Even Cairo, the meteorologists say, does not have a light as pure as this. There is nothing like it, except the light of the Red Sea. Kosta, of course, does not accept the Red Sea.

So the coasts of Greece burn. We are suddenly conscious of the elements—earth, air, water and fire. It is a liberation to the senses. The towns are dry and clear, their houses are separate and could be counted like beads dropped through the fingers. Even looking at Athens from the sea, at its tens of thousands of houses scattered for miles across the tilting plain under its white mottled mountains—even here you could pick out the buildings one by one. At least one of the gifts the Greeks have retained since ancient times is their curiosity. Has their light made them see too much? Have they—a people easily distracted—been too distracted by the equal distinctiveness of everything they see? Yes, they have, Kosta said; this light has the quality of their passion for "pure reason."

There is another quality that follows from the candor of the Greek light. Looking at the wild and silvered mountains of the ragged coast of Greece, you get the impression of an incinerated and tormented land striking out violently into promontories, wounded by gulfs and inlets, throwing out scores of rock islands into the Aegean and Ionian seas; yet, except in the very early morning, and in the sudden storms of a changeable climate, there is no mist in the gorges and valleys. There are simply degrees of fire, degrees of shadow, a light shadow laid on a dark.

These scenes appeal less to the eye than to the hand, or indeed the whole body: as if you could reach out, touch, feel the shapes and hold them. This light is for sculptors, not for painters, a light for rock and stone. And you remember that the one great Greek painter was El Greco, who found something of Greece in the landscape of Castile and painted a sculptor's rather than a painter's forms.

"What are the modern Greeks like?" I used to ask Kosta.

"Exactly like the ancient Greeks," said Kosta. "Talkers, quarrelsome. There is no difference."

They all say this.

"Look at the map," he said. Well, we had no map, but we spread one out in our heads. We saw the Balkan mountains descending from the north, the passes difficult, the people poor, only old people left there and young Communists who cannot get passports. The stormy mountains divide into valleys inaccessible from one another, and shredding into a coast so indented that it used to be—and often still is—quicker to take a boat and go by sea to get to your neighbors. And if you went to your neighbors it was to contradict and fight them.

To the north, Kosta said, are the "barbarians"—the Yugoslavs, the Albanians behind their Russian barbed wire, the Bulgarians, who owe the Greeks a war indemnity and are industrializing faster than Greeks like to think—all Communists, mainly Slavs with the traditional Slav longing to get to the Mediterranean and Aegean and to feed on the wealth of the Levant. On the East are the Moslem Turks, the old enemies, who occupied Greece for centuries. "But," Kosta said reluctantly, "we are beginning to get on better with the Turks." (The two enemies are in NATO, heavily supported by American money, because they are at the key strategic point of the Middle East.)

"This is a ragged country," Kosta boomed out. "In every generation the sons grow up without remembering their fathers, for the fathers have been killed in war—the Balkan wars, wars against the Turks, the Italians, the Germans, and the civil war at the end of World War II. I did not know my father: he was killed by the Turks. My father did not know his father. My own son will not know me. Now everything is fine—but for how long? I give us ten years and then—once more! All Greeks know this in their bones and have always known it from the beginning of time."

No tragic look, no shrugs, but a light, reckless sound of excitement, a sort of curiosity, was in Kosta's rhetoric.

"We are indestructible," he said. "You know what the Greek poet said"—

I forget the name— " 'The Greeks are like yeast. You bite a piece off and it goes on growing.' "

It was half past eight, the rush hour; people were pouring out of the shops and offices—for Athens closes down at one o'clock until five in the afternoon, and only then is this hot, noisy, dusty city quiet. But now the cafés were packed. People were eating ice cream and drinking water. In spite of the great heat people walked briskly, for they are nervous, active and volatile in temperament. The men and the women looked sturdy and their eyes were alive; but beauties and handsome men were rare—and I saw no Greek profiles, none at all. But if you speak to anyone, there is a sudden change. These sun-darkened, sun-eaten beings, the well-fed or the thin and harassed, who walk along expressionlessly shut up in their thoughts, will light up dramatically with an avid yet gentle dignity and grace. Sympathy in their first impulse, inquisitiveness the next, along with a quite unguarded openheartedness, and all contained within a natural sense of fineness and consideration. The Greek is all yours, but not obsequiously, intrusively, nor by calculation. You would think that a people who are such demons for trade and a real nation of shopkeepers and bankers, who in fact ran the commerce of Turkey for the Turks, might be out for the main chance in some direction or other. But no, their manners are their very skin—a form of perceptiveness, a foreseeing, a manifestation of their cleverness, which they delight in exercising. Besides—if nothing else—you are their thriller and their story. And for a story they will do anything.

There was an air of wealth and luxury in the middle of Athens. Greece has recovered from the starvation and ruin of its civil war. American money has come. Greece is a NATO power, its army is one of the best small forces in Europe, the shipyards of Niarchos thrive, thousands of foreigners bring in their money, and the Karamanlis government has been continuously in power for the incredible period of six years (there were twenty-six governments between 1946 and 1955). The government has succeeded in stabilizing the country—but what problems there are! One of the lowest per capita incomes in Europe; a fatal decline in the chief export, tobacco, which used to go mainly to Germany. (America introduced the Germans to Virginia tobacco after the war, and the Greek peasants now have tobacco drying on the fences unsold.) There is great illiteracy.

143

About politics, the favorite topic of conversation in Greece, I came away with these conclusions: Karamanlis, the premier, is a practical man who has done well, but he holds his power because most Greeks fear the Communists, who overbid their hand at the last elections and have, in fact, only 10 or 15 percent of the voting power. The Party is outlawed, but known Communists are openly in the opposition parties. The reforms of Karamanlis have been sensible, but he is now up against the fact that the boom has benefited only a few thousand people directly and that there is rising unemployment. The old ELAS Communist movement of the civil war has disintegrated; the peasants are violently anti-Communist—but something like Communism is noticeably increasing in cities like Piraeus, Athens and Salonika. Wages are low. Seasonal emigration to prosperous countries like West Germany has started on a large scale. In short, to get Greece out of its fundamental poverty will be a long and painful business. The government claims to have solved the problem of the refugees—that is to say the huge Greek population turned out of Turkey after World War II, the massacre and persecution of Greeks having been traditional with the Turks for centuries and for political and religious reasons. Hostility to Greeks is the Turkish anti-Semitism. The Greek government has built houses for thousands of refugees; but they number a million and a half, and no one who has seen their shacks on the way down to Piraeus from Athens will think the problem solved. Still, something has been done.

The Greek lives an open-air life in a hot climate. The mass of people rarely eat meat more than a few times a year. They live on fish and vegetables and fruit. Olive oil is their butter; honey is their sugar; wine or water their drink. They have goat's milk and cheese. Their life is simple but ceaselessly active.

"This is a country," a one-time cabinet minister said to me, "where the rich are ashamed of their riches and the poor ashamed of their poverty." And yet position and wealth are irrelevant to them. Not a Greek but thinks he has the greatest ability. The merest boy will go into the boss's office and tell him with entire confidence that he could run the place. He thinks it is simple bad luck, not lack of experience or capacity, that stands in the way of his being prime minister. Politics are in the blood. But—and this goes back to ancient Greece, when the city-states were shut off from one another by the mountains—the Greek does not vote *for* something; he votes against. A vote for Karamanlis is a vote against the Communists, not a vote for him! A vote for the Communists is a vote against American influence. And as for going Communist, the overpowering feeling of Greek nationalism is against it, and so is the old, long-headed Greek mistrust of putting all your eggs in one basket.

"We are," said this politician, "by nature a people who are *éparpillé*. We scatter our interests. We cannot bear monotony."

The Greeks are a people of mountain and sea.

"Leave this noisy place. It is an ugly modern city; one hundred and fifty years ago it was only a little market town. Get out to the islands and the sea!" Kosta used to shout at me. The islands! They are always in sight. You would say they were leaping over the sea like schools of huge dolphins in the sun, passing and effacing one another, old islands vanishing, new ones appearing to take their place.

To reach the islands you go down to Piraeus—it is only half an hour in the bus from Athens and is really joined to it by suburbs strung out along the road—to white Piraeus with its cliff and its harbors and its markets and its Communist mayor. It is early in the morning. In dozens of cafés and eating houses the market workers are eating their stew, some mess scooped out of the huge pans on the counter; on the broken pavements, outside the tattered, sun-rotted buildings, the crowds have found broken chairs and rickety tables to sit at. The buses disgorge. By the quay are the ferry steamers, always coming and going, always full, always people struggling up the gangplanks. If these people are poor, they are not passive; they are eagerly alive.

The harbor stinks of fish and drains, the heat is already slapped on, the flies buzz, but on the steamer all is easy and spick-and-span. You drink your coffee, eat cold cheese patties, and cast off to the noise of radio and accordion. You are packed in with families of all kinds. The fat boy next to you is being taught French by his mother—Greece is a country of fat boys; the old peasant woman is sitting on her bundles; the doctor is discoursing.

Soon the distant islands begin their dance, sliding one after another into view. In an hour or so you will call at one of them. They are rocky and barren, mere pasturage for goats, except at sea level. At Poros, you could imagine yourself to be beside the painted houses of a little harbor on the Italian lakes.

A powerful woman comes out on a balcony and combs her thick black hair, watching your steamer arrive. The cafés on the quay are crowded with idlers. There is a blue-washed church. Olive trees lean as though in a ballet. There are a few vines, and the black paintbrushes of the cypresses.

Beyond Poros, as you pass through the straits and plunge into open water again, island rocks appear, little Gibraltars of the Aegean, and you are heading past other islands for Idhra, that perfect island town, an island of mountain, almost uninhabited. There is only half a mile of rocky road in Idhra; the rest is donkey track, promontory, precipice, and the utter island silence. You look down on emerald water, grinding and frilling to white continually round the rock, and clear to the golden rock floor of the sea. Idhra has a deep-set harbor and the town stares like a still stone face of inspecting windows. It is as complex as an abstract painting. And very silent, for there are no quayside crowds here. A few people sit in the little cafés, eating their honey-soaked cakes. The fishermen spread out their golden nets. The back streets are sedate and white and hot. They are like part of a miniature Capri before Capri was ruined by tourism. Idhra is secretive. Its houses, you notice, are plain but fine; this was once a rich island. The houses belonged to sea captains whose wealth came from piracy, for all the Greek islands were natural hiding places in the perpetual warfare of the Greeks against the Turks. Idhra was the chief port of the Greek insurgents in the fight for freedom in the 1830s; its money began to give out in the War of Independence, finally vanishing when sail gave place to steam. It is now a faraway place for a few people.

Aegina, Poros and Idhra are the nearer islands, a day's journey to and from Athens; the longer journeys are to the Cyclades, to Crete and to Rhodes. But you notice that these farther islands have their own life; little boats are always phutting off to other islands, taking fishermen or peasants. You could pass months traveling from one to another, dodging the Aegean storms, caught in the sun's blaze and the blue, the indigo, the wild emerald of a strong and drugging sea. In each island there is a steep little town or village of closely built stone, erected centuries ago.

Food is not plentiful. You eat "island food"—that is to say, what is in season—tomatoes, cucumbers, black olives, goat cheese, mullet, hake, some fish or other. When the island's melons or tomatoes have been eaten there are no more till next year. There may be kid or pork. There will always be *retsina*, the resin-tasting wine that varnishes the tongue but is light and refreshing. You eat in the simple *taverna*, as you do on the mainland, going straight to the kitchen in the Greek manner, to choose your fish or to pick out what you want from the pans simmering on the stove. There are some delicacies from which no doubt you withdraw   the stuffed fish head, for instance, in which the *bonne bouche* is the eye.

The enchantment of these journeys lies in the continual surprise of the harbors, in the silence of sea and sun, the swimming islands, blue on blue. Fire, air and water—you are reborn among the elements. And nothing, nothing at all, thank heaven, has been done to attract people to the smaller places, though hundreds go to great islands like Rhodes and Corfu. There is only the felicity of their untouched existence, and the fine simplicity of the people who are very old in the knowledge of living.

But at the back of our minds in these sea journeys, and in every Greek journey, there is the sense of something echoing and recognized. The dolphins leap, twist and dive sportingly, like wheels spinning across the sea; we think of Apollo the sun god in a chariot drawn by dolphins; of Poseidon, and the "wine-dark sea" of Odysseus; of Aphrodite, born in the island of Cythera. We are in their very hunting grounds. This sea is Homeric in its storm and in its gaiety. Out of these waves and mountains, these rocks and trees, the myths of our civilization were born. (And how Greek and changeable they were: Aphrodite now a goddess of fertility, now, since she was born out of the sea, a protector of the seamen.) We have known the Greek stories from childhood, we have seen them changed by the Romans and in our own minds. They move from the tale to the myth, to allegories of nature, to the first serious ordering of the Western mind. In the story of Oedipus we have found a psychological pattern of human fate.

These myths, these legends that were history, have actually laid the foundation of the Western mind. We are different from the Asiatics because of Greece, for the Greeks taught us democracy when they set themselves apart from the tyrants of Asia. We owe our Bible to Greek-speaking Semites: in Athens, in Corinth, Saint Paul spoke; in Patmos, Saint John wrote the Book of Revelation. The myths, the legends, the histories of other cultures and civilizations have far less to say to us. Thor and Wotan are nothing compared with Zeus; we catch a glimmer from Celtic tradition, but no more; we derive slim nourishment from the legends of India; neither North nor South America has any profound Indian revelations to offer us—the gods of Hiawatha, of the Mayans, the Aztecs, the Incas or the African Negroes are little more than curiosities for us. Yet we turn to the Greeks and find they are buried or extended in ourselves.

And so, as we travel in modern Greece, we lead a double life. The memory of even the most ignorant camera-clicker is stirred. He has heard of Apollo and Olympia. "I know nothing about politics or philosophy," he says immodestly and, without knowing it, is speaking Greek. Gradually ancient Greece makes us conscious of ourselves; and when we visit the sites, we are suddenly shocked into the recognition that all we heard or read was not a story, but often quite literally happened to *this* person, in *this* place, before human eyes; and that these people were the most intelligent people the earth had known. The Greek journey is a recivilization.

It is a hard journey, but I do not think there is anything in Europe to equal it, either in the wild scene of mountain and sea or in what they evoke. I think of the days on the road from Athens to Delphi, from there the sea passage over the Gulf of Corinth to Dhiakopton, Patras to Olympia; and then the giddy and exhausting journey along precipices, over passes, to Mycenae and the tomb of Agamemnon, to Epidaurus where Asclepius practiced the art of healing, and the plain of Argolis to Nauplion—the old capital of Greece and unlike any other Greek town—and so to modern Corinth and the corniche back to Athens. It can be done in five days at a rush, but you need strong nerves and a resistant body; and if you understand nothing else at the end of it, you will grasp the toughness of the Greeks.

You go racketing out of Athens down the modern boulevard toward the sea, and at once the mind splits. You are on the Sacred Way, you pass the site of the temple to Demeter, who brought the fig to Greece; you are driving through burned-up land of scanty grass. There lie the shipyards and the oil refinery—but also the sacred lakes; beyond are the soap works, the cement works—but there also is the place of the Eleusinian mysteries.

In this industrial corner of a burned-up country, the corn goddess came to seek Persephone, her daughter; here the myth of spring and winter originated: the seed lying in the darkness of the earth and coming to life. You drive past the red soil of the olive groves, you rise to the new forests of pines. If much of Greece is bare of trees, the Turks must be blamed. They were soldiers and colonists; they let everything be eaten by the goats, as they have also done in Turkey. Here at this very crossroads, Oedipus unknowingly slew the man who was his father, a lashing driver on the road; there, in the scrub near the roadside, are a village's white beehives, for Greece is the land of honey; there are melons in the fields, and walnuts on the trees.

There is no water in the riverbeds; they are wide and stony. But you pass from wilderness to fertile plain where there are cotton fields. The trucks are loaded with sacks of cotton for a new factory making cottonseed oil. And then you come to Thebes, a prosperous town but shockingly housed, where the main street seems to be on fire with the red berries of the shrubs that are planted down the middle of it. And so, on and on, rising until you are in the clouds, and under Parnassus is Delphi.

Two thousand years have tamed ancient Greece in our minds; we forget the wildness, we forget that civilizations are pauses of balance in continuous conflict. The ruins of Delphi do not impress at first as, say, the sea temples of Sounion or Rhodes; Delphi depends for its effect on the awe, even the terror, the command and secrecy of its site. Almost hidden under its precipices, it looks down thousands of feet on a sweep of mountain, a wide concealed stairway of hills to the spear of silver water that comes into the immense plain of olives at sea level ten miles away. From below you cannot imagine how you will reach this terrifying point of power—for Delphi was the dynamo of Greek rule—and from above you marvel at the resource, the authority and subtlety of the whole political proposition of an oracle so absolutely placed and so ingeniously manipulated. The scene is noble, savage and ominous, the minds that used it were of the highest sophistication.

The little village of Delphi has been moved down from the site of the temple and theater to the edge of its ferned and flowering cliffs. It is a place of flowers, for give a Greek a yard or two of earth and he will grow flowers in it and trail his vines. One of the enviable things on earth is to own a terrace garden there, built out into the sky and surveying that point where the wild ravine under Parnassus descends and widens into the spectacular valley. The village smells of thyme, the fig hangs over walls that are covered with morning glory. Rocks fall down from the hillside onto the road. The dogs bark at night. The air is cold.

The valley floor appears to be covered by a close green carpet of scrub or kale, but when you drive twisting and twisting down to it, you find it is not that sort of vegetation at all but an immense grove of olives, planted in ghostly alleys miles long, its trees a thousand years old, and the red soil beneath them turned by the mattock as it has been for centuries. It is one of the oldest olive groves in the world, a place spectral and haunted. I shall not forget how still it was. There was great wealth, there is still great wealth, at the foot of Delphi.

At the harbor, on the rich Gulf of Corinth, you catch the ferry. You had heard its anchor go down in the stillness of the mountain night. And now you are in the blue flame of the Gulf of Corinth. I remember the cattle lowing, the truck drivers asleep in their cabs, as the ferry took us down the gulf. We called at little painted Galaxidion, which the Turks once destroyed, and then moved slowly past the chasms and ravines to the opposite coast, past the mountains that looked as smooth as lions' backs but turned silvery white when the sun reached its blinding force. For a little short of a hundred miles you could drift along to the Ionian Sea and say again that Greece is all rock, water, light and air, and that all seem to turn to fire.

You land on the far side of the gulf in the lemon-growing country, where people sit under awnings and the donkeys trot. You drive through flowers, beside fences of oleander, into Patras, the currant port, where restaurant tables are laid out in the street. This is easy traveling. You are making for Olympia, away from the rugged mountains into milder country. Olympia lies in a bowl of thyme-scented wooded hills, a place of vineyards, flowers, and of shepherds who water their sheep in the river, the course of which was altered last century to reveal the astonishing and entire site of the Olympic Games. Under the oak trees on the hill called Kronion, Kronos—that is to say Time himself—fathered Zeus, "the president of the immortals." I know of no more restful rural spot than Olympia; and peace is its tradition, for the Games were the four-yearly truce in the continual Greek quarrel.

After two days you are hurled (it is the only word) across those violent mountains of the Peloponnese to Argolis, Nauplion and to Corinth. It is a journey in which the road seems always to be on the edge of some violent gorge. You climb to the top of a pass and then take the next gorge and travel from precipice to precipice. There is rarely a town, and when there is it hangs down the mountainside; the town square will be built out on stone or steel into the sky. Down you go hurtling, night falls, and high above you see small lights moving. They are not in the sky. They are the trucks zigzagging, hairpinning upward—it is the same road as yours. You will spiral, up and up, round the lights of a village, come back to it again when you think you have left it for good.

On a lonely stretch a policeman and a girl ask you for a lift. Stolidly, hour after hour, they drive with you and you wonder about the lives of these mountain people: about, say, the priest you saw walking up and down with—was it the mayor?—in the village square, or the youth who brought you coffee in the café. And then, at the end of the long day you are across the Peloponnese to the rich orange groves of Argolis, in the fertile country of wild Agamemnon. You are in Nauplion.

I used to sit—it was too hot to walk far—on the long quay of Nauplion. This town was the seat of the first Greek government after the liberation from the Turks in 1829, and it is one of the prettiest towns in Greece. It has the neatness and dignity of some prosperous Western European town of the seventeenth or eighteenth century. It stands by a spacious lagoon of quiet, enameled water where the fish swarm and polyps, like breathing footballs, come wallowing in flotillas along the quay. All day the youths threw out their fishing lines, the sailors played cards in the bars, and people sat out of the heat in the deep shade of the trees.

In the town, you notice Turkish fountains and a mosque—now a cinema. Outside, in the orange groves, the cotton and tobacco fields, you have seen the peasant women with their scarves wound over their mouths, hiding their faces—a survival from Turkish times. They say they cover their faces because of the heat of the sun, and the dust; but really it is a memory of the times when Greek women concealed themselves from the Turks or copied the semiveiling of Turkish country women. In the towns the women dress as women do anywhere. The position of women in Greece is far less independent than in northern countries, at any rate on the surface. The ruling factor in their lives is the dowry system, for the Greeks, like the French, believe firmly in money. It is the rigid obligation of the males of a family to provide their marriageable females with dowries. A brother may not marry before his sisters are provided for. In a poor country this means long delays in marriage. "I cannot marry yet because of my sisters," a young man will say. And I have heard of Greek immigrants in America who have reached old age unmarried because there has been one more girl to provide for back in Greece. The rapacious son-in-law turns up a good deal in family gossip. There are tales of bigamous dowry collecting.

The dowry system is not a passing custom. It is a national preoccupation. After the war, the new queen of Greece instituted a public fund called the Queen's Fund—it gets some of its money from a tax on cinema tickets—partly to provide dowries for poor girls. Yet, among the country people, there are surprising instances of hidden wealth. Only a month or two ago I read a report in a paper of a country marriage where the bride was endowed not only with linen for a lifetime but also with a sum equal to $3000 in gold coins! The peasant would not trust anything but gold.

The Greeks speak of romantic love, but only as one of the many aspects of love, unromantic love being regarded as more desirable. Our romantic temperament of the north does not appeal to these people who have a very unshocked, worldly, pagan eye for ways and means. Both nature and necessity make the Greek aware of the value of money, so that one meets in many Greeks a strange mixture of idealism and expediency which they call compromise, arrangement and realism. The illicit love affairs of Athens, like those of Paris, have a discreet money basis. The Greek is not resigned to his poverty. The ill-paid bank clerk turns accountant in the evenings and does the accounts of several shops; a typist will become a cashier in the evenings; a professor will earn some extra money as a consultant.

Life is like that everywhere in the Mediterranean, but there is a fundamental difference between Greek and Latin life. The Greek is different because he represents the Eastern branch of the Christian religion; as the mosque of Nauplion reminds you, he was for centuries under Turkish rule. The Greek church is a church of holy pictures, not of holy images. People wander in, light their tapers, kiss the picture of a saint. (An old woman stands by to wipe the picture after it has been kissed.) The tapers are put into the sockets of a candelabrum. It is a religion without drama, and the church is not militant. It does not proselytize. Unlike the Roman church it is, as its priests will tell you, a passive faith. Ninety percent of its congregation is behind the Iron Curtain, and its Patriarch is in the totally hostile Moslem city of Istanbul. "We are a pathetic church," a priest once told me; he was using the word in the strict, archaic sense of feeling, passivity and suffering, and saying this with pride. "We dislike militant religions," he said. "Our passivity enables us to understand Eastern people much better than Westerners do."

But if the Greek church has nothing like Catholic Action, Opus Dei or Catholic trade-unions, if it does not pronounce against birth control and divorce and remains detached from society, educational policies and party politics, it still has one very important role in Greek life. You have only to see the gorgeous procession for the patron saint of Athens (a procession largely military), to see that the church is close to the reality of Greek patriotism. When the Turks conquered Greece, the Orthodox priests became the natural custodians of the Greek spirit of independence. They conserved the cultural traditions. They taught. They came to be regarded as the arbiters. And so, in times of national crisis, when the factions cannot agree, or in times of war, the Archbishop of Athens steps in and takes charge until the politicians settle their differences. Once government is re-established, he retires. When Winston Churchill came to Athens during the civil war of 1944, he negotiated with the Archbishop. In its independence, in the fact that its priests are usually married, the Greek church has rather more resemblance to the Protestant than to the Roman Catholic confessions.

I left Nauplion for Athens on one more of those spectacular Greek journeys. You travel from the milky lagoon and see the mountains above Mycenae—shaped, they say, like the head and body of Agamemnon still ruling after thousands of years in the rock. In old Corinth the men are out in the cafés under the trees, the butcher is chopping up a kid, a pig is roasting on a spit in the street; in new Corinth, there is the dust of the trucks loaded with currants. Then you cross the terrifying cleft of the Corinth canal—a little Suez Jr., joining the Ionian and Aegean seas—and you are out on the coast road that twists and tunnels. The stupendous sunset colors the long, changing islands. Two hours away in this clear air you see the prickle of the lights of Piraeus stretching into Athens itself.

And in Athens, in some simple *taverna*, you will sit outdoors in the soft night, served by poor thin men who smile with dignity and inquire with avid interest. About what? About every detail concerning yourself, your health, your feelings, your thoughts, your marriage, children, illnesses, work— everything except your money. Questions about money are considered very indelicate, for that is a most intimate preoccupation. You will sit with friends who will talk their heads off about their lives, their politics, their amusements, and always about the distraction which is Greece itself: friends you will find again in the morning, thinking of something to give you simple pleasure, something to remind you that whether you are fat or starving, there is nothing like gossip, storytelling and being aware every minute that you are alive and in the sun. For life is short. And so you bring up two chairs in the Greek fashion—one to sit on, one for your feet—and you wonder why you live anywhere else.

[1961]

7

The Secret People

Once more the disturbing German experience begins.

"Anti-Germanism is a cliché."

"The Germans hate themselves because of what they have done."

"The Germans long to be loved."

We have been listening to the talk of German acquaintances, and sentences like these stick in the mind.

We are in Cologne, looking at the luxurious shops, the jewelry, the travel goods, the dresses, the Americanized restaurants, the glossy packs of automobiles in the car parks. Half the city is old Germany; half of it is sparkling, rich and new. We are pleased to see it like this. Then we go down to the banks of the Rhine and there we try to collect our thoughts. We are standing in a country that, twice in a lifetime, has wrecked our civilization and brought humiliation upon itself; and yet each time it has recovered to look us in the face with childlike candor, as if it remembered nothing. We may be wrong in that last phrase: we hope we are. But we stand there, under the enormous shaft of Cologne Cathedral, which rises like the figure of some great Gothic emperor turned to stone, before a people that are an enigma to us. And—more alarming—an enigma to themselves.

At Cologne the greatest and richest of the Western European rivers flows fast and choppy in the wind. The Rhine is busier than the Hudson and, I would guess, busier than the Saint Lawrence. The heavy barge and seagoing traffic goes crowding down to the Ruhr factories, the seaports of Holland and Belgium. This is the most densely populated region in Europe and, quite probably, in the modern world. The oil and gasoline barges, the coal, coke and wine go up and down one a minute (by my counting), often in convoys or fleets, with the German, Dutch, Belgian, French and Swiss flags on them, and the house flags of Krupp and Shell. They are not dawdling barges; they go at speed and there are small seagoing ships among them. The Rhine flows through factory land, pasture, wooded cliffs, past dozens of pretty little spas with their rose beds and parading lime trees and dozens of grandiose villas, past imitation castles and cherished ruined ones, past vineyards and manufacturing cities. Over the high steel bridges, the very efficient trains are racing to Düsseldorf, symbol of the German "miracle." Northward in the Ruhr is the monolithic private empire of Krupp's hundred and fifty factories—Krupps who were the servants of German militarism, and who now build harbors and steel mills for Africa and the Far East and have opened an office in Moscow; farther north are the shipyards and docks of Hamburg; southeast the freight trains clatter on to Frankfurt, Munich and Basel. Close to the tracks are the dangerous autobahns, packed with cars on an almost American scale. Whatever else we shall have to say about the Germans, there is a foundation of toil and power, and of wealth that flows.

Today is Ascension Day, a holiday, and sometimes called Father's Day, for Germany is the land of the Father. No mother country here: fatherland.

On the Rhine and to the Rhinelanders and the industrial millions, this is the day for the Rhine trip. The crowds troop in their thousands onto the river steamers for the long trips up the beloved river. For hours they will be drinking beer, gallons of it, or the wines of the Rhine or Moselle. They will be shouting and singing. The majority will be cheerfully, harmlessly, bawling drunk. The young men will wear comic straw hats and carry light swagger canes for a lark. Some will have fixed bicycle bells to their canes, to make as much din as possible. Male choruses! Female choruses! Groups of stout women—to be middle-aged and robust and stout is the popular ideal for women—will toast one another and sing vehemently. At each little town, where some of the crowd get off and a new swarm comes on, these flushed ladies will be singing *Auf Wiedersehen* with an energy that recalls the turbine. The British crowd on holiday in England is just as rowdy, of course; it is just as noisy, and it is bawdier. In England, fights soon start up. Things get smashed, shops are wrecked. In Germany, no; the beer orgy is not pretty, but it is blameless. No one fights. Everyone laughs. There is a fundamental domestic good nature. And there is another thing which makes the Germans differ from most other Europeans: on holiday, as on every working day, they hate casualness of dress. On holiday, they are in their best clothes. The little boys will wear suits and white socks; the little girls their party frocks. Germans are always neat and correct, indeed correctness they admire above everything. One of the things which really humiliated them in the early postwar period was having to dress roughly in whatever clothes they had left. In the previous pre-Hitler generation they had been deeply shamed in their persons by the ruin brought by inflation.

Look around at those who are not drinking. They are eating. They eat their "fricassees," their enormous dishes of potatoes and pork. (I have myself been faced by a dish which consisted of a slice of old ox—called veal—covered with lobster, lobster sauce, shrimps, crab, tangerines and cherries.) The German orgy requires a hardy stomach, as well as lung power and thirst. Here are people notorious for working themselves to the bone and who also thrust an animal energy into their pleasures. It is odd to see the deferential, fussing, slaving, detail-loving office worker turned now into a machine of a different kind—a machine that is boisterous.

I don't say that all Germans are as boisterous as those boatloads of trippers. There are the quiet families. Looking down the long reaches of the Rhine, you see not only the flotillas of barges, but the crews of scullers and canoeists who delight, as so many Germans do, in river and lake life. But I think it is fair to say that in most Germans there is a tendency, at some moment, to burst at the seams. All these people around us probably get up before seven in the morning on their working days, they go to work far earlier than most of us, they have constructed a country that hums with the smooth, busy efficiency of a power station; and yet, essentially, they are bursting, romantic extroverts. The word *Deutsch* means tribe, and tribes move back and forth knowing no set limit until they are exhausted or are stopped. They overflowed, in the last war, over a great part of Western Europe—all except Britain, Sweden, Spain, Portugal and Switzerland. Before the First World War, Germany extended south into Alsace and Lorraine and through Prussia beyond Königsberg (now Kaliningrad) in the Baltic. A large part of what is now Poland was ruled by Germans. Now Germany has shrunk. What is now called East Germany extends to the door of Lübeck in the north, bulges westward, swallowing Thuringia, and southward until it is only some seventy miles from Frankfurt. The frontier then turns back toward Czechoslovakia beyond Plauen. Leipzig and Dresden—two cities that, like Hamburg in the West, were hostile to Hitler—are now in the Eastern zone. In the West are Lower Saxony, the Ruhr, the Rhineland, Westphalia, the Palatinate, Württemberg and Bavaria. Some 74 million Germans are now divided into 57 million Westerners and 17 million Easterners.

In short, the Germany of Bismarck and Hitler is broken—not, indeed, into the fragmentary kingdoms and principalities of the early nineteenth century, but into arbitrary pieces. There is the West or Federated Germany, there is the East; there is West Berlin, there is East Berlin. And here arises an immediate difficulty in discussing Germany with Germans. To any question their answers over and over again begin with the words: "The Germans, they are—" The rest of us identify ourselves with our nations. But so often the German splits into two: he thinks of himself privately as a man of his region, which is more important to him than the nation as a whole. He is a Rhinelander, a man from Hamburg, a Nuremberger, a Bavarian, a Swabian, a Berliner first. He is a refugee from the East. He is a Catholic or a Protestant. He is a man who loves to work, who loves domestic contentment, who has an almost pagan love of nature, but he bears on his mind the scars not only of the last two wars but of all the ferocious wars of German history. Despite a stolid appearance and an ingratiating manner he has the thinnest of European political skins; under his humility and kindness he has a temper and an arrogance that arise—in the manner of overcompensation—from the wound he cannot forget. The sense of a double life, privately wounded, publicly without definition, lies at the root of German life.

"The differences of English, Welsh, Irish and Scots are deep, but they are fertilizing," my Hamburg doctor says. "In Germany the differences between, say, Hamburg and Nuremberg or Munich are violent and separating in their effect."

My young playwright friend in Cologne, as gay a fair-haired, blue-eyed German as you could wish to see, confirms him vehemently. "The Germans are infatuated with history," he says. "People like myself are a minority. We always have been."

If we put contemporary history aside for the moment, this double character of the Germans seems to have been long established. The cathedral at Cologne is one symbol of this dualism. It is a power symbol. The edifice is heavily medieval, with that speared, bucklered, helmeted and gargoyled Gothic detail which we expect. It stands like Charlemagne, a Knight Emperor armored in stone. And yet nothing like the whole of this cathedral genuinely belongs to the Middle Ages; it had been small and incomplete for centuries, though the promise of scale was there. The fact is that the most ambitious and successful part of this great mass was created in the late nineteenth century, when German nationalism, fed on the wealth of modern industry, was at its most aggressive and exuberant. Industrialism came late. A newborn modern nation, united for less than thirty years and suddenly very rich, had chosen a medieval emblem. And not out of nostalgia for an unknown past, like, say, the Gothic architecture in the United States, which is pastiche and artifice; nor like, say, the House of Commons in England, which was the product of a literary Gothic revival; the German choice grew from an ineradicable attachment to military feudalism and feudal authority. The men who completed Cologne, like the men who built the empires of Krupp or I. G. Farben, were authoritarians. The relation of Emperor to Minister, of industrialist to worker, of man to man, had this medieval basis of authority and hierarchy. Germany is the country of the strict father. It was as if Germany, coming very late to the modern world, had expertly copied the appearance but was hostile to its essential spirit.

There was nothing new in this. One hundred and fifty years ago, long, long before German unity, nationalism and industrialism were dreamed of in Germany, foreign travelers saw and felt very much what we see and feel. They noticed how the relics of chivalry abounded in the country in perfect condition and to an extent unknown elsewhere. As Mme de Staël, Napoleon's great enemy, said during her long exile from France, the onetime wandering world conquerors of northern Europe had long left all this behind them when they passed into other lands. They went to other countries; behind hem they left only a museum of knightly images. The effect is romantic, but it is funereal and (she said) "painful." These are death images. Even now, in spite of the destruction of the last war, the medieval house, spire, hall, fortress, wall and city gate abound in Germany; the skyline of mercantile Hamburg is all spears and helmets, and just when we are charmed by its picturesqueness, by the gaiety of chivalry and the care of preservation, we have also the inner feeling of a buried drama and know the pain of living in two violently different worlds at once. And when we talk to the German engineer or the slaving executive dictating letters in the train, we find that something of the medieval ethos rules his mind. He likes to feel anonymous before authority. He likes to command and be commanded; he reveres the curt utterance. In the rest of Western Europe, that has died out. The Renaissance broke it; the French Revolution broke it; the gradual growth of democratic practice broke it. Only in Spain does anything comparable to the German outlook survive in Europe, for some of the same reasons.

When we look at a German we realize that he is only recently and still nebulously German. In 1800, Americans, British, French, each had a country; in what is now called Germany there were still at that time 77 major principalities, 51 Imperial cities, 45 Imperial villages and 1475 territories ruled by Imperial Knights. Serfdom was not effectively abolished in Bavaria until 1848. By 1871, when Bismarck succeeded by war and *Realpolitik* in creating the German confederation and Wilhelm was proclaimed emperor in Versailles—a characteristic piece of tactless vainglory—complete unity still had not been achieved. Essentially, feudalism survived in Prussia until after 1918. Moreover, in the midst of the liberal nineteenth century, the German constitution was imposed from above; it did not grow out of "the will of the people." The minority who represented the democratic view knew politics only in the abstract. One part, perhaps the most intense part of the German we are talking to, belongs to his region and his old lost principality; it is the part of him which has had few lessons in self-government and which waits for orders—the orders of the ghost Prince of the past on the one hand, and the orders of the military caste on the other.

If you ask why your German's ancestors were obliged to obey the orders of the Prince, the answer usually given is that it all dates back to the frightful destruction of the wars of religion. As Mme de Staël said, the Germans admire power because they see it as Destiny; and the Princes were the only power to whom the disorganized and fragmented people could turn. Absolute rule looked more practically effective than self-government; a sound administration—and the Prussians were brilliant bureaucrats—was more urgent and promised more stability than elective choice. It was left, for example, to the Princes to decide, quite arbitrarily, whether their little States should be Protestant or Catholic. The Thirty Years' War had created a great lethargy. While clever young men in seventeenth- and eighteenth-century England and America turned to parliamentary politics, their opposite numbers in Prussia became administrators. They were stern and brilliant administrators. I was in Hamburg at the time of Adenauer's retirement, when he was succeeded by the liberal Erhard. People spoke of Adenauer with a mixture of awe, admiration and amusement. They said that he had the mind of a typical provincial mayor. They grinned at his famous administrative intrigues, his tenacity and his dictatorial habits. They were, in a way, proud of him. He was in the tradition. For, they said, he was the quintessential old German type: the strict father who rules his country as severely as he rules his family.

How do our generalizations apply to Germany now? If they were true when Bismarck, Wilhelm II and finally Hitler galvanized this extraordinary people, how must they be modified to fit the case of postwar Germany risen from ruin, joined to NATO, in the Common Market with France and trying to make a parliament work? The moment one crosses the frontier one is conscious that this is a country where the scale of things is large. Except for the monster statues to Stalin in Eastern Europe, the famous Bismarck monument overlooking the harbor at Hamburg is on a scale no other country gives to its great men. Its churches are taller, their pillars are vaster; even when they moved from the Gothic to the Baroque, the German architects built to inordinate size. The beautiful Micaeliskirche in Hamburg, perfectly reconstructed after its destruction in the war, startles the visitor by its princely proportions; and when the old palaces survive it is noticeable that every petty prince desired nothing short of an imitation Versailles in the eighteenth century. In their regard for the large—and not in that alone—the Germans are the Americans of Europe. The *Kolossal* is essentially a German notion. Even the beer halls of Germany are built, like cathedrals, for mass life, for huge congregations. It is as if Germany had always built for large gatherings of men and not for wayward individuals. The German takes to mass life. He forgets his uncertainty and his scars when he becomes part of a group.

In Cologne men drop into bars at seven in the evening on the way home from the office. They are soon shouting and laughing. Already there are a few drunks toppling about in clownish fashion—serious businessmen behaving like simpletons or boys. In Hamburg the air is graver. Talk is quiet. The bars are sedate. Few people are in them. Grave men walk home briskly along the pretty paths of the Alster in the hard northeast wind, carrying their briefcases. Groups of athletes come running by or go sculling on the lake. Hard work at the office, exercise, and then home—that is the Hamburg day.

"Other Germans complain," says Doctor X as we sit in the privacy of one of the city's excellent restaurants near the water, "that Hamburg is calm, soft and tolerant, liberal and Londonish."

They also complain of its staid regard for wealth and its phalanx of ruling families. And about that Doctor X says: "We are conscious of status and hierarchy—all over Germany. The professor is still the most respected person in society. Your status in your profession is important—and it is immensely important to your wife. One rank defers to the one above and our hierarchies are rigid: student, assistant teacher, teacher, headmaster, professor are strictly separated ranks. It is so in all trades and professions."

"That is very military?"

"Or a medieval inheritance," he says.

"Softness" is not well thought of; outside of Hamburg, at any rate, "hardness" is the thing. And although Germans are ingratiating there is an automatic formality in their manners: the greeting to the stranger as they sit next to him in the restaurant, the faint click of the heels and the brief bow as they leave.

Hamburg is one of the beautiful cities of Germany. It is Hanseatic, deep in the mercantile tradition. It has always had a liberal past. It stood out against the Nazis. It has a large resident foreign population. Whereas Cologne and the Rhineland towns look southward and are Frankish if not French, Hamburg is an Atlantic city, looking to sea trade, London, Rotterdam, Amsterdam and New York. Hamburg might as well be Dutch or English and has often been derided, by other cities, as "the English agency."

The large Alster Lake in the middle of the city, edged by imposing villas and apartment houses, might be New York's Central Park turned to water. You go home from the office by water bus. You sail your boat in the regattas. In the beautiful shaded avenues you see a domestic life that might be a copy of Kensington or New York's fashionable East Side. A London autumn and a Hamburg autumn are indistinguishable. (It is a bitter irony that the German city which most certainly belongs to what we call Western civilization, which has no eye for the traditional eastward march of Germany, was terribly bombed during the war.)

Hamburg is the city of protest. It is the home of famous papers like *Die Welt*, *Der Spiegel* and *Die Zeit*. And it was the editor of *Der Spiegel* who was arrested in 1962 (but never tried) for collecting facts about German rearmament. His imprisonment without trial was one of the scandals of the Adenauer regime; it led to the further scandal over telephone-tapping by the police. The matter appears to have been dropped and the editor is at last out of jail.

The action of Adenauer reflected the fact—depressing to democrats—that the Germans are not great newspaper readers. Circulations are small compared with British and French circulations. The Germans, it seems, are book buyers rather than periodical buyers. There is no really national newspaper. One interesting point emerged when I was discussing this with the editor of one of the Hamburg newspapers (which are very good). We were talking about the great loss to Germany caused by the Jewish massacres and emigrations. The Jewish businessman never returns; there has also been a great loss in German medicine. But to journalism, especially to literary journalism, the Jews have come back. They give a high quality to this part of the German press.

Hamburg does not take antiliberal acts lying down. (It is considerably more sensible about East Germany than is, say, Berlin or Munich.) For example, Bertolt Brecht is not universally admired in West Germany owing to the West's built-in angst about Communism. But in Hamburg they were playing Brecht's opera *Aufstieg und Fall der Stadt Mahagonny* in the very fine new opera house when I was there, to the usual packed and elegantly dressed audience—every German city has its opera house and it is always packed. When, in the middle of the opera, Brecht's line about the law was spoken— "The Courts are as rotten as they always have been"—there was loud applause from a part of the audience. (Perhaps I should mention that to interrupt an opera in Germany is like protesting in church.) It is in Hamburg that you hear most of the talk about the activities of Nazi judges still in office; about Government interference in justice; about the "three secret services" in German life, with old Gestapo men still in them. Many Germans in Hamburg—and in Bonn—drew the moral of the Profumo case. Profumo resigned and has not returned to office. In Germany, they say, he would have been back in a few weeks. This, to them, indicates that public opinion in Germany is still not a serious force. They shake their heads sadly: "It will take years to educate us for democracy." It is in Hamburg also that one meets the emphatic phrase: "The Germans—they will never change," as if the Germans were other Germans of other regions and not themselves.

In fact, the Germans do change—if I judge by a tale I heard from a young foreign student, though his case may simply illuminate the traditional spirit of Hamburg. He was an Arab who had been so chivvied by the French police in Paris during the Algerian war that he had moved to carry on his studies in Hamburg. There, once more, he got into very serious trouble with the police. I shall not go into the facts of his case for I do not wish to identify him; but it was grave enough to get him a prison sentence. He swore he was innocent. The matter came to the notice of lawyers, and others, who were far from having the usual German docility. They saw at once the flimsiness of the evidence brought against the youth; the sentence looked like an example of racial prejudice. This does not go down in Hamburg. Several citizens took up his case. There was an appeal, and the sentence was quashed. There are, of course, few colored people in Germany, even if one extends the term beyond the Negro to all southern people of dark "non-Nordic" skin; but a considerable number of colored opera singers who say they cannot get jobs in the States are now singing in German opera.

Whether the old Rosenberg notions of the superiority of the so-called Nordic or Aryan race still exist in the background of any German minds, one cannot tell. Whether most Germans, or only some Germans, knew about the extermination camps, all Germans knew about the virulence of anti-Semitism which had existed as a political force in the nationalist and center parties long before Hitler. But the Nuremberg trials, the subsequent trials in the German courts, the trials in Frankfurt, the educative films and exhibitions exposing the history of anti-Semitism, and, above all, the Eichmann trial, have had a cumulative effect on the German mind. In Cologne there was an impressive exhibition called the Monumenta Judaica which gave a full account of the work of the Jews in the Rhineland for two thousand years. It included a great many objects of Jewish craftsmanship, a large number of ancient documents, and a great deal of well-displayed statistical material exposing the fictions of anti-Semitism. The exhibition ends with the awful pictorial story of the camps. Lecturers were taking groups of young people around every day; the place was crowded.

On the subject of racial persecution, the Germans appear to have had their eyes opened. They are aware of their guilt. One must suppose that this is a good thing, though in German literature there does seem to have been a traditional and morbid interest in having guilt for its own sake. All the young people I have met are shocked not only by the horrors but by what they call the "stupidity" of their elders. And from time to time one hears questions about *how much* guilt they ought to feel. They are bewildered. I used to go to a cozy, ugly little *Bierstube* in Hamburg, a place where small businessmen and clerks drop in for a sausage and a beer in the middle of the day, under the eye of a massive lady wearing creaking shoes and an old-fashioned starched apron that stretched stiffly from her chin to the floor. The place filled up with the old-style German characters who obviously survive from generation to generation in provincial life. There was, for example, the classic white-haired, rosy-faced, roly-poly old man, gazing like a clown out of large, doleful blue eyes, who sat giggling and joking with everyone.

One morning a returned Chicago-German came in to tell his friends about America. Suddenly I heard him mention Birmingham, Alabama, and he said cynically, "Yet the poor bloody Germans can't get away with anything." I am not sure what the moral of that remark is. It may have been a protest about self-righteousness, it may have just been a salesman's meaningless barroom swank. It may have had something to do with simple literalness of mind. For that *does* crop up rather often in Germany. Against the electric-light switch on the wall of this little bar there was a very fine enamel plate with the boldly engraved words "Light Switch" on it.

This literalness is puzzling. There is a fussy, myopic, rule-of-thumb element in it. In this old-fashioned *Bierstube* the good lady made out a small check for every drink and placed it with the others, which were arranged on the bar counter in a chessboard pattern. The checks covered most of the bar. When you paid for your drink, she searched her chessboard for your check. A simple, thorough, orderly but pettifogging method. In banks and hotels I have often met the same cautious, patient and maddening regard for bureaucratic detail. When the operator is pigheaded and arrogant, the effect is awful. What is even worse is that if you raise your voice and shout as though you were giving an order, the effect is magical.

I had not been to Hamburg for six years. That is to say since the high moment of the "German miracle." Old Hamburg was still in ruins then, but the new city was rising. Now most of the domestic building is down, but huge office blocks are still going up and districts change from week to week. Some of the new work is harsh and crude and has not yet settled into the scene, though I noticed that Unilever has put up a fine building, every bit as good as its remarkable building on Park Avenue, New York. Six years ago shipbuilding was booming; in 1961 there was a bad slump, but the superb harbor, one of the best on the Continent, was busy. St. Pauli, the famous Montmartre of Hamburg, still goes in for striptease; the tarts still sit in the windows of the brothel street, looking far more mercantile than their domesticated opposite numbers in Amsterdam, and having the grim *soigné* look of models in a dress-shop window.

Hordes of provincial tourists, especially Bavarians, parade the streets with cameras strapped, *à l'Américain*, or stand rollicking drunk arm-in-arm, a dozen or so at a time, on the tables of the Bavarian café where the bands play and everyone bellows *Prosit!* The *Tanz* bars and cabarets of all Germany have a certain harsh, electric efficiency. Pleasure is one more form of money-making work. The modern Germans love the glittering surface.

They were born for costume jewelry, fluorescent lighting, snack bars, neon and the twenty-four-hour day.

"Have you noticed," a young student said to me when we were sitting in a new Espresso—a place not much approved by the older people of Hamburg but filled with elegant young boys and girls from the university— "Have you noticed that the Germans never eat a real meal? They go through the day eating a snack here, a sausage there, a sandwich, a hamburger, on and off; they like to be always nibbling and on the move. It is the continual eating of small tidbits from morning until late in the night that destroys their figures."

True. The number of people who go along eating a cake or a sausage or an ice cream in the street is extraordinary. This young man was French; he was not as smartly dressed as the German students for, as he said, the German university student usually comes from the well-off middle class. He found the young Germans delightful and (he thought) very different from their elders; to him they represented a real break with the past. (Later on, this was also my impression.) They are benefiting from the breakup of the particularist or regional spirit. The thing that baffled him in German life was that there was no "*politique*," that is to say no continuous stream of analyzed political thought. Where the political man ought to be, there is a vacuum. "They do not reflect between one action and the next. They are always taken by surprise," he said. And at the moment, he said, they realize there is something artificial in their political situation: it depends on two "false friendships," one with France, the other with the far-off United States. These "false friendships" make them apprehensive and the fear stops them from thinking. The curious thing (for him) was what he called the two faces of the German, the "they" and "we" difficulty I have already referred to. In private, he said, he had met with warm, sincere and incredibly solicitous kindness. People had gone to great lengths in helping him in serious, intimate matters, without being asked. If he was ill, they nursed him. If he was poor, they fed him. But the Germans he ran into casually had a public face, cold, arrogant and aggressively hostile. In their formal social life he had found them stiff and without intimacy, as if they lived by rules. When it was not their turn to speak, they folded their arms in frozen silence; if you spoke to them out of turn, they looked startled, gave a small offended bow, raised their glasses politely but said nothing. General conversation on these public occasions offended and even bewildered them. I could hear his next phrase coming: "They long to be loved," he said. And since love is something one gives only by one's own choice, this longing seems overweening, demanding and eventually oppressive. They realize this and swing to the other extreme: self-pity. That remark about Alabama, which I had overheard earlier in the *Bierstube*, was perhaps an example of German self-pity.

I have set out this young Frenchman's view at length because it seemed penetrating, if partial. It confirmed what I have often noticed in Germany and what I have heard put forward by Germans themselves. Yet I must say that little of this applies to my close German friends.

Up on the hill with a view of the harbor, in a quarter which was terribly devastated in the war, is the old Saint Micaelis Church. An elevator takes you to the belfry and from there you can see the whole of Hamburg. This church was hit by bombs and gutted. It is now completely restored. It is—to use a German epithet that often comes to mind in this country—a princely church, like an opera house in its dimensions. Only in some of the very much smaller but carefully preserved small churches of the United States—there is one in Princeton that I especially remember—have I seen a comparable polish, comfort and care: German and American attention to the material things of life run hand in hand. With its starch-white walls, its gilded Corinthian columns, its delicate state boxes or loges, its pulpit like a cornucopia of marble and Saint Michael leaping in gold on the canopy above, this church has all the classical order and self-consequent invention of baroque art on the grandiose German scale.

One sees similar architectural rhetoric in certain churches in Munich. One realizes that the German imagination is an imitative and borrowing imagination, but one which borrows primarily for aggrandizement. Here, in Saint Micaelis, was a harmony acquired from abroad; the native things were the elaborate galleries for the princely or mercantile hierarchy, and the ambition. The organ pipes seemed to flame against the wall of the loft, as dramatically as they do in all old German churches. How dramatic, how theatrical, these seemingly rule-of-thumb manufacturers are!

I listened to the organist and it seemed to me that the ingenious variations

and dreamings of organ music perfectly expressed the wanderings of the
Teutonic mind; a mind liable to the liquid, lyrical flight or the military blast;
a mind laborious, practical and energetic, and yet at the same time drifting
off into a cloudland of unanswerable questionings. And between this metaphysical cloudland—whether it was fine or sinister—and reality there was
no connecting link. We were back at what Mme de Staël had detected: that
there is a gap between what is felt and what is done. A morose and grubby
young man operated the elevator to the tower. We looked down on the factories, the docks, the screaming road to the autobahn and the men shoveling
away at the brick rubble that had fallen into the water of a dock.

One generalizes. One says, "The Germans are this or that." One talks of
"typical Germans." Doctor X teases me about this. He says the "typical German" is a woman. The fatherland, he says, has two million surplus women,
due to the losses of the war. He brought a very pretty girl to lunch.

"What is it like to be a German girl?"

"Well—just a girl."

"A girl is a girl is a girl," says Doctor X.

She drank a glass of orange squash and later a little Moselle, and ate
strawberries and cream. She had come to Hamburg for the day, from the
Ruhr, to get a job out of Doctor X. Quite gracefully, but very firmly, she
worked on Doctor X; when he evaded, she tried to enlist me to work on him
for her.

"There you see the modern German woman," he philosophized. "Work
—that is to say, earning their living—is the most important thing in their
lives. No other country in the world, and I include the United States, has so
high a proportion of wage-earning women. Every second woman has a job."

The average age of marriage is very late—about twenty-seven. After
marriage this woman would probably still go on working. The crèche system looks after the children. The divorce rate is high because divorce is easy,
but that does not seem to worry anybody. The ideal is not youth but middle
age. To be middle-aged, have a job, run a family: this appears to be the general desire. And although the popular notion of the German woman is of the
docile *Hausfrau*, this seems to be no longer quite true.

It used to be said that what a German woman liked was beating carpets
and using a scrubbing brush. She had physical energy and liked to work it

off. She is still a great tidier. I have seen women in Bavaria sweeping every speck of sawdust in the street outside their houses after the log-cutting season. Last week more than once I saw women beating carpets in their gardens outside Düsseldorf. It was a hot day. But in a big store in Hamburg I also saw a sinister sign of the times. There was a male robot, standing over a washtub, working a mechanical scrubbing device. Whether one has to buy the robot or the machine I do not know. But on the placard beside him was the fantastically un-German sentence: "The day that father does the wash." I can't believe that day will ever come. The German women are too brisk to let it.

I talked to one intelligent early-middle-aged lady who had been in Berlin all through the war. She was a beauty in the heavy manner; young, she must have been seductive, but determination was written all over her.

"The Russian troops were no trouble," she said, in formidable style. "It was easy to scare them off."

Hamburg has its urbanity. But all German cities stand alone. One thinks of Germany as a collection of city-states, each complete with museum, opera house and churches. Only Berlin seemed in the past to dominate. It was the one city that was not provincial. If it is not now the capital, it still has the relics of the cosmopolitan air. Maimed though it is, it has the resistance, the detachment, even the nonchalant air of a ghost metropolis. It is the cleverest, the least natural, the gayest of the German cities. It is the obvious symbol of the West German situation: the Wall itself has given it that macabre dignity. It is at once an island, a Mecca and a political fiction—or, rather, a pair of political fictions—a gesture floating free in space. You have either to fly into it (at a restricted altitude), or, if you go by train or bus, you must enter the Eastern zone at fixed checkpoints where the Russian-controlled East German police do everything possible to delay and depress the traveler. Thousands of West Germans travel overland because it is cheaper, and endure the boredom and the uncertainties.

The inhabitants of West Berlin have the nervous sparkle of people who live on the flank of an active volcano; if it is true that the Germans worship the idea of Destiny, here is Destiny itself utterly mysterious, perhaps even satisfying between the alarms. The crises come and go. Some people leave in panic; but from the outside, at one time from the East but now from the West, others pour in to replace them. The city is traditionally the home of the garment trade and after the war the owners of the garment factories moved to the Rhineland; the workers refused to leave their city, so the employers had to return. German regionalism and devotion to the native city has triumphed in Berlin. The Berliner feels himself to be superior; he is attached to his ghost, to the precarious joke of his situation. The city is his dreamland. He feels he is untarnished by the notorious materialism of, say, Frankfurt or the Ruhr; and if East Berlin thinks it is holier than the Western sector, West Berlin thinks it is holier than the rest of the country. (It is quieter, incidentally, than other German cities because it has fewer motor cars. A Berlin Sunday must be the quietest in the industrial world.)

To these distinctions there is added another one—corroding, embittering, boring but somehow energizing: the distinction of the Wall. It is true that last Christmas thousands of Berliners were allowed to go through and visit their relations briefly; and although some returned overcome by the experience of meeting and parting, the tension has slightly lessened. But the Wall is a monument to man's inhumanity to man; it even resembles a moral symbol of the struggle between light and darkness. It is also a tourist attraction and a point of pilgrimage. Against that wall (ironically enough) it is the Germans' turn to wail. Crowds come from Europe and America to look at it. The tourist buses run in to East Berlin several times a day and the passengers come back silenced, emotionally poised between dislike and boredom. They have had their morbid sensation. They report well of the reconstructed Opera House in East Berlin which (the older ones say) looks much better than it used to in prewar days. They report a certain amount of new building. Things are getting a bit better in the East, they all agree. But the East German police! They are the Nazis reborn. Compared to them the Russians are easygoing and pleasant. The Russians have often a saving incompetence; the East German police and the Party have all the cold efficiency, the blind order-obeying cruelty of the bad German military and official heritage. Many West German students go on trips to East Germany and they see, better than any history book can ever show them, what it is the outside world has always feared in the German character. They also see the unabashed survival of Stalinism.

That West Berlin retains a pleasant calm despite its dismaying neighbor is partly due to the flatness of the city. It is as flat as a board, as flat as an Oriental city under a lifeless sky. The place has no vertical skyline. The spear and helmet, the armored, medieval look are absent. If either sector of the city had been on a hill and so overlooked the other, the calm would have sensibly diminished. As it is, one has the illusion that the "other side" is itself an illusion: so much do we live by the eye. I suppose the only people who get a depressing view are those who live on the top floor of the high apartment block called the Giraffe, near the Zoo.

The calm changes as one approaches the Wall; it turns to a nasty, gunbarrel stillness where the no-man's-land of dead grass, bomb sites, hunks of broken buildings and tank screens begins. Up near the Potsdamer Platz only two new big buildings have been put up on the West Side: a printing works and the bizarre Concert Hall—lonely taunts at the East. And then, as low to the view as a front-line trench in the First World War, is the obscene structure itself, winding like some gray concrete worm, with rusting wire on top. It wriggles mostly through a wilderness, though occasionally along the backs of houses, silent on either side; its sentries are out of sight except at the narrow checkpoints through which so many brilliant escapes were at one time made. There is a meanness about the Wall, mean in the sense that the organization of Buchenwald and Dachau was mean and disorientated. The builders of the Wall are the heirs of those who built the extermination camps; they have worked with a similar pedestrian and wearying malice. The Wall is the dreary monument to the natural affinity of Stalinism and Nazism. The only relief is the American name of Checkpoint Charlie. As one of my Berlin friends says, there ought to be a dance tune called The Checkpoint Charlie Blues; for such a tune, as macabre as Harry Lime's whistle, plays continually in the backs of Berliners' minds. I have noticed once or twice, out in the pretty suburb of Dahlem, how the sound of a police car going by at night will make people look up from their card games for one short frightened moment.

One turns back from the Wall and the gloom vanishes. The trees of the Tiergarten are growing tall now. A wide, fast road system has been built in West Berlin, too grand and fast for the relatively small amount of traffic; traffic in the East can be said just to exist, but that is all. One goes back to the Kurfürstendamm—the Prince's street, again reminding one of how important the Princes once were in forming German life—to the crowded cafés of a northern Paris. For Berlin is light and witty in the Parisian manner; it is more spirited than any other German city. Berliners, people say, think only of Berlin and no doubt Bavarians think only of Munich; but the pride of Berlin is cosmopolitan and worldly, and quickens the city tongue, even though it is only the broken shell of what it had been in the twenties and thirties.

What strikes one now is the mass of young people. Many of them come in from West Germany—some of the boys to escape military service. The young German has always been a banjo-carrying animal (banjo, or guitar, or saxophone); groups of lively young men and girls will sit on the sidewalks and strike up a tune for the delighted crowd. The sidewalk artist laboring at his compulsive portrait of Brahms or Beethoven or his abstract masterpiece in chalk amuses the passer-by. There are Arabs, Spaniards, Italian working men and students about. A buffoon dressed up as a rollicking bear lures ladies to be photographed. All day and late into the night the cafés are packed—and mostly with the young; though here and there, especially at Kempinski's, one sees one of those impassive, monocled old Berliners staring into vacancy, or those pairs of very masculine-looking widows dressed with a severe elegance that suggests a mixture of old Prussia and old Boston. The women are fashionably dressed. There is a smell of caraway and cigars.

There are several kinds of popular Berlin rendezvous. There is the common *Bierstube*, where the atmosphere is very much like that of a London pub; everyone talks to everyone in a friendly way; you are at home, so to speak, with a larger family than your own. Or there are the huge restaurants, usually heavily upholstered in the American manner—it was the Germans, after all, who brought to the United States the notion of furnishing everything, of creating the "conspicuous waste" of comfort. Germany as a whole has a passion for tablecloths and curtains, cushions, anything—however revolting—that can create "coziness"; not satisfied with a mere bar stool, the German demands a velvet-cushioned bar stool with brass or copper fittings. Everything is desirable that keeps this most house-proud of peoples continually polishing, cleaning, brightening every inch of floor, seat, table and wall. And in the winter, when the hard winds blow or the sleet and snow drive down, one understands why the German wants to insulate himself inside a cocoon of Things. He may be by nature an out-of-doors man but he is determined, once he gets inside, to take his ease and keep anything as inclement as air and nature out.

The mass eating-places are packed, noisy, steamy and rough. A perpetual eater, the German worker stands to his sausage and his beer or his plate of thick bean soup, jostled by other bodies. The massing of Germans is phenomenal. Most of us get swept into the crowd at some time in our day and suffer bewilderment or resentment as a result. Not so the lonely German; unsure of himself, he finds his identity once he is shouting in a group. The group—from a foreigner's point of view—is most agreeable in the old-style taverns which abound all over Germany, where one sits together perhaps with ten or twelve others at a scrubbed beechwood table. Talk is immediate and kindly. One is in a club, among passing friends who bow politely before they join the common table and bow as they leave. In these places the Germans reveal themselves without shyness. No English reserve, no French discretion, no American air of being on the alert and on the job. A sort of explosion takes place in the German personality. A region, if not a whole nation, unbuttons in all degrees of amiability from the boisterous, the preposterous, the sentimentally amorous or the absurd to the grave and engaging.

Most people who go to Berlin spend an hour or two in Hardtke's, the place for the traditional German dishes: the pork, the huge steaming knuckle of ham, the platters of liver and veal are planked down, in a cloud of steam, on the board before you. At the counter, glasses clatter and one watches the one thing that in Germany never stops: the sacred, slow dripping of the draught lager being brought to perfect condition in the waiting glasses. No vulgar shouts of "Where's my beer?" "*Es kommt*," they will say reproachfully, tenderly watching the foaming head like a poem that comes slowly word by word. At Hardtke's one sees all the German types; the fat man of folded neck with the great Brünnhilde-like woman, her blue eyes flashing like the German lakes; the classic German anecdotalist, crowing out his story in a simmering tenor voice like a cockerel inflamed by the sunrise; the actress got up not merely like a gypsy but like several gypsies at once; the shouting groups of friends; the quiet serious German up from the Rhine on some business deal worrying about his nine-hour bus journey home.

It was at Hardtke's one morning that I had one of my most interesting en-

THE SECRET PEOPLE

counters with young Germans. There were four of them, good-looking and well-dressed young men who were students reading economics in the famous school at Cologne. They had arrived from Moscow and Warsaw just an hour before, after two and a half days of what they described as primitive, sleepless train travel. They had been shocked by the incompetence and backwardness of the things they had seen in Moscow and outside it; they had been bored by the lectures the Russians had given them; they had been charmed by the Poles: "The Poles do not lecture." They had gone prepared to be told of the German war guilt and—in Poland particularly—had been shocked by what they had seen and been told. But to them the German guilt was something they already knew and felt. "We knew about it intellectually, of course," one said. "Now we saw our guilt with our own eyes." It was the first time I heard any German speak of "our guilt" as distinct from "their guilt." But what they could not stomach was the assumption of the East Germans that they were not Germans themselves and therefore had no guilt. The East Germans had convinced themselves that only West Germany had a Nazi past, yet the East Germans were in fact Nazis still in spirit. These young West Germans were going in either for industry or for academic work. They knew all the chief foreign books. Two had read Rolf Hochhuth's play *The Deputy* and disapproved of it: in blaming the Pope for not intervening in the persecution of the Jews, the playwright had given the Germans the chance to say, How indeed can we be blamed after that? (Many other Germans said the same thing to me.) We were joined by three workmen who had just come back from a sightseeing tour in East Berlin and who were indignant about the beer, the prices and what they had been told about conditions of work. Although the big boom of the fifties has slackened, West German wages are still rising. One of the workmen read out bits of propaganda from an East Berlin paper, amid shouts of laughter. On top of that, they had been held up for two or three hours, on some pretext, at the checkpoint. But one thing the West Germans do concede: the best German opera is to be heard in East Berlin.

There is a certain tension—so people say—between the Hamburgers and the Berliners: the latter feel exposed to Communism and untouched by the miracle. The Berliners' attitude is close to the American hysteria or—to be polite—tenseness about Communism: Hamburg reflects the more pli-

175

able attitude of the rest of Europe. But both parties have the sort of alarm about the Bavarians which the British once had about the Irish or the Yankees have about Southerners. For the north German, Bavaria is headstrong, violent, engulfed in dangerous political rhetoric, and has never really got over its separation. Strauss, the onetime defense minister, is a Bavarian; and non-Bavarians are relieved that he is not now in office. You hear people say: "The Bavarians hate us," but in fact one is up against the vast differences of temperament in different German regions. One forgets how violent the mild-sounding Germans are underneath. One is told in the United States that one cannot safely generalize about Americans because of the size of the country and the varying racial and social strains; a parallel complexity exists among the Germans. Germans recall that Hitler first succeeded in noisy, histrionic, egocentric Bavaria; but I fancy that north Germany is more diverted than anything else by Bavarian exaggeration, play-acting and emotionalism. They think of Bavaria as a carnival afloat on oceans of beer; and indeed at the Oktoberfest it is something like that. The sight of thousands of men and women comically fuddled, flopping red-faced into each other's sweating arms, singsonging, passing out, vomiting, and relieving themselves when and where they feel like it has a medieval coarseness. They do not quarrel. They sing and declaim nonsense and roll harmlessly into the streets.

The wine-tasting occasions in Munich are more seemly. There in the wine halls they sit in groups at their tables, but this time the group-life of the scrubbed beech table is solemn and silent as they consider the vintages of the white wine. Hundreds sit there in the high-beamed, stone-flagged hall; a man will rise formally and "call" on his friends politely at another table; indeed it would be a fatal solecism to fail to see or greet a friend. These social duties are taken formally and seriously. And the high spirits of the wine drinker have a certain fantasy and refinement. I have wandered around Munich at night, in the falling snow, with a chance German acquaintance who has stood reciting poetry in a loud voice and with great feeling at street corners, while we were converted into snowmen; for under the braggadocio of the Bavarian is the eloquent comic sense one notices among the Irish, but without the Irish bent for quarreling. Bavaria is the beautiful, Alpine, recalcitrant kingdom, the enemy of the old, Prussian-enforced unity. And Munich—once more rebuilt, regal and romantic in its outward air—is, after all, one of the three great cities of Germany. Italy is just over the mountains, the airs of the South blow in, the famous northern "hardness" and severity are not there; the German speech has less of the sergeant-major in it and is either rhetorical or caressing.

Dangerous, they say, in the north; fantastic notions rush to the Bavarian's head, orators bowl him over—as Hitler did—and the Bavarian tribe hangs enthusiastically together against the outsider.

You come back to trim little Bonn. It is often derided because it is a prosaic university town where there is nothing to do. Like so many German small towns it has beautiful trees; it is decorous in architecture; in the spring the flowers in the park and gardens are beautiful.

You sit in a café under the deep German chestnuts listening to the chatter of the handsome young people who are drinking their beer or their Coca-Cola. They look and sound gay and free. They certainly claim to be freer and happier than the older generation which is haunted by its past.

You ask the old questions. Can we trust the Germans not to try and destroy the world again? Have they really changed? Will they ever discard the military or despotic traditions and learn to become a genuine democracy? Will they cease to be the dangerous adolescent among the European nations?

These questions are unanswerable. We are told that the Germans have a profound moral need to assent, to say yes. This goes far beyond the everyday habit of ingratiating themselves. There is a real need to be governed by some large idea. In the early "good" Germany of Goethe, the Idea was philosoph ical and had touches of idealistic internationalism, and I have often heard it said that the old Germany is still alive in the minds of many. But they are consciously a minority. The worst aspect of the desire to say yes was seen in the tribal roars of the Hitler period and in the perversion of the international longings. Moreover, democracy is not built on the principle of assent, but on the dissenting spirit: the freedom to say no. It is extraordinary, for example, how few strikes there are in Germany. Only sixty thousand working days were lost there in 1959; in England, France and the United States, the figure is well over five million. Obedience still means a great deal to the German.

When there is no overwhelming Idea, the German turns his back on politics and thinks of nothing but material contentment. The general complaint that Germans are now apathetic about what is serious and are simply out for a good time has something in it. But if an Idea *does* seize them, then one can only pray that it will not resemble the idea of dominion expressed by German nationalism since 1870.

What really worries the Germans is the division of the country into West and East. They know this is likely to last for at least another generation, and they are resigned to it. But they hate the lack of "dialogue" between the two parts, the lack of any real human contact. They fear the two parts of Germany are hardening into a dangerous, explosive civil hate. What they really fear is the atmosphere of the wars of religion, which smashed Germany two centuries ago. The two Germanys may be separated forever, but at least they should know each other. There are fanatics on either side of the frontier. The wise minority in Germany does what it can to reduce the German weakness for categorical utterance, by creating the thing they have had so little of: public opinion. What the thoughtful young German says is that his parents must have been either mad or stupid, but that he has been subjected to too much propaganda on behalf of democracy and has had nothing like enough education in it. The most hopeful thing is that this younger generation is at any rate not sick as the Hitler generation was.

[1964]

8

The Irish Character

There is one in every bar in the world, waiting for me to come in, expertly gauging my capacity to listen, his tongue as sly as a hook and baited with a phrase that I shall not be able to resist. There was one, for example, sitting next to me in the parlor car of the train that was just drawing out of Vancouver, in British Columbia. We were passing through the docks, and presently a group of grain elevators came into sight.

"They've built those elevators quickly," he said.

"Are they new?"

"Sure the old ones were burned down two years ago," he said. "I set fire to them myself."

"Go on!"

"Anyway, they said I did. They accused me of it. I backed a truck into the cable."

"Were you hurt?"

"Not at all." (Scornfully, but the gentle voice was delighted.) "There was a powerful explosion. The elevators were burned to a cinder."

The quiet, soft, precise voice musically considering the event, the half-evasive, insinuating encouragement to conspire with him in a vision of some transcendental piece of destruction, mark the man infallibly. "They were an eyesore," he says.

He is an Irishman.

You are caught, on such occasions, in one of the English-speaking world's most hackneyed jokes, the one that begins: "An Englishman, a Scotsman and an Irishman were sitting in a train." It ends: "And Paddy said—" Add a Welshman to it and the joke vanishes and becomes a serious historical imbroglio.

By what devilish inspiration of historical fate were these four ill-assorted, quarrelsome peoples stuck on a couple of small islands off the wet and foggy Atlantic coast of Europe, outside the sweetness of civilization, and forced to live in one another's pockets for nearly two thousand years? And how is it that the Irish personality, to say nothing of the Irish race or nation, has always emerged with total recalcitrance and distinctness from the other three, despite all the entanglements of their common history? The simple but very unsatisfactory explanation is that the Irish have an island to themselves and that the Scot, the Welshman and the Englishman have to share one; for if we go to the United States, Canada, Australia, New Zealand or any other English-speaking country where the adventurous peoples of the British Isles have settled in any number, it is the Irishman who stands apart, who retains the consciousness of his race, his nation, his two religions, and his peculiarity, and who is never quite assimilated. Certainly there are great Spanish and Spanish-American families with Irish names and descent, who have been distinguished in history. They have been assimilated. The Irish make much of this, for the flight to those countries was caused by the Irish struggle against the British—but the Scots and English also have given their names to foreign families and have likewise lost their identity. But the British generally survive only in the institutions they create; the Irishman-born or the man who is Irish by descent survives in his racial person.

In certain weathers, especially in the west of Ireland, where the clouds seem to have been just that minute born out of the sea and to drift about not knowing where to go, Ireland itself almost seems to be newborn. A child could have dabbled it out in simple colors from a paint box. It is more than an emerald isle—it is an ephemeral one. This is, we know, a trick of the Atlantic climate and its light, for there will be hours when the trick is not played—long, gray, heavy hours when the island looks sullen and *is* sullen. No other island is so moody and variable in aspect, so likely to pass from the earthly to the unearthly before our eyes.

The Irish air is Atlantic air, but quite unlike, for instance, that of Maine; it is all empowered by the west wind, moist and rain-smelling, the lethargic air of heathery islands that are surrounded even more by air than by sea. One is excited and half asleep by turns. I was leaning one day on the loose stone wall of a little field in Connemara, where an old man was making the hay. "There's been a lot of sleep made in this field, too," he said.

Meteorology says that the changes in atmospheric pressure to which a human being has to adapt himself in Ireland are more sudden, more extreme, and far more frequent in the course of a day than in any other country. One moment our Irishman is walking as lightly as a deer; the next the sky is weighing on him. In Cork I have rarely been able to get up before eleven; and Limerick—as the famous John Mahaffy, the Trinity College wit, used to say—was the only city in Western Europe where you could see a bittern standing undisturbed in the main street at half past nine in the morning. That fantasy is impossible in modern Limerick, which is close to the new industries of the Shannon, jammed with salesmen, engineers, German technicians and transatlantic passengers, but the bittern could easily inhabit one's mind at that hour.

To the extent that climate forms character, one can see what the Atlantic island climate has done for Irishmen. The air, the constantly changing sky and light, that will turn green hills to gold, to purple, to blue and dreary gray in the course of an hour or two, will cause a man to notice the evanescence of things and keep him in a state of daydream or dismay. This will be as true of the mountain landscapes of Cork, Kerry and Galway, where the kind of country changes in every few miles of road, as it is of the brown bogs or waving meadows of the midlands, where the country is luscious and the farms are rich. And the fact that, in beautiful country of fine trees and rich land, the villages and little towns are gray and ugly, points to another aspect of the dreaming life. No one could be troubled, in the short time he was awake each day, to build better. These places are the work of people, you would say, who resented having to live in bricks, stone, slate and mortar. The old Irish race never built a town—so we are told by Arland Ussher, the Gaelic scholar, though the assertion is naturally disputed—and one of the more ingenious grudges held in Ireland against the British is that they never taught the Irish how to do so. Much of what the Irish had—the castles, mills, warehouses, forts, churches, farms—was ruined by wars and by abandonment, so that when we turn from climate to history, we are passing through a land where, in the name of some violent dream or other, real things have been destroyed.

The first generalization, then, that can be risked about the Irish character is that the tension between dream and reality is fundamental to it. The fact that the Irish claim to be realists confirms the view: no one has so cold and startled an eye for reality as the man who suddenly wakes up. Bernard Shaw put the misanthropic view of this character in the words of Larry Doyle, in *John Bull's Other Island*, and as usual in an Irishman's outburst, the lines are a collection of piercing half-truths:

> *An Irishman's imagination never lets him alone, never convinces him, never satisfies him; but it makes him that he cant face reality nor deal with it nor handle it nor conquer it: he can only sneer at them that do. . . . It saves working. It saves everything except imagination, imagination, imagination; and imagination's such a torture that you cant bear it without whisky. At last you get that you can bear nothing real at all; youd rather starve than cook a meal, youd rather go shabby and dirty than set your mind to take care of your clothes and wash yourself; you nag and squabble at home because your wife isnt an angel; and she despises you because youre not a hero. . . . And all the while there goes on a horrible, senseless, mischievous laughter. . . . laugh, laugh, laugh! eternal derision, eternal envy, eternal folly. . . .**

That is a good passage of Irish self-laceration. An imaginative talker has suddenly got an idea on the great central subject of Irish talk: the "unfortunate country"—itself a remarkably evasive understatement about a land that has been racked for centuries by big wars, little wars, enslavement, po-

*Quoted by permission of The Public Trustee and The Society of Authors, London.

litical murders, executions, starvation and treason—and made the jail the
home of honor. Certainly the Irishman is imaginative and cynical, angry
and laughing, but Larry Doyle is being glib: the Irish mind is also ancient
and humane in its acceptance of savage fatality and the human delin-
quent—outside the dram shop and even in it. The streak of cruelty that runs
through the Irish mind belongs to a pagan world that younger civilizations
have overlaid: it is the cruelty of pre-Christian tragedy.

Still, it is no good running on like this before we know who the Irish are
and what kind of Irishman we are talking about. For myself, an Irishman is
a man born in Ireland or born of Irish stock. I see no fundamental difference
between an Ulsterman, Protestant or Catholic, and any southern Irishman.
They are variants of the same mixed races.

Here the trouble starts, and every Irishman's eye is alert. Even after forty
years of freedom in Éire, and of solidarity with the British in Northern Ireland, a few fanatics keep the issue alive, though nowadays much more in
America than in Ireland itself. The theory is that several million of the Irish
millions are not Irish at all! The British, who are mongrels themselves, look
across the water and see another collection of mongrels who divide into
Protestants and Catholics—a crude view, but the British utter it out of bewildered politeness and to save time. Americans divide the Irish into two
waves of immigrants: the early wave of Scottish-Irish Protestants whom one
finds among the poor whites of Tennessee, the Southern colonelcy and the
upper reaches of industrial and academic life; and the later wave, usually
Catholic and "native" Irish who emigrated in millions after the terrible fam-
ines and criminal evictions of the 1840s, a pure peasantry to whom ward politics are second nature.

These divisions are far too simple. The Irish are more conscious of tradition and history than any other race one can think of; more even than the
Jews. Most Irishmen feel themselves to be aristocratic, either because they
are clansmen or because they descend from conquering invaders. Clan chief-
tainship becomes kingly in their imagination; colonists become—and it is
their word—Ascendancy. All are born great, and greatness is the stuff of
myth.

Your Irishman may claim descent from the Milesian Kings; I know one
who lets his mind run back without difficulty to the year 1600—yes, but 1600

B.C. There is no reason why he should not. The traditions of the Irish people are the oldest in Europe north and west of the Alps. Ireland is in fact the only Celtic state left in the world, and every Irishman will tell you—indeed cannot be stopped from telling you—that, in 350 B.C., Britain and Erin were the last of the Celtic conquests. Until 1066, the famous year, Erin ruled all Scotland, Wales and the north of England to the Midlands.

The sense of the remote past is strong in Ireland, and it creates in the mind a historical dreaming to match the dreaming of everyday life. So does the sense of the near past: Elizabethan; Cromwellian; Williamite; the loss of the Irish Parliament in 1800; the famine and the struggle for freedom from Irish landlords (mainly Protestant) and English rulers in the nineteenth century. So that when we ask, "Who are the Irish?" we are invited to decide whether our man is Celt, Gael, Norseman, a mixture of Norse and Gael, a Norman, Anglo-Norman, Welsh-Norman—the last three being called "old English"!—how they intermarried, which side they took in the Reformation, and whether they were of the upper or lower class. There are Normans who turned Protestant; there are Catholic Normans like the Joyces. And one would need to know why a twelfth-century Joyce should be less "Irish" than the famous native O'Flahertys, known as "the ferocious," from whom the city of Galway prayed to God to be delivered and who, at last, after hundreds of unavailing years, have got one of their family elected mayor of the city. Which of two famous modern writers—James Joyce or Liam O'Flaherty, both Catholic-born but fiercely anticlerical—is truly Irish?

Of course, we can simplify and say that any settlers or invaders who came after the English or Welsh-Normans—that is to say, Elizabethan, Cromwellian and Williamite English, lowland Scot or Huguenot French—are not "native" Irish. Then Swift, Grattan, Parnell, Shaw, Lord Dunsany, Plunkett, Yeats, Lady Gregory and O'Casey would not count. Nor Maria Edgeworth, the novelist. Nor the glorious philosopher, Bishop Berkeley. Two, three or four hundred years, in this land of genealogists, do not do the trick. The oddest offenders are the Ulster Protestants, transplanted between the reigns of Charles II and William of Orange from the lowlands of Scotland and without question cousins of the "native" Irish, if not of the same race. The northern Irish Protestants were all "colonists." Were Americans less American when they were colonists? The character break with the native country is always immediate, even if the political break comes much later. Test any colonists by their mother countries: the Anglo-Irish with their half-English accent are markedly un-English; the Ulster Scots with their half-Scottish lowland accent are markedly un-Scottish.

But we still haven't done with the matter, for there are large numbers of Irish who claim to descend from the shipwrecked Spanish sailors of the Armada and who can be added to the old claim that the Celts originated in Galicia, in the northwest of Spain. Of all such assertions this last is the most sympathetic: the rainy climate of Galicia, the moodiness and cleverness of the inhabitants, their wit, their drollness (at the very word *gallego* every Spaniard begins to laugh), their spirited yet negligent character, and the fact that they play the bagpipes and have sad, lyrical, nostalgic songs, combine to identify them with the Irish more surely than does any other racial speculation.

We have added racial history to the Irish dream and only one certain thing emerges: it was unlucky, since Ireland lay at one remove from Western Europe and a long way off, that the decisive European invasions of its soil were not dense enough to form a welded community. Britain was thoroughly conquered and settled; Ireland was not. In any case, large parts of the country were for long periods wretchedly poor. The facts of modern Irish history are really better seen from the points of view of the struggle of classes: Shaw was realistic about that. And the younger generation of liberated Irishmen today are more realistic than their elders, the nationalists who—with high imagination—fought for freedom. The Irish nationalist is going out fast. The old "unfortunate country," romantic in its martyrdom and sorrows, exists as a historic fixation, chiefly in the sentimental minds of Irish-Americans who have lost touch. The young Irishman does not dream—or not so much.

Anyone who has known Ireland over the last forty years must be struck by its modernization and by the emergence of new Irish types in the cities and farms. The long political struggle with the British was corrupting. The intelligent and active were either frustrated if they had office or power, or were sooner or later called collaborators. Independence has meant a class and technical revolution. Its effect on the land is obvious. Rural Ireland is much trimmer than it used to be. It is rare now to see the peasant cutting his own turf in the bog and going off, with his "private ass and cart," to stack it by the wall of his cottage. There are now turf-cutting companies and the work is done by machine.

In some places the primitive peasant life has been vastly changed. The culverts that used to break car springs, upset carts and jar the spine on the narrow Irish roads have gone. There are plantations of firs—to my personal regret—on the once totally bare Dublin mountains. The big estates are broken up and the "landless men"—the wildest of the old militant organizations, given to crime and arson—have their holdings. It is one of the unforeseen ironies arising out of the deep peasant mind—that the new owner will rent out the land to bigger operators who work it. The Irishman is a natural landlord. However poor, he likes rent.

I stayed recently in a small country house built in the late eighteenth century and surrounded by a demesne of splendid trees and the usual long gray walls which give a fortified appearance to so much of the Irish landscape. It had been for generations in an Irish family that gave famous generals to the British army. The latest general could no longer afford it and had sold it to a working farmer who had done very well in the last thirty years. He had sold his original farm in Kilkenny to a West German speculator for an enormous sum. The new farm was no out-of-date old homestead. It was not a gentleman's run-down estate. It had the latest equipment.

In cities like Dublin, Cork, Limerick and Galway, the busy and active young men are practical and positive in mind. They have access to money, to real political power or influence. There used to be something sad about the young man who stayed in Ireland; he was often little more than a convenient servant of a neglected estate, often embittered, often phony and gradually going downhill. He had a dozen excuses for his lassitude. This is no longer true, especially not in the last five years. He can now run new industries. They are small, but it is a beginning. He can fight his own government. He has made successful war on the squalid Irish cabin. The airlines, motor transport, the hydroelectric installations have turned a romantically dead city like Limerick, where the hotels were heavy with Dickensian dirt and the streets dead and idle, into something with a crowded modern sparkle.

I don't say that some of this modernization is not superficially dramatic. As I was leaving a Limerick hotel last year, the hall porter was affronted to see the lift boy idling with a friend. "Get that lift moving," he shouted. The startled boy—not long off the farm, I would guess—got into the lift. It shot up, shot down, shot up again—empty. But at least honor to Action and Efficiency had been done—albeit metaphysically, in the classic Irish tradition. It was a distinct advance over the time, forty years earlier, when in that same hotel—now unrecognizable—I saw the drunken waiter throw à plate of bacon and eggs at a customer, after a night when "the boys in the hills" had been machine-gunning the town.

At any rate, the modern Irishman is struggling with himself. The British are not there to blame; and there is—perhaps disturbingly—a new wave of foreign land speculators, hotelmen, industrialists and farmers coming in to buy up properties cheaply and display the cold, impatient efficiency of central Europe. A young Dublin acquaintance of mine talks about being "polluted" with work; he is an excellent executive but he feels almost literally polluted: it would be less corrupting to the soul to go fishing.

His industry is by no means acceptable to many of the older generation. The efficient young man is dismissed by them as a conscienceless and selfish operator. In Dublin last year, a young Canadian Irishman was raging against the young Irish who "have sold their souls" to the British and the Germans. But when I listen to those who still dream of De Valera's Ireland as a small peasant state using the Gaelic tongue and suppressing all the literature that disturbs the closed mind of "holy Ireland," and when I hear the young dismissed as mean-spirited opportunists—I remember with relief that the Troubles are indeed over. The young businessman is keen not to appear too religious. He may remark—to incredulous ears—that he is "not very Catholic," just as in the north he may say he is "not very Presbyterian." They are beginning to hate the accusation that, now that they rule themselves, they have become a byword for provinciality and dull fanaticism. It is now the Irish who begin to teach the Irish the painful lesson that a country had better not persecute its intellectuals. A slow business: a librarian I know tells people to *dare* to ask for the book they want, and he guarantees to get it for them. That is a modest but very startling change.

The difficulty is that the Irish mind has a strong authoritarian bent. Its religions are authoritarian; its tastes are soldierly; its intellect responds to abstract ideas. This militant authoritarianism comes out strongly in the banning of books. The power behind that is ecclesiastical. But as soldiers who live by orders are notorious for being "old soldiers" when it comes to getting round the regulations, so one is always able to buy the banned books—for example, Shaw, Tolstoy, the French Catholic novelists, Graham Greene, D. H. Lawrence—in Dublin under the counter. In other words, the Irish authoritarian will not compromise over the doctrine but he will usually, in practice, wink at circumvention. There is nothing even the most fanatical Irishman likes so much as a successful sin—except sexual sin—so long as you don't interfere with the theology.

The Irishman is by nature one of the world's great talkers—passionate, oratorical, vehement, easily roused to rage, easily appeased by wit. Yet I suspect that silence is really his natural habit; he is, about what truly concerns him, deeply reserved and watchful. Unlike the Englishman, he does not wear his heart on his sleeve and rarely discloses his real feelings. The emotions he reveals are mainly sentiments. He is utterly unromantic. His eyes are on the realities of life, defending them from his ardent fancies and—whatever he may say to beguile either himself or you—he has an unchanging fidelity to the beliefs he has been brought up in. There is a hard, silent being inside the actor's costume; the Irishman who does not talk much is very impressive.

Men of this kind, cool of mind, intellectually entrenched in the absolutes that entrance them, have been remarkable in international politics. The rise of Irish figures in the administration of the U. N. and their action in the Congo, point to the emergence of talents that have been romantically wasted by the soldiers of fortune in the past. This temperament, at its highest development, makes the Irishman the most signal example of that rare thing: a citizen of the world. I would put Conor Cruise O'Brien in this class; also an earlier courageous figure, now forgotten, Seán Lester, who stood up against the Nazis in Danzig before the Second World War, a modest man, no talker, but of iron.

You drive out of Dublin across the center of Ireland to Galway and the west. The romantic hills of Wicklow are left behind; you are in rich farming land; fine parks of the departed landlords appear, and their houses gaze back through the breaks in the beautiful trees. There is little traffic on the roads, but you may find yourself held up by a mile-long procession of cars going to an Irish country funeral: the size of a funeral is an important mark of social status. You pass many little cars containing pairs of neat red-faced priests looking like young blackbirds. Occasionally there is the trim spire of a Protestant church out in the countryside, and in the middle of a village will rise the enormous, ugly Roman Catholic chapel. (There was wholesale destruction of Catholic chapels in the time of Catholic persecution, and whereas the Protestants had the benefit of the English architectural tradition, the Catholics had to rebuild in poverty and in a period of poor taste.)

If it is a market day, splendid sows will be dozing on the pavements: the town will smell of animals and turf smoke. You will notice that the country pipe smoker has a small tin lid on his pipe to protect his tobacco from the strong wind and the rain. There are fewer donkey carts than there used to be. There are small new housing developments. The little pubs and inns are often grubby and bare, but the hotels are becoming smart; you'll eat good plain pork and mutton, and the wine is often excellent. You notice advertisements for the local dances—one of the few diversions, outside of television, in the lonely country life. The high television masts are for picking up the British stations and, in this country of Atlantic gales, the masts are strongly supported by struts.

Social life also means: men in the pubs, women and children at home, or drinking "sessions" that go on until the small hours. It means fairs, where the gambling is the great draw. There are wild country horse races, with the fights, the fleeing bookies, the loud shouts of "Objection!" after every race, the deals going on with jockeys in the corner, the drink flowing, and the crowd dribbling home.

After Athlone the country begins to get milder, the trees scarcer and bent over by the wind. Families of tinkers are camped along the stone walls—the wildest-looking people in Ireland, though occasionally a noble-looking figure stands out. The land gets rocky, Lough Corrib burns blue, the salmon fishermen are out, and in Galway you see those lordly fish lined up like small submarines in the shallow water, worshiped by the crowd looking over the walls. This superb city, on a bay, that is unequaled in the west of Ireland, is thriving; and it has one of the best restaurants in the country. I forget how many liners call at Galway but the people are proud of the port, and one realizes, as one hears Limerick or Cork pulled to pieces and hears "Cork men" and "Limerick men" spoken of as rival clans, that there is a sort of underground and very masculine war of character between the Irish cities and that it is passionately waged.

Galway is a rich place. In the evenings, at the best hotel, the survivors of the old upper-class life turn up—remarkably dressed women of a certain age, horsy, sporting, excitable in the Irish fashion. There is an easygoing dash in their appearance, and a marked eccentricity if one compares them with their more stolid opposite numbers in Cheltenham or Bath, knitting or sleeping over their novels. There is a touch of outrageous gaiety. You hear flattering phrases—the first duty of man and woman is to charm, and to hell with the rest. The feeling for amusement and for the sparkle of pleasure goes deep. Life is dull, but luck may change it. And even if you know there is "nothing in luck," you'd lose a lot of the pleasure of life if you didn't kid yourself that you believed in it. You can't live without excitement. With rich and poor it is the same—though there are misanthropists about too.

I used to sit on a wall with an old peasant in the mountainy country near Clifden while he let his greyhound off to put up a hare. If it came off, he would be shouting with excitement: "He has him! He has *not!* He has him! He has *not!* He has him beat. He has him destroyed in the corner. He has *not*, he's away over the wall." And so on. An afternoon came pelting to life for a poor man living alone with his rags, his whiskey bottle and his dog.

The west of Ireland has been turned into holiday country now and is better off. But its habits don't change much. It would be hard to find anything approaching the pages of Synge—anyway, he invented that poetic language—but one still sees the women in their long brown shawls, walking two or three miles down the road to Mass on Sunday mornings. Apart from the race days it is the one time when those treeless, rocky roads come to life with people.

Out of the conflict between imagination and the sense of reality springs the Irishman's quick intelligence, his wit, his genius as an actor; and from the clash of languages—up to the end of the eighteenth century the greater part of the population spoke Gaelic, and, if they knew English, had inherited it from the Elizabethan invaders—his often superb use of words and his power of oratory. When the Galway peasant asks, "What's strange beyant?" for "What is the news?"; when he asks, "Is the stranger within?" inquiring after a visitor; or, speaking of some exciting sight he has seen, says, "Twas powerful," he is uttering possible lines of Shakespeare. Words like "desperate"—"I was looking for a reel of cotton everywhere; it was desperate"— have the excess of older English. Anyone who is critical of Ireland is called "bitter." I have heard a political woman described as being "pickled in the vinegar of her own bitterness"—in a public speech. The range of language is wide and its utterance orotund. Years ago someone painted on the long gray walls of a demesne near Dublin, in huge white letters, "Vote for Duffy." The opposition added a sentence in letters six feet high: "And Ireland's dead will rise and curse you." It ran for a couple of hundred yards.

Sententious fantasy haunts the smallest incidents of life. The drunken "Captain" swallows his whiskey in the bar and orders another. He declaims to his friend the priest that the damned English doctors told him he had a coronary condition. "So I came to Dublin and saw an Irish doctor, and do you know what he said? 'Not at all!' he said." At this the chef comes out of the kitchen, a huge fellow like a heavyweight boxer, and calls out: "Come on now, Captain. Will ye come on! You have us destroyed in here." Getting people out of bars being one of the problems of Irish life, and promoting them to military rank being one of the rhetorical devices for moving them.

It is fashionable to deplore the "stage Irishman" and to pretend that he is a fiction. He is not; he is as old as Cuchulain, the prodigious hero of Irish legend. Synge's "playboy" is a fundamental Irish type. The clowning of a Brendan Behan is not an isolated performance; Shaw was a variant of the word-intoxicated man. And in my youth, I heard Yeats's voice rise from the conversational to the declamatory as he spoke of marching down O'Connell Street at the head of thousands of men and said, with relish, "We broke four thousand pounds' worth of plate glass!"—(How much finer were the words "plate glass"—spoken with the Irish short *a*—as a final phrase than "shop windows"; the poet and Irishman knew the value of the *sound* of words.)

From the sense of the personal role and the sense of language derives the long line of Irish dramatists who, after the Elizabethans, dominate the English drama—from Farquhar of *The Beaux' Stratagem* to Congreve, Sheridan, Shaw, Wilde, Synge, O'Casey and O'Neill. To that list can be added a long one of minor dramatists. And the gift is not to be confused with exhibitionism or bombast, in life or in literature; it is there because of Irish self-consciousness. The Irishman is well aware of the act he is putting on, the "lie" that he is telling, and is therefore an artist in the act. The well-known despondency into which he falls after his best performances is a sign that exhaustion and self-criticism have destroyed the dream and brought on—as Larry Doyle suggested—a bleak awakening to self-mockery.

I do not disparage the stage Irishman. He can rise to feats of inventive brilliance as well as descend to depths of sentimental vulgarity. He rarely deludes himself.

In most Irish minds images and ideas are in collision, and collision is the essence of wit. A jaywalking lady dashes through the traffic and waits halfway across, beside the policeman.

"That's a terrible risk ye took, ma'am," says the policeman.

"The traffic's desperate this morning, officer. I thought I'd be safe with you in the middle of the street."

"And with me, ma'am," says the policeman, "you'll only be middling safe."

For such conceits, punnings and ripostes the Irish are famous. Obliquity of mind and speech is second nature to them. They never miss a trick of word-play, and the quickness is embellished by a love of fantasy for its own sake:

"Did you ever taste my grandmother's curry?" asks Flurry Knox. "Well, you'd take a splint off a horse with it."

The lines come from the writings of Somerville and Ross, but you can hear sentences as good any day in Cork, Galway or Londonderry. The wit also has the advantage—but only in Ireland itself—of containing overtones of political and religious insinuation. It is also an expert way of evading dangerous subjects. An observant Catholic friend of mine who has indignant moral differences with the priesthood and, with Irish evasiveness, never lets on even to himself how far he can go, was lamenting the defeat of a team of Irish riders at the Dublin Horse Show in 1962 and the very bad luck of the American team, who were only just beaten by the Italians. He murmured that politics keep some of the best Irish riders out. "Anyway"—he winked to avoid that awkward subject—"it was a good day for the Pope." A remark that quickly laughed off the whole Irish quarrel.

One of the great burdens the Irish have to bear is their reputation for being unconsciously funny—a fine self-consciousness and self-awareness being their pride. It is often indeed argued that this nation of wits have almost no humor. The Irish pride in the "leg pull" is tedious, and it is one of the few matters in which an Irishman deceives himself. He is too egoistic to be a good psychologist. But Irish literature, from Goldsmith to Frank O'Connor and Samuel Beckett, makes nonsense of the notion that the Irish are not humorous. Ordinary Irish humor depends mainly on horseplay, leg-pulling, foolery, disasters and deceptions, and in this there is a genius for farce and knockabout. Although a novel like James Joyce's *Ulysses* is a great comic book, a compendium of all the comic situations known to man, it has more intellectual or fantastic sharpness of tongue than humor commonly has. It is the humor of a grammarian, and so is Beckett's, which is irascible intellectual farce. There is also a deep humor of roguery, for to rogues the Irish are notoriously merciful—as they are to sainthood. it appeals to a strong masochistic strain. A great deal of Dublin laughter is a mixture of the festive and malicious: all one's friends turn out, in this gossip, to be cynical frauds.

And snobbery plays its part. The Irish brogue—so alluring to foreigners—is a matter of delicacy; though singsong Cork, dogged Wexford, melancholy Galway and the lowland Scottish hootings of Ulster have their distinct regional dignity, the rank and adenoidal accent of Dublin is riddled by class differences and vulgar snobberies. The lower-middle-class accent of Rathmines; the painful division between those who pronounce "gas" with a short *a* and those who use the long one; the harsh, sneezing voice of Georges Street, with its inserted aspirate; the would-be English sound of Ball's Bridge—all have comical overtones of social afflatus. Being a man for language, the Irishman picks these things out with relish.

The once-ruling or Ascendancy Protestants mocked the brogue and still do, but themselves speak an English that has a clearly un-English inflection, being softer where the English speech is crisp, clipped and hard; but it is indeed a distinction of the educated Irish—whatever their class or derivation—that they give back to English its modulated beauty without fashionable or vulgar distortions—and of the uneducated that they give it vehemence and color. This has made them masters of English rhetoric and prose and, with the Welsh, custodians of the language.

In humor, this acute Irish ear is merciless to the affectations of language and goes far beyond the narrow scope of English U and non-U; it is silent before the Elizabethan dignity of some peasant speech, but it revels in the mockery of social pretentiousness, provincialities and gentilities. And these abound, for putting on scorn is in the blood. Since the Irish place such value on awareness, they exploit any signs of social delusion in their neighbors.

In the days of the cult of the Celtic Twilight and, later on, of Sinn Fein, the funny Irishman was held to be a wicked British colonialist invention, and it is true that colonialism always defends itself by regarding the "natives" as comic children. (The Negro is "funny"; in London factories today the colored workers are known as "smoked Irish.") This humor is usually defensive and insensitive, but one bears with it because it is part of the international rough-and-tumble. Russians and Poles, French and Italians, Americans and British, all go at it; and the Irish aren't so sacred that they can escape.

But there is a comicality that springs from the pursuit of abstract thought and logic and its clash with sense or fact: the Irish do produce that. I was traveling by train to Cork during what, in sublime euphemism, were called the Troubles, and we were held up for hours because a bridge had been blown up and the train was to be diverted. Eventually there was a hopeful bustle at the station and I asked the guard, "Are we starting now?" He replied, "We haven't started starting yet"—a sentence that may be a witticism at the expense of railways, or the utterance of a man bemused by a fine semantic or metaphysical point. Again, it may be an unconscious absurdity. Whatever it is, it is funny, and if you were solemn enough to press the point you would come off second best in the exchange. The Irishman always has the last word.

The Irish comic gift arises a good deal from the tradition of evasion. The Church, for example, used its influence—an influence that goes into every detail of southern Irish life—to get the pubs closed around lunchtime, so that the workers would be forced to go home to eat. The closure was at once nicknamed "the holy hour."

Irish grandeur has had its periods of aristocratic elegance of the careless kind, especially in the eighteenth century, and that has left a strong mark; but carelessness is the qualifying word. To appearances the Irish are indifferent. Ireland is a good deal smarter than it used to be, but you still get the country waiter who seems to have slept in his suit; for the Irish sense of style is inward, not outward, an attribute of the imagination. He is a man for the warmhearted social occasion. Sociability is his triumph and sometimes his ruin. Folly attracts him, luck he prays for; if he is a southerner, his goddess is Fortune. Like the Spaniard, he likes passing the time of day with anyone he happens to meet, for he loves turning life into talk and manners.

A girl is taking a long bus journey to Lisdoonvarna, a spa in Clare. "I talked to everyone on the bus," says this broth of a girl, delighted with herself. "You couldn't do that in England."

"Why not? Don't they talk there?"

"Oh, they do," she says primly, "but they get familiar. They've no manners."

Propriety and manners, to these egoists, are for keeping a distance. Their sociability achieves a kind of poetry —think of Irish songs about "the gaiety," and so on—but it is also a preserver of inner retreat. The word "decent" is often heard. I wrote down this quotation at a station in Galway. A girl was leaning out of the coach window eagerly looking for someone, anyone, to talk to. She caught sight of a young man and she chattered in high spirits: "Were ye ever in Cleggen? Were ye now? Did ye know Michael Linden? Did ye not! Well, did ye know Patrick Joyce? Did ye not! Were ye ever in Ennistimon? Were ye not! Were ye ever in Cashel? Were ye now? Did ye know Bartley Hehir? Did ye not! Well, good-bye now. We're off to America."

It was like a poem of the continual hail and farewell of Irish life, the meetings and partings; it sang of pleasure, of acquaintance without intimacy, ranging wide, filling up time with light words.

The paradox is that this gaiety is both decorous and high-spirited—at ten or eleven at night O'Connell Street in Dublin is gayer than any city of provincial England—but it can turn, if the black mood comes on and the drink is flowing, into fighting. Why do you see so many black eyes in the Irish quarters anywhere? There comes a moment when the Irish face turns dour: "Would you mind repeating what you just said?" The inflection is unmistakable. One lives on a hair trigger. Is Ireland really so light-hearted? Country life is lonely, the priests keep a sharp eye on dances and social gatherings. The rain pours off the brim of your hat, the cold gales blow. I have often spoken to Basque fishermen who turn up in Kerry from time to time and who are appalled by the melancholy of the people, their puritan religion and their suspiciousness. They are shattered by the number and squalor of the pubs and by the sharp tongues of the girls. And the Irish fisherman thinks the Basque a fool for sailing as far as Ireland and even as far as Iceland. The Irish fisherman lives for the day.

The cure for melancholy, for listlessness and boredom is violent action, and in Ireland this is embodied in sport. The horse has always been the heroic solvent of Irish evils, and I half believe that any Irish man or woman would as soon be a horse as a human being. After all, in *Gulliver's Travels*, Swift portrayed the Houyhnhnms as an equine master race, though in fact he was satirizing the rational man. Animal spirits of the athletic, hunting, racing, chasing kind; the rushing of the blood; the excitement of dangerous physical effort; the actual suffering and pain—these awaken and delight. The Irish hunts are known for their recklessness. The knowledge of horses is immense; the animal is worshiped and cared for as no human being is. Of course, there is money in the horse, and the favorite kind of money: luck or the money of the long-headed deal. But the mere sight of the animal excites the whole population.

The annual Horse Show in Dublin is a national feast and it is run by an ancient society—the Royal Dublin Society—which spends the rest of the year sponsoring lectures on the arts and the sciences—an extraordinary uniting of study and stable. The crowd contains every type that Ireland has to show and astounds by the individuality of the people: they are no sheep-like mass. They could be mistaken for no other nation. The sun stings, the rain drives—but an Irish crowd is indifferent to the weather; it has to be. One notices the clear eyes, the pink skins or those delicate ivory skins of the raven-haired types; but no skin leathery or dead. Whatever else the climate does to the people, it gives them complexions that cannot be concocted and bought in London, Paris or New York. And on this occasion the national kindness and generosity come out, and the instinctive democracy. The gasps of admiration before fine jumping are expert and ecstatic, the groans of sympathy for an unlucky rider are deeply felt. There is no derision for the stupid mistake. And in that week Dublin is up all night and one of the most energetic spots in the world. "I'm not going to the ball tonight. The Galway Blazers have arrived," a friend of mine said. "I don't want my arm broken." The city becomes like a great country house by the sea, in the old days, alive with hospitality.

To the outsider, all this has the natural ease of life in a happier age and suggests that, if we except the northeast corner at Belfast, a good deal of Irish life is really going on in a lost early Victorian paradise. It has, for this reason, a sort of mannerly innocence on the surface—very different from the life of industrial countries. It is without the sinister and nasty things we are used to. Even the appalling slums of north Dublin, where every fanlight is smashed and the children swarm on the stairs, are Victorian—indeed Dickensian. There is another, deeper innocence which is most difficult to define but which the Irish themselves lay claim to; a form of mysticism. The foreigner is aware of something fey and "elsewhere" in the personality even of those large, scowling, truculent, black-haired, pale-faced Irishmen, or in the shrewd eyes of plump old Irish ladies, or the young girls whether they are wan or spirited.

The Irish are proud of their chastity of spirit, of a "holiness" that runs through their life from their imagination to their religion and their sexual morality, even when they are patently and professedly unholy. To them the Americans and the British are overfed libertines and materialists. The Irish ate better than the rest of Europe during the Second World War, but food is of no great interest to them. It was the only European country where you could see anything approaching the traditional figure of John Bull. Although thought of as the land of hunger, Ireland is a country where, perhaps owing to the climate, appetite declines. Poverty—the island has few minerals, no oil, little coal or iron—and their peculiar Roman Catholicism, which is puritanic and removed from the urbane religion of the Mediterranean, may account for the inner austerity of the Irish. But, in fact, both in the north and the south, Protestantism has a similar character, being moralistic, nasal, prating and forever watchful.

Religion has great authority in the authority-loving Irish mind, and Latin paganism has little part of the religious inheritance. Although the Irish respond to France, Spain and Italy, it is more as matter of cultural or aesthetic pride than of deep affinity; and the Irish cleric, like the exile, has usually the spirit of the mission. This in no way conflicts with Irish "wildness"—mystics, it has been noted, have a cynical vein and a power of dissociation—but something in the Irish temper is shy of the sensual man. The odd thing is that the Catholics are still afraid of the influence of what they call Protestant "libertinism"—as they see it in England and America—and that the Protestants dread Catholic "corruption"; both parties in Ireland are equally shockable and, at heart, on guard.

What any traveler in Ireland notices is the emptiness of the land. It is underpopulated; its population declines at a time when, in every other country, population is increasing; and emigration is not the sole cause. The average age of marriage in Ireland is later than in any other civilized country— thirty-four for men, twenty-nine for women—and the marriage rate is the lowest in Europe. A study published a few years ago declared that only 30 percent of the population were married. The people had become either so canny or so continent that they did not want to breed.

Did the Famine have a traumatic effect that has lasted generations? Is poverty the cause? Hardly. The poorest countries breed fastest. When the Irish marry, their families are large; it may indeed be the fear of the inevitably large family that holds the Irish bachelor back.

Among the peasantry, is the land system the cause? One of the charming sights of the country is that of a man and his wife and their son working together in their little field, "saving the hay." But where are the other sons and daughters? The farm can support only one son. The others have gone away. The remaining son is really a hired laborer; only when his parents are dead—and they will live to a great age—will he have the farm, and he cannot easily marry before he does. The girl whom he may be courting will be courted for years and will be mature before she bears a child. And anyway, she will not be married unless she brings a dowry. You can pick up the local paper and still read one of those "comic" Irish breach-of-promise cases; they are in fact bleak:

> Miss X said she never saw the defendant until he was introduced to her by Mr. Y. He came to matchmake and had a bottle of whisky and the young man asked her to marry him. She told him she had £100 fortune, £140 being asked but £40 was knocked off by the matchmaker. She was over 30 but under 40. But neither party turned up when the ring was to be bought.

The young man said he would marry her any day if he got the money. Was there no love at all in it? asked the judge. "Ah. Sorra much," says the old reluctant Lochinvar, for the cash was not forthcoming. Loud laughter but it is a sad tale.

But the Irish are not all peasants, and according to John O'Brien's book, *The Vanishing Irish*, the reluctance to marry is general in Irish communities all over the world. Some people blame the country priests, the denunciations of courtship and of the dances where boys and girls can meet, and the religious rage against sex. And Irish rage is real authoritarian rage. One would have thought that Irish alcoholism was a far more serious difficulty than sexual promiscuity. Quebec has many resemblances to Ireland, but there the population increases and love is not dishonored. Yet those who blame the Irish Church must remember that its priesthood springs from the Irish peasantry.

The country is made for men, not for women, and the personable fellow in the small towns or in the Irish districts of London prefers to hang about with his pals, to gamble, follow sport and cut a figure. You rarely see a woman with him. There is a long tradition of the spendthrift husband who "lives like a gentleman," like Joyce's father or O'Casey's Paycock. The house is kept together by a hard-pressed, strong-minded mother who is idealized by the son whom she rules like iron, right into old age. The very vocal, easy-going and gallant spirit of Irish life covers an inner caution and pedantry; and one is more struck by the jeering between the sexes than by their amity. Yet the evocations of love in Irish poetry are tender, romantic and nostalgic; and perhaps nostalgia explains a lot, for it is an emotion that fills all Ireland like the air one breathes. The songs are made out of it; and it is more than the nostalgia of a scattered race; it is the nostalgia perhaps for lost centuries, the unearthly distractions at the back of the minds of a very realistic people. One has to reconcile this with the dashing Irish gallant and famous Irish *amou- reuses* who crop up in European and South American history — though scarcely ever in Ireland itself.

The legend of holy Ireland has always seemed a paradox in a people who oscillate between idealism and cynicism. As idealistic rebels, fighters for liberty, visionaries of liberation and justice, soldiers of fortune, they have had a gift at once noble and strangely personal. They have a passionate sense of principle, and their intransigence comes from their devotion to an abstract idea. In the management of the British Empire, they almost always showed more intelligent personal sympathy and curiosity than the British, who are more responsible but less responsive.

The Irish constitute one of the world's great secret societies, with branches everywhere. It is a very public secret society, visible to all, with no special purpose beyond preserving the racial imagination of a scattered people, and with no mysteries beyond the general family mystery of being Irish. But this secret society does unmistakably have a Grand Master. He is no less a figure than the Devil himself, to whom their cousins the Scots are also profoundly attached. Literature and speech proclaim him. In Scotland he is no more than the "puir wee devil" who has had a terrible time at the hands of Scottish theologians and needs all the help any dear kind soul can give him. In Ireland, he is stronger; he is a brave boy, full of life, who gets on with everyone.

The Irish habit of mind owes everything to the insight that all men and women have a bit of the devil in them, and that it behooves us all, therefore, to admire the devil first of all, then to be charitable and—if we can't do this—at least to take the precaution of being extremely polite. The devil is good luck, bad luck, the incalculable, the incurable; inseparable from you like your ragged shadow. In one sense he does not need to tempt you. You tempt him. You take him over for a spell. It amuses him. He was bored in Hell.

I once spent some hours with an Irish priest, and when I told him I came from London, he told me he had been brought up in Chicago, where his father had been a politician. "He was so corrupt," the priest said, "that he would even give an Englishman a job." You catch the accent of the Grand Master in that little speech, and the ethos of the secret society. It is because they are a secret society that the Irish have preserved their singularity in lands other than their own. Where indeed most of them live.

[1963]

9

The Americans
in My Mind

The inhabitants of the United States are the most restless and gregarious people in the world, a race of nomads voracious for sights and facts, who turn up in tens of thousands everywhere from the Angkor Wat to Stratford-upon Avon, from Moscow to Colombo. They are the only race to upset the balance of nature by achieving sexual inequality, and their docile males, wearing cameras as accessory sense organs, follow obediently their vivacious and moaning females. This moan (my American women friends frankly say) is a "secondary sexual characteristic," and is persistently mentioned in the novels of Henry James. American soldiers even took their cameras into battle with them in the Pacific war, according to the author of *From Here to Eternity*.

Caricatures of this kind can be done of any people seen out of their environment, but what are they like at home? Of the Americans, that is difficult to say. The European who arrives in the United States is astonished—and assuaged—to find it full of Americans who no longer look alien and who have homes of their own. But generalizing about the American character or temper is a perennial international game; in the last twenty years or so it has become an American industry. I have read more books by Americans on the American scene and character during this time than by writers of any other nation about themselves; and one thing has struck me immediately—what for generations we Europeans have called the boastfulness of Americans was really the self-dramatization of a lonely people, an acute and often painful consciousness of themselves.

Any foreigner who goes onto the international stage and offers a few quips and asides about the American character ought to state his qualifications. I have only one. I was, for a moment, nearly an American. Last year, at the Pennsylvania Railroad station in Philadelphia, I was mistaken for the governor of Texas, to whom apologies. My disqualifications are serious. Man and boy, over a period of forty years, the total of my several visits to the United States amounts to only fourteen months. These have been spent mostly in the East, never in the Deep South, never in Texas, never in the Middle West except for two days of blizzard in Chicago, which I could hardly see. It is true that I have watched the Chinese mists crawling over the branches of the live oaks in California, but in that ebullient state I have lived mostly in the shelter of the skeptical universities. Though they may have their twenty thousand students, they are nevertheless islands in the rough-and-tumble of American life. My most curious American experience was walking, when I was young, through the mountains of North Carolina and Tennessee roughing it and collecting unusual words. This was hardly typical. But is anything American typical?

My America is a personal fantasy, a chaos of impressions: I see a continent of suburbs, of prettily painted small buildings, sharp roofs, glossy sunsets. I see enormous invading armies of pines and firs, drab cities, quiet and beautifully shaded towns, garish highways slicing through what is (for a European) an empty countryside. I see New York, a mortal Babylon, a collection of the stumps of a petrified forest by day; by night a lantern hanging from the sky. I see San Francisco scattered like confetti around its Bay. As for the people, they are a bizarre procession made up of all nationalities and with serious, unrevealing faces. Either they look like boys and girls or they are middle-aged—how and when does that sudden jump occur? A brisk and specialized population, one would say, with that jerky walk one used to see in old-fashioned films. I have sat with tobacco chewers in the country stores; I have tried for a word from silent, elderly conductors on trains. I have interrupted overworked professors at their typewriters. I have been bowled over by the charm and earnestness of students. I have eaten strange rice dishes on my knees in the bright and tidy homes of motherly ladies. I have been delighted by the waltzing bandleaders in the parades. I have had sensitive conversations with Puerto Ricans and have had abrupt relations with dictatorial children. I have had highbrow talks with cab drivers.

And then, there are my restful personal friends who think, talk and feel much as I do and who differ from me only in being more patient and considerate than Europeans are, who talk rather more slowly, who sound lonely outside their work, and who are more interestingly worried than I am. They have "problems." Their nerves are tauter; they are more "strung up" than I. They are boundlessly hospitable. They perpetuate the eighteenth-century doctrine of Benevolence. They are excited in welcome, enthusiastic in farewells. Always on the move themselves, and inclined to loneliness, they have perfected the rituals of greeting and parting. I see some puritanic British racing motorist has lately said that American good wishes are transitory. You are soon forgotten. Henry James said in one of his short stories, "The Point of View," that indeed American social life was a process of "innocent jilting." Possibly: America expects you to keep moving on your own because that is what America was invented for; and it expects you to be serious and flexible about it.

My final disqualification is that I am British. We British tend to imagine that, because we were founder members, have the same language, literature and close bonds of religion and law, America will be simply an extension of ourselves into greater space. This is not so. We are simply the descendants of the first of the many European father figures whose rejection in every generation has made American civilization different from all others in the world—a civilization that is at odds with itself about the principle of authority. We are islanders packed in to a density of, say, seven or eight hundred to the square mile; Americans are continentals, land-mass people, only fifty to the square mile. We live intensely, privately; Americans relax in the ease of great space. In America (again as Henry James said) everything is for "the people," not for the "person."

In some respects American life has more in common with the life of central Europe, of the northern European plains and indeed of Russia than it has with British or Western European life. Food is very German; technology and efficiency are German; higher education—with its great influence—is basically German; the brightness, workableness and cleanliness of American homes is German. Americans, like Germans, live by the will. Even a certain emotionalism, a certain aggressiveness, a self-torment and modesty are German. (I say nothing of the male haircut and the specializing mind.) These influences are, of course, due to immigration but only partly so: the real influence is that of the great land mass on energetic people to whom living by the will has been an imperative demand. How else could they have constructed a powerful country so rapidly? And from a blueprint.

America is on the move (many Americans have said to me) but has no idea of its destination. Does a nation have to have a destination? How can you define a temper that will fit New York and Texas, the Deep South and California, the large half-assimilated populations—the Mexicans, the Puerto Ricans and above all the Negroes? Look at the holiday mob at Pennsylvania Station in New York; there is no homogeneity. Even one's friends seem to live on islands against which the vast mass of America washes like an incomprehensible ocean. The violence and intolerance in American life show that people have shut themselves up in groups for self-defense. This is unanswerable and yet, though I accept the picture, I suspect the reasoning. There may not be an "American character," but there is the emotion of being American. It has many resemblances to the emotion of being Russian—that feeling, traditional in both countries, of nostalgia for some undetermined future when man will have improved himself beyond recognition and when all will be well.

Only two regions of the United States (according to the historians I have read) offer marked variants of that emotion: the Deep South and, strangely enough, Texas. The Deep South has retained a colonial, pseudo-aristocratic tradition—to reverse Henry James, everything for the person and nothing for the people. Texas seems to have been on the verge of becoming a naturally independent nation and without the difficulty of "rejecting the father"; there was no father to reject. I offer the fantastic suggestion that the Texan is the nearest thing to a European the United States can supply. He could easily come from Barcelona.

In spite of the enormous changes in American life during this century— the great increase of wealth, the rise of the masses and the assumption of a financial world empire and its military commitments—is there anything in the modern scene that is not simply a huge extension of what Henry James had found in 1907, when in old age he came back to the United States and wrote *The American Scene*? His psychological observation is, at any rate, still very telling. My opinion is that there is a deep, even defensive dislike of definition among Americans because it would limit and work against the American sense of possibility and becoming. It is profoundly part of the energetic and moralistic American tradition that a man may, indeed must, become something else and that he not only has the right but must have the resilience necessary to the heartrending pursuit of life, liberty and happiness.

A heterogeneous, thinly spread nation, living in a land where nature is unfriendly to man, where climates are, in most places, extreme, a nation at odds with the principle of authority, is kept together by a paradox: a deep emotional sense of freedom, generated by the extent, opportunity and wealth of the land, has to be adjusted to its opposite—the standardization of human beings. This yea-saying country, emotionally free, is mentally the most conformist. The "good guy" who never questions is enshrined. An English friend of mine in California was given a friendly warning that he was "too individualist." And, in fact, when I return to Europe from the United States I am myself almost irked, for a while, by the obstinate individuality of Europeans. In them the private, personal life is strong and concern for "the sense of the meeting" is far less so.

But the basic difference of character between the Americans I have met and the Europeans is that the former are indoctrinated and the latter grow organically in their species. Americans—even those who live on private islands in the American ocean—are conscious, walking contradictions. Their habit of mind was formed in the eighteenth century: the American tradition is an abstract idea. Puritan teaching, especially in its Calvinist aspect, encouraged one to examine minutely the approaches to perfection and the lapses from it: in the engine room of Puritanism there is a machine whose function is to produce moral and material success. Failure must be sin. In a new country it was indispensable that the community should succeed, and when the great immigrations began, it was essential that the newcomers be indoctrinated and made to conform. There were grave spiritual losses in the process, but these losses introduced the immigrants to pragmatic American humanism: the belief that you can build your life and work it out, conscientiously, bit by bit. The task is enormous; it is often dulling; but that is the price you willingly pay for believing in the perfectibility of man. There is no conception of tragedy; something just went wrong.

One unexpected result of rejecting the father, and believing in the freedom to construct consciously one's own life, has been the rise of the mother and the establishment of a formidable matriarchy. During the last war, when I was among American soldiers, it struck me that they often talked about their dads but never about the sacred figure of mother; among British and French soldiers the talk was always about her. Father was the ruling figure they did not often mention. I have heard anthropologists argue that the American male is often at a loss through having to carry about with him a "feminine conscience."

But there is no point in generalizing in a void like this; I fall back upon my own fantasies of American life, and out of the confusion there emerge three or four vaguely human shapes: American prototypes. I see bits of them in most American men and women I know.

The first I will call Sam Robinson. We met forty years ago in Tennessee, in the middle of a stream. He was crossing by stepping on stones from his bank, I from mine. In the middle we balanced unsteadily, with the water splashing into our boots, and challenged each other. He was an oldish man in black clothes, with white hair bushing from under a broad-brimmed black hat, and he shouted out in a singsong voice words which I carefully wrote down afterward. I was collecting speech, and I found it curious that he used a noun as a verb:

"Howdy! Pretty day. Yessir. What's your name? Where do you all come from? Where do you all expectation to end? I am Sam Robinson. I am a preacher. I go everywhere. I belong to no one and no one belongs to me. I belong to myself. Sam Robinson—remember—he don't belong to no one. There's right smart of Robinsons in the next creek. They raise hogs."

Samuel Robinson—the perpetual, quintessential American Pilgrim, though less dry than the usual Pilgrim Father. Independent, religious, a ruthless old cuss, restless—the prototype of the wandering American who moves on, scrapping things, answerable to none, the custodian of the famous American libertarian Dream, knotty in conscience and yet issuing the jaunty, general optimism of the country, an optimism that survives disillusion. When that occurs he strikes camp and leaves his litter behind him—a ghost town, a dust bowl, the rocky fields of New England; in modern times, an exhausted oil well, a wife or two. He is a complete man, a wiseacre perhaps, but not an eccentric. His community does not like the nonconformist: a slight deviation from scriptural norm and he may be called a Communist. He is, you notice, practical and he likes a deal. And he likes to announce it: remember—his family raises hogs. As T. C. Haliburton's New England peddler, Sam Slick, put it in *The Clockmaker*, "Braggin' saves advertisin'." He is far more conscious of other Robinsons (his family) than his opposite number in Europe is.

Hundreds of thousands of Sams now are moving to California, the Promised Land of sun, electronics and the bomb. And there, the Dream manifests itself in strange religions, strange theories of education and behavior: in violence, but also in an extraordinary dreamy soft-voiced gentleness of manners. They are the best automobile drivers in the world. They are churchgoers. I am always astonished, after the empty churches of an English Sunday, to see how packed the American churches are. I do not know if Americans are more pious than the British, but the American community likes church attendance. Sam Robinson hangs on to the Victorian Sunday; but, unlike the Victorians, he is cheerful about it, and devotes another part of the day to the real American religion: shopping. Henry James said that an American would lose his self-respect if he failed, on any day, to shop. On second thought, he was referring to Mrs. Sam Robinson, not to her husband.

Sam Robinsonism, in its serious sense, is responsible also for expatriation. He does not always move West: he often moves East. Just as he left Europe for America, to realize, in freedom, the beautiful American Idea, so many other Sams leave it and return to Europe to find the lost reality. They feel the ideal Republic has been betrayed and that America is a wilderness. These Sams are very often intellectuals, for the American intellectual complains bitterly of his isolation in the American community—with some justice. He is not in business and is often made boisterous fun of by the businessman. He objects to the commercialization of values and to fanaticism, and he has one great achievement to his credit: he helped (if he stayed at home) to make the American Civil Liberties Union one of the strongest in the world. He is the American conscience. If America is now emerging from a long period of intolerance, it's due largely to the influence of the egghead. When they are stirred to face fundamental problems, Americans do face them.

The Sam Robinsons who return to Europe are indignant, idealistic and pernickety. They idealize foreign cultures, they join foreign political causes: they are always searching. Yet they still "belong to themselves" in whatever territory they "light out" into. Years ago, walking in short, skipping steps down the Boulevard du Montparnasse, a pale, spry, shabby American used to pass me with a cigar in his mouth. I knew he was an American because he wore lighter clothes and lighter-soled shoes than a European does. He was a disillusioned fighter from some old Balkan War, now a punctual, efficient yet dreamy journalist. Poor—what a lot could be written about that little-known type, the "poor" American—he lived frugally, respectably and chastely in a modest hotel that was a notorious house of assignation. He was amused and concerned about me because I was young and he wished to cure me of any tendencies I had to be a capitalist, imperialist enemy of the ideal Republic and the brotherhood of man. He was kind to the whores and to people down on their luck; he was always helping people out with small loans of money. He was never without a cigar, he was always taking pills, he always had an ulcer and a wintry smile.

He had one secret passion into which he flung himself with true American romantic enterprise: on Saturday afternoons he got in touch with "the other side," so full of notabilities and (no doubt) the final home of the ideal Republic. Usually he got in touch with Shakespeare, and with American thoroughness he typed out what Shakespeare said. Although a dedicated atheist who deplored the way things had gone in the United States, he played the organ in the American church on Sundays and Wednesdays.

I have met such seekers of the ideal Republic all over the world. They often run into a dilemma if they marry a fellow seeker in Europe. For the European seeker is bound to believe that the Republic is in America; and this kind of American is bound to think it is in Europe. A very American secondary trait is marked in these Sams, who impress Europeans by their innocence and idealism: perpetually disappointed, they manage to be innocent and cynical at the same time.

I have said that Sam Robinson was "poor." Really, he was simply not well-off. The real poor in the United States are the Negroes, the Mexicans, the Puerto Ricans and the cotton peasantry of the Deep South. One of the evils of an affluent society is that it shuts out the real poor, blaming them—as the British Victorians did—for being unindustrious; also the affluent are in terror of them. Yet in terms of sensibility and civilization I have often found, say, the Puerto Rican elevator man, barman and so on, a more rewarding individual, more thoughtful and imaginative company than his standard customers. And better mannered.

A second fundamental character-shape comes groping toward me out of the fog of my American fantasy. He is none other than Hiawatha as we see him in Longfellow's poem, the hero who can do anything: crush rocks with his magic mittens, stride miles at a step, create maize, build a canoe, destroy disease, install the reign of peace and culture. In contemporary form he is the practical man and technician who—under Longfellow's guidance—tells you how he does everything. There are university Hiawathas; there are Hiawathas in bars, planes, trains, ships, libraries, laboratories and at evening parties. Like Longfellow (his apologist), he has the mastery of slow, deliberate, inexhaustible utterance. He is a founding figure of the American Saga who inherits his art from the long lonely evenings of the log cabin. It appears that every American is born with the inalienable right—if he cares to insist on it—to total monologue. Hiawatha's influence on vernacular literature is enormous; indeed he invented it. On a higher level, he manifests himself in the novels of Melville, Faulkner and the later works of Henry James.

He also has had an influence on American social habits, for he has made the anecdote supreme in American talk. There is no common ground between anecdote and conversation, for the latter depends on interruption, whereas the anecdote demands reverent attention. In private life American manners are notoriously good, and the European who forgets himself and interrupts the slow blossoming of an anecdote by saying, for example, that he, too, knew a man who filled a jumping frog with lead pellets and induced a mutation in the spawn—the European who commits this kind of outrage will be kindly treated; but by the patient looks on the faces of the company, and by the fact that the original anecdote will be taken up at the precise point at which it was interrupted, he will know he has committed a ghastly solecism and that Longfellow is turning in his grave.

Hiawatha is basic American because he loves a fact. "The fact," Robert Frost has written, "is the sweetest dream that labor knows." (I may be asked if Frost was being ironical. I doubt it; but on the exalted face of a poet there is sometimes a smile.) Hiawatha's facts are dreams: there lies his spell. I would be willing to speculate on the influence of Hiawatha on the pragmatism of William James, but I will take the humbler example of a Texas oilman with whom I spent a few days at Manaus on the Amazon.

American practicality occasionally meets a challenge. The town of Manaus, in Brazil, is such a challenge to all Hiawathas; it is the practical man's dream, for every stone of it was brought across several thousands of miles of sea, river and forest from Portugal. My friend's name was Wilkins, and his parents, foreseeing in their shrewd American way that they had brought a master technician into the world, and wishing to free him from distracting personal inconveniences, efficiently named him Wilk. Wilk Wilkins: it is like sleeve and piston, nut and bolt. Wilk Wilkins was expert in building oil refineries. And as we chugged up the Amazon, Wilk uttered the saga—and Longfellow could not have done better—of how one built an oil refinery. From the foundations upward. Indeed, Wilk could be said to have built a whole refinery for me that morning, pipe by pipe and girder by girder. I was exhausted by the amount of concrete we put in. If ever I build an oil refinery single-handed it will be because of the thorough grounding he gave me. At the end—remembering some affront he had received from one of his employers—Wilk went into reverse and pipe by pipe, girder by girder, pulled the whole thing down again. If ever I pull my refinery down I shall do it exactly as Wilk taught me.

After a short lunch, we moved on to other feats. Wilk could build houses, so we had How Hiawatha Built Him a House, not omitting radiant heat, water supply and drainage, and we did it room by room. That done, there was How Hiawatha Built Him a Better House. This brought up the subject of why you want a house. And so, inevitably, we moved on to Minnehaha, Hiawatha's Wedding, or rather to his Next Wedding—there had been more than one Minnehaha in Wilk's life—and, to get that straightened out, we had to go into his Other Wooings. With the same technical skill he took these ladies to pieces to show how they worked, and since he had an impartial mind he did the same for himself. We had Hiawatha's mother, Wenonah, another dominant American type, whose husband had not done right by her; in true American style, Hiawatha fought and defeated his father. But that left him with Wenonah trouble: Hiawatha's Problem with his Mother, his consequent Drinking and Not-Drinking, his Illnesses; and so on to Psychiatry and Time Off for Fishing and Hunting. Finally we got to that very un-American problem, Hiawatha's Plan to Prevent his New Minnehaha from having a car of her own. His solution was, characteristically, constructional. Hiawatha Built Him a One-Car Garage.

I believe the Kinsey Report is now out of date, but an interesting ambiguity appeared in the character of Wilk Wilkins and I have often asked myself whether it has any bearing on the love of activity, the strong development of will, the feeling for enterprise and power that lie behind the technological and constructive genius of Americans; and especially whether it has any bearing on their relations with Minnehaha. The ambiguity came out in this way. There is a famous opera house in Manaus and Wilk Wilkins worshiped it. The sight of its dome made his buried emotional life burst out. We would turn street corners and he would look back to see how the dome looked now. We gazed at it from the river, we gazed at it from the forest. He adored the thing helplessly. It would come into view as if it were following us, and once more he would exclaim—and he must have done this fifty times a day—"There she goes, the old son of a bitch."

That seems an odd conjunction of noun and pronoun.

The function of Hiawatha's imagination (Tocqueville has written) is "to devise what may be useful and to represent the real." He faces situations frontally, in the classical manner, and mistrusts the oblique approach. He will build, he will pull down, he will change. His emphasis on the will exposes him, under stress, to breakdown—hence the outbreaks of hysteria in

American life—but he is equal to that. He thinks failure is wicked, so he turns to psychiatry, for in it he finds another kind of engineering—one for treating the psyche as if that, too, were a machine. More and more consciousness is what Hiawatha admires, and in this he builds on the traditions of humanism; though, by a paradox, psychiatry can easily be a way of evading moral issues: to be told one has an ill-adjusted ego is flattering to one's self-regard; to be told one is self-destructively selfish is not so flattering. Mechanical repair seems more practical than moral overhaul; and Hiawatha is a practical optimist.

I have personally known a few people in England who go to psychiatrists. They do so for some serious reason—a real breakdown or criminal action. In America I have known many more who are on and off the psychiatrist's couch for trivial reasons—business disputes, lack of social success and so on. I am told it's the rage among schoolgirls. In Europe one goes to the psychiatrist in despair and, if the man is a Freudian, to face devastating revelations; but Hiawatha goes optimistically in search of the power more consciousness will give him. Hiawatha has removed the pessimism from psychology, just as some American religious sects remove the central idea of the drama of suffering from the Christian myth. Hiawatha is looking for more extroverted activity, more opportunity for the will, and he presses forward, even when he gropes, on the humanist's path believing in perfectibility *tout court*.

Hiawatha is not sad. I think sadness is not valued in America. Or rather, the only people who retain sadness are the immigrants; they are looking back on emotional losses. Their children will not know sadness. They may know disappointment; Hiawatha is often disappointed. Disappointment sits like a dismal bird on many shoulders in the crowd of the New York subway. I repeat there is no place for failure, for sadness and the tragic, but when these inevitably occur, the victims look discarded and superfluous. They have worked and willed too much, like those phalanxes of aging, pensioned men and women who pack the benches of the cross streets on upper Broadway in the summer, with the dust blowing past their expressionless faces, looking at the traffic. America is a kind country; but its ethos has no use for the casualty or the old. And age is premature.

Hiawatha has built two fine cities: dramatic New York and beautiful San Francisco. I am told New Orleans qualifies also; I wish I had been there.

Most of his other cities are not, frankly, a success; he has a fatal weakness for sameness. Compared with the European, the American urban scene is not squalid, but it is drab, uninteresting and impersonal. It does not surprise after the first encounter. His new small towns, run off the assembly line, are poor packaged goods. On the other hand his suburban architecture is intimate, charming, restful and gay; his nineteenth-century and early-twentieth-century domestic buildings are far more attractive than the same thing in Great Britain or in France. I hope Hiawatha's passion for tearing things down will not destroy what he did well.

In my lifetime I have seen America move out of the swaggering, self-righteous and hectoring mood of the twenties, into the humiliation and revolution of the thirties, and finally into the startled discovery that it had become a great world power. Great powers are always respected, even distantly admired, but they are not loved, as the history of Britain, Spain and Russia shows: they protect but they also limit the freedom and swamp the lives of weaker peoples. The desire to be loved for themselves is an anxiety of the rich; but in the famous American desire to be loved there is something else, and I am not sure what it is, except that Europeans are without it. Some American writers put it down to a desire for reassurance: to be unloved or only partly loved is a point marked up against one, a sign of failure. If this *is* an American trait, it is obviously childish; it may go back to the anxiety Americans feel for the prestige and *success* of their children and to the idealization of childhood. Europeans—but we must except the Italians—are usually accused by Americans of over-disciplining their children, yet children like authority, order and knowing where they stand. It has often struck me that Americans put a great strain on children in demanding success of them, and perhaps that success is demanded because the father's role is secondary. Criticism is not liked in America; it is a masculine trait. Mother does *not* like it; she thinks it is an attack on her person.

Since Americans enjoy being Americans, they must get something pleasurable and positive out of this anxiety—perhaps the feeling that anxiety and self-examination avert catastrophe. They are very patient and tender psychologists; very truthful in human relationships, almost laboriously so. The pursuit of truth is activity. It has the sanction of being work. "Why do we do it?" I have heard an American mother say when she was being martyrized by a spoiled child and had yielded once more. "It must be," she said, "to satisfy some very deep need." It does; as a troubled perfectionist she believed in the future, and the future is embodied in the child.

Still, catastrophe cannot be averted. American history is the story of a great success at the cost of enormous casualties. Huck Finn is one. He is a vagabond child who has lived through horrors. There is even a romantic and anarchic American tradition—dating from the lonely forest and mountain life—that society itself is evil (see Fenimore Cooper and Thoreau), that the meaning of life is in its terrors and horrors (see American Gothic novels). There is an irreverent, sardonic enjoyment of disaster that is opposed to Yankee moralism. (As Josh Billings said, "Americans like Caustic Things.") The pessimism of Ambrose Bierce, the anger of Mencken, the iconoclasm and comic diatribes of Henry Miller, the large number of Americans who enjoy giving you macabre hints of life's awfulness from a highly cherished, suicidal, intensely private corner of themselves, are a refreshing and important corrective to the blandness and flavorlessness of standard American life.

The nation's films and its popular literature revel in violence, gangsterism, sadism, alcoholism, drug addiction and sexual misdemeanor, and these, when exported, give a horrifying picture of American life. It is no doubt not a real picture; but it is an account of fantasies that are going on in the hard-pressed public mind. Perhaps real life is dull.

So my third American fundamental type emerges: Sebastian, descendant of the saint. He arrived on American shores with the Discovery, when he faced all the terrors, the moral chaos and the loneliness of those who leave established societies. As he courageously, ruthlessly, laboriously established himself his character changed. The original Saint Sebastian is usually shown by our sadistic painters suffering agony from a shower of shrewdly aimed arrows. The new democratic American Sebastian—he has dropped the aristocratic San or Saint—does not wait romantically or resignedly, posing for martyrdom. He is a technician. He has ingeniously invented an invisible apparatus for shooting arrows into himself.

In the fifteen years preceding the Cuban crisis, the United States was loud with the cries of the self-wounded. A lot of this self-criticism was very healthy. Intelligent people had got sick of being called Communists just because they thought for themselves. People had got sick of that lie in the soul which, I'm afraid, I heard more than one respectable person utter in defense of the late Senator McCarthy: "I don't like what he's doing, but someone had to do it."

I remember hearing that sort of thing in Tennessee in the big-time days of the Ku Klux Klan. Self-criticism pointed out how preposterously the idea of freedom had come to mean almost exclusively "economic private enterprise." The attack on the backwardness of American education up to the age of sixteen, and on the deadening, hectic cramming system at higher levels afterwards, is good, as is the current frenzy to catch up. My clever and charming students at American universities were almost all Sebastians, agonizing in a system they found frustrating. They had the usual American illusion that European life, especially the British, is more leisurely. The opposite is true: there is nothing more relaxed than automatic cramming; it induces the stupor of the hum of the machine.

Ask any modern immigrant his first reaction to American life. "Everything is so easy here," he says. It is. But the American Sebastian knows that life, to be creative, first has to be intense and difficult. He may fear to stick his neck out in a conformist society, but he at least begins to see he is a coward.

There is a bad side to Sebastianism. That prayer one often sees in American hotels, printed on a card (generally beside a huge menu) and showing Uncle Sam on his knees begging for forgiveness, is an absurd piece of self-indulgence. Sometimes it is hard to distinguish Sebastian from Narcissus. "We are great bleeders," says one of my New York friends; to call oneself a coward may be no more than self-protective. Such a bout of self-criticism is likely to turn, in the end, into its opposite and become cock-a-hoop.

Like the Mississippi, the main stream of American life does not seriously change. For myself, the first attraction of America is in the diversity of its peoples. The immigrants have electrified the nation. The hard Anglo-Saxon, who is money-minded, adventurous, politically austere, law-abiding, sternly conventional in his social life, is saved from his own conservative insensibility by the humanity of the Irishman and the Italian, the sensitive or dynamic Jew, the wistful Puerto Rican, the tragic or splendacious Negro, the intelligent Greek, and so on. They bring temperament, genius and vitality. Relatively new countries fall quickly into decadence—as the history of the South American nations shows—unless there is a steady renewal from outside in every generation. New countries work people to death: the stress on youth means early aging.

The final attraction of America for me is in the popular tradition and the figures of American folklore—the gorgeous liars, the muckrakers, the storytellers, the homespun philosophers, and so on, who have created something of the Elizabethan spirit of Bartholomew's Fair—and although they belong to the vanished world of the frontier, their spirit still walks.

My last American type is, therefore, the shade of Barnum. In his sense America is, indeed, the greatest show on earth, and Barnumism is indigenous. He celebrates the "free-for-all" of American life. He conducts the colossal scandals. (The taste for the great scandal is one that binds Americans closely to the Russians.) Barnum has an instinct for circus; he runs elections, parades, the sporting crowd. His vulgarities always have a stylish, preposterous air. My American friends often reproach me for enjoying these shows which stop at nothing; in California, not at death itself. Barnum celebrates the enjoyment of total loss of dignity (the uproar when the Mona Lisa was exhibited) and exploits the native irreverence and exhibitionism (Father's away: let's have a party).

Barnumism goes very far. I was often told in McCarthy's time that I was quite wrong about the significance of McCarthyism, that it was just one more American circus, one more saturnalia. I cannot regard the Ku Klux Klan, the John Birch Society or McCarthyism as circuses—and my list includes the Congressional investigation committees, such as the House Un-American Activities Committee, which are much more significant than the KKK today: they strike me as being illnesses. Perhaps, in Europe, we are too doctrinaire. These things apart, however, the genial hullabaloos are some sort of manifestation of folk culture, maybe also a perversion of it. In Britain we used to have bear-baiting.

There is a certain American solemnity that calls for relief. Jazz is a triumphant American invention, and its appeal to the rest of the world has been irresistible. The Negro, the most serious casualty of American life, has after all done more for America in this sense than all the enlightened people of New England and the highbrow Middle West put together. Two generations ago Rudyard Kipling pointed to the enormous dynamic potential of the Jew in American life; his foresight has been exact. The despised Irish have produced a president.

The European Ego eventually explodes and goes to pieces in the United States and has to be reassembled. It is only fair to add that the American Ego explodes and disintegrates in the same way in Europe; but it is never really reassembled. All one can say, in these days when the world is smaller, is that little groups of the like-minded, with the same tastes and affections, find it is easier to change places in both continents and to meet. They must not be deluded. An American friend in London says the difference between America and Europe is that "in Europe you prune your trees in order to train their growth; in America we let them grow." Europe has grown by saying no, America by saying yes. Opposite points of view: foreignness is an important, life-giving and, fortunately, ineradicable essence.

I never agree that the distinctive quality of American democracy derives from social equality, or that this exists no more strongly in America than in other advanced countries: the distinctive thing is equality of contact.

"Lousy day," says the chirpy New York waiter when he brings me my breakfast; he might be a cheerful brother who has suddenly turned up in the family. It is an old saying that there is more fraternity than there is equality or liberty in the United States.

I enjoy the waiter's greeting, but in enjoying it, I realize I lose something of my private identity, and so does he lose something of his. But this brotherliness is a pleasant, amorphous family feeling. I think of America, in the end, as a huge, scattered, mixed-up family from which father vanished years ago leaving no address. The family are on their own.

[1963]

10

Across the Vast Land

From San Francisco we flew north: out of the sunny city into the struggle with Nature. Clouds bowled over Oregon, darkened over Washington, the rainstorms began and, below, the forests came tramping down in endless wet armies to meet us. The sea turned gray, and it seemed that it, too, had its forests, for when we looked out over the water, innumerable wooded islands, like schools of whales, were nosing northward with us into dirty weather. The sea turned sallow and then rank ocherish where the Fraser River stained it far beyond its delta with the silt of the Rockies; until, in a sudden vertical mix-up of mountain, cloud, sea, forest and long, straight streets of bungalows and green lawns, we bumped down into Vancouver. From the runway Nature lowered stormily on the city and looked stupendously rock-thighed and high. We were at the beginning of the four-thousand-mile journey across Canada, and the Rockies stood like a lion in the path.

Were we in a new country? The immigration official had a Chinese face; the waiters at the hotel were Italian, German or Hungarian; there were Irish in the streets. So far, we might still be in the United States. But small things showed we were not: that first hot, full-bodied cup of tea in the hotel, tea drunk as a stimulant, not as a sedative; thicker, woollier clothes, provincial shops, an American accent softened by the quiet British intonation. A quiet, calm country, evidently not as rich as California. Anyone wanting to swear used British profanities. The girls with the "natural" European look, rather than the American artifice. Smaller cars on the streets. An impression of restraint rather than exuberance; of tidiness: Vancouver cares for its gardens. In general, a mingling of British and American traits. One could say, outwardly American, inwardly British, yet perhaps Canada is the reverse of that. Perhaps Canada would turn out to be Canadian? Would this identifiable, distinctive Canada be revealed to us?

It was too soon to say. But a story by Thomas Carlyle and his wife came into my head, a good Scottish story, and almost anything Scottish has a bearing on Canada. An earnest metaphysical lady, in the midst of an argument with Mrs. Carlyle, had been driven into a corner. "All right," she said, "I accept the universe." This was reported to Carlyle, who said, "She'd better." From the beginning of their history until even today, the inhabitants of northern America have been in a similar situation. They have had to accept Nature—not the mild, friendly Nature of Europe, but Nature wicked, relentless and hostile. And Nature has, on the whole, been far harsher to Canadians than to Americans.

From the beginning the men of the northern pincer movement of exploration on the Saint Lawrence tended to move south or southwest, into a kinder climate. When the United States was prospering rapidly, with seaports open all year round and an easy contact with Europe and the wealth of the Indies, the Canadians were frozen in. The gods that rule the Canadians are the Greenland icecap, the frozen polar sea and the lasting effects of the Ice Age. Changeable as it may be, and very hot in the summer, the Canadian climate is rudely northern. Of the whole country the part of British Columbia where we stood was the only mild region, where the rose blooms in every season and the azalea and rhododendron flourish, where flowers can grow to the full. (All across Canada we were struck by the smallness of the flowers.) For an enormous portion of this second-largest country in the world is a barely inhabited Siberia. Until the great advance of modern technology,

Canadians were locked in a grinding struggle with the climate, with exhausting distances and, at last, with the Rockies. The Canadian passes were almost insuperable; Nature there was at her worst.

For nearly a century longer than in the United States, life in Canada has been struggling to emerge from the epic stage; it is still pretty well in that stage in the Arctic, despite the airplane, the diesel engine, electric power and the opening up of enormous mineral wealth. Until the railway and the plane, Canada was opened up by the canoe and the heavy labor of portages; even now at Fort Smith Rapids, on the Slave River, they are carrying ships on trailers across country to rejoin navigable water. From west to east, the most thickly populated belt is only two hundred miles wide, and of the nineteen million people, the greater part live in the Toronto triangle and the province of Quebec; and trees, mountains, grass and the water of tens of thousands of lakes crowd down on man. The machine has conquered the climate now: the country people are moving into towns, but when one asks what is the distinctive quality of the Canadian, the old trauma is at the back of his mind. "It is," as the historian Jean-C. Falardeau wrote, "the allegiance of the solitary to his solitude." The winds come down the central corridor from the north into the cities; the north is always in people's heads. The short summer and long winter impress Nature on the mind even in cities, where, one might think, Nature could be forgotten.

So in June we stood in Vancouver, in the long, straight American-style streets, and could feel the north in our backs. The warm weather was late in coming—and Vancouver can do better than this, as one realizes when the sun bursts out. It is not a handsome town—what can one expect? Eighty years ago it was a rough little lumber port; now it is the third city of Canada and has a fine university. It has a stupendous situation. The fjords and channels of Victoria and Vancouver are one of the most powerful sights of North America. The clouds storm over snow peaks, the wild forests storm down to the sea, which here has a sort of herding, animal force. I do not mean storm in the sense of thunder, lightning and gale. I mean that they affect the senses and the imagination in that way, like wild, romantic poetry.

The people of Vancouver are expansive. They take to the sea. It was not long before we were cruising in the sounds, the fjords and among the islands near the city, listening to the news of the weather fronts on the radio and running for quieter water. And there, as we penetrated these deep inlets, mile after mile, the wildness of the country, the sense of animal freedom, was brought home. Forest everywhere, forest at every turn, forest behind forest, mountain behind mountain; in some new stretch of water, sea and forest would seem to have been laughing together as we came in, and to have fallen into a watchful and not well-intentioned silence, as we dodged the floating timber and forest jetsam.

Here and there, on some steep slope, the forest was gashed, and that was a symbol of Canada—the felled trees, the logs rolling into the water. One saw the man with the ax, one heard the scream of the power saw and the weird sound of a tree falling. Here the logs were just waste matter, but on other rivers we would see those orderly rafts, floating silently, like fast geometrical propositions, from the forest to the mills or to the harbors. The log rafts, the log piles of Canada give to the inexhaustible savage landscape the first heartening signs of craftsmanship and the skills of civilization.

This coast begins to have that sunny sophistication which is typical of the Pacific from Valparaíso and Lima to Monterey and San Francisco. The new villas have the California originality, and one can see, in the luxuriance of Victoria and Vancouver, why the people exuberantly dream that this is the site of a new Mediterranean civilization. So it may become—though I would have thought that the Scandinavian is the more likely prospect in this latitude. But for the present there remains the fact that eighty miles up the Fraser River, and once one is out of the rich farmlands, Nature begins to flower. Through the terrible gulches of this savage river, in 1857, the disheartened miners came down to found Vancouver; the old military trail is now a fantastic motorway, yet one still feels the warning in rock and tree that one feels all over Canada when one turns north: do not go too far. In a step you will be in total solitude, where leaves turn into eyes. And as you sit comfortably among the businessmen in a Vancouver club, watching ships load wheat for China and Europe and the timber that supplies half the pulp of the Free World, your mind wanders off northward and you ask what people are doing a hundred, two hundred miles away.

The answer is peculiar. To begin with there are very few people. But there is an odd official statistic claiming that Canadians make more telephone calls than any other people on earth. Up there, then, they are talking. Stay for a few days in a forest cabin and you will remember only two sounds: the scampering of chipmunks on the roof and the daylong shrilling of the party line that links the solitaries of the wilderness or a forest. The Canadian is not a talkative man: the shrilling bell asserts that, among the billions of trees, a human being exists. Possibly alone.

All this is far less true of the cheerful, gregarious, outward-looking life of cities like Vancouver. At one time British Columbia might have drifted into the American Union; this is now impossible, and no one in British Columbia would want it. But there is a close affinity of temperament with the people of the American Pacific. They share what South Americans call "the Pacific sadness," which is not sadness at all but a sense of having got to the limit you dreamed of. You are in heaven at last. *Now* what do you do? You dream no longer, which is a loss; so you enact dreams. Hence the exuberance, the fantasy. (It is not surprising that Vancouver, its dreams lost, should have taken over the illicit drug trade from Montreal, though perhaps that is the old tradition of the China trade.)

Steady-minded people from Toronto and Ottawa enjoy this breath of heaven for a while; then suddenly they get worried about education and their children. A solemn Nova Scotian in Winnipeg said to me, "In Calgary it's all hoopla; in British Columbia they're mad." They pack up and return East, for education does better in purgatory than in heaven. Something like this occurs in California too. But if British Columbia has its taste for gorgeous boosters, for lotus-eating and pleasure, it takes pleasure more strenuously. The escape is to the sea, to the camp and to those overwhelming Canadian passions—skiing and fishing. Canadians are men of the open air. When Nature relents in the struggle she soothes them with sports. The Canadians use their dry, sunny winters as skillfully as the Swiss use theirs.

There is a brotherly bickering between Vancouver and San Francisco, farther south: a shopkeeper said, "My American brother-in-law is killing himself. He has a hardware business and he's always there from early morning to late at night, every weekday. 'Why do you do it?' I ask him. 'I have to do it because my competitors do it. I would soon be out of business if I didn't.' You see, he can't stop chasing the dollar. It isn't that he needs it; it isn't that he is greedy either. The fact is, he *enjoys* making money; it excites him to make it and spend it. It doesn't excite us quite so much. We don't live to work. We want to get some fishing in."

Here we were on the fringe of the perpetual Canadian question, which gets more and more complicated the more one looks at it. Personal relationships across the border are excellent. They are made so by Nature itself; life in each province runs on a natural north-south axis, within Canada and outside. That is the way trade goes. But historically and politically Canada is a confederation of regions running from east to west; on the face of it, Canada is a nation living against its own current. When he looks across the boundary, the Canadian sees the prodigiously wealthy American nation of 180 million people prospering under the simplicity of the American Idea, while he himself, one of a population roughly one tenth as large, is struggling with the knottiness of the Canadian Conundrum. There is a smile of success on the American face; on the Canadian brow there is a notch of admiration, envy and puzzlement. Looking up from his struggle he feels a mixture of attraction and repulsion about everything in the United States.

In the euphoria of the postwar boom that ended in 1959, the Canadian felt he was standing up fairly well to the cultural and economic and political alternative that America offers to his life. Since the slump, he has realized how much of his industry and the new mining wealth is in American hands.

It is often said that he prefers to invest his own wealth abroad rather than in Canada itself; this is a habit of old-style mercantile finance. In the nineteenth century he held out successfully against the doctrine of Manifest Destiny; how is he to hold out now against a peaceful penetration by American business and American ideas that often differ profoundly from his own? He is not American. He is not British (and in Quebec he is not French), for the attachment to Britain is no more than a respectful emotion; nowadays the United States puts in far more capital and takes out more goods than Britain does or ever did. Yet he is enough British, American and French to be lost when he asks himself what a Canadian is.

In consequence, between the time you board the train at Vancouver and get out of it three or four thousand miles away in Quebec, you will have crossed a continent of doubt. "We are a negative country," or "We do not know who we are," such remarks are made right across the continent until one gets to Montreal. There the French Canadian—the Canadien—*does* know, but chiefly in a rhetorical way, who he is. The doubt sounds bad. But Canadians are proud of their doubt. It is the expression of that deep Scottish caution that is a marked strain in so many of them. In their dilemma they find a certain vanity and, it seemed to me, a strength of the kind that sends down roots slowly.

Canada (it has been said) is a country held together by two railway termini and four thousand miles of telegraph wire. You get into the train at Vancouver and soon learn what distance means in a country with a small population. On the opening journey to Banff, for miles up the broad yellow Fraser, we were in the comfortable farmland. Hours go by. In the melancholy twilight across the river one sees not the lights of a city but those of an occasional few houses; or a boat tied up by the river at sunset, the loneliest sight in the world. There were few tourists on the train so early in the season; the passengers were a working crowd. At night, as the climb begins into the Rockies, one is among the trees; in the morning, on the mountains, there are more trees. The names of stations raise hopes. But Rogers is a ruined lumber mill and two or three boarded-up shacks; Beavermouth is a woman's face looking out of the window of the frame house as she washes clothes; Golden looks like a camp—it's a scattered township with a frame hotel, a timberyard, hundreds of pale-blue cars. They must have come in from hidden settlements. The trees flicker by; the armies of firs relieved by the stippled poplars, burned by frost, hour after hour. The flickering hurts the eyes. Occasionally one sees two or three elk standing under the firs, senatorial and stupid.

The train is running beside the coppery, foaming, rocky water of the Kicking Horse River up to the pass that takes the mind back to the Gold Rush tales, and by now the mountain walls are standing out, greenish-gray and naked, snow-slabbed, with their terraces arranged by Nature in dreadful precipices.

When, later on, one gets out and stands looking at these mountains, one has conflicting sensations. They are noble like massive cathedrals; they are brutal in their mass; they are silent and indifferent as if they were looking through one with empty eyes set in ice and granite above the tree line, and the sky looks clear and cold as the long evening goes on; yet to the imagination they crowd upon one with a sort of inner noise.

They are less friendly than the Andes—they are grayer; they lack the urbanity and—I may as well say it—the intelligence of the Alps. This is absurd anthropomorphism, I know, but I am thinking of the poverty of human association in the scene and I realize that, in general, Europeans have to be trained to feel the emotion aroused in North Americans by the stupendous North American geography. We lack that feeling for plain scale. I thought of Mackenzie, Fraser and all the others who canoed across Canada and fought their way through these walls. Canada was out of luck again: the passes in the American Rockies were much easier. It was a feat getting the railway through here to Vancouver, and (with national pride driving them) it was as great a feat getting the transcontinental highway through in 1962. It is one of the spectacular rides of the western continent.

Again and again, the talk on the train is all about settlers, the newness of everything. (It must have been like this in the U.S. West after the 1840s.) The Poles and Italians are admired for going out to the harsh places. The Germans and British are technicians, doctors, and so on. The Americans—who keep to themselves as they do all over the world—are in the oil fields of Alberta. The Dutch? Opinion is unanimous: they are by far the best settlers. I have found this opinion in South America too. The Dutch are patient and unromantic. In Banff I found a young Dutchman working in a bar, and his life story epitomizes everything the immigrant of these days thinks and feels. In Holland he had been a butcher. "I came here five years ago," he said, "because I was fed up with army service in Indonesia. I chose Canada rather than the United States partly because of the fuss about entering the States— the forms, the questions and all that—but chiefly because there is more scope for the individual in Canada."

Canadians often stress this: sometimes they mean that the Canadian is more individual than the American, which is true; at any rate the feeling for uniformity is far less pronounced. At other times they mean that the individual is freer and has a better chance in a country that is still in the stage of being opened up.

"Wages are not as high in Canada as they are in the States. Life is duller. But living is cheap," the Dutchman went on. "Everything is very easy. Of course the food is poor, all this canned stuff and no fresh vegetables like you get in Holland, and my wife complains about that. And education is not really good—I mean compared with Holland. My eldest son, who is ten, already suffers from that—no foreign languages. In Europe he would be learning French and German and English as well as his Dutch, and speak them as I do. The youngest is far behind what he would be in our country, but it does not affect him because the Canadian school was his first. They speak English perfectly."

"But Canada is supposed to be bilingual," I said.

"In theory, yes. In fact, no. Only for the French," he said, "in spite of all the bilingual notices. I'm sad when I see my children forgetting their Dutch; they speak it only at home and only when their friends are not about. They would be ashamed. You have to swallow things like that. They have a fine open life. They are skiing half the day; we don't see them till they come home in the evening. Life is very free. In Holland if you are a butcher, as I was, you have to be apprenticed and certificated and it takes years; you are fixed in your trade. But here life is open. You can be anything. Of course there are losses. You wince at the vulgar advertisements on television. Life is perhaps a little dull. It is not gay. I used to go to the south of France every year, and for pleasure and civilization there is nothing to beat that. Still, you get wonderful sun in the winter in the Rockies—people forget the sun and clean dry air of the Canadian winter. It's healthy. There is wonderful fishing; I have never had such fishing in my life. My family in Rotterdam keep telling me to go back to Holland, but I've made my decision, I don't regret it and I shall stick to it."

The Italians, the Germans, and so on, give much the same report. It is always the scope for the individual they stress; though at the top of the tree, the Canadian executive in an American-controlled firm complains of the impersonal efficiency and of a boss whom he does not know and who gives him orders from outside Canada. The same complaint—the complaint of the distant, unknown boss—is heard in the United States, and I conclude that Canada still largely belongs to the opening-up period of development; the United States has passed out of that into the rule of the organization man. The Canadians for the most part live in a world where it is possible to be individual, and individuality is what one notices most about them. Their silences, hesitations, doubts, the strongly individual lines taken by various provinces emphasize this.

You cross the continental divide. This country is all national park. The site of Banff, within the Banff National Park in the Rockies, is spectacular. The town looks very Scottish, clean, trim. The Bow River flows under its granite bridge as gravely as does the Tweed. The celebrated lakes add to the sense of the Scottish highlands magnified. The Fine Arts School in Banff—Canada's painters are more notable than its writers—and the excellent Indian museum reflect a sort of Scottish seriousness. Basically Canada is Scottish and French—as one can see in the place names. And the Scottish traits come out in the careful, frugal attitude to money, the strictness of religion, the caution, the tenacity, the sentiment and even the superstitions. The dourness, a certain conceit in virtue, and the protective melancholy one often notices when a Canadian is doing well, are Scottish traits. It is said that Canadians are slow to quarrel, make friends slowly and are less highly strung than Americans. But if they do make friends it is for life—and if they do quarrel their passion is violent. I once asked a Canadian with a Scottish name if Canada might one day join the United States. He went white with rage, turned his back on me and sat muttering with anger. I feared he was going to call out the clans.

Banff is a playground, unspoiled by commercial vulgarities. It is full of healthy, cheerful young people, and their faces have a northern openness and candor. Their minds are on the ski runs. But I am not a mountain man, and the Rockies impressed me most from a distance, as we got out of them into the prairie, where the country in June is kinder, where tall grass grows, the poplar replaces the firs, and cattle are grazing. One is still over three thousand feet up at Calgary, and the country rolls. The wheat was springing out of the black soil, and at this cheerful city one sees the first signs of great wealth—the wealth of the cattle and oil men. Alberta and part of Saskatchewan float on oil and natural gas. Many a British family who sent a remittance man to these provinces sixty years ago must have some rich relations there—if they could ever be found—though most of them must have finished among the wreckage of colonization. (It is odd that we Englishmen go to the Americas to look for descendants, whereas Americans and Canadians come to us for ancestors.) Within living memory tens of thousands of settlers moved out of Manitoba, and from farther east, to these provinces, stuck out their early days in holes dug in the earth and covered with sods of turf, and struggled against drought, flood and blizzard. It broke thousands, but cities rose out of the struggle—Edmonton, Regina, Saskatoon with its university. And now people no longer fling themselves against Nature with their naked hands.

No, I have never been much of a mountain man—not, at any rate, since I escaped from Romantic literature. People forget how much the late eighteenth century and early nineteenth century have inflated the reputation of the mountain scene and have declared that the plains are monotonous. For myself the Canadian prairie, considered as a sight to the eye and an emotional experience, shares the spell of the Polish and the Russian steppe and has probably already produced people who have much in common. Most of the Dukhobors live in British Columbia, but there are some on the plains. There are also Hutterites. In this landscape you are likely to develop a sensibility to the Unseen and an impenetrable inner life. It is a region made for such sectarians who see homespun visions and who combine the chaotic and primitive injunctions of the Old Testament with Utopian views of society. But what absorbs the eye of the passing traveler is the subtle coloring and texture of the prairie country—those greens turning to madder and yellow, to grays and blues of intricate delicacy—and the land mass itself flowing from fold to fold, from horizon to horizon as the light changes and the wind moves over it. The wild duck fly up from among the prairie flowers and the hidden rivers, for one does not see a great river like the Saskatchewan until one comes suddenly upon it in its wide gully; a human being is no more than a dot of a pencil, a house or an elevator can be seen for an hour as one travels toward it. Look back an hour later and there its shape still stands like a ship one has passed at sea. There is no mist. The only sound is the wind. And the simple meeting of empty sky and lonely earth on the horizon's circle fills one with exaltation and fear.

The summer is hot. At Medicine Hat—"a wonderful clean town, just become a city," said the Negro attendant on the train; by "clean" he meant no crime or misdemeanor—temperatures go up to 110°. In the winter, at 50° below, the prairie must be a nightmare, though all Canadians speak of the winter sun. Wallace Stegner, who was brought up in Montana and Saskatchewan (in this region Americans and Canadians are indifferent to the frontier) has written in *Wolf Willow* a fine, precise and dramatic account of the prairie winter and of the madness of the thaw. He is no friend to frontier life, having lived through it in childhood; his contemporaries are of the same mind. They are moving fast into the towns. But the land has formed them so that they will never be like the people of other provinces.

The epic period of Canadian life is always near to one's mind, even when it goes back to the seventeenth and eighteenth centuries; perhaps because such a small population stands between oneself and the past. The Bow River flows into the Saskatchewan, and the waters of the Saskatchewan into Lake Winnipeg and Hudson Bay: it is extraordinary to think that the great river was discovered within a few years of La Salle's journey to the mouth of the Mississippi. In 1690 the French *voyageurs*, the fur traders, were making their way across the continent. "A man in the Canadian service," runs a Hudson's Bay Company report in the eighteenth century, "who cannot carry two packs of 80 lbs. each, one and a half leagues loses his Trip, that is, his Wages." I heard the same weight-carrying boast from a stumpy little métis, aged twenty-five, not so very long ago in Quebec. It is an irony of history that an American, the famous Peter Pond of Connecticut, was one of the first men to find an east-west route across the continent by way of the Saskatchewan. His discoveries were unknown to the treaty makers after the American Revolution, who were preoccupied with the eastern territories. So Canada, as we know it, got a chance to be viable and survive.

At Winnipeg the flat country was still with us, but now there were sappy scrub and long coppices of aspen, poplar and cottonwood. This is traditional wheat country, a continuation of North Dakota and Minnesota. Winnipeg is still called "the gateway to the West." I met a wiry, complaining old chap who had been thrown out of his job in Toronto and was working his way West "to get more scope for the individual." He was cheerful and kindly, but I could not tell him that his "trade" in industry was done for owing to automation. He would become a cranky "little man"; he came straight out of the Cockney seam in Canadian life and Canada would preserve his wiry eccentricity. He was driving a taxi in fighting form, through the dust of one of the ugliest and historically most interesting cities of the country. It has the ugliness of the English industrial Midlands, relieved by fine trees and by some pretty streets in the suburbs. The days of the great wheat fortunes are gone, and Winnipeg complains that Americans "dump" their wheat in what were

Canadian markets: it is an episode in Canada's struggle with American over-production. But since the Canadian sale of wheat to Russia last year, the position has improved. So Winnipeg still sells wheat but now has also turned to making clothes.

In this hot, dusty growing city of half a million, one meets at last a real, well-rooted Canada. Winnipeg is not as polished as Toronto or anywhere near as sophisticated as Montreal, but it is as individual as all other Canadian cities and puts the fundamental Canadian case. The first things to catch the eyes are the onion domes of the Russian Orthodox churches of the Ukrainians. Here the non-British immigrant becomes important. The Ukrainians came here in 1900 from the richest wheat-bearing lands of Russia. The older men still wear the long beard and sheepskin coat; the older women are still weather-scarred like Russian peasants. Up at Selkirk, on Lake Winnipeg, are the Scandinavians and Icelanders: in the city itself is a new Jewish population, as well as the German and Italian settlers who arrived in the last few years. The original population includes a very strong outpost of French Canadians, the descendants of French marriages with Indians and of the men of the fur trade. Their churches across the river in Saint Boniface and their seminary are the best buildings in the city. Winnipeg's money and power are in the hands of people of British stock, who are now less than half of the population. In other words, on the face of it, we have a melting pot.

But no. Canada does not easily melt. Until now its pride has been in *not* melting its population, in letting the minorities go their separate ways, in leaving people alone. The tradition started by the British, after the fall of Quebec, the tradition of noninterference with French customs, religion and education, has lasted. Indoctrination, Canadianization does not exist as a principle or practice, as Americanization does in the United States. Once more, the Canadian is proud of his respect for individuality and of his theory of the bilingual confederation: once more he has chosen the difficult course. It has been easy up to now in this huge country to let people go their own way; but will it go on being easy? The children are now being taught French in the schools. Will they be taught Italian and German too?

This delightful state of academic speculation has been brought up against some hard realities since the war. In the last ten years Canada has had an enormous increase in population—four million—chiefly Poles, Dutch,

Germans and Italians. Immigration has dropped now because the boom is over, but when the Canadians cry out for people they really mean the northern Europeans. There is a waiting list for Italians: why, one cannot imagine. They are one of the cleverest breeds in Europe, and the tens of thousands of them who have come into Toronto since the war have had a lot to do with livening up that very staid city. One thing immigration has done for Winnipeg is to give it some excellent restaurants. Good food tends to civilize.

A city like Winnipeg is really a workers' society and almost classless. The granite houses of the wheat millionaires stand under the trees, but those days are done. Boss and worker belong to the same clubs, go fishing or spend weekends in the lakeside huts which—as the saying is—"everyone" has. They like the ballet, the theater and that very Canadian institution, the choral society. As for the race question: Winnipeg has a Ukrainian mayor.

Flying out of Winnipeg you get one more shock to the eye. First of all, the city spreads for miles as if it were printed on the land. The print moves out to the scrub and forest of the Shield, the enormous slab of Precambrian rock that stretches to Hudson Bay. The north-south depth of forest across Canada ranges from 600 to 1500 miles—half the distance across the Atlantic. The second shock is the sight of thousands of lakes, gay eyelets of blue looking out of the face of vegetation, and you realize how much of Canada is wild water. It is forest and lake all the way to the Great Lakes, and hardly a road anywhere. There must be trails of some sort, for occasionally there is the white speck of a settlement. The Great Lakes themselves are forest bound. One understands why this country was crossed by water first, not by land; and that now it is the airplane that is opening up the northern and northwestern territories. How else could one get there? It is the plane that has made possible the exploitation of Canada's mineral wealth—the greatest single factor in the country's growth in the last few years. "You'll never understand Canada," a distinguished French-Canadian scientist said to me, "until you've seen the Arctic mining towns. They are fantastic examples of how modern technology has got its foot on the neck of the climate. I go up there once a year to meet intelligent people who prefer the life there to the boredom of city life."

The Rockies, the prairie and now the Great Lakes and the greatest of the Canadian rivers, the Saint Lawrence, the jugular artery of the country: the traveler's capacity to react to geography has to be stretched once more to meet this astonishing scene. The blue inland seas, silvered by the wake of steamers, stare up like vast wind-smeared mirrors from the earth. The earliest dramas of the penetration of the continent strike up again in the mind. La Salle, Jolliet, the absurd Father Hennepin, the Indian wars come to life in one's head; the character of those early North Americans was formed by something new to Europeans—endless forest, liberating rivers, inland oceans. The continental emotion moved in on these men and has remained ever since in the North American mind. It seizes every newcomer.

Ontario was Canada's stroke of luck; a northern but tolerable climate, good farmland, a countryside that would seem very English to the English and comfortable, at least to the Scots. Here in Toronto, and on up to Ottawa and Montreal, we are in the most densely populated, thriving and industrialized part of Canada, the richest market, where the British background is strongest. Conservative, solid, cautious, a region of long stockings, Ontario could be southern England except for one thing: a certain staidness. Toronto thinks Vancouver mad and dangerously nonconformist; Vancouver thinks Toronto conformist and dull. Until the immigration of the last twenty years, the shake-up of the boom and the last war, Toronto was in the grip of Presbyterian rectitude. Its Sabbatarianism and propriety were notorious all over the Commonwealth. Perhaps new countries require this rocklike self-righteousness; it makes people work and saves them from the moral collapse that afflicted large numbers of the earliest explorers and settlers.

The first thing the Toronto man tells you today is that all this has changed. Even so, when I asked for a drink to be sent to my luxurious hotel room, I was told that this was illegal—but that I was now, under the new licensing laws, allowed to drink very expensively in the bar below. Canada has had great difficulty with its liquor laws. It has a higher percentage of alcoholics even than America and maybe even than Sweden. Boredom, loneliness, the worship of work—the Puritan illnesses—surely account for a lot of this, as well as the innate violence of the Anglo-Saxon. But—putting the special Canadian problem of alcohol aside—Toronto is obviously a happier and livelier city than it used to be. Intellectually it has awakened. It now produces poets and—above all—satirists. It has begun to laugh. It is the center of publishing and here, of course, the Canadians clash with American influences.

Both the best and the worst of American periodical literature pour into Canada. And out of every ten books bought in Canada, seven come from the United States. Canadian writers cannot earn a living in their own country. A new novel by a Canadian sells only a thousand copies, and the writers are faced by the far more highly developed American culture, which long ago left the pioneer and the provincial stage behind.

Although Toronto has been a very British city, it is becoming Americanized. Canadians are attracted, with a part of themselves, by this. But something in them also tenaciously resists. They are proud of their separate history; they have never disliked the long colonial period, indeed they have had many benefits from the gradualness of their evolution. It has suited them emotionally and morally. There is a basic difference between Canadians and Americans which goes back, of course, to the Revolution. The Americans made the first indispensable gesture of the creative mind at the time of the Revolution, when they rejected European authority. They did so under the tutelage of the Age of Reason—that is to say, in the name of an Idea. The rebellion was a mixture of the cynical and the lofty; it created an irreverent and confident spirit of "free-for-all" which at various times led to an inordinate amount of lawlessness and corruption, but it also gave opportunity to adventurous and finer minds. To the Canadians, on the contrary, the principle of authority was everything and still counts heavily. There was no desire to be "free." There was no desire for a continental nationhood until about a century ago, and even then it took the panic at the sight of the American Civil War, and the American threats that lasted into the 1880s to give Canadians a rudimentary self consciousness.

The Canadians are moralists, but without the sense of guilt that harasses but also stimulates the American mind. And although Canadians frequently accuse themselves of having an inferiority complex in their masochistic way, they are relatively free of that desire to be loved which haunts Americans. They indeed ask often, "Do you like Canada?" with a wondering detachment. It is one of the rewards, perhaps, of sticking to authority. One effect of this attitude was that Canada became a parliamentary democracy on the British model and not in the Revolutionary sense. (America resembles Russia far more than Canada ever will.) Canadian politics, outside of Quebec, are clean; even rigorously so. The law is respected. When the

United States West was a scene of crime, the figure of the lonely Mountie became a symbol of the sudden reign of order north of the purely mathematical frontier line. Authority has made the churches powerful in society: it has been said that almost every Canadian is a church member. Family life is dominated by the father, not by the mother as in the United States, and domesticity reigns. Not so long ago there were only sixty divorces a year in all of Canada; now there is one divorce for every twenty marriages; in the United States there is one divorce for every four.

The soldier in Canada has a status he lacks in the States. He has never fought in a serious civil war. His wars have been foreign and in the Commonwealth interest; and although that might seem to mean a loss to a purely national consciousness—not to mention the terrible loss of manpower in the First World War—it has had exactly the opposite effect. Many Canadians from Vancouver to Ottawa have sat in their offices telling me this with a quiet conviction. One very frank political adviser in Ottawa, sitting in a Victorian room that might have been in the British Foreign Office, said, "Perhaps Canada was unlucky in not having gone through the crucible of civil war, or at any rate, of national violence. We have benefited from the British political skill and wisdom which steered us clear, without our having to earn our security ourselves, without having to forge ourselves into shape. Against this, it is certain that the men who came back from World War II discovered they were Canadians when they were out of Canada. Britain and America did not interest them anymore. They had found themselves. This we had never had before, and it has lasted."

Authority has its influence in education. A Canadian student of mine at an American university intended to become a schoolteacher. I asked if he would stay to teach in the States.

"No," he said with that shy, cautious purposefulness which I have often noticed among young Canadians. "Of course, life is more enjoyable here in the States and I would be far better paid. But in American schools, ideas are always changing, and the teacher is interfered with by parents' associations. He has no authority."

Again, authority shows itself in the socialistic tendencies of Canadian life. Canada is not as progressive as the United States in its antitrust laws and gives far less support to agriculture. But there is a National Health Service in

Saskatchewan; there are "family allowances"; the government operates the national broadcasting system—although there are also private broadcasting systems—an international airline, a national railroad. The provinces are taking over the ownership of hydroelectric power; the province of Alberta owns the telephone system, and the new and vastly important natural-gas industry is run by a public-utilities board. Socialism worries Canadians far less than it worries Americans.

Authority—but this time it is perhaps reflected authority—is shown in the intense Canadian concern with foreign politics. Some sage heads wonder if here Canada does not overbid its hand, although this active concern does set Canada *apparently* apart from the United States. As a colony, a Dominion, and finally a member of the Commonwealth, Canada was always politically more conscious of the rest of the world than the United States was until 1914. Neglected or remote Canada may have been, but there was never anything comparable to American isolationism—a period in which the United States was concerned only with its own development and wealth. There is more foreign news, even today, in the Vancouver press than in the papers of San Francisco.

This tradition of looking out on the world is a necessity so long as Canada is an exporting country; and it would outlast the influences of the Commonwealth if that were to break up. It has the side effect of encouraging Canadian nationalism, which, like all nationalisms, has its self-deluding aspects. Lying between Russia and the United States, Canada cannot help being in the American orbit in matters of foreign policy and defense; but Canada, like every other nation in the Western alliance, is jealous of its independence, especially in its new self-conscious mood.

Toronto has a substantial red-brick Victorian charm mixed in with its American innovations. Its villas with their sharply curved gables, always shaded by avenues of maples, are pretty. It is a well-painted place, and like all Canadian cities, very distinctive. This is very noticeable in Ontario—Windsor, Kingston, London are all different from one another. The journey along the long shore of Lake Ontario and up the Saint Lawrence at this time of the year is meadowy and charming. The farmhouses are substantial and the barns are impressive. Years ago a whole village would turn out for a barn-raising—that is, to lift the great beams of the structure in place. After the noble barns, the curious church spires catch the eye. They are commonly hexagonal and built of aluminum—for Canada has more of this metal than it knows what to do with. This unlikely material gives a blinding, piercing originality to the churches and they are one of the aesthetic sights of the province. The barns, the metal spires, the split-rail fences in the long fields that go down to the Saint Lawrence—this is the constructed Canada I shall remember.

The country is crowded where the train branches off into the woods toward Ottawa. The bell of the diesel rings continually for stations and crossings, and when one reaches the wide Ottawa River and sees the green copper-roofed granite of the capital on its cliff above the water, one exclaims with affectionate recognition. This is not Durham; it is not Aberdeen; but in its determinedly Victorian way, it has character. Here at last is a city with a skyline. And if one grins at the French château architecture mixed in with the Victorian, at the general air of Balmoral and granite, one remembers that this is a sign of how much later most Canadian architecture is than American architecture. Canada began to build when, alas, the lovely classical architecture of the American Revolutionary period was going out.

There is one exquisite Victorian thing in Ottawa. It is in the Parliament House, where Scots burst into tears of patriotism when they see the Trooping of the Color. I am thinking of the library, with its little pink-sugar columns in the dome and the delicate carving of the bookcases. The inside of the Parliament House has a miniature charm; the outside is forbidding and Presbyterian, redeemed only by the picturesque folly of the green copper roofing.

The Canadians have a genius for making parks of all sizes—the Gatineau Park at Ottawa is as fine as any wild park one can visit near a civilized city. Even the great rafts of logs, that remind one of the realities of Canadian life, seem to drift down the river in silent, dreaming islands of blameless utility. But the trees and the timber here begin to belong to another Canada, which one had first seen as an outpost in Winnipeg: the Canada of the French. Here the Canadien, as distinct from the Canadian, makes himself felt. People think little of Hull, the suburb just across the river, blocked out of view by the mountains of logs in the timberyard, but it has the best restaurant in the city, one of the most charming on the whole continent, and it is totally French.

Hull is a modest suburb of red-brick houses with green-painted doors and windows—red and green are the signals of the Canadien—and with curious outside staircases of iron or wood that make any row of houses look like a set of cages. These outside staircases are general throughout the French part of Montreal, also, and they are the mark of the immovable frugality, economy and attention to custom that set the Canadien off from Americans and Canadians alike. The staircases are outside to save interior space and to conserve the heating of the houses. Once he has conceived a system the Canadien, like the French, sticks to it forever, as to a logical proposition.

In the streets of Hull, and in the street market of Ottawa, one hears Canadien French—seventeenth-century French, in some respects, in which English mingles. There was a strike on when we were there, and the pickets carried signs inscribed in the mixed jargon that Canadiens scornfully call *jonal*:

STRIKE, PROFIT DE LA COMPAGNIE. 13 MILLION.
RIEN POUR LES EMPLOYEES.

As one travels along the Saint Lawrence to Montreal through the pretty, crowded country, the French character of the towns becomes strong. At Rigaud, the fine seminary takes one's mind to Tours or Poitiers. "What is that building?" I asked my Canadian waiter. "A classical college," he replied respectfully. The word "classical" defines the Canadien ideal. It conveys the idea of authority, and in that, Canadien and Canadian have something in common. There were wine drinkers on the train. At Vaudreuil one might have been on the Seine, for the beautiful lake passes into little channels flecked by the mirrored birch and maple; in the gardens the beans were neatly growing. Monet could have painted the watery scene, as if the intimacy and the light of France had been brought here.

In Montreal, the most exciting city of Canada, one arrives at the mass confrontation of two races. One has entered the vast province of Quebec, and Montreal is the metropolis of Canada. An industrial port, it has a Londonish air about it, as it lies under the smoke of the liners in the docks. It is a place of weight. At night, the high buildings are slabs of electricity in the sky. By day the traffic surges across the great bridges of the superb Saint Lawrence, the streets are packed. You climb up to the hill that stands like a volcano in the middle of the city, through streets that are alive with interest. In the French part of the city, the outside staircases, the crowded balconies where families sit on rockers in the shade of the maples, give an originality to the architecture. There are fine churches, and there are two famous universities.

The Anglo-French mixture in Montreal is bizarre. It is curious to lunch at a French-Canadian club which looks entirely English in its conduct and decorum. It is a pleasure to see *tavernes* instead of the forbidding Licensed Premises of the rest of Canada. An elderly man came out of a *taverne* near the Place d'Armes, having wined rather well, and he made a fine flourish with his hand and shouted, *"Vive la France!"* at us, with all the *esprit moqueur* of his people. The theater is always active and in a state of change and agitation. There are some excellent actors. I saw Feydeau's *Hotel Paradiso* in a little outlying theater, and the performance was superior to one I had seen in London years before. The family audience loved it; no sluggish Puritans there. Montreal has something of American luxury, the sagacity of London, the briskness of New York, the *sans-gêne* of Europe.

The very tension between the two cultures and religions is exciting to the mind even though, outside of political and business circles, the two peoples interpenetrate very little. They are like separate currents of two rivers that have been joined by events that happened two hundred years ago—indeed, if one goes back to the fur trade, much longer than that. The French Canadians are a third of the country's population, the oldest historically established in the northern part of the continent and—here's the rub—they have nothing like a proportional share of economic power. Until only a few years ago they were resigned to this. Now they are not. The race of peasant farmers who had formed a frugal, stagnant community, the only true peasantry on the European model in North America, who had scarcely changed a custom or an opinion since the seventeenth century, whose politics were rhetorical and corrupt and whose education, directed by religion, equipped no one to live in the modern world, has been transformed since World War II and is likely to force great changes in the balance of Canadian life. Quebec has become the most interesting province in the country.

Perhaps the critics of French Canada in America and Anglo-Canada ought to take a second look at French-Canadian "stagnation." For two hundred years the French Canadians have successfully resisted Anglo-Saxon influences, by sheer passivity. They have stuck, unmoved, to their beliefs and habits. The North American restlessness has not touched them. And they have been able to resist because of their language and religion, and above all by the invisibly powerful influence of the French family system. One day I was chatting in Quebec with Jean-C. Falardeau, the historian; we were looking from the Citadel to the enormous expansion of the city, and he said that the French Canadians were really "a vertical people," like the Jews; that is, they conceive life not as a relation to society, in the Anglo-Saxon manner, but as the relation of an individual to his destiny. The French Canadian, like the Jew, is deeply rooted in his cultural heritage. He belongs to the pre-Revolutionary past of France, and his insularity has intensified the separateness of his life.

The Canadien has always been an awkward member of the Canadian nation. The symptom of his unease lies in the fact that, while he is bilingual in a theoretically bilingual state, very few Anglo-Canadians are. To be fair, they are trying to alter this among the young. What really woke up Quebec was the sudden industrialization of the province during and after World War II. The peasant went to work in the factories, the old system run by the parish priest broke up. The success of the very radical Social Credit Party is a sign of the confusion that the change has caused. Now the Canadien is asking why he is still a second-class citizen when it comes to the leading positions in industry. When Maurice Duplessis, the political boss who had run French Canada, died a few years ago, his elaborate political machine broke down, and there was an outburst of self-criticism among the Canadiens. Clericalism, the old "classical" education, had failed to train them for industry and science: that was largely why they had not had their share of economic power. There has always been a strong strain of cultural nationalism in the Canadien; but now it has sharpened into an attack on the Anglicized jargon that has crept into his French. But the more able and less rigid Canadiens now begin to work beside Anglo-Canadians, especially on the university level, instead of standing aloof; and they are discovering that the two mistrustful peoples have many things in common.

"What about separatism?" one asks people in Montreal. Do the French want to become a new independent state? There is always a separatist movement among the French-Canadian young in every generation, and so far it has always faded. But the Algerian movement has offered an example, and in the past year extremists have shown an ugly hand with the bomb. (There has also been some gangster violence in Montreal in the last few years, and it has always had the reputation of being a violent city.)

There are two overwhelming arguments against separatism in the minds of the Canadiens. One is the fear and dislike of everything the United States stands for, especially of America's attitude to its own minorities and the principle of Americanization—the melting pot. Someone said to me in Quebec: "The Americans and the Anglo-Canadians are naïve; *les* businessmen are just boys who have not grown up. And abnormal boys at that." But however much a French Canadian may criticize the British and the Anglo-Canadians, he invariably ends with the same sentence: "We owe a debt of gratitude to British tolerance." And indeed they do. In what they most valued, the British left them alone. The second argument is more subtle. It is based on a fear of themselves. A shrewd, young, ebullient and very successful Canadien brusquely denied there was any real revival in Quebec. He said it was just a lot of talk among a few intellectuals and that the masses had merely been addled by television. There may be something in that, but his key sentence was: "Give us independence and we would have a military dictator on the South American model at once—and he would sell us to the Americans."

Canadien anti-Americanism has its half-baked aspects. There are many French Canadians in New England who are very happy there; they frequently reproach Quebec for its ignorance and provinciality. And, after all, like the rest of Canada, the French have become conscious of a Canadian nationality, or rather of the reality of a dual nationality. Even the worry about their identity as a nation, their lack of a flag, and so on, is comfortably shared by both parties, and the lack of decision is seen as virtue:

"Our nation has become adult through patience and without color," Falardeau has written. "It has had the sober beginning of a '*mariage de raison*' between two parties who did not choose to live together. Consequently we should not make the effort to create artificially the symbol of a national life which history has refused us. . . . Perhaps, in a not too distant future, in a world where national boundaries will have become meaningless and national arrogance catastrophic, we may be envied by many other nations as 'the country without a flag.'"

So the Canadien and the Canadian rub along as best they can, divided by the Anglo-Canadian possession of the biggest share of the wealth and the rival moralities of Anglo-Saxon and Latin. The situation is exacerbated by the company towns along the Saint Lawrence, the towns created for the paper mill or the mining products, where the workers are not allowed political action. Mining, in all the Americas, seems to be run very often indeed on this paternalistic system, and where the executives are Anglo-Saxons and probably Protestants, and the owners often not even Canadian, one can see why the Canadien resents his situation. In my twenties I spent a little time in one of these company lumber camps. It was run more or less on military lines. The French lumbermen were a glowering lot. Their only pleasure was to get leave to go to Quebec and get drunk. The company arranged even that and collected them later from the jails.

But the city of Quebec has one advantage: it is almost entirely French. The tiny Anglo-Canadian minority go to their church in the middle of the city and have little contact with the Canadiens; though I have met people in the university who do make contacts. I find the Québecois excellent company, very genial and far from insular. The charge that the French Canadian is humorless is nonsense; he has a good deal of the *vieille gaieté française*. I do not know if there is a Canadien tradition of the tall story, but I know one rumbustious man in Quebec who can tell many a good one about wolves and girls.

What a contrast there is between Vancouver and Quebec. Here Canada, and the Saint Lawrence that now takes ships one thousand miles into the inland seas, are guarded by a fortress that was strengthened every generation until the nineteenth century. A real fortress in the old European style. Quebec is the only really European city in North America; its life is untouched by the tourists who flood in in search of the picturesque. It is as European as Poitiers, and only the citadel of Cartagena in Colombia can compare with it.

From its cliff, the sight of the wide, forested river is stirring to the imagination. The gray stone of the city has rudimentary colonial primness and harshness. The appearance is a mixture of the severe and gracious, and the trees are tall and fine.

Above all, old Quebec does not look excessively preserved or even preserved at all. There is no "ye olde" note in the *tavernes*, nor, for example, in the shabby little square on the quays where the sailors' church of Notre Dame des Victoires stands. The famous seminary of Laval, founded in 1663 and externally altered in 1820, is a fine classical object; but the most attractive thing is the intimacy of Quebec's shops and restaurants. But if one comes away from Quebec with the impression that it is simply a picturesque spot that leads to the playground created in the Laurentians in the last thirty or forty years, one is quite wrong. The industrial region outside is full of life.

Quebec ought, in a poetic way, to be the terminal point of the transcontinental journey across this bilingual nation. But it is no longer the fortress commanding the entrance to the interior. The real Land's End of Canada, the end of the transcontinental railway, is the port of Halifax—by sea the closest point to Europe. If sea war is a test of importance, the vast harbor of Halifax was the assembly point of Atlantic convoys in the last war; and for eastern Canada it has the added importance of being, along with Saint John, the only port open when the Saint Lawrence is closed by winter. Halifax has some character as a Victorian Anglo-Scottish town; it has fine hospitals, Dalhousie University and many colleges, and its environs are romantically pretty. There are many lakes and rivers among the forests and farms of Nova Scotia.

But Canada is all paradox, and once again, in these Maritime Provinces, the Canadian Difficulty appears. These provinces, and Nova Scotia particularly, are a natural continuation of Maine, but they are at once the most deeply British and the most anciently American part of Canada. The inhabitants speak of Canada as if it were foreign to them. They were not ardently for the Confederation, which (they say) has ruined them. They are on their own pursuing an un-American and un-Canadian, unmodern British way of life. They are living still in something like the easygoing colonial existence of the early eighteenth century. Money counts for nothing—except inherited money; caste, not cash, gives a man distinction. To be poor is no disgrace, indeed it is a matter of respect. Nova Scotia strikes one as being rather like Ireland, the Scottish highlands or the eccentric parts of Cornwall.

The Maritimes represent a happy indifference to everything North America stands for; these provinces boast that they produce more men of brains, more leaders, than any other part of Canada, that their culture is deeper and that theirs is the happiest place on the harassed continent. The little ports and villages are peaceful, the rocky shores are wild. A little Dutch-German town like Lunenburg, with its white frame churches, its droll charm and its small boatbuilding yards, is a gem. The frame villas have their verandas and balustrades; occasionally, on an older one, one sees the widow's walk. All through here is the land of the lobster and the famous Gaspé salmon; fishing—incredible to European ears—often is free. True, the temperature drops to 25° below in the winter, but there is sun.

Now in spring the lupines were growing wild in the fields, the late lilac was in the gardens. More than 150 years ago William Cobbett wrote with fervor of this country, where he fell in love with a local beauty and wanted to work a farm when he was a younger man. It is probably less prosperous and less populated than in his time, but it pleases. Six stocks, unmelted by the New World, live here side by side; the old Highland Scots, still speaking Gaelic on Cape Breton Island (it is taught in the schools), a few French, German-Dutch, the descendants of the old Loyalists, the Irish and the British. What the earliest settlers—refugees from New York and the Revolution—wanted to do was to perpetuate colonial life; the only thing wrong was that the exquisite classical period of New England architecture had passed. Victorian architecture that unaristocratic style had come in. But apart from that, Americans find here the New England past.

The Maritimes and the Atlantic provinces have depended on the Newfoundland fisheries and their own, as well as on trade with Great Britain; both have declined. The enterprising have gone west, immediately to rise to the top of the Canadian tree. They take with them more feeling—the fruit of a well-rooted culture—than is common among Canadians; a passionate, well-wrought character. The recurring undertones of their voices are more Irish, Scottish and English than is usual in Canada. The prospects of the Maritimes are not bright—perhaps that is a blessing in disguise—though there is long talk of cutting a canal from the Saint Lawrence to Saint John, which would shorten the sea journey to New York. But that would not please Halifax. There is a quiet war of ports going on all around North America: San Francisco competes with Seattle and Vancouver; Winnipeg would be vastly tempted to send its grain, not to Vancouver but to the summer port they talk of enlarging in Hudson Bay. The Seaway traffic, which has not had the tonnage so optimistically expected a few years back, would feel the competition.

One cannot tell how Canada will grow in the next few decades, when the present phase of belt-tightening is over. The mines of the Shield and the far north are enormously rich, and Canadians, like the Russians and the Americans, are making great efforts in their Arctic regions. At the moment Canada needs a new flood of immigrants. In the last generation, the Canada which had been written off as a stagnant playground has surprised and disconcerted Americans by the strength of its distinctive personality. At one time it was possible for Americans to regard Canada as an eccentric and touching survival of British imperialism, a country fading until, one day, it would become indistinguishable from the United States. Older Americans—and some older Canadians in the rich areas of the Lakes—still think in this fashion. It is out of date. The moral strength of Canada derives from its struggle with the Canadian Difficulty.

On the Canadian side, there is truculence about the nation's status as a military base and buffer in the struggle between America and Russia, and about the American economic invasion, although basically Canadians are more aware of the fundamental things they have in common with the United States. On the other side, the United States is not famous for its understanding of its satellites. The American economic imperialists of today carry a large, unconscious luggage of isolationism. In Canada they seem to forget that Canada became politically viable largely because of British tact, tolerance and respect. It is very noticeable that Canadians are intimately at home when they go to England, although they may be greatly attracted to the United States. They are far nearer to England and even closer to Scotland than Americans have ever been, and in spite of Canada's Queen Victoria worship, Canadians do not romanticize England, as many Americans do.

We can expect American-Canadian relationships to be more restive as Canadian personality defines itself; and this is a good thing, for the history of Europe shows that variety has been the fertilizer of that powerful civilization which, after all, created the New World. The Canadian spirit is cautious, observant and critical where the American is assertive; the foreign policies of the two nations are never likely to fit very conveniently, and this, again, is just as well, for the peace of the world depends on a respect for differences.

The real nightmare of the Canadian is not fear of economic swamping by the rich neighbor with whom he has so much in common, but the old fear of disintegration. This is most strongly felt when the Quebec question has one of its dangerous outbursts—people who speculate about an eventual union of Canada and the United States always forget this intractable matter. The Canadians have, on the whole, managed, step by step, to overcome the disintegrating tendency; and wise Americans are as glad not to have the Quebec question on their hands, just as Canadians are relieved not to have the Negro question on theirs. Although they are at different stages of historical development, the two countries share a common geographical position on the exposed Arctic frontier of Asiatic disturbance.

[1964]

11

London

No Londoner can be exact or reasonable about London. This place with the heavy-sounding name, like coal being delivered or an engine shunting, is the world's greatest unreasonable city, a monstrous agglomeration of well-painted property. The main part of the city, 120 square miles of low-lying and congested Portland stone, yellow brick and stucco, slate, glass and several million chimneys, lies a few minutes' flight from the North Sea. There are immense acreages of railway track, and the subsoil is a tangle of tunnels running into scores of miles. Such is the mere core of London; another 700 square miles of what was once pasture and woodland is now continuous red-faced suburb. People talk loosely about the number of London's inhabitants: there are certainly nine million. To the police it seems much more.

It is impossible to be exact about London because no one really has ever seen it. Once in, we are engulfed. It is a city without profile, without symmetry; it is amorphous, like life, and no one thing about it is definitive. A natural guess, for example, is that it is as gray and yellow as it looks; yet, from any small height it looks entirely green, like a forest, with occasional stone towers sticking out. The explanation is paradoxical: by preserving trees the Londoner, by far the most urban living creature, convinces himself he is living in the countryside.

Of the world's capitals London has been the most powerful and important for a good two hundred years, the capital of the largest empire since the Roman. It is now the capital of a Commonwealth. But to be a Londoner is still to be immediately, ineluctably, a citizen of the world. Half of the mind of every Londoner is overseas. If the French government falls, if there is dock trouble in New York, a riot in the Gold Coast, even the charwoman cleaning the office will mention the lugubrious fact. There is an old story that someone was once mad enough to ask a Cockney whether the London he came from was London, Ontario; the Cockney groaned "Nah! London the whole bloomin' world." Truculent, proud, even sentimental, yet the old hypocrite was piously complaining of the weight of the world upon the London mind.

Perhaps because of the weight and the worry, London is the least ostentatious of the world's capitals. It has little of the rhetorical architecture and the ambitious spacing of monuments and temples to be found in the capitals of the new democracies; none of the marble splash endowed by patriotic planners. Napoleon would turn in his grave in the Invalides if he could see Nelson's urn crowded among painters and bishops in the crypt of St. Paul's. The Houses of Parliament and Buckingham Palace are among the few great edifices to compose a view, and so—thanks to German bombers—was St. Paul's cathedral for a few years during and after the war; but, for the rest, though London has its fine quarters, its monuments, palaces and even a triumphal arch or two, these have been eased into the city and are not ornately imposed upon it.

London excels in the things that segregate and preserve an air of privilege: the lovely terraces of the Regency, the sedate faces of the squares and of the moneyed or modest Georgian and Early Victorian streets. These are not collectors' pieces; they are the routine of central London. The Londoner is purse-proud and shows it in his domestic property rather than in imperial splash; and if in a moment of vainglory he builds a Pall Mall club that looks like the Foreign Office and a Foreign Office that looks like a cross between a

Renaissance palace and a Turkish bath, he redresses the balance by putting the Prime Minister in a small private house called No. 10 down a side street and with only an iron railing—and a couple of policemen—to prevent us from putting our noses against the window.

But I am writing as if I had *seen* London, when the confusing fact is that I have only lived in it most of my life. I have just looked at the smear of gray sky through the window of my top-floor flat. It is in one of those blocks of pink structures which went up like so many vending machines in London between the wars, when architecture broke with the Victorian rotundity and the cheese-colored stucco of 150 years before. I closed the window to shut out the noise of the buses. Look at my hands. Already filthy.

I find myself siding with Henry James, who noticed the filth of London as soon as he arrived here, went on to say that it was not cheerful or agreeable, added that London was dull, stupid and brutally large and had a "horrible numerosity of society." Was anything left after that? Yes, he said; there was magnificence.

London is a prime grumbler. The weather, the traffic, the smoke, the dirty color get us down and we feel our life is being eaten up in those interminable bus and tube journeys through the marsh of brick—eaten up before we have even started to live. But gradually we begin to feel the magnificence that rises out of the gray, moody, Victorian splodge. We felt it in the sound of Big Ben growling like an old lion over the wet roofs in the silent, apprehensive nights of the war. Where Paris suggests pleasure, Rome the human passions of two thousand years, with assassination in every doorway, where New York suggests a ruthless alacrity, London suggests experience.

The manner of the city is familiar, casual, mild but incontrovertible.

London has this power not only of conserving the history of others but of making one feel personally historic. A young bus conductor, a youth with Korea in his face, said to me the other day: "That's all a thing of the past, like everything else nowadays." He was feeling historic already at twenty-five. Perhaps in all the very large cities of the world at the moment, people are beginning to feel they only have a past; the future seems short. But London has always turned the mind inward. Londoners vegetate.

The city also is something you get on your lungs, which quickens and dries your speech and puts a mask on the face. We breathe an acid effluence of city brick, the odors of cold soot, the dead rubbery breath of city door-ways, or swallow a mouthful of mixed sulfuric that blows off those deserts of railway tracks which are still called Old Oak Common or Nine Elms without a blade of vegetation in sight for miles—we breathe these with advantage. They gave us headaches when we were young, but now the poison has worked and is almost beneficent to those born to it. So herrings must feel when they have been thoroughly kippered.

On top of this there is the climate. That is in itself aging. We are, for example, ten years older since eight o'clock this morning, for we woke up to fog, saw it melt into feeble sunshine, watched white clouds boil up and then stand still like marble. A thunderstorm? No, the temperature changes, shoots up, drops down, the sky blackens. At midday the lights come on in flats and shops. All those thousands of green desk lamps in the banks of the City are switched on. What does this mean? Snow this afternoon? Or rain? Probably rain but who can tell? We can't. In the next twenty-four hours we shall have lived a lifetime's weather. We shall have seen a dozen hopes and expectations annulled; we shall have been driven in on ourselves and on the defensive. We shall talk of what it was like yesterday, of the past.

Yet when Henry James used that word "magnificent" it was the London sky I at once thought of. London generates its own sky—a prolonged panorama of the battle between earth and heaven. For if the lower sky is glum over London and sometimes dark brown or soupy yellow, it is often a haze of violet and soft, sandy-saffron colors. If the basis is smoke and the next layer is smoke and fog banked up, the superstructure of cloud is frequently noble. White cumulus boils up over the city against a sky that is never blue as the Mediterranean knows blue, but which is fair and angelic. The sky space in our low city is wide.

And this sky has had another magnificence: it has been a battlefield. I never see a large white cloud now, against the blue, without going back to that afternoon when the Spitfires dived into it like silver fish, as the sirens went off over the British Museum. And many times in 1940 I saw the night sky go green instead of black, twitching like mad electricity, hammered all over by tens of thousands of sharp golden sparks as the barrage beat against it like steel against a steel door. The curling ribbons of fire that came down from heaven were almost a relief to see, with that unremitting noise. One was glad of silence, even if the silence was alight. One cloudless August afternoon green snow fell in dry, unmelting flakes in Holborn. We picked this new venture of the English climate off our coats: a V-2 had just fallen nearly two miles away in Hyde Park and had blown the leaves of the trees into these mysterious smithereens.

London is an agglomeration of villages which have been gummed together in the course of centuries. It is a small nation rather than a city, and its regions have never quite lost their original identity or even their dialects. The City of London, the administrative heart of the city, which begins at Aldgate suddenly, like a row of cliffs, is a province in itself. Yet a large part of central London is not muddle at all, for here it was planned in the late eighteenth and early nineteenth centuries, when the squares were laid out between Bloomsbury and Bayswater. The habit of making tree-shaded oases, in squares and private terraces, gave a respite from the vulgar uproar and ugly building of the general commercial scramble. The railed-in lawns and the green enclosures of the Inns of Court betray our love of privacy and privilege, and for delectable cliques, clubs and coteries, just as those acres and acres of little two-story houses show how much we like a little property to ourselves. This has been the despair of urban planners.

There are immense cheese-colored areas in Bayswater and elsewhere where Bernard Shaw's tall Heartbreak Houses have pillars like footmen's legs. Chelsea is one kind of place. Westminster another. Inner London is gray or yellow, outer London is red; that is about as much as can be said of the Victorian jungle, unless we name the slates shining like mirrors in the wet.

In that tired air, always heavy and often damp and lethargic, the grass grows green in the black soil of the gardens, the shrubs grow dusty and the dappled plane trees grow black. In the summer evenings we listen to their leaves turning over like the pages of endless office ledgers. We hear the ducks fly over from some pool of filthy water left on a bomb site to the wooded lakes in the parks. We hear the starlings at St. Martin's crying down the traffic. We hear owls. We even hear sheep in Regent's Park in the summer. A city so countrified cannot be megapolis.

We are tree lovers. In the winter the London trees are as black as processions of mourners and, like the weeds of some sooty gathering of widows, their higher branches are laced against the mist or the long, sad sunsets. The thing that reconciled us to those ruined miles in Holborn, Cheapside and round St. Paul's were the trees that grew rapidly out of burned-out basements where the safes had been kept; and the willow herb that grew in purple acres out of commercial brick.

The London tree grows out of poisoned soil, its roots are enclosed by stone and asphalt, and it breathes smoke. There is one heroic creature, raising its arms between two overtowering blocks of office buildings and the church of St. Magnus the Martyr in Billingsgate. Typewriters clatter among its branches instead of birds; and a boy who climbed it would come down black. Its survival shows how firmly Londoners cling to nature and, in life, to some corner of what has been.

Except in the curve of the river between Westminster and St. Paul's, there are no large vistas in London, and our small ones have come to us by luck and accident. I have a typical view of the London muddle from my flat. There is one of those Victorian streets of carefully painted small houses, with their classical doorways and their iron railings. (The Victorians did not know what to do with all the iron they produced and simply caged up everything in it.) I have counted 270 chimneys in a couple of hundred yards—cheap coal, cheap servants to carry it up from those basements. Now only about ten of those chimneys are smoking; we run on electricity and gas; but this population of London chimneys remains like millions of sets of old, unwanted teeth.

The street runs into a decaying square where the first publisher I knew used to live and poke his small Victorian fire in the late twenties; he wore button boots and believed in Animal Magnetism. A furniture depository has wrecked one end of the square. At the back of it are the mews: one smart mews flat, several garages with the chauffeurs cleaning and polishing and one of those doubtful "caffs" where the police are always asking questions. Until the espresso bars started there was a certain affinity between London coffee and crime.

Turn back, across the main street, and you are walking through Thackeray's *Vanity Fair* and *The Newcomes* into the country of the Victorian new rich and the pretty houses of their mistresses. Dickens lived near here in state. But close to their back doors was and is the toughest street in the neighborhood, a place for those fantastic fights between women who have had a pint or two. I once saw a lady pulled off her prey by three or four men. "I can't take the 'ole ruddy lot of you on," she said, misunderstanding their intention. "I'm not an elephant."

The quarter has its gin palaces, its television shops, its cinemas, its plastic bars, a reputation for smash-and-grab, and the ripest old London music hall. There are only a few left. The idea is to go there, full of beer and with the family, and to laugh from the belly at mothers-in-law, double beds, perambulators and love from the point of view of the sexual treadmill. No Puritans here; on the other hand, not much art either. London has always liked its jokes to be common, full-fleshed, dirty and sanguine and its chorus girls to be pink, broad and breezy. It likes Britannia on the loose, with her helmet over one eye and her trident unspeakably meaningful.

The eye tours the slate roofs of the horizon and, presently, it stops short: there is that new aspect of the London skyline, the sudden gap. Ten or twelve houses went down over there in a cloud of dust during the war. These gaps and gashes are everywhere in London; some of them startle us. We see our ghosts. Up there (we say), where the sky is now, I used to dine with the So-and-so's. Or, there in that space were my first lodgings: the landlady used to tipple. Or, there, about thirty-five feet in the air, I was in love with a girl who read my fortune in my hand and infuriated me in predicting that I was to be the least important of the three great loves of her life. The back room where I wrote my first book is a piece of sky. To have survived such total destruction by ten or fifteen years makes one feel irrelevant. It makes life seem very long. The gardens of these destroyed houses are now haunted and sinister wilderness.

These gaps bring back the strangest thing that has ever happened to London: the silence of the city at night during the war. Only one writer has described it: Elizabeth Bowen, who sat it out in her cracked and boarded-up Regency house in the Park. One walked in those days down empty streets that stared like sepulchers, hearing only the echo of one's own heels. Voices carried far, as if across water. I remember two painted old ladies sitting up late on a bench in Lincoln's Inn Fields, and I could hear their solitary chatter from across the square. They were, of course, talking about the distant connections of the Royal Family.

LONDON

Ever since that night in December 1940, when the City was burned out, the black crowds marching over London Bridge to their offices have seen a lifetime's seriousness made nonsense of. It was dumfounding to lose one's working past, affronting to pride and good sense. There has always been pride in trade and in London it was commemorated in the plaques and urns and epitaphs of Wren's churches. Men working in the city—selling shirts in Cheapside or insurance in London Wall—knew they were working in the birthplace of modern capitalism. They were heirs of Defoe and Lloyd. A guidebook to this part of London is useless now. Streets vanished. Neighborhoods vanished. North of Cheapside one wanders in an abstract wilderness of streets without reason, for no buildings stand in them. London Wall is brick frieze three feet high to prevent one from falling into the cellars. Tears come into my eyes when I see the blackened husk of Bow Church. I suppose because the place had been made human by the nursery rhyme so suited to the children of merchants:

> "When will you pay me,"
> Said the bells of Old Bailey.
> "I do not know,"
> Said the big bell at Bow.

One thinks of mere impedimenta: the desks, the telephones, the filing systems, the teacups of the sacred quarter-of-an-hour for office tea, the counters and tills, the lifts that some people spent their working lives in. All gone. That wilderness north of Cheapside is misery; in the winter, when the snow is on it, or under the moon, it is the Void itself.

The wastes gave space and perspective to a city which the greedy middle-class individualism of trade had always grudged. All the fine planning in London, and any nobility it has, is aristocratic and royal; the rest of us, from the small shopkeeper to the great bureaucratic corporations, are consumed by the tenacious passion for property. The true Londoner would sooner have property than money; he would certainly sooner have it, no matter how muddled, than air or space.

This muddle of property, however, has its own richness. I worked in pungent London when I was young. Pungent London lies eastward of London Bridge. In the Boro' High Street, where you can still eat at one of those gal-

leried inns that you probably thought existed only in the drawings of Cruikshank, I mooned in the heady smell of hops; in Tooley Street it is the Scandinavian trade in butter and eggs; in Pickle Herring Street, dry salted hides,
rank and camphorous. Australian leather is being pulled off the lighters at
Thames wharf, where the cranes sigh in their strange, birdlike communities.
There is a strong smell of pepper, too, and the sour-mutton odor of wool. We
dodged the crane hooks and got startling earfuls of the language of carmen,
who are noted for their command of blasphemy. The cranes, the anchor
chains and winches are clattering across the water, and steam and smoke go
up dancing in the river wind. There are one or two public houses with terraces on the river, sitting as neat as pigeons between the warehouse walls.
London is not a very self-regarding city; these wharves are its innumerable
windows looking on the faraway world—to Africa, the Indies, China or the
Levant.

But, for myself, Bermondsey was the place. There on the south bank they
refer to London as the place "over the water." We worked in the stink of
leather, listening to the splitting machines and the clogs of the hide men. The
slum kids used to climb up the bars on the office windows and make faces at
us and tie the swing doors so that we could not get out. When we caught
these children their mothers turned up: "You take your bleedin' hands off
that bleedin' kid." The Hide Market has been knocked silly now; Bermondsey and Rotherhithe are burned out, and where there was once a jungle of
little houses, there now is London's naked clay, filling up with thousands of
prefabricated huts that look like sets of caterpillar eggs. There are new ten-
ements. One notices a rise in tone. At the Caledonian Market, where they sell
everything from old clothes and worn-out gramophone records to antiques
at the top West End prices, a good many stall holders talk the new B.B.C. English. "No, madam," one hears the incredible accent, "the date of this salt-
cellar is 1765, not '75. One can see by the scroll."

In Throgmorton Street, we used to see the stock jobbers thick in the
street. Inside the Stock Exchange we looked down on the littered floor and
saw again what a passion for the market London has. For the stalls marked
Diamonds, Industrials, Mines, and so on, are really gentlemanly versions of
the vegetable market at Covent Garden, the meat market at Smithfield or the
fish market of Billingsgate. The only difference is that a boss at the Stock Ex-

change puts on a top hat when he visits his banker; at the others, he sticks to his white dust coat, his cap or his bowler. The population of bowlers in London has declined, but in the conservative city clubs they can still be seen rowed up by the hundred like sittings of black eggs.

In Carlyle's London Library or under the dome of the whispering Reading Room of the British Museum, one may forget that London has the habit of markets and auctions. But at Christie's, the world-famous auction rooms of pictures, silver and china, they will knock down a Picasso or a Matisse, a Gainsborough or a Raphael, at a nod no one can see. The crowd is well-dressed and silent. Knowingness irradiates from inscrutable faces. It is like a chapel service, and the auctioneer is up to all the tricks of the sinners in the congregation: "I must ask you, sir, to stop preventing people from bidding. You turned round. Three or four times you have made a face." Such is the sensibility of this secretive business that a mere raised eyebrow can cause doubt. Where all are mad, all are cunning. It is the same at Sotheby's. You realize in these markets that London is composed of cliques, coteries and specialists, little clubbable collections, causeries, exclusivities, snobberies, of people in innumerable "games" played on secret knowledge, protecting people "in," keeping others "out," with dilatory blandness. It is untrue that we are white sepulchers. Our sepulchers are rosy.

In London, whatever you do, you have to be a "member." I have no doubt there are cliques at Covent Garden or Smithfield. It is different only in those instantaneous, outspoken markets of the street, that mark more clearly than anything one district from another. Berwick market for the foreigners, junk in the Portobello Road, dogs at Bethnal Green, pictures on the Embankment, jewelry and diamonds being sold on the street at Hatton Garden.

Petticoat Lane, just past Aldgate off the Whitechapel Road, is still the richest; this narrow mile, gashed by bomb sites and hemmed in by the East End sweatshops, is London's screaming parody of an Oriental bazaar. It is a mile deafened by voices that have burst their throat strings years ago and are down to tonsils and catarrh. "Nah then, come on closer. I'll tell you what I'll do. What's that? You're not my bloody sister. My family's like me, ugly as hell. Nah then, will any lady or gentleman present this morning do me the favah of lending me a pound note?" Or: "I'm not taking money this morning, not two pound, one pound, not eighteen, seventeen, fifteen, twelve shilling but"—bang on the book—"five shilling and sixpence for these beautiful cut-glass vases, the last. I'm frowing them away."

The crowd is dense here. You move six deep, chest to back, an inch at a time, jammed in by Cockneys, Jews, Negroes, Lascars and Chinese off the ships. And, head and shoulders above all, there will be that pink-feathered Zulu prince who can be seen any day anywhere between Aldgate and Tottenham Court Road, selling his racing tips and making the girls scream with his devouring smile. There will be a turban or two and, moving through them against the crowd, will come that tall, glum specter of the London streets with his billboard high above his head, denouncing the Jews for their wickedness in trading on Sunday morning. "The Wages of Sin," the notice reads, and people make way for him, "is Death." He passes the stalls where they are serving stewed eels by the cup and black-currant cordial by the glass. He passes the hot dogs and the sugared apples, the stalls of china, socks, watches, handkerchiefs, blankets, toys. A yell comes up from your boot. You have almost trodden on a little fellow who has sat down there suddenly in the middle of the street and is crying out, as if he were on fire: "Ladies! Ladies! Nylons a penny a pair!" And just when we are crushed and cannot move even our chests, there is the tinny sound of kettledrums, the wheeze of clarinet and trumpet, the boom of a soft slack drum. The blind men's band, with its one-legged collectors fore and aft, moves sternly through us all, raking in the cash.

For a year or two the City and the London market used to tempt me. There is a torpid pleasure in custom and routine which give their absorbent power to great cities. You could spend your life in those acres of desks under the thousands of green-shaded lamps that hang over them. There was that little temple in the middle of Lloyd's great temple of insurance, where the Lutine Bell was and still is, and where the red-robed and black-collared attendant in his velvet sat calling out the names of the underwriters like psalms throughout the day. You never realized before what a passion for guarantees the human race has and that London was the steady guarantor. I have never heard that Bell ring, as it is supposed to do, once for Bad News and twice for Good, and I am told that they have given up ringing it for Bad News because nowadays it would never stop ringing. They did ring it twice lately because some coastal steamer in the eastern Mediterranean and given up for lost had just crawled into Tobruk. Nothing happens at sea in any part of the world, but London suffers a seismographic tremor.

And then the spell of working in London owes something to its lingering medieval habit of working in districts; the tailors in Savile Row and their cutters in the Whitechapel Road; the car dealers in Great Portland Street; there are streets sweet to international banking, others committed to insurance; a street for merchant shipping, the "rag" or mantle trades round St. Paul's, as near as possible to Defoe's Cheapside—what is left of both—newspapers in Fleet Street. Even the Law splits up among the lawns and chambers of the Inns of Court, into Law and Equity. This is pleasant and, by middle age, one has gathered that London lives by and enjoys its inner self, purveying the careful illusion of leisure and the pretense that its business is private. But for a young man this was all privilege, mystery and a bore. One gets restless.

One morning in the First World War, a carman called Ninety burst into the office and shouted "Air Raid!" across the counter to us boys, and to show he had a proper respect for white collars, added the inevitable "Please" (I have heard the reception clerk at Broadcasting House say the same thing in the Blitz twenty-five years later—"Air Raid, please"—to call the boys to close the iron shutters). It did please. What a relief from the monotonous London rumble to hear a sound like doors banging in the sky. We left our desks. A flight of German aircraft flew as steady as mosquitoes in a clear May sky that was pimpled with gunfire. Black smoke was going up from Billingsgate.

Our boss, a white-bearded old lion of eighty, with the telephone in his shaking hand, was saying breathlessly to the head clerk: "Have you heard the news? The *Dunnottar Castle* has just docked. Send a boy to me." There were no boys. We were on the roof. It was about this time I decided that if I wanted to see the world London had so much experience of, the sooner I stopped seeing it from weighing slips, delivery orders, the foreign mail and the secondhand bookshops of the Charing Cross Road, the better. London would make me less impatient once I had got back from Paris, Rome, Madrid or New York.

What does strike me when I come back from these places now is that London is a masculine city, a place for male content and consequence. The men, I notice, dress better here than anywhere else; none knows the curl of a hat or the set of a shoulder better or wears clothes of finer quality. It is just as well, for the absurd variety of English chins, teeth and noses needs some redemption, and people who run so easily to eccentricity need strong rituals and conventions. This is not the idiotic London of Bertie Wooster and the Drones, for the man-about-town is an extinct type. But, we have a dandy for Prime Minister, and there are tens of thousands of less eminent males doing what Henry James called "the thing" properly.

Coming out of the cloakroom of a hotel during the war with my hat in my hand, I saw Sir Max Beerbohm give me a historical look. "In my youth," he said, "it was not correct to uncover one's head in an hotel." How low we had sunk. Such men suffer for us all. They bear the cruelty of the mirror of Narcissus with fortitude.

That young undersecretary to the Cabinet Minister who stands, without overcoat, in the biting January wind, outside Brooks's Club talking to a friend, knows that if he dies of pneumonia tomorrow he will have caught it, properly costumed, at the right address. It will satisfy him and we, who are not impeccable, know that he is suffering fashion for us. Just as the Guards are when they stamp at the Palace.

Nor does this London vanity afflict only a small class. Detectives and barrow boys, bank messengers and the man in the shop have it as a matter of *amour-propre*. I used to know a London leech gatherer who went barefoot, with his trousers rolled up, into the ponds on his strange search, but he always wore a white lining to his waistcoat and a carnation in his buttonhole when about his duties. Old Mr. Cox at the London Library, who knew every famous writer and scholar of the last sixty years, used to say with deep London approval: "I knew Mr. Pater. Very particular about his clothes, Mr. Pater was." Sartorially, we like to burn like Mr. Pater's "still blue flame."

Foreigners say that Londoners are less honest than they were before the war, but find us startlingly kind and clever since we have put aside the imperial mask. It is true, I am sure, that we are less starchy; but I am far from noticing any disastrous decline in our complacency, our traditional habit of lazy and vocal self-congratulation. It is also true that once we went out to the Empire; now the Commonwealth comes to us and adds to the polyglot vivacity of our streets.

These strangers come, of course, in the summer when London is green and the smoked white clouds boil over the sultry brick. Then the center of London becomes a foreign city. There are summer mornings at Victoria or Waterloo when the platforms become African or South American. The African tribes appear in all their topknots and shaven blackness: the Moslem turbans gather in the underground railway. The universities and schools have always had a large number of Hindus, Moslems and Chinese and, indeed, it is from their lips mainly that one hears authentic Oxford English. There have always been maharajahs at Claridge's, Africans at the British Museum, Canadians, Australians and New Zealanders in the Strand; and we would be hurt if there were not.

What surprises us is that the real foreigners now come to visit us, not for trade, but for pleasure. There are posses of Argentines in the art galleries of Bond Street. There are days when Piccadilly is German. Crowds of Scandinavians sit on the steps of Eros in Piccadilly taking photographs. Most astonishing are the young French who pour over for the pleasure of eating the *cuisine anglaise* in the Corner Houses! Most familiar, for they have always come here, are the Americans. We do not know and they do not know whether they are foreign or not.

The change is remarkable. Once visited for the power we had, we are, as I say, now visited for our pleasures. The effect is most notable in the police. It has been said that every Englishman desires to be a policeman, a just, tolerant, self-commanding man, and the police may be considered martyrs to our desire for what we call "the sterling qualities"—the stoical, slow and resistant. But, inevitably, the policeman becomes a giddy tourist guide; he begins to rock on his pedestal into a state of informative frivolity. He has always been good-natured; now he becomes witty. And so with other groups. Conductors get off buses—in defiance of regulations—to show a stranger the way; taxi drivers throw away their misanthropy; all barmaids, waiters, doormen, porters, club servants and chambermaids appear to have sat up the night before reading their Dickens, in order to turn out next morning as authentic characters from *Pickwick* or *David Copperfield*. The foreign touch has always ignited the strong inner fantasy life of the Londoner.

The desire for a Dickensian London is strongest among Russians and Americans. This has its dark side. The Russians search for cotton mills in

Piccadilly and expect to find children starving to death up every chimney. There are Americans who expect to find the roaring hungry chaos of the home of the Industrial Revolution. The American student, like the American soldier, gets to know something more like the real contemporary London. The American Dickensian visits the shrine in Doughty Street, follows the ghosts through the quadrangles and the alleys of Lincoln's Inn Fields and the Temple, drinks a glass of warm beer in piety at that old coaching inn in Southwark and looks hopefully from London Bridge towards Rotherhithe for the fog to be coming up the river. He returns to his hotel and, as I say, finds the perpetual Dickens there, if the staff are not all Poles, Czechs, Italians or Irish.

Americans, too, are strong Johnsonians and are familiar with Wine Office Court and the Old Cheshire Cheese. Do they look at the Doctor's statue under the trees by the burned-out church near the Law Courts? They know Westminster Abbey, St. Paul's, the museums and galleries better than ourselves. Do they know the exquisite Soane Museum in Lincoln's Inn Fields with its collection of Hogarth's paintings? London is still Hogarthian underneath.

When they come from seeing the Italian paintings in the National Gallery, do they risk their lives in the middle of the traffic south of Trafalgar Square and regard one of the few beautiful statues in a city notorious for its commemoration of nonentities—the equestrian figure of Charles I gaily prancing down the street of his downfall? Do any go into the church of St. Stephen in Wallbrook, the perfect small classical seventeenth-century building, or consider the blue octagon interior of St. Clement Danes?

I would send my American friends down St. Peter's Square into Chiswick Mall, to go out to Strand-on-the-Green, to walk for days in the London squares, to drink at Jack Straw's Castle or The Spaniards on the Hampstead Heights, where one can look down at the whole London mess and get a breath of air. At Gravesend, you can get even a touch of the sea from the Thames estuary, and from the window of an inn built for an earl's mistress in the Regency, you can watch that magical procession of the ships of the world proceeding seawards, two or three a minute, at the top of the tide.

What the right-minded American comes to see in London is what we enjoy most ourselves: the sideshows. The city of markets is also a circus. We never know when we are going to run into the Brigade of Guards up to some ceremonial antic—I heard the Horse Guards this morning trooping off from the stables to the palace, and yesterday there were the royal and golden coaches picking up an ambassador at St. James's as if he were a piece of wedding cake and not a commissar and one-time graduate of the London School of Economics. They buried an ambassador this week too. The Guards came across Bryanston Square to the single tap of a muffled drum, their arms reversed and like votaries of death itself in their gloomy Russian busbies. The minute gun went off in Hyde Park, the pigeons flew high off the hotels. It was well done and with pride.

The State never gives up a sideshow, a privilege, a title or a yard of scarlet or gold. In the House of Commons, before the free-for-all of Question Times begins, the Speaker walks like a specter in his silken knee breeches, with the Mace borne before him. We half grin at the solemnity and then, unaccountably, we straighten our faces. Our religion? Clearly we are ancestor worshipers; at any rate we worship their clothes and emblems.

There is humbug in this, of course. There was a good deal of clever humbug in *Alice in Wonderland*, and that book is the best guide to the inner life of London because it catches that London mood which is half solemn and half comic. A man will make jokes about some medieval office of vastly symbolical but slender real meaning, but in some private sense he will think the farce serious. We catch the feeling that, to relieve London of its crushing importance, we must have dreams that are half absurd, half elegant; we could hardly live under this weight without some grotesque or fancy. It is perhaps shady of us to be like this. John Quincy Adams thought it was plain hypocrisy. When the English are behaving badly, he said, they always pretend to be mad. At the House of Lords I heard a packed and humdrum collection of peers debate the outrageous fact of their existence in a democratic state. When Lord Salisbury said he could not offhand think of a logical defense of the hereditary principle and, for this reason, was disinclined to give it up, he was properly adjourning to *Alice in Wonderland*, and asserting the necessity of the London dream.

The clash between scarlet dream and pin-stripe reality is frank in the courts. They are the best booths in the London circus, easier to walk into than a news cinema and the only toothy bit of Dickensian London left.

Dickens had the feeling for the London Wonderland. You can begin at the bottom with the police courts, a place like Bow Street. And here, as so often in this city, you are distracted and have to break off, for you are in a characteristic London muddle. For they have put an Opera House as fine as Milan's and the toughest police court of the city into the middle of Covent Garden vegetable market, so that you have to dodge the Black Maria and step over squashed oranges and cabbage stalks before you can see Fonteyn dance or hear Schwarzkopf sing.

Behind the market lorries is a church famous as a burial place for actors. The best collection of theatrical prints outside the museums is on the walls of the saloon bar of The Nag's Head public house, and at five in the morning the bar will be packed with market porters. One of the minor pleasures for women in London is to walk through Covent Garden early in the morning to a serenade of wolf cries, whistles, blunt suggestions, and the crucial bars of love songs from men of powerful voice. And here, in a strong smell of disinfectant, the Law hauls in its morning catch of thieves, prostitutes and drunks. People put in an hour at Bow Street before the pubs begin to open at 11:30.

Bow Street is crude casualty and is not dressed up. London's *Alice in Wonderland* really begins at the law courts of the Old Bailey, under its golden sword and scales, and continues at the Queen's Bench. When I was a child I used to sit at my father's office window watching the crowds queue for the murder trials at this ugly temple, which they put up in place of disreputable Old Newgate. This is a region of ghosts, doubly so since the war. In Dickens's time the Law was housed in eighteenth-century buildings and behaved with Gothic oddity; now it is housed in nineteenth-century Gothic and behaves with a disturbing decorum. Yet pale oak paneling, with its suggestions of parliament, public libraries, choir stalls and the halls of modern universities, has not killed the waggishness of the Law. Wigs and scarlet robes, ermine and starched bibs, look alarming against this color. The real thing here is ourselves, foolish in our ordinary clothes but also rather aggressive, vulgar and impudent. There is nothing like the sight of a truculent witness, in a navy blue suit and with a bad accent, stonewalling Learned Counsel. The air is motionless, dry and tepid. A small cough, the turning of the pages of briefs, the quiet voices of lawyers, conducting as it seems not a trial but an insinuating conversation among educated friends—these stiffen behavior. A very thoughtful game of chess is going on at dictation speed. The Pawn goes into the box, Queen's Bishop stands up, King's Bishop sits down, a Knight scratches under his wig with a pen. Wrapped in his scarlet, that untakable piece the Lord Chief Justice, an old man with a face as hard as a walnut, restlessly moves his waxen hands.

The Law is a patient, tedious occupation and in London it relieves the boredom by its own little comedies.

"And you may think, m'lord," says Learned Counsel, "that it is not without significance that when the prisoner signed these cheques he appended the name of Ernest Stoney, a reference possibly to the circumstance that he was at that time without funds."

"Not one of your best, Mr. So-and-So," says the judge.

"An inadvertence, m'lord, an inadvertence," murmurs Counsel. He is satisfied. The calamities of legal wit are to be borne like the loss of Bishop's Pawn: the prisoner gets eighteen months. We laugh, the Usher calls silence in Court and we turn to look at the confidence man who tricks the colonials in some Strand hotel, the boy murderer with the vain smile on the lips—the Lord Chief does not frighten *him*—the row of conspiring company directors, respectable corner-seat men of the suburban train, the women of a lifetime's convictions, empurpled now by the uncomprehended load of her enmity toward us. We look at the newcomers since the war: the Poles, the West Africans, the West Indians who bring the angry pathos of their uprooting before the soft voices of their alien judges.

London is prolific in its casualties, its human waste and its eccentrics. We see that blowsy red-haired woman with the gray beard who dances and skips about the pavement in the Haymarket. A well-known trial to bus conductors, the woman always carries a spare hat concealed in a brown-paper bag for traveling by bus. She changes her hat and then sings out:

> *He called me his Popsy Wopsy*
> *But I don't care.*

And drops into a few unprintable words. We are very fond of her. There is the pavement artist who conducts a war with other street entertainers, especially those who use an animal to beg from the thousands of dog lovers, cat strokers, pigeon and duck feeders, the chronic animal lovers who swarm in London. "Worship God not animals," he scrawls in angry chalk on the pavement. There is the Negro bird warbler, ecstatic in his compulsion, and the King of Poland in his long golden hair and his long crimson robe. There are those solitaries with imaginary military careers and the frightening dry monotonous gramophone record of their battles and wounds. They are compelled, they utter, they click their heels, salute and depart. A pretty addled neighbor of mine used to mix up the washing of the tenants in her house when it hung on the line in her garden. She was getting her own back on the Pope, who had broken up her marriage to the Duke of Windsor. One has to distinguish between the divine mad and the people pursuing a stern, individual course. The elderly lady who arrives in white shorts on a racing bicycle at the British Museum every morning, winter and summer, is simply a student whom we shall see working under the gilded dome of the Reading Room. The taxi driver who answers you in the Latin he has picked up from the bishops he has been taking to and fro from the Athenaeum Club all his life is not consciously doing a comic turn. He is simply living his private life in public. As Jung says, we are dreaming all the time; consciousness merely interrupts. It was what Dickens noticed in Londoners a hundred years before.

We live in localities where we sharpen our particular foibles. The "local" public house is one gathering point, although television is emptying the pubs in the working-class districts. The London pubs are all different and live by character. For the stage, I think of the Salisbury, where a stage-door keeper the other day suggested to me that gin and eels made the ideal nightcap; El Vino's for the journalists, the York Minster for the French. We live on strong beer and gin and drink them standing in moody or explanatory groups. At a pub we like to reveal ourselves suddenly and at length to a few new friends; but we respect privacy too. I have seen a man sitting in the midst of a packed and roaring pub reading *The Economist* from cover to cover, unaware of the quarrel between the sailor and the tart, the racing talk, the slow description of a hospital operation or the whispers to the girl having her neck stroked. He was simply insulated.

People began to say before the war that London was becoming continentalized. So it was, in a superficial way. You can buy pizza in the mass restaurants without going to Soho and espresso coffee in the bars. Popular London lives by its mass diversions. For generations the city has been the world's capital of ballroom dancing, and its "pallys" are packed most of the week to see the exhibitions. Africans and Indians color the popular crowd and the great dancers are watched with a critical devotion that I have seen equaled only by Spaniards at the bullfight. The thousands who go to the ballet at Sadler's Wells or Covent Garden are a race in themselves.

And there is gambling; London is almost silenced in some quarters on Thursday nights, when people are doing their football pools, and again at six on Saturday when they hear the worst. There are the greyhound tracks—London's night betting machine; under the white floodlight that chemically green oval suggests the roulette tables of Monte Carlo. The mob goes to these places, the toughs, the spivs, the workers from the factories; but in the hot, carpeted bars of the people who are in the money you see the full heat of gambling, its secretiveness and its fantasies, as the floor is littered with betting slips. Living in London all my life, I had not met these Londoners before: the swarthy, brash, gold-ringed men, the Oriental-looking women in their furs or these startling blondes on the bar stools. Once more I had found another race, as I did when I followed the crowd who go to hear *Tosca* at Sadler's Wells or Shakespeare at the Old Vic, who have heard all the plays and all the operas you can name a dozen times over and call out for their favorite actors and actresses by name in an orgy of local religion.

Another London race is the race of arguers. We can never resist an argument. There are the human cockerels at lunchtime in squares like Lincoln's Inn Fields, crowing about every conceivable kind of political new dawn. But Sunday is the day for this essentially Puritan pleasure. We revel vulgarly in free speech. There are not only the dozen main meetings under the trees in Hyde Park but there are those earliest known manifestations of dialectical life on earth: the conjunction of two men standing nose to nose, with two or three idle friends attending, each proving the other wrong, not in rage but in quiet and disparaging parliamentary calm and pith. ("You say the Buddha is living—how do you know the Buddha is living? Have you seen the Buddha?") From a distance the shouting of Marble Arch sounds like a dog show. The red buses go round the Arch and add the uproarious, band-playing suggestion of merry-go-rounds and racers, but nothing can drown the argument. "My friends," the speakers shout, "believe!" Half a dozen voices call back, "Get on with it. You said that before." And some wit yells out, "Where was Moses born?"

"Believe! Believe!" What are we asked to believe? Some well-informed man is telling us that there are millions of gallons of water up in the sky— "What? Up there, Dad?" comes a voice—and that there will be a repetition of the Great Flood. We are asked to believe that Ireland will be free, that Russia wants war, that America wants war—or that they don't—a hymn strikes up next door, all the Truth societies are at it like mongrels, a lonely fig- ure disputes the Virgin Birth relentlessly, an elderly man, gnawing at a bone, tells us the Pyramids hold the key to human destiny. And then we hear the melting Oxford voice of a colored man from the Gold Coast five yards away: "If I become Minister of Commerce in the Gold Coast—" What is he going to do? Something unpleasant to London, just as the Irish are, the Egyptians, the Russians, the South Americans, the men of God.

Insult, doom, destruction are offered to us. The crowds stand round grin- ning. The Guardsmen stand pink with pleasure. Sailors are delighted. The police stand by like hospital nurses. For nurse is never far off, gossipy at the moment, but always with an eye open. There is a nurse in every Londoner and nurse says things have got to be fair. One would be relieved if, as in wicked countries like France or Italy, things could be unfair—just for once. It is our weakness that we cannot manage that. "No," someone shouts out to an interrupter. "Let him say what he thinks. Go on, mate, say what you was going to say."

The Park is Babel. But in Trafalgar Square, at the foot of Nelson's Col- umn and under the patriotic bas-relief of the Death of Nelson—for the British god is a sea god—you hear the Voice of the People. (They have put amplifiers on the noses of the lions there, which gives these soapy figures a new professorial look.)

The Irish poet W. B. Yeats, who used to wander, tall, remote and lonely, about the London streets when he had woken up from the detective story he had been reading in the Savile Club, despised Trafalgar Square meetings and once told me that in Dublin he had led a procession up Sackville Street—since re-named O'Connell Street—and had smashed ten thousand pounds' worth of plate glass. Such exaltations haven't been heard of in London—not since the days of the Duke of Wellington.

You have been looking at the Piero della Francescas in the National Gallery, watching the crowds there resting their feet on the sofas. You want some air and so, stepping over the face of Greta Garbo and the other Muses which have been done in mosaic in the hall, you come out into the Square. It is all pigeons, peanuts, prams and children getting wet and dirty in the capricious fountains; but round the plinth are the packed, studious-looking crowd, and the lions relaying the indignations of the speaker. He is almost certainly insulting the House of Commons and all those government offices down Whitehall. He is sickened by Downing Street. He is sarcastic about some "noble lord," for if we love lords we also love being rude about them. He is appealing to us, the People, to lift up our Voice and say no to something or other.

We look up at the sky. The appalling London pigeons fly round from their dung heaps on the top of Nelson's Column, the Gallery, the Admiralty Arch or St. Martin's. We listen to the babies crying. We stare at the advertising signs on the ugly buildings to the south, which remind us that if things are as bad as the speakers say, we can emigrate to any corner of the world. Most Londoners who look at those signs have relatives who have done so, and minds wander to what Jack is doing in New Zealand now, and how many years it is since Sis was in Durban, Saskatchewan or Singapore.

Yet we do not emigrate. We accumulate. More of us are pumped day and night into the tubes, more of us lie under the heavy trees in the parks in the summer, more of us greedily parade past the Oxford Street shops, more of us queue for the cinemas, cram the hotels and burst the buses. It is notorious that the English, who founded colonies and peopled new places, now do not fill the emigration quotas and do not care to move. Crowd life is intense life, and what the Londoner misses elsewhere is intensity, for intensity keeps him solid and obliges him to be clever. We have become the great urban nation which is bored by the open spaces. London is our macrocosm. It is no longer the nightmare city of the early Industrial Revolution; it has moderated though it continues to be vulgar and exuberant. It adds to the London spell that the future of this monstrosity, which never has more than a few weeks' supply of food in its store, is a gamble.

In any case London is traditionally free of hysteria, stoical and disciplined, but not beyond the resources of nature. Publicly powerful and often hated for that, London has always valued private life most. It is a place where whims have their rights, where nerves are not exacerbated, where one is at ease, where standardization of behavior is disliked and where the tone of casual conversation is affectionate. There is regard for what can last; this can be called vegetative, sentimental, unrealistic, muddled. A Londoner himself would call this feeling: passion.

[1956]

12

The Island World

"... *this little world*": in that phrase, from the famous passage in *Richard II*, Shakespeare defined England simply and forever. The smallness of England is absurd, frightening and exquisite. It is a little sea garden. It is the toy country of millions of small, neatly painted houses with millions of small polished windows shining after rain, thousands of little green fields of little green woods. The gardens are small, the famous rivers are small, the distances between villages and towns are small; no hill rises to much more than three thousand feet and most are less than eight hundred. Small motorcars travel down narrow, winding roads, small locomotives draw small railway wagons. A man living a mile from a village or a few miles from a town considers himself to be in solitude.

How has it come about that an island so trivial and so private, a mere six hundred miles long, and, at its widest, not much more than three hundred, should have become, until fifty years ago, the wealthiest and most powerful in the world? And if that is not true now, the most densely populated country in the world after Belgium? The traveler who looks at the English landscape and considers the English character ought never to forget this. The moment he flies into the mist that on most days is streaked across this island, the moment he faces the long array of chalk at Dover or picks out the statue of Drake on the Hoe at Plymouth, or passes the Needles off Southampton, he is about to enter a country where people are shoulder to shoulder. The desire for privacy, the gambits for avoiding acquaintance are understandable.

When Columbus discovered America he can be said to have created Britain also, for he moved the island to the center or crossroads of the world. Since then, all sea traffic across the Atlantic has had to come this way for its shortest routes; the situation has been little changed by air travel. Set free by Columbus, the British discovered their Atlantic, non-European countenance.

As a result, the Englishman stands between two worlds, living by both. He is a European with a difference. You can prove to him that he is a European who has got his civil institutions from the Anglo-Saxon north and his Christianity and culture from the ancient Mediterranean; but he will insist that he is a fortress afloat off the European coast, unconquered since the eleventh century, and looking across the Atlantic to the countries his race has founded, or his ancestors have explored and exploited. He is a man facing two ways. In this, where he is chauvinistic, he has a national pride; he knows by long experience what it is to be admired, envied and hated, to make profits, commit crimes, to forgive those he has injured, to take punishment and laugh at himself. The songs of the Gilbert and Sullivan operas are full of national self-mockery. For behind the figure of the British as a figure of power, there is another: the kind, good-humored man of the small island.

Islanders who live close to the great land masses develop an intense defensive, local individuality; they live in continual fear of conquest. The British are nationally united because, in the last four hundred years, they have been in terror of Continental despots like Philip II of Spain, Louis XIV and Napoleon in France and, in our time, Hitler. Fear of this kind creates resolution and the spirit of aggression. In the late Middle Ages, the British were continually invading France, and when the long effort failed, their energies turned toward the New World. In milder times this aggressive spirit has become no more than a fruitful outburst against the claustrophobia which affects people on small islands, and especially one where the gray and relatively sunless climate turns the mind in upon itself. We are liable to burst out. The man who delivers my whiskey dresses up like a gentleman once a year, to let himself go in Monte Carlo.

Another important basic fact is that no place in Britain is more than seventy-five miles from tidal water; the frontier is the sea. One can see how much of British life has looked outward by the names of many of the little suburban villas: Durban, Poona, Kimberley, Nairobi, Waterloo. Or by the names of the streets in the seaports.

The main overriding difference in England is between North and South. The river Trent cuts English character in two. It passes through Nottingham—the region called "The Dukeries" because so many dukes have estates there—and turning northeast, runs into the Humber near Hull, the port for the Baltic. The North makes; heavy industry is there. The South rules; the Queen and the government are in the South. The Queen speaks in the standard southern English accent of the upper classes. Oxford and Cambridge are in the South.

The Southerner is gentler, more leisurely in manner, wittier, more self-concealing, more formal, politic and reserved than the Northerner. He is a bit of a snob, in all classes. If he is well-off he conceals the fact. He is inclined to disparage himself. The Northerner calls him "soft." But if this north-south division is true of the people in a very general way, the landscape division of the country is really made by a line drawn from the mouth of the River Tweed on the northeast to Lands End in the southwest. The hills and mountains are mainly west of that line. East of it lie smaller hills, green plains and marshes.

Yet east or west, pastureland or sea marsh, moor or mountain, the delight of England is in the intimate and continual changes of a manmade landscape. It is the most gardened country on earth. The roads are rarely straight for more than a mile or so; there is always surprise at the next corner. One moment the land is arable, the next it is water meadow or heath. We are in an island of oak woods. The beeches have their tall aisles in Buckinghamshire close to the Thames; the willow hangs over the small rivers and mill-races of East Anglia, the counties of Norfolk, Suffolk and Essex that bulge out into the North Sea or "German Ocean." The poplar whitens against the slaty sky, the ash hangs in all the lanes, and the elm, the chestnut, the syca-more and hornbeam are in every hedgerow. The South is a country of haw-thorn hedges. We live in a place of hanging woods, coppices, brakes and dells. Only in the flat country of the Fens southeast of Lincoln—a very Dutch part of England on the east coast protected by dykes—does one see trees scattered singly, like separate people in long vistas, with the east wind and the dyke water between them.

The English counties are countries in themselves. Begin at Canterbury in Kent, in the extreme southeast, in the fruit garden of England, and work your way through the widest stretch of southern England to Cornwall in the extreme west. The River Medway still traditionally divides the legendary Kentish man from the equally legendary Man of Kent—the man of the cherry orchards, netting his trees to keep off the birds, in agony about the late frosts—the "frosties," as country people call them—that are the curse of English agriculture. The russet towns and flint oast houses or hop kilns of Kent change to the birch woods of Surrey, adjoining Kent on the west, a county given to stockbrokers and those golden, hearty, tennis-playing girls whose forearm drives John Betjeman has celebrated in his poem "A Subal-tern's Love Song":

> *Oh! full Surrey twilight! importunate band!*
> *Oh! strongly adorable tennis girl's hand!*

Vast Hampshire, just west of Surrey, has its sandy heaths and those lovely houses on the Sussex border that some think as remarkable as the châteaux of the Loire; it has also its large nondescript population of squatters, eking out a hard independent living on a few ugly acres. In Hampshire are the chalk downs and the hangars on wooded cliffs where Gilbert White wrote the most English of small English classics: *Natural History and Antiquities of Selborne*. White is a model for the eccentricity of the English country clergy—the oddest race in the country. All through Kent and Hampshire, and adjoining Sussex, Wiltshire and Dorset run the bold chalk downs, rising like smooth green whales from the beech woods. Pause at Jane Austen's

Winchester, in Hampshire. It is vivid to me, not only because of the cathedral but because there, the only time in my life, I saw a judge put on the black cap and condemn a man to death. It was a scene of horror from Thomas Hardy, but brought up to date in macabre fashion by press photographers who walked backward, like a court, before the mother of the murderer and the mother of his victim as they left the courtroom. I can still smell the brilliantine on the hair of the police. Soldiers were singing in the barracks nearby and the afternoon traffic of the cathedral town spanked on its way to Southampton.

Those chalk downs run north to Salisbury Plain, to Avebury and Stonehenge (they are pimpled by scores of burial mounds left by the people of the Stone Age and the Bronze); and southward into Hardy's Dorset, where the Gothic-looking stone cottages remind one that part of the variety of the English villages depends on the fact that they were built in styles, changing from century to century, by local men using local brick and stone. All these counties have their vestiges of dialect and their own accents. The radio is leveling this out; but the traveler who buys a postcard in a village shop or listens in the village pub, will notice that the people talk two languages. They fall back into the dialect of their childhood (English people fall very easily into the talk of childhood) when they drop into craftiness or are telling comic stories against each other. Rustic phrases like "Be'e talking to we?" are the language of succulent local comedy. It keeps the stranger at arm's length too. I once saw a la-di-da fellow go into a seaside taproom and call out cheerfully to the players, "I see you like playing shove ha'penny heah." The fishermen went on playing and, after a very long and freezing time, the oldest of them took his pipe out of his mouth and replied: "Some of us buggers be bloody artists at it." It was the war of town and country, between local and stranger.

The mass life of England is not prim; indeed one wonders how Puritanism ever got started here. It was strongest on the righteous eastern side of the country, where the earliest Christian missionaries and abbots installed themselves. Rural England all over is free-spoken and earthy and lazy-voiced. As you travel westward you notice the "I" changing to "Oi," the r's burr richly; in Somerset "cider" still becomes "zoider" and the words soften. Traveling in a straight line westward through Berkshire, Wiltshire, Somerset, Devon to Cornwall, getting off the Wiltshire chalk onto the brilliant pink soil of

Somerset and then onto the deep chocolate soil of Devonshire, you notice that speech has dawdled almost to a dream on the lips of those pink and creamy-skinned Devonshire girls with their dark-blue eyes and dimpled, double-chinned smiles. They call you "dear" and "love" in the shops and you almost believe they love you.

The village inn is still the place to see the main country types. The evening is the time when the beer flows and the pipe tobacco is strong. I think of a Wiltshire inn in a valley of water meadows, bad in the winter fogs. One of the first in is an old man who is one of the few surviving thatchers in the county. He is notable for his huge boots and distorted feet, and likes a joke about them. In his youth he had walked all over England from job to job and had a few fights on the road, but now he and an old widow, who polices him and her neighbors from the cottage window, are mostly at home looking at TV. That does not keep him from his couple of pints—a couple being five or six. There is the tall lean woodcutter, father of six and of many by-blows, a handsome fellow and in the money. There is a gardener who was a shepherd in Patagonia and speaks Spanish. The talk is dull at first: the estimates of the weather which absorb so much of English talk (for it changes every few hours), the eternal talk of onions and broccoli. The cricket team enters in flannels and blazers; the garage man plays bar billiards. Four van drivers are playing darts, and at harvesttime there may be men traveling from farm to farm with their combine. The inn is run by a man from Cumberland with a pretty wife who is the queen of the local dances. Their daughter is a fashion artist. There is the usual strange English spinster in pullover and trousers, guarded by a huge Airedale dog. She is mad about horses. A lady, she enjoys "drinking up" with the men. There is the deplorable Irish lady with her blue, doll's eyes, her racing tips and her jockey.

Next door, in a private bar full of flowers, are two respectable women from the post office drinking a glass of black stout which makes them swell into an even greater appearance of respectability. It is needed. For they must affect not to hear the language or notice the behavior of the eccentric cavalry colonel who has a compulsion every few minutes to shout—even when stone sober—"Stand to your horses," as a mysterious, deeply private contribution to the talk. It is a tolerated madness. He has a test pilot with him, a dandy who likes to kiss the ladies' hands and offer them a large door key. It is, he says, "the key to my heart." Before addressing the colonel he always uses the old R.A.F. catch phrase: "Colonel, may I drop the 'sir' socially?"

These people are well on the way to becoming "characters"; as for the villagers, they are a canny clan; all are related; all know every detail of one another's lives. The men have, most of them, been overseas. It is the publican's distinction that he was once asked to a circumcision party in Turkey. "Ah felt awkward," he says.

Rich cities strung across southern England, like Canterbury, Winchester, Salisbury, Wells and Exeter, establish the type of the cathedral town. The achievements of moneyed men, not the merits of the saints, are celebrated in the elaborate epitaphs and tombs of the cathedrals. The British worship position and power. New red suburbs and factories surround the city; closer in are the Victorian parks, the botanical gardens, the beautiful green circle of the cricket field with its white pavilion; in the center are the older narrow streets and the cathedral with its close, as ripe in its red brick as the faces of old men in Reynolds's portraits. The small shops were mostly built in early Victorian times, but their line will be broken by the vermillion and chromium plating and the neon signs of the twentieth century. There is always one good old-fashioned family grocer with his black-and-gold tea canisters.

But the contrasts are violent. That handsome town house is no longer the home of a wealthy family; it has become the office of the Inland Revenue or the Electricity Commission now. The Milk Bar and Cafeteria stand by the old-style cretonned teashop which always has its ladies at the proper hour. The TV aerial rides on the seventeenth-century gable. Market day crowds these towns with food and junk stalls and cattle. The place is a sallow sea of raincoats and peculiar tweeds washing round the stalls, and of spick-and-span double-decker buses. And then, almost suddenly, between five and six o'clock, the shops close, thousands of bicycles rush down the streets taking the people home, and a city has become deserted and silent. There may be a few girls going to a dance at the Corn Exchange, which was a real corn market 150 years ago, or a few Teddy Boys and lost soldiers hanging about in doorways, but that will be all. The Teddy Boy with his long jacket and very narrow trousers is the postwar version of the adolescent corner boy or loafer.

A stranger could die of loneliness at this hour. The public faces of the English look sad when pleasure approaches; a worried mulish kindness is their

275

expression when they speak. They "break out" only in intimacy. Eavesdrop on their conversation and you will notice how often the word "right" occurs. "It is all *right*." "I don't think it is *right*." "She has no *right*." It is the sad official *hypocrite* refrain of English speech. English life is lived in the home in the evenings. The Englishman must be pursued to his armchair or his back garden.

The town will not wake up again until 10:30, the gloomy hour when the public houses close and the buses pick up the cinema crowds. (The Englishman—it is astonishing to find—spends far more hours in cinema-going than the American; on reflection, this seems quite natural, for we spend a good deal of our privacy, and our avoidance of one another in this crowded island, in daydreaming.) For half an hour or so the buses and motorbikes roar, the fish-and-chips shops do their trade, the people queue up talking quietly; a group of youths, with the beer in them, will go home singing very flat; the fantastic old ladies who sit like tropical insects in the hotels, and who are an English specialty, put down their brandy and go to bed; the cathedral bell strikes eleven, the last dogs and cats are called in—the day is over.

After eleven o'clock if you want to eat, or drink a cup of tea, you will have to dig out some soldiers' or lorry drivers' "caff" on the outskirts of the town. These "caffs" are shacks. They are not very clean. Busy, steamy, motherly women and slatternly girls pour the strong tea and serve some fry or sandwiches. One of these disheartened places looks snug but may have a sideline in petty crime. You can't tell. There's a pale, breathless man called Pop on the West Road, known to all the lorry drivers in England—as far as I can make out—who is always called "more sinned against than sinning." He had the ill luck to be put "inside" for some black-market offense years ago, and the drivers are indignant. ("So 'e 'ad a fiddle? So what?") There is a dear old lady sitting in a tiny shed on the same road outside Bath who starts business at four in the morning to catch the long-distance truck drivers with a cup of tea. About six at a time and a tired policeman can squeeze in.

The Great West Road from London to Bristol is the road of Fielding's *Tom Jones*, and when a Wiltshire squire is weaving down it, and the heavy lorries are pulling in at the "caffs," and the fruit pickers or harvest people are on the move, it seems to me that the mock-pious, ribald England goes on, not so differently from the England of Fielding's time. It merely moves faster.

Southwestern England from Devon into Cornwall is warmer, wetter and richer to look at than the rest of the country. One feels the air softening and, on the Atlantic side, getting stronger. It becomes so strong that it drugs the stranger with earth and ocean smells and reduces him to indolence and sleep. The soil becomes red; the short, sharp, steep hills pile up, crowned by their tors of rock; lanes twist and deepen between the high banks and the gray stone walls that run beside the woods, and these walls are mottled with delicate mosses and are rife with ferns. The oak and the ash close in on sudden ravines where fast black streams worry and curdle among the rocks under old stone bridges. The rhododendron empurples the woods; flowers seem larger and the leaves of the woods shine.

We are on Exmoor, in the north of Devon. Down in its gorges is the hidden country described in Blackmore's *Lorna Doone*. Toward the south is Dartmoor, where the fogs come suddenly down; that south-coast air is relaxing. We drop down hills that fall one foot in four, with the grasses and wildflowers brushing the fenders of our car, and we pray we won't meet a car coming up.

On the north side of Devon and Cornwall from Hartland Point all the way down to Lands End you are on the most dangerous and violent coast of Western Europe. It is the open Atlantic coast of wrecks. The sea has smashed up the cliffs and the rocks, and has broken the coast into enameled and dangerous coves; if we climb over the shore in the bad places, we see the rusted plates and iron wreckage of lost ships, old mines and old torpedoes. Two hundred years ago this used to be the coast of the wreckers and smugglers; and it is still a place where the country people know the important legal difference between flotsam and jetsam—between the wreckage that is still afloat and can be claimed and the wreckage which is thrown on the shore and belongs either to the Excise or, possibly, to the lord of the manor. They brushed up their knowledge profitably in the last war. Granite breaks through the coastal fields, and in the lanes the ragged robin and speedwell grow hedge high. On the high lands the Atlantic gales have stunted the dark-leaved trees and land is poor; but in the deep dales all is suddenly rich. In Cornwall each little field is enclosed by banks and fortified against the wind and the drenching Atlantic squalls.

Devon and Cornwall are the seafaring counties. Most of the great seamen from Drake onward came from this part of Britain. You can see from the statue of Drake on the Hoe at Plymouth that this is the sea-traffic gate of England and can understand why this naval city suffered frightful destruction during the last war. The Devon towns grew rich not only on wool and their orchards and farmlands but on sea traffic, war, piracy and the prizes. In later times, Devon has been the county of the retired Empire builder: he can be seen, in his tweeds, in places like Budleigh Salterton, Sidmouth and in the exotic Victorian architecture of Torquay. He sits on his property, sun-reddened and shrewd, dreaming of curry and Bombay duck, gazing sleepily at the red cliffs and the hot coves and the boats on the long Devon estuaries.

The peninsula gets wilder as it pushes out into the sea toward Lands End, the color of the soil changes again and we are out of England, strictly speaking, and in Cornwall. There is a sudden change in architecture. The villages are slate-roofed, and built in gray or whitewashed stone in the manner of Welsh or Irish buildings. They are odd and severe to the eye. The richer English have far more taste for domestic style. The large country houses in Cornwall seem to belong to a wilder, older and poorer economy. Seamen, tin miners, workers in China clay, small farmers, the Cornish have seen the traditional trades dwindle; the Cornish miner who was working in the time of the Phoenicians now turns up in Johannesburg, in South American and African mines. He has been in all the world's gold rushes. His own land is very much a place for the holiday-maker now; and since he gets the warm weather much earlier than any other part of England, he also does an enormous trade in cut flowers. Not only the daffodil and the crocus but the fuchsia and hydrangea belong to this country.

The stranger feels something mysterious about the Cornish. There is a long tradition of the fairy tale and Celtic superstition, and like all the Celts, the Cornish are remarkable natural storytellers. Theirs is reputedly the country of King Arthur and the Round Table. By the singsong sound of voice and words used, by a certain excitable restlessness we can tell these people are not Anglo-Saxon. They are engaging in their ordinary address. They use words curiously. The postman talks of "going up-along" or "down-along" the steep streets. On buses, in pubs, in shops, you are called not "Sir" or "Ma'am" but "my dear" or "my love," caressingly, as if you were a member of the tribe; for the Celts always wish to endear and please at first sight.

Wesley, the great preacher, had a total success in Cornwall; his rhetoric caught the Cornish taste for romantic phrase; they became Methodists overnight. Severe in custom, they close public houses on Sundays, just as the Welsh do. The innumerable chapels are packed with hymn singers; in England proper—so pious in Victorian times—the churches are poorly attended and the decline of Methodism and other nonconformist sects has been general.

I was standing on the quay at St. Ives, a pretty fishing town in North Cornwall. It is now a holiday place and has been famous for two generations as an art colony. As I stood there I heard two fishermen shouting at each other and moved closer to see what the quarrel was about. Of all things, it was about religion. One was crying out: "But it says in the Bible, 'By Grace ye are saved.'" You would never hear a public row going on about Grace and Works in England. The English would be ignorant of theology. Nor can the English sing hymns with the fervor of the Welsh or the Cornish, though they have wonderful choirs in places like King's College Chapel in Cambridge or at Canterbury Cathedral. Ordinary English singing when the pubs close is like the dying of cows; and in the ordinary churches the singing sounds as if the whole congregation were dragging out a bad cold in the head.

The Cornish have been overrun by the English; their customs die. They are still notable wrestlers. Some loneliness in the life has produced many eccentrics. They like practical jokes and carry them to farcical lengths. There are jokes which are really private charades and which last for days on end. They are sometimes carried further by theatrical disguises. If the telephone rings and you are told that your lawyer or the chief constable or some important enemy is speaking, do not believe it. Reject the story he ingeniously concocts. If your neighbor's grandfather comes to tea, do not believe that either: pull his wig off. The Cornish live a good deal in their imaginations and manias, and the strong Atlantic air and the violent changes of a drugging climate make one uncertain of the borderline between reality and dream. The solid kind of Englishman, who is humorous rather than witty and has no time for fancy, never gets the hang of these people and is fair game.

If we leave wild, wind-polished Cornwall and go north back into solid England, to the lovely terraces of Beau Nash's Bath so favored by retired naval officers and readers of Jane Austen's *Northanger Abbey*; if we press on north to Bristol, where the Cabots sailed from, the port for the American expeditions, the slave and the tobacco trades, we are in the valley of the Severn. The yellow stone of this country has been got out of its hills. Again, up the Severn, the people change; and the country changes too. Celt and Saxon are well mixed here, for we are on the Welsh border. In the Welsh towns the people smile and in the English they do not. We see the mixture of two antagonistic races abusing each other at the top of their tempers for lying, thieving and hypocrisy throughout the centuries. Language and blood have profited.

"You've come back with the bloom on you, as ripe as a plum," cries the old Shropshire farmer to the beautiful girl who has come back from some city to be married. And with a wink at her young man he says to her: "If that young devil don't keep you quiet, I'll be upstairs in a jiffy." This is merry England, fleshy, sensual, shrewd and uproarious. It loves to see the girls blush and the men drink. It gets round the law. It crowds to the cattle shows. Its small towns rock to the gossip of love affairs. You eat the Severn salmon and don't ask whether it has been caught illegally; if you do you will be answered by a look as pious as a Methodist chapel. This is the country of A. E. Housman's *Shropshire Lad*, of lovely towns like Ludlow on its cliff, of Clun, Much Wenlock and Church Stretton.

But we must turn now and face the important fact that England is an industrial nation and that we have been dodging it. Ninety percent of its people live in towns; and of those, 40 percent live in the huge industrial conurbations. It is all very well: the most intelligent, alive and interesting people belong to the industrial population. Oxford dispels an illusion: an industrial city has engulfed the university, and the student body is formed, not by the privileged classes but by poorer clever boys up on scholarships from the redbrick suburbs and the industrial towns.

At Stratford, on Shakespeare's birthday, the long American cars of the diplomatic corps pack the streets for schoolboys to admire. A town councillor told me, as we watched the swans of Avon turning on the river, that he had never read Shakespeare until he came to Stratford. But now he had discovered, as a businessman, that "Shakespeare had the answer to every question." That's the spirit of the Midlands: practical.

Its capital is Birmingham, that huge concentration of engineering works, where town runs into town under the smoke, where the ground subsides over the coal fields, until we reach Arnold Bennett's Black Country. That is a region to see at night, when the kilns and the furnaces glow; it is inhabited by a race apart. Yet once these industrial wildernesses are passed, we realize that they have emptied the countryside and left enormous empty panoramas of moor and mountain. The north is the one part of this unspectacular island which is dramatic.

Suppose you drive up from Derby, where they make the Rolls-Royce engines, toward Manchester: you are traveling through ravines of the Peak District.

"What's life like in Derby?" you ask the man at the garage.

He gives you the set industrial look. "Dead," he says. "You coom here for the money and the work."

The North, you realize, means work, the love of work, the cult of work, the scorn for those who don't work. When you drive through the Peak to Buxton, looking down at the green curling River Wye, watching the water go over the weirs like glass, and passing through the spacious parklands where medieval Haddon Hall with its battlements looks across the centuries to Chatsworth, you see the busloads of industrial workers out on holiday. They have come out to see the spa waters blessed at Buxton, to hear the town band, drink pints of beer and eat potato crisps. Sheffield, with its steel and mines, is not far off over the hills.

A hard climate here. There is less sun than in the south. Snow blocks the roads in the winter. Hedges have gone, grass is poor on the hills. It is a country bony with rock. The bare fields are chained by loose, blackened stone walls; and from now on in the North, the stone wall will have taken the place of the hedge and there will be few flowers and grasses close to them. From the top of the high country you see Manchester lying twenty-odd miles away under a white chemical fume that makes you cough the moment you drive down into it. You have re-entered the poisoned-climate twentieth century.

When you stop to ask the way, you notice the accent has changed from the short, flat tone of the Midlands to one broad in its vowels and cutting-sharp in its consonants. They know how to pronounce the letter *r* in the North; indeed, in Tyneside, the miners and shipwrights use the only guttural *r* (very much like the French *r*) known in the Kingdom. The northern demeanor is different too. No southern obsequiousness, no flattering desire to please.

If you come to a crossroads and you stop to ask a passerby for a direction he will not say, for example: "Turn sharp right." He will say: "Turn stoomp raaight," touching the "stump" of his arm as if going through an emergency amputation, or as sharp and brutally right as having your arm chopped off. He likes the brutal physical image; but the voice, though hard, is kind. The dramas that occur to a Lancashire man or his neighbor in Yorkshire—from the raids on Berlin to a singsong down at the local pub—have to be compressed in a few words of poker-faced understatement. He will say: "We 'ad a bit of a do," to describe the Normandy landings. If pressed he will add, "It were nowt." Compliments are rare and based on practical observation. The young man said to his girl: "My, th' mother keeps tha nice." The whole of England is a man's country run by men for men; Dad rules, Mum cleans. This is above all true of the North, which makes for a quizzical, practical, hardheaded kindness between the sexes. When she went up to Haworth to see old Mr. Brontë, Mrs. Gaskell observed how slowly the affections moved in these people; but that, once moved, their passions, in antagonism or love, were violent and for life.

I stood in the garden of a Lancashire man's house, on a ridge of the Pennines, looking down on the industrial plain. He was a blue-eyed, fair-haired, pink-faced man as men here always seem to be—ebullient, laughing, talking, with the sardonic northern edge to his voice, a scholar and a wit. In the South his counterpart would have been harder to know, more cautious and less immediately hospitable: I would have been shown the ancient buildings. But this man had taken me to all the modern buildings of the city, its schools, halls and galleries; he had taken me on a tour of the rich manufacturers' suburb and had talked about the ups and downs of fortune in the cotton trade. He was more American than southern English; for the Northerners have immense civic pride.

There is dash, energy, a love of gambling and a touch of fantasy about the Lancashire people. They are famous for their music-hall comedians and their popular singers and for laughing at themselves. "Clogs to clogs in three generations," the mill hands say; humble men have piled up fortunes and spent them fantastically.

All across the North you are in something like a democracy; you certainly are not in the South. You are "lad" or "lass," not "sir," in the North. They are outspoken, laconic, love a coarse word; they test you out, hit hard, hope to be hit back. "Nowt for nowt" is a Yorkshire saying; nothing for nothing. Men and women work together all their lives in the mills; in one of the small mill towns of the Pennine ravines, it will be the men in the quarries, the women in the mills. The passion for work is joined to a passion for cleanliness among the women. In the evening, you will see women polishing their brass door knockers, whitening their doorsteps and window sills, cleaning windows, scrubbing floors and children. My Yorkshire grandmother used to seize us southern grandchildren and cry, "Eh, ah a doubt but what tha moother lets th' run about like a gooter lad." My indignant southern mother would snap back in Cockney: "You'd scrub the inside of a goose, old girl." My grandmother, undefeated: "Eh, ah never could abide London moock." Such altercations shock a southern sensibility; to the Northerner they are inoffensive, the life blood. And after the working and cleaning and the downright words, there are the huge northern meals to mollify the temper. Tripe and pig's trotters, hame and sausages and pies, cakes and twenty kinds of bread—a variety far beyond the southern imagination contents these aggressive people.

Yet here I am generalizing about the North, when there is all the difference in the world between the Lancashireman and the man from Yorkshire. And in Yorkshire a great difference between those of the West Riding and the East: the western part of Yorkshire is the more intensely industrialized; the eastern part remained for longer in the hands of the landowning aristocracy. The East—the Westerners say with contempt—are gentlemen. If Lancashire is likely to spend, Yorkshire is cautious and canny and likes to save. "Ay," an old lady said to me in a moorland village, "they've got a lot of brass felted here." To "felt" is to hide and "brass" is money. A child born of Yorkshire and Lowland Scottish parents is impregnable in finance. Yorkshire has more reserve, self-regard, less imagination than Lancashire. The Yorkshiremen are an obstinate, critical race. They like to say, "Ah won't boodge." I stood in the signal box outside the railway station in York during the war. The city had just been bombed. The signalman nodded to the towers of the Minster rising above the city.

"Hitler says he's going to be married up at t'Minster next spring," he reflected. "But . . . ah doan't knaw."

I still hear the slow broad Yorkshire voice dawdling its unsmiling irony along the words.

The mountains and the moors are the lungs of the North and they come down to the very ends of the streets in the Pennine valleys. Here are the panoramas. The hard long ridges of the moors drop into the wide-wooded Dales with their lovely rivers and rise again to the Fells, the peaks of the Lake country and the Cheviots on the Scottish border. Until August comes, these moors are green with young bracken and dark with heather and tussocky grass; small streams trickle in them. Then the heather blooms and they are changed to a spacious and rolling sea of purple. The heights seem great—once you are used to the English scale—the treeless ridges are austere; you hear only the wind, the cry of the curlew and the baa-ing of sheep. You come down into clean gray towns of wintry stone.

The beauty of England lies in all its small towns. The cities have drawn away the growing population and have left the towns in their perfection. There is the market square, the parish church—almost always interesting: a Norman crypt perhaps, some superb murals of the fifteenth century as at Pickering near Scarborough in the northeast, or angels and bosses in the vaulting—there are the red-brick or cream houses which so often turn out to be the patchwork of the centuries if you go down an alley and look at the backs of them.

I think of neat, stone Kirby Lonsdale on the way to Westmoreland and the Lakes, with its warm little square. It was one of Ruskin's favorite places. There's a lively blacksmith at Kirby Lonsdale whose family has worked for generations in wrought iron and who made the lovely gates of the churchyard. He is a TV "character" now, but he is a real craftsman and wanderer: he has ridden all over the sheep drives of the north into Scotland, and they have hardly changed since Sir Walter Scott wrote *The Two Drovers*.

I think of perfect Helmsley in the Pickering valley on the eastern side of Yorkshire. It is six o'clock in the summer, but it is cool enough for a big fire. People are sitting round it in the inn having tea. Two silent men are playing darts in the bar, and out of the window I can see the elegant gray square, empty, without a building to distress the eye, unchanged in gravity for centuries. Do not misunderstand me: the age of a place means nothing. Helmsley retains a perfect moment of domestic civilization in silvering stone.

We used to climb the Fells and look across to the higher mountains of Westmoreland and to Solway Firth under their changing cloud. We were looking at what the Lake Poets have made into official romantic scenery. The traveler who leaves Lancashire or West Yorkshire for these little lakes has to prepare for those days when, as the people say, the weather is "damp-ening on"—as good a piece of English understatement as I have ever met. The caprice of the sky, the changes from wet to clear enhance the grace and variety of the scene as one drives, say, over the Kirkstone Pass into Patterdale and Ullswater. Into that lake, red deer from the oldest herd in England will sometimes come down to swim. The Lakes are the country for walkers and climbers. The inhabitants are hardy, good, plain folk and taciturn; they have the Celt and the Viking in them.

The observant and thirsty traveler will have noticed by now how many inns are called *The Lamb*, *The Fleece*, *The Woolpack*, and so on; he will have read that the Lord Chancellor is said to "sit on the Woolsack." When you turn from Yorkshire and away from the machines and begin your journey down the eastern side of England from Durham to York, and then on to Lincoln and finally to that bulge into the North Sea which is called East An-glia, you will be traveling back in time to when the wealth of England was based on wool.

When we learned to weave our own cloth in the fourteenth century, the beautiful wool towns of East Anglia were built and, in them, some of the fin-est churches in the country. I think of the churches at Lavenham and Stoke-by-Nayland, of lonely Blythburgh on its sea marsh and of the great church of Long Melford. I think of Norwich and the water-color painters who learned from their almost-neighbors, the Dutch, and who were moved by the immense light of this flattish country which has been cleaned by the pre-vailing east wind. It was always a place for churches. Suffolk is called *selig Suffolk*, which is nowadays pronounced "silly"; but the word means holy and describes a land of monasteries and abbeys. The Anglo-Saxon is almost pure here. I went to school in Ipswich when I was a boy and we always called each other "boa"—their German *Bauer*—instead of boy; and in the sing-song speech of the county we said, "Farewell, boa" instead of good-bye.

Of all the East Anglian towns Bury St. Edmunds, I think, is the most beautiful. It is little known to travelers. The majestic Abbey churches and the vast ruin of the old Abbey in the middle of town have given the place the grand style. It has fine squares and streets, whose eighteenth-century façades very often conceal back ways and building of a much earlier time. It has the serenity of something fixed forever. It is a place of steep hills.

As the cars and motor bicycles roar through the town on a summer evening, the people walk into the Abbey grounds and there is the complete English summer scene. Couples go in for that expert examination of the rose garden which few Englishmen can resist, for they know the names of roses as they know the names of cricketers. Boys are swimming in the river, girls are playing tennis, youths are playing rough-and-ready cricket and quarreling about whose turn it is next; and on the bowling green, that lovely close-cut lawn which is an English specialty and a sacred object of contemplation, sly men are rolling the big black balls.

"How does that smell, Tom?" the butcher calls as his ball rolls toward the pin and gives its sudden turn.

"Strong!" calls the draper from the other end of the green.

The decorum of the people, the quiet, the evening scents, the silence of the courting couples—for English courtships are sedate in public—the rich shadows of the elms, take your mind off the white scribble of the soundless jets in the blue sky. It is a thing we have got used to: the island is a fortress and you cannot drive many miles without coming to a runway.

I have written only about England and Englishmen, not about the Welsh or the Scots. It is all nonsense really; there are only the British. The English are a cultural fiction, the descendants of an early melting pot of Celts, Norsemen, Saxons, Teutons, Danes and Norman French, with an allowance of later Huguenots and the European immigrations of the last thirty years or more and the continuous inflow of the Irish. We now have West Indians too.

We have seen in the Englishman a barbarian who has been tamed by a mild climate.

Hippolyte Taine, the French critic who came here in the middle of the last century, did not agree that we were a silent and reserved race. He found us quick, affable, talkative, easily unbosoming. Our leisurely manner was a necessary pose. God help everybody if we abandoned our self-control.

Taine found us unexampled in our individual relation to society but poor in personal relationships; our unrelaxed nature was deeply private, he said, and this privacy found its supreme expression in English lyrical poetry. For the rest, we were too closely packed, shoulder to shoulder.

I don't know. A few months ago I was standing on the walls of York looking over the rose gardens to the towers of the Minster and listening to the sound of the great bells. There were two bells, deep-sounding bells that

hummed powerfully, covering all other sounds in the city. One was profound, grave and masculine, its note pronounced, impervious to argument.
The other, though strong, was pitched a little higher, like an echo, still grave
but feminine. I was listening to a colloquy of towers, a dialogue between
those two aspects of the English nature, the outer and the inner, the govern-
ing and the private or poetic. They spoke for a long time and seemed to me
to speak of the division that lies in the sober English nature.

In the end, if we ask what an Englishman is like, we have to say that he
changes more from county to county than he does from class to class. The
confident aggressor of the nineteenth century has become the peculiar, considerate and self-disciplined being of today who so often sacrifices his obli-
gations to his emotions and whose teenage children show regular signs of
wanting to burst out again. His fortune was once made out of wool; then out
of coal, steel and ships; his skill—and skill he fosters and values far more
than happiness—now has turned to the air and atomic power. If he accepts
now a great deal of the standardization imposed by a mass society, he pro-
tects himself by a great tolerance of eccentricity and of what passes for madness. (All the English, Hamlet said, were mad.) He is a man who has always
thought his own past was alive in him. It has been his fate to live in the crank-
ish intimacy of that "little world" Shakespeare spoke of and yet to act com-
pulsively on a far larger world outside in every century. It is the fate of the
islands.

[1958]

13

Thames River of History

River life is male: Father Tiber; Old Man River; Father Thames. On the banks of rivers, civilizations are begotten. English civilization is the Thames. It is the preeminent British river.

It is small, but the British specialty is, notoriously, smallness. The Thames could be swallowed whole by the Rhine, the Danube or the Volga; from its estuary far down on the east coast of England, to its source in the west among the hills of Gloucestershire, it is only 209 miles long; it is only 50 yards wide at Oxford, 250 yards at London Bridge, and 700 at Gravesend and Tilbury. Twenty-odd miles farther down is the estuary and the Nore Light Tower where the river ends its journey to the sea.

A ship bound for London will pass the Nore Light and pick up the river pilot off Gravesend Pier, where the river narrows. There are another twenty-four miles to travel before she can dock in the Pool below London Bridge in the center of the City. The pilot will take her past Greenwich on the south bank, and the Isle of Dogs—an island of docks, in fact—on the north, where Limehouse Reach begins. Beyond is Tower Bridge, cutting the Pool in half, and beyond London Bridge she cannot go. The journey farther up must be done by river steamer or launch. These craft pass under the bridges of Blackfriars, Waterloo, Westminster, Lambeth, Vauxhall and the rest, until we breathe less polluted air in the suburban greenery of Kew, Hampton Court and Richmond.

At Teddington the tidal water and the rule of the Port of London Authority end: then we are free for the pastoral river—for Windsor, Hampton Court and Richmond, for the pleasure waters of Maidenhead, the straight racing mile of Henley and its regatta, for Goring and Oxford and so into the west of England, through Lechlade, Cricklade to the source.

The secret of the power and prestige of the Thames lies in its location; the estuary is immediately opposite the mouths of three great rivers of continental Europe—the Elbe, the Scheldt and the Rhine. Handily placed at the crossing of the sea routes, the Thames turns the port of London into a huge warehouse and center of transshipment. Half the being of the river is mercantile; it is heavy with wealth and the advantages of trade and politics. To follow the Thames from estuary to source is to cut through the dense accumulation of English political history into the vegetative rumination and poetry of English life.

So we can say that the Thames is really two rivers: London river, which is the river of merchants and government, and, above that, the "sweete Themmes" of poetry and pleasure. Let us look at London river first. It stretches from the Nore Light Tower in the estuary to London Bridge, just over forty-seven miles of muddy and polluted water poor in oxygen—a River Policeman told me there is none at all—where no fish live. They get five hundred tons of driftwood, broken boxes mainly, out of this part of the river every year. The water is sometimes sadly silvered, but most often it is brown to look at, like dark ale, and very murky, fit only for rats. Indeed, a pair of kestrels made a nest and brought up a family in the roof of the Savoy Hotel in the Strand a year or two back, and lived off the rats of the Thames mud.

Toward the end of the day the dirty water takes on a ragged and weary gravity, for there is nearly always mist in London to blur and take the hard edge off a skyline or a warehouse wall. Sometimes, as it sweeps between Blackfriars and Westminster, or again by Chelsea, the river looks tawny, leathery and majestic. Smoke, fog, mist, all the umbers and purples of London haze, paint elaborate and baroque sunsets which suggest the back cloth of an unbelievable melodrama with a sentimental ending. What a place for a murder, a suicide, some life-and-death gesture, the river looks in these moments. One thinks of the low balustrade on Waterloo Bridge, which suicides are said to prefer—the police reckon they save half of them—or the peculiar fragment of an anonymous London love story painted by some passing amateur on a piece of iron on Hungerford Bridge, just above the red light that marks the channel: "John, come home to 63 Elm—" The rest is undecipherable; it was daubed there years ago, and the author evidently had an obsession, for it is repeated fifty yards farther on—with a change of address.

Sinister, its darkness glossed by scarves of golden light and the pinkish black of the London night, the Thames has in these hours some quality which I can only call imperial. The river has known everything; in the Blitz, bits of it even caught fire.

As with many important English things, there is nothing appropriately grand about the entry to the river from the sea. The estuary is wide and open, but narrows to five and a half miles at the Nore Light Tower. Joseph Conrad has described what it's like to bring a ship into London. The pilot comes down to meet you, he says, and takes the ship through Queens Channel, Princes Channel or the Four Fathoms; sometimes he comes up to the Swin from the north. Conrad said that, of all the rivers he knew, this one lacked romance and grandeur in its outer approaches. Its quality, he said, was mysteriousness. There was no sign of a great city, no clatter of work, but the silence of low seawall and marsh, broken here and there by chalk bluff. His ship, he said, went deeper and deeper inland as if it were being lured. He saw more sky than land.

The entry is most mysterious in a light sea fog, when an extra brush stroke of unearthliness may be given by the sight of the high brown sails of one of the few remaining sailing barges of the river—some "bricky," low in the water, still surviving against the competition of the roads, making for the Essex or the Kentish brickfields, or carrying a cargo of rubbish and clinker. Tall, melancholy, these stained and rusted sails rise over craft that seem to be standing still until, as you pass one, you can just hear the whisper of the water at the stern. I believe there are not more than half a dozen of them left. Presently, as you move upstream, the oil stores, the power and gas plants appear in the marshes, standing up like cathedrals. If you should ever walk across these flats you will come upon gunnery ranges, forgotten lime workings, factories abandoned generations ago and broken up; this desolate country is a natural scene for the writer of thrillers.

It is not until Gravesend, with its old fort on the midstream island and the thickening of industrial chimneys, that the Thames really begins. This was the nearest point to the sea at which the river could be defended by shore batteries. The Norse raiders and invaders got this far without hindrance; after that they met trouble—although, as we know, some of them settled down: the "hythe" of the nearby river towns of Greenhithe and Rotherhithe is their language.

At Gravesend the sea pilot drops off and goes ashore to the Pilot Station at Royal Terrace Pier. Here he reports, no doubt, to the officer known as Ruler of Pilots—with no definite article, as if he were Ruler of Heaven and Earth. He has a den in that green-painted row of offices on the pier down which the north wind blows. You will notice a strong smell of tea here. There are hundreds of parked bicycles: you are confronting the touchy bureaucracy of the river, with its ancient pomps, privileges and jealousies. The Port of London Authority founded in 1908, now rules, administers, preserves and improves the Port of London as far as Teddington, the tidal limit; but the old hard-won rights and privileges, dating from the time of the trade guilds of the Tudors when every trade defended itself by charter, still have their place. Trinity House is represented among the governors of the Authority, but it sticks to its ancient roles: sea and river pilotage and the buoying of the Thames. The fixed lighthouses between Gravesend Reach and Galleons Reach are in the control of the Elder Brethren of Trinity House—"the guild or fraternity of the most glorious and undividable Trinity of St. Clement," founded by Henry VIII in 1514, when the royal shipyards were at Deptford. (Sir Francis Drake's *Golden Hind* was built on the Thames.) Trinity House also has interests beyond the Thames; it controls the lighting and buoying of a good part of the coasts of England and Wales.

Just above the Royal Terrace Pier is the Gravesend Ferry, and on the opposite shore is Tilbury, the first dock one reaches coming up the river, where the Oriental liners lie at rest, flashing white like new hotels. Here begin the cement works, the paper mills, the power stations: the drab processions of wharves, dock gates, warehouses and factories will continue for twenty-four miles to London Bridge, in the middle of the City. It is a long way—a packed, populous, smoking, clattering stretch, with only one or two patches of green and no fine building to relieve the eye until Wren's superb, cold, grand Naval College at Greenwich, and beside it, the first Queen Elizabeth's charming house at the end of its classical vista.

Gravesend is a pretty little town, with a good deal of Regency about it and the air of having been drawn by Cruikshank and populated by Dickens. Indeed, all this part of the Thames is full of Dickens—from Rotherhithe, where Bill Sikes hanged himself, to Gadshill, where the novelist lived; from Rochester to the Medway, from which Mr. Micawber hoped for something to turn up. At Gravesend the shops sell shrimps, cockles and winkles from the estuary flats. There is talk of "up-anchoring" in the pubs. River life has even affected the parking lots, for on the wall of a boat house are the words "Please park pretty." Customers in the bar of the Clarendon Royal raise their tankards and, as they do so, cannot resist a sideways glance at the river to note the ships going by, two a minute at high tide, and to listen to the peremptory blasphemies of the tugs.

From now on up the Pool there will be no silence on the river, but a day-long, nightlong cacophony carrying briskly across the water; an orchestra of phutting cranes, rattling conveyors, shovelings, chuggings, whinings, the clanking and croak of anchors, the spinning of winches and the fizz of steam—broken every now and then by the whistles of ships' officers to their crews or occasionally by a plain human voice uttering an unprintable word.

The last time I came up from Gravesend by water was on a tug. It is a good way to see how the Thames works. A dirty damp light was breaking on a cold morning. To climb from one tug to another as they lie doglike and close together at the jetty is not easy, especially under the faraway gaze of a tug's crew. In fact it is a delusion that there is anything faraway about the gaze. It is strange, too, to find yourself steaming up the river in a barnyard cackle of radio telephony: "Calling *Sun 17*. Take the *Florian* and go in with her, over. Calling *Sun 16*. Has that little Spaniard moved? What's the matter with her? O.K. I'll be back."

Our job is to take the *Florian* up to Millwall. There she lies, white and clean as a new castle in midstream, home from the Persian Gulf. A grinning Irish officer and the unsmiling Persian crew in their astrakhan bonnets look down on us as the anchor groans up. We put a waterman on the Jacob's ladder and he climbs up calling for his breakfast, and then the tow is thrown and the tug's crew grabs it. It takes three men, with gloved hands and all their strength, to get this tow in and lock it down with a mallet. In a moment the *Florian*'s siren blows, the tug curses back twice; ship and imp are talking and we are turning the monster round.

"Been on for forty-eight hours," says the skipper. He has had to bring his wife and a television set because he never knows when he'll be home. For a few hours, as we move upriver, we stand stamping our feet in the smell of oil, taking lungfuls of coal smoke and wharf smells that blow across the stream. Those warehouse doors and yards breathe out strong: gusts of raw timber, clouds of coal gas, camphor and the rich gluey smell of bulk sugar. The Thames smells of goods. Ahead of us are ancient names of ugly places. Poplar, Stepney, Limehouse, Wapping, Shadwell, Deptford—where King Henry VIII had his ships built—the dockyard at Woolwich, the Isle of Dogs—where the royal dogs were once kept—Blackwall, whence Captain John Smith sailed (fourteen years before the Pilgrim Fathers left Plymouth), to found the colony of Virginia, and Cuckold's Point, where a king of England, one of the Henrys, once gratified a loyal innkeeper by seducing his wife. But we are still a good hour or two from there, staring at a gasworks, watching the iron ore being grabbed out of the lighters at the Ford plant, seeing it travel overhead to the furnaces and pour out in red liquid. As the skipper says, with that special bitterness river men have when they think of road transport, "It comes in by lighter and goes out on wheels."

The lighters are the distinguishing craft of the Thames, marking its difference from all other rivers. They are moored by the score, all over the stream, forming vague low islands and archipelagos. It is the commonest sight of the river to see a tug rushing along with a double row of these poor, black, blind hulks behind her; they never sheer or get out of the line of tow; they pass under bridges and dodge the traffic with the ease of skaters. The big ships must unload in the docks, but whatever can be dropped overside onto lighters saves port dues.

It is surprising to stare at one of those ugly, seemingly rotting islands of craft which look as though they have been lying there for years, and then suddenly see a couple of tugs appear and a dozen men spring off. In a few minutes of shouting and rushing work the island splits into pieces, and in a quarter of an hour it has gone. They are mostly "dumb," these barges—that is to say they have no engines. One of the grotesque sights of the Thames is to see a barge adrift and askew on the tide with one or two men in the stern, steering with their long oars. Their job looks hopeless. The lump looks as though it will foul all traffic and blunder into the piers of any bridge in its way. But the Thames waterman has not just tumbled into his job. He has been apprenticed; he has had to earn his license.

The waterman at his long oar reminds us that at one time the Thames was London's only convenient or safe road from one end of the city to the other. The whole population used it. Kings and queens went up by river to the palaces at the Tower of London or at Greenwich, for royal and naval London lay east not west until the eighteenth century. The royal barges, graceful gondolas in green and red with golden canopies, lie in the National Maritime Museum at Greenwich. The present queen has twice made a royal river progress—at the end of the last war and again at her coronation. Shakespeare's Globe Theater was on the South Bank between London Bridge and Blackfriars; the actors and the theater crowds, who mostly lived on the north side, had to go "over the water"—a phrase still used in London life. The wherries were the taxicabs of those years: indeed when the roads became safe and coaches and carriages came in, the London watermen were powerful enough to prevent these interlopers from getting licenses for more than a generation. The Thames was marked by "stairs" and "gates," where the wherries picked up their passengers. Many still exist: Wapping Old Stairs, for example, and the stairs at London Bridge where Nancy took the boat in *Oliver Twist*. The old trick was not to tell the passenger his fare until he was in the middle of the river and at the wherryman's mercy. These rows and quarrels and blusterings were, and are, perpetual in British life; British liberty seems to be based on bloody-minded acrimony; this mild race has a talent for digging its toes in. The old Watermen's and Lightermen's Company, founded in 1555 to stop these arguments about fares, still licenses the apprentice lightermen under the Port of London Authority. The pretty Georgian building of the Watermen's and Lightermen's Company, crammed between fish warehouses down in Billingsgate—London's treasures are often stuck away in terrible places—has a portrait of one of its Masters whose lonely distinction it was to be called "The Honest Waterman." Honesty was a matter for astonishment, till the River Police were started at the end of the eighteenth century: they claimed to be the oldest police force in the world.

Shakespeare's actors were a particular thorn in the flesh of the watermen, but in fact the uneasy alliance between stage and wherry was eventually celebrated in a happy fashion in 1715, when an actor called Thomas Doggett founded a prize called Doggett's Coat and Badge for an annual rowing race of Thames Watermen. The race has been held every year since then, although wherries are no longer used: it is now rowed in gigs, from the site of the Old Swan public house near London Bridge to Cadogan Pier at Chelsea, and it is claimed to be the oldest and longest rowing race in the world, the course being four miles, seven furlongs. One of the early winners was the old prizefighter John Broughton, known as the Father of British Boxing and the first to introduce the gloves. The prize is a brilliant red coat of the period, with a large silver badge on the arm bearing the white horse of the house of Hanover. This glorious piece of apparel can be seen in the hall of the Watermen's and Lightermen's Company at the bottom of St. Mary-at-Hill in Billingsgate and there, drinking your glass of sherry at eleven with the courteous gentlemen who are up to their necks in the Thames shipping trades, you can also consider the portraits of past Masters going back centuries, the lovely Adam ceiling and chimney piece of the Court (all City companies are administered by a "Court"), the remarkable clock that was once stolen, and other treasures of the ancient Thames from days when it was not so respectable as it has become. There is even a large painting of the ceremony, with the latest Doggett winner in the foreground and, among the crowd of notables, Mrs. Eleanor Roosevelt.

But I am not drinking sherry down at Watermen's Hall. I am still freezing on the bridge of the tug *Sun*, as we lead the *Florian* into Millwall Dock.

The skipper was more silent than his prototype in the old stories of W. W. Jacobs, the great writer of comedies of Thames-side life. The Scottish engineer, who had been up all night, was having a sleep in the wheelhouse, and the cabin boy brought up those huge white mugs of tea which you can always see being carried about on tugs as they pass by. Working England runs on strong, very hot tea, and would die without it.

It was when we had the *Florian* in tow again at the dock entrance, waiting for the drawbridge to go up, that I saw the beauty of the maneuver, and why there is all that delicate waltzing, pulling and slacking off this way and that. The tug had to persuade fifteen thousand tons to do a series of sharp right-angle turns into lock and dock basin, without touching a quay or any other craft by so much as a graze. The skipper was playing a game of chess with wind tide, current and traffic, a matter he described as being partly instinct and partly the art of somehow seeing two moves ahead. When he nipped down the ladder to bolt a chop in the galley and said the job upsets the digestion, I could believe him: it is the malady of artists.

The docks break up east London into grimy little Venices. How do you imagine the Isle of Dogs? It is about three miles down the river from Tower Bridge—a collection of high black prison walls and streets without feature. Over one of these walls will appear, perhaps, in huge white letters the startling single word *Philosopher*, or some other just as strange: you are looking at the name of a ship whose black bow overhangs the wall of the graving dock, dwarfing trains, buses, houses, everything. The funnels and the masts stand up between the new blocks of flats that have gone up since dockland was burned out during the Blitz. It is exciting to see ships, lightly domesticated, careless looking, gay and trim, rising with the clean paint of the sea among London's dirty brick.

There are havens on the Isle of Dogs—such as The Gun, one of the few remaining public houses with a terrace on the river—where on summer nights you can look at the water and its hard reflected lights, listening to the clatter of the chains and conveyors of industry, and wait, with a glass of beer, for that peremptory, half-melancholy, half-majestic sound of a ship blowing as she silently glides out fast into the night, almost through the pub yard.

"Nice boys. Very nice fellers they were. And spent a lot of money," says the woman at the bar, looking toward the sound of the ship she cannot see. There will be no more singsong at the piano in the river room with that lot now. They have gone.

The destruction on the Isle of Dogs during the war was terrible, but no one could get the inhabitants to move. This was true of all the other dockland neighborhoods—Stepney, Limehouse, Poplar, Wapping, Deptford, Woolwich and Rotherhithe: the river people are as tenacious and as closed to the outside world as villagers. They have grown out of a rich and picaresque past, in which honest work went on beside the piracy and pilfering enjoyed by gangs who were subtly divided into river pirates, night-plunderers, light-horsemen, heavy-horsemen, scuffle-hunters and mudlarks.

The amount of thieving on the Thames in the days before the docks were built in the nineteenth century was due to the enormous congestion in the Pool below London Bridge: the docks and the River Police brought it slowly to an end, or nearly so. You hear tales today of ambitious rogues making off with a lighter of copper, or modest ones collaring a few cans of rabbit. But the bloodcurdling tales of the Ratcliff Highway and Limehouse Causeway; the general atmosphere of robbery, murder and brothels; the story of Execution Dock, where pirates were left for three tides to pass over them—all this is history now. The Town of Ramsgate pub, where criminals were given a good feed the night before their execution, still stands snugly at Wapping Old Stairs, and still does a good lunch. Limehouse Causeway has no opium dens: it is a collection of modern flats—one, I believe, is called Bethlehem House. There is still a Chinese quarter in the West India Dock Road. It still has the best Chinese restaurant in London.

Wapping High School is a mile or more of wharves and warehouses, where you duck under the cranes, and hear the warehouseman's old chant: "Lower. Lower a bit," and see him bring out his double hook to catch the bales. But if there is hardly a dwelling house in the street, there is a handsome region of apartment houses just off it. The Turks Head was bombed; the pretty Prospect of Whitby has become modish. It is the same over the river in Bill Sike's Rotherhithe. Paradise Street is still an alley but I don't suppose they ever sing there now:

> You robbed every tailor and you've
> skinned every sailor
> But you won't be walking down
> Paradise Street no more.

—which I have heard London sailors sing in Liverpool, but have never seen printed. And The Angel in Cherry Garden Street, where Pepys used to gather cherries when all this dock area was countryside, has been modernized. The New Jolly Caulkers by the Surrey Commercial Docks commemorates the site if not the actual house of Dickens's Three Jolly Fellowship Porters. The past of the whole region lives on in street names, with their whiff of sea life: Dockhead, Muscovy Street, Cathay Street, Pickle Herring Street and Shad Thames. There is Free Trade Wharf, dating back to the battles fought by the river folk against an old monopoly; there is New Fresh Wharf, where the banana boats unload in the middle of the city, just as the bacon and butter and hide trades are unloading on the southern side opposite. Down near London Bridge is the site of the Old Clink prison. The approach road to old London Bridge—Pepys described the houses burning on it in the Fire—goes through the churchyard of Wren's beautiful St. Magnus the Martyr, and anyone on a tug or a police launch will show you how the water breaks a little, a few yards east of London Bridge, over the site of the old piers.

This "absurd old bridge," as it was called, with its four-story houses, stood unsteadily for 650 years. If things are unsteady enough, they last. It was deadly to navigators and some of its arches used to be jammed with the bodies of dead starlings. Starlings have nowadays moved westward with civilization to Trafalgar Square. The old houses came down in 1750; the present London Bridge, packed tight with City clerks ten abreast at eight-thirty in the morning when the suburban trains get in, was finished in 1831. T. S. Eliot recorded these clerks in *The Waste Land*:

> *Sighs, short and infrequent, were exhaled,*
> *And each man fixed his eyes before his feet.*

Kipling was sardonic also:

> *Twenty bridges from Tower to Kew*
> *Wanted to know what the River knew.*

Tower Bridge, that strange Victorian Gothic contraption in stone and steel—fake fortress, part cathedral, part machine, which suits well with the Tower of London nearby, is the first bridge you meet as you come upriver. Below this point, the Thames is crossed by tunnel or by ferry. There is an old foot tunnel in a sad little garden in the Isle of Dogs, which comes up at Greenwich, near the spot where the veteran sailing ship, the *Cutty Sark*, stands in dry dock to show us what "sail" was like. The builders of the Tower Bridge must have had their doubts about the river pilots, for a tug with steam up stands beside the bridge, ready to go to the rescue of ships. It has been standing there by statute for sixty-five years, and only three times has it been called upon. The mugs of tea that must have been brewed aboard in that time!

This corner by the Tower is the most intense point of the river, the Pool; intense because the river work is thickest here, but also because the Tower exists as a lasting image in the minds of all who have been children in London. Those school visits with the history teacher. Your armor period; your Crown Jewels period; your spy and prisoner period; your almost traumatic preoccupation with smothered children, executioners' axes and heroes unjustly passing to doom under Traitor's Gate. Somehow the Thames looks sinister and greenish under the low arch of Traitor's Gate and one winces at the half-sly smile which the wobbling reflection of the water makes on the stone archway. A good part of the bloody history of England is contained in this fortress, and I confess to getting a nasty thrill out of the thought that spies have been sent here in the last two wars.

But it is not until the Londoner has grown out of childhood and got over the boredom of guidebook history, that he wakes up to the fact that the Tower is one of the marvels of Europe. Every time you see it, it seems to have got larger, and its walls, curtains, screens, towers and ramparts, built of a stone as gray and cruel as frost, give you the fright of something impregnable and of enormous weight. It is said to be the largest and most complete surviving medieval fortress in Europe. A king's palace and court in flushed royal red brick, are at the center where the ravens walk like dilapidated Tudors on the lawns; a belt of medieval town is set about the court; and then the outer belt of fortress with its screens and moats. In its hollow, the Tower is dwarfed by office buildings; but how many such modern steel things were blown up or burned out eighteen years ago, while the Tower stood?

And as you stare at the Tower, as your eye catches the speckled river running toward the sea beyond it, as you think of what is going on in the world beyond the Thames estuary, this old building ceases to be simply something out of a child's tale, and becomes a part of modern life. We have returned to the age of judicial murder, traitors real or false, political imprisonments, banishments, tortures, executions and the slow wasting away of unlucky men. . . . The Tower has become disagreeable and actual, and a whole lot of Beefeaters, looking like geraniums, do not keep alive its innocence for me anymore.

My temperament is the trader's. I keep a glance for the Tower, but thousands of hours I must have passed staring at the Pool. I always have to take one more look down the river at the cranes: twenty-four miles of cranes—forty-eight if you reckon both banks—from Gravesend to London Bridge, and they are thickest in the Pool, like a nation of grasshoppers sticking up against the sky. I wait, in a stupor, for one of these insects to move a leg or alter the angle of its antennae; and then for it to drop a bale into a ship's hold, as dead straight and sudden as a die. Pernickety, pedantic, doctoral things these machines are; I worked in one or two of the hide wharves in Pickle Herring Street when I was a youth, and the hiss of these insects put a touch of excitement into the hot, smelly hours I spent in wharfingers' offices. Ceilings are low, light is poor in these rooms, and the trucks rumble all day long on the floor above like trains. And by smell, I mean something between the aromatic and the outright stinking: sharp camphor, hides and wools like meat "going off," pleasant barks, soaps, bacons; nutmeg and pepper to relieve the nose; or that faintly dungy smell—rather childishly agreeable—of leather.

These river work places have not the sacerdotal calm of banks or the dry, light chatter of computers and typewriters, all nerves, of "modern" offices; wharf clerks are jammed in with draymen, dockers and watermen, who barge in breathing beer, cursing about their delivery orders and arguing about short weight, water damage, and stuff that has heated in the holds, while some hooting tug outside drowns the conversation. Certain river men I remember: Ben who never made a mistake and was always giving his notice; Bill who never got anything right; Jack the foreman with the fancy writing who could quote us half of Boswell and who went out on a three-day drunk once a month; sexy 'Arry Atterbury—his name sticks—with his fourteen children and his annual remark: "Nother nice little present from the missus, this morning."

But whether you have spent the morning in the wharf or standing in the modern offices of the Port of London Authority or some tug company, it seems natural in the lunch hour to hang round the open-air meetings on Tower Hill and listen to the political speakers haranguing about the state of India, China, Israel, Africa or the Indies.

The last time I was there, some bowler hat in the crowd asked about the situation in Fiji. A very natural, urgent question. They were talking about the bread and butter which the river brings. And if the speeches get too mercantile or worldly there is the ancient church of All Hallows, close to Tower Hill, a spick-and-span church, burned out in the war, with its seventeenth-century memorials, but now rebuilt. It is not altogether an unworldly shrine—none of the City churches is; there is a notice in the doorway saying: "Not all have been converted who enter this Church. Mind your handbags."

They take ships up to ten thousand tons into the Pool below London Bridge, but as we move on above the bridge commerce thins out, the State and the Law impose their Portland stone. Modern architecture is leveling the Victorian skyline of low-built cities, but the Thames has St. Paul's on its hill and all Wren's pigeon-gray spires. We pass Wren's little house squeezed behind wharves near Blackfriars. It has a bright red door now. We pass under the bridges at Waterloo, get one more salute from a passing police launch, and look at the noble façade of Somerset House in the Strand, once a duke's mansion, now a mixture of university, Record Office and the home of those sad, dedicated mathematicians, the Commissioners of Inland Revenue, the stateliest building on the Thames, indeed I would say the finest in London. This curving reach of the Thames to Westminster impresses, though the South Bank is mostly an industrial mess. On the north bank the Victorian outline, the Victorian statues and monuments predominate, there is something heavily Londonish and official about the Embankment. In this stretch the Thames lacks the grace and lightness of the Seine, but the flowers in the Embankment Gardens and the lawns, like all southern English flowers and lawns, are beautiful. Coal lighters go up past Westminster to Chelsea, and even far beyond, and there the river sweeps beautifully, often silver, to encourage painters, and there is green on the banks. We go on to the rowing and sailing clubs at Putney and Chiswick, and the Thames of sport and pleasure has begun at last.

We are in the waters of the Oxford and Cambridge boat-race course, where in March the crowds climb on the walls, run shouting along the towpaths, and spit down from the bridges, as people do—by some peculiar human impulse—from all the bridges in the world. We round the big bend to Kew and Richmond, and it is well to go ashore here and climb Richmond Hill, for there we have the finest of all the views of a silver river curving with elegance through the parkland and sumptuous woods of its valley. And so to Hampton Court, Magna Carta Island, the mass of Windsor Castle, and Eton College. The associations are overpowering. We are looking at the "sweete Themmes" of Spenser's poem at last.

Nor is Spenser so remote, for whether we English have embellished the river with palaces, courts, great houses and pretty towns, or ruined it with industrial suburbs, some regard for nature is still left in us. One ice-clear winter afternoon I was looking at Hampton Court. It is a ruddy-faced, comfortable, quietly splendid palace like some agreeable wine-fed king, with its small Tudor panes like tears of cold in old eyes. The red sun was dropping into the mists that rise early here in the river valley, breaking into lilacs, violets and grays so soft one cannot speak of them. The green of the riverbanks grew more vivid as the evening closed; the miles of wiry willows were gray and brown; the air still and the straight river like a low stairway rising to some imperceptible entrance to the sky. And then—I saw them: Spenser's swans coming down the stream, their eyes and necks seigneurial and their bodies like boats beneath them on the water.

> *So purely white they were,*
> *That even the gentle streame, the which them bare,*
> *Seem'd foul to them, and bade his billowes spare*
> *To wet their silken feathers, lest they might*
> *Soyle their fayre plumes with water not so fayre,*
> *And marre their beauties bright,*
> *That shone as heaven's light,*
> *Against their Brydale day, which was not long:*
> *Sweete Themmes! runne softly, till I end my Song.*

Day after day of your journey up the Thames you see them. They belong to the Queen. On the last Monday in July every year the quaint ceremony or lark—whatever you like—called "Swan-upping" begins at Romney Lock, where the river turns north to Windsor. It simply means that the young swans are caught and marked, and nicked on the side of the beak by emissaries of the Dyers' and Vintners' Companies who have some historic right under royal license to the birds they can catch and nick. To catch a swan takes some doing and, since all unmarked birds belong to the Queen, her property increases every year under the genial incompetence of the lark.

From Putney to Henley the Thames is a pleasant resort, as packed in some places as the lakes of Berlin. Sometime in the last quarter of the nineteenth century the office workers, shop workers and factory hands became aquatic, taking to the river on weekends. Today, painted houseboats with jaunty names, cabin cruisers, tied-up barges and converted troop carriers, landing craft and torpedo boats are littered along the towpaths. There are the shack cafés and bungalows of the weekend parties, with radios and record players going hard, and the riverside pubs that have had to enlarge their bars to cater for the busloads of tourists. The grand mansion façade of Ham House, a fine example of seventeenth-century architecture and now a museum, looks down between the trees and through its great iron gates, upon a river that at times resembles a merry-go-round.

On hot Sundays, the punts line up by the hundred to go through the locks, their occupants cursing the wash of the flashing cruisers or the packed steamers that ply regularly from Kingston to Oxford. The Londoner is a water animal—Henry James noted it and, taking time off from his addiction to country-house visiting, he was surprisingly delighted by the vulgar gaieties of the river.

To hire a punt, after haggling with a rosy, sentimental and rapacious waterside dealer who looks as innocent as honeysuckle—and then to pole or paddle the craft along under branches of overhanging willow, with a girl, a sunshade and a radio, is a kind of heaven—if the sun doesn't go in, if the midges don't bite, and if insensitive bargees don't wreck the affair with their wake and with brutal comments on love, which seems to have no appeal for them. Punting on the Thames enhances the beauty of the male. Tall, sunburned, in flashing flannels, he is Hamlet's waterfly in person as he stands poised on the small platform at the stern of the punt, silhouetted against the sky and the luxurious summer trees. He lets the long pole slide vertically between his hands, until it just taps—he hopes—a gravel bottom; and then,

303

adeptly moving his weight, he pushes effortlessly yet forcefully on the bottom and, as the punt glides forward, draws in his shishing pole at the prettiest low angle to renew the stroke—without, he hopes, getting a quart of water down his sleeve, or soaking the lady, or without any of those accidents that come to the self-admiring, such as being hung up on the low branches of a passing tree, or getting the pole stuck in the riverbed so that he remains, slowly sinking at the top of it, while the punt and its heavenly load shoots on like a passing smile of farewell, beyond him.

Two hundred and nine miles from the Nore Light Tower, in the softer and wetter climate of the west of England where the hills rise higher, there is a soggy meadow and a tree on which someone has cut the letters *T. H.* Not far off is a dried-up Roman well, and near that the embankment of the Fosse Way, the Roman road from Cirencester to Bath; under the embankment is a small tunnel. They have called the culvert Thames Head Bridge. Somewhere here is the source of the river, the childish stream that is to grow into the Father.

In its progress from here to the sea it has its pastoral, its academic, its poetic, its sporting, its royal and its mercantile phases. Pastorally, it is a curl of silver clasping the parklands and the great houses, running through fields of buttercups and cooling the cows. It has its odd villages and odder churches; at Dorchester Abbey there is an epitaph to a lady who died "a martyr to excessive sensibility," uncalmed by the rural stream. Oxford rules its academic and poetic life: there it belongs to poets and undergraduates—and there, by some freak of English pedantry, tradition or local tenacity, it changes its name to Isis. Why? Was it a splitting up of the old name Themesis or Tamesis? Or a corruption of the common English names for a river—Ouse or Isca, so that people said Thames Ouse or Thames Isca for Thames River? Here, too, when it does not belong to the undergraduates who go to Salter's boat landing to talk of dinghies, gigs, skiffs, scullers, randans, whiffs, Roy Roys, funnies and other such vessels, it belongs to the poets.

Shelley heard a skylark at Bablock Hythe, Keats planned Endymion's journey hereabouts, Southey "sailed unskillfully" at Nuncham, Pope translated the *Iliad*, and Wordsworth listened to that oldest and most delicate of Thames sounds, "the dripping of the oar suspended."

But if we start drifting down the literature of the Thames or indeed its historical anecdotage, we shall never end until we pass Falstaff dining at his inn at Windsor, Wolsey filling Hampton Court with four hundred guests, Henry VIII calmly stealing the property from him, and Magna Carta being signed at Runnymede all over again.

The sky is the least of the things that are reflected in Thames water; the light on its water is the long light of time itself. It bears away British history and habit of life. No great falls break its course: no high mountains dominate; it runs into no lakes; has no great islands; its weirs are mild, its locks domestic, its bridges without drama. It has no splendor, no wildness and no mythology. It is simply a sly, idle stream that has enticed a civilization and a lot of swans.

[1960]

14

The Appalachian Mountains

Overture to a Mountain Theme

The southern train had cannoned me loudly over Virginia into Tennessee. And after an eventless waiting at a junction there, I was tugged under difficult steam up a light railway into the mountains of the North Carolina border. I had seen the blue lips of these mountains before, briefly arched over and beyond nearer hills.

To live in blue mountains, I began to think; to alight in that horizon unawares and extravagantly to plunge one's body in it! And then I was drawn over narrow steel into those very mountains. They circled by as we trudged. We invaded their gorges, serpenting through them, striking arcs into their townships, outlining their bases. And as we passed, echoes like unleashed dogs ran barking up the mountain sides and were lost in the woods.

The hills were at times huddled like sheep, at times scattered and grouped like herds. The sunlight was golden on them, the gold of laden furnaces, but the deep shades sunken between the ridges had the winding, varying blue of turf smoke. The processional hills trended back and down and away; new ones came before old ones had been grasped or regretted. I wished for the power of a king to halt them; and for the gifted hands of a poet to grasp them and pull them into myself. For a mountain is something high and blue within one.

We pelted into N——, galloped in like mountaineer horsemen and reined in sharply at Jenkins's store. N—— is highly set, like a pool on a mountain summit. There is a low, surrounding ridge of woods and the village itself has twenty timber shacks of all kinds, and about fifty-three inhabitants, including children. Of these, all the men sit on the platform of Jenkins's store, accompanied by "Zeb" Jenkins, and wait for the daily train to arrive.

I remember the men, fifteen of them, taller than corn, but scarcely stouter, wearing blue overalls and wide black hats, with brims flapped this way and that with the challenging nonchalance of raven's wings. There were no exceptions; each man wore blue overalls and a black hat. Each man was thin and nasal, drawling to canny length, with a startling amount of bone, with a reach as long as the dawn.

Each man had blue eyes and fair hair. It was as though these mountaineers were wearing a uniform, and my sensations were like those of Rip Van Winkle when he came upon the Dutchmen. As I watched these fifteen men, long and thin as turnpikes, looking wordlessly at me, and with their idle lengths of leg hung over the platform of the store, a fear seized me that by a general conspiracy of men, trains and blue mountains I had been thrown into an outlaw stronghold, and that the outlaws were just taking their time.

I found myself listening for their thoughts, trying to meet their spare blue gaze. But impossible. The main thoroughfare of N—— was the railway track, by which stood a few shacks and a sawmill, and as I turned back to escape this way I could feel that fifteen black hats, cocked at all angles of defiance, had turned with me, that thirty blue eyes turned and perforated me; and that the silence was refining to its ultimate frigidity. Oh, for a stout man!

As though answering, a rotund fellow came from behind a wagon and smiled at me, seized me and undertook my defense, strode over railway tracks and fields, gave me a bed for the night, and fed me on corn bread and chunks of salt bacon, and dippers of spring water. The strangeness of blue mountains departed and they attended my walk that night with so warm a familiarity that I did not even think about them. It was dark, and as I reconnoitered the tracks and the store, there was not a man of that lanky band to be seen.

The world had been blackened out by the heavy charcoal of night. There was no moon. But the sky was vaguely luminous, a dome of light in which the stars swung, and their keen votive smoke brought involuntary tears to the eyes and dimmed them, as wood smoke will. The white stars burned at a far, heatless distance. On that sky they might have been the white-hot and minute cinders of diamonds, which the wind had raked down, blown and scattered.

The hills which had waited with heads raised, like lowing cattle, during the day, were now straightened and flattened into a one-dimensional rim circling the world, and bluntly standing out against the light of void thrown up from beyond it. The earth was like a black caldron swinging over the reflected glow of the night fires of space.

I found a dimmed road and followed it to the liquid pulsations of the crickets. There were shrill encampments of these insects blotted in the fields and hills. Their notes were the sizzling of the caldron. Over the floor of silence ricocheted the sudden barking of dogs. A fan of yellow light opened across the fields, from the porch of a house, and in the porch two men were talking.

I heard solitary words drop on to the air and eddying briefly down, extinguish into the dark. I passed closed doors, and windows in which oil lamps burned sparingly and laid a film of yellow light on the heads of talking people. A hand moving the light would start a whirligig of shadows over the walls, like the wings of big moths; and settling would cast and fix a new fantasy.

I passed a shack on a hill, and out of its window was hopping the skirl of a gramophone. But the trees broke up and subdued the noise, and the black silence crept closely in as though it had been the breathing of the earth. I blotted myself into the woods, led on by a light which I discovered to be the lamp of a white frame church standing up naïvely like a child's toy.

In the church a wide voice was preaching, and words of the sermon jumped out of the open door into its funnel of light and fell out of the light to earth like the turning leaves. There was singing, a reverent monody. After, a deep silence, and I expected to see the lights put out. But a long silence of vacant dark. A chestnut aimed to earth.

The lights clicked out. The preacher came out of the church and by the light of a storm lantern walked with a dozen men and women between the trees. The preacher, seeing the star smoke above, sang out courageously the tune of a hymn, till a woman's voice stopped him with,

"Right smart o' chestnuts bin fallin', Mr. Cooper. Last night one fell and hit Doc McDowell plum' on the head."

The high nasal comment from Doc:

"Yes. And I hain't never seen no chestnut the size o' that-a-one. Seemed like it kind o' fell searchin' for me."

Then the moon rose, yellow as candle light, and I could see the group by the boles of the columnar trees. The men were wearing black hats and blue overalls.

An Aside on the Mountaineers

After hearing Doc McDowell's widely drawling voice tell how the bursting chestnut hit him "plumb on the head," I hurried home, feeling the ice of mountain strangeness had been cracked by this small wedge of overheard speech. But I awoke the next morning to see the immutable highlands waiting for me. They seemed to be mirrored in the air, like glass, to resist anything but a surface acquaintance.

North Carolina is proud. Proud of having less than 1 percent of foreign blood in its stock. Proud of its pure Scottish, Irish and English blood. There you hear a strange dialect, not an acquired twang, but a traditional, custom-hewn brogue, something which hovers naïvely between a Devonshire accent and the Oxford manner.

In these border mountains of western North Carolina, in the Unakas and Blue Ridge, it is said you may hear the English of Shakespeare and Chaucer; though in my wanderings to the remote parts of these mountains I did not experience the happiness of noting anything so rare, except the name Leander.

Sitting in his storm-thinned and weather-split shack in one of the highest ranges, fifteen miles from a railway and eight miles from any road but a rough wagon trail, was Leander, tall, shaggy, unkempt as a furze bush; and his brother Beaumont. They could neither read nor write. Beaumont and Leander Wiggins, who gave us apples and asked, "Now is you-uns kin to ol' Uncle Moses P—— on the yon side o' Little Rock Creek?" That is as near to Shakespeare as we ever got!

The mountaineers are perhaps America's only peasantry. These men and women have been shut up in their loved mountains since the coming of the first settlers, and have conserved their rough, antique modes of living. The mountains still hold more of mysterious life than a stranger can quickly penetrate.

The scattered huts shelter men almost startled by their own voices. Their speech has the intonation of solitude. Within the last two or three years roads have been carved into the mountains, and it is possible for the avid to "do" them at anything up to forty miles an hour. But the mountaineers accept the change suspiciously, keep to where one can travel only on horseback, and often only on foot.

One sees the tall blue figures, with narrow heads looking to the ground, with hands in pockets, and gun laid across their arms, behind their backs— one sees them stalking along in depths of thought beyond the length of our conventional-sounding chains.

Is it as grim as it appears to be? What does this brooding betoken? The thoughts of the mountaineer flow in deep, evasive channels. One is warned of the suspicious nature and lawless tendencies of these men. But I am safely back in New York to testify that a more hospitable and genial people does not exist, that they have what Pío Baroja—who would have been enthusiastic about them—would call a "dynamic" sense of freedom, the unconfiding, unadministered freedom of bears and squirrels, and that like the rest of us they do not want outsiders to meddle in their affairs.

I became involved in no feuds. I discovered no stills—about which hearsay has brought forth a vast brood of exaggerations, though there was vague evidence of both feuds and stills. But, even in these desperate matters, I prefer to remember these men are living according to the customs of 150 or 200 years ago. Better education and roads have only begun to penetrate their retreats. They have been a law unto themselves, have lived as clansmen and hunters, shot, hewn and eaten for their own bare needs in solitudes where even the echo of an ordered society has not been heard.

Knowing only the stark changes of life, the unexplained varying of sun, wind, rain, the diurnal infusions of light and darkness, and the sporadic labor of the open air, the mountaineer obeys instinct without discriminating. Though unconsciously he carries within him, as he breaks into the laurel, that primal instinct of all, the instinct for law.

The mountaineer fights hard for his liquor yet, and will do so until his adventurous impulses and his active mind are given occupations measuring up to his powers. Meanwhile, he is shrewd enough to let his children take advantage of the better opportunities for education which are now offering.

I heard of one aged mountaineer, whose wild career had become a byword in the country, but who fell upon hard times and was forced to live in the corner of a sawmill shed throughout a severe winter. When strangers commiserated and asked how he spent the long, bare evenings, he said he taught his two grandchildren to read and write. "Thar never hain't bin no ignorant Perkinses," he said proudly.

All this and "a right smart piece" more—as they say—I have discovered since that morning when, hesitating before the start, I saw the mountains indifferently, signlessly waiting like furred animals with the casual, upward forest marked on them. The moist, alluring blue had gone from them. They were gray-green, real, ponderous. They exhaled odors, the humid odors of sap and clay.

The noon heat swayed over their hollows. Chords of wind moved in white vibration over their ridges. There were the short, warm smell of fields and the smell of damp earth under trees. There were the tang of thickets, the hanging odor of laurel or rhododendron, the flavor of stripped bark. The torches of corn rattled dryly like paper. The air weighed like the air of a warm barn, the rafterless barn of the sky to which the steep fields of corn and rye reached and attained.

Blue rainclouds, sagging and weighty spheres of vapor, were forced over the ridges and, listing heavily, rolled over upon us with staring, electric clarity. Their enormous movements were defined powerfully in white curves and blue bodies of polished thunder. They bulked in silence.

"Hit hain't rained since the spring o' the year. What way was it whaur ye came from?" commented and asked the first man we met on our way. Large and single circles of rain, slate blue, tapped the dust; and as we turned up our first creek, we heard ahead of us, lumbering wagons of thunder jolting stolidly down from the gaps.

On the Trail of Alison

Unknowingly we were on the trail of Alison, the grandiloquent Alison.

Vagrant unshapely audiences of cloud moved before the sun, broke up, obscured and then released the main force of his light, giving the earth an inconstant, vaporous glaze. We walked through a valley for miles and miles, among sumac, goldenrod and Michaelmas daisies.

Finding the mountains now built into ranges of loftiness, like green naves; the hills like chapels and chapters around them; and the ranges themselves supported by flying buttresses, ridges; and windows of light shining with the soft restraint of sun-wakened hills, the scene changed for us. We turned up one of the least habited creeks, as though it were the aisle of a cathedral. We climbed, as it were, turret, stairs, ridding ourselves of the weighty valley sun, and breathing a more agile air.

A man getting corn out of his barn told us we could spend the night at his sister's house. He had a grandiloquent figure, filling his overalls to an ample blue like a bombastic sky, wearing his black hat—through which his hair stuck like ears of wheat at the side of the crown—more as a tilted and permanent gesture of expatiation than as headgear.

He was delighted with life. As we walked with him toward his sister's solitary shack poked onto the brow of a hill, he pointed out to us high lifts of land and askew triangles of corn and rye and pasturage which he owned on the ridge.

"Nat Pearcy is my name. Yessir. I didn't catch yours. Oh, yes. Why, right smart of them folk living in Gap Creek over Cloudland. There's Ned, and Doc, and Tom, and Commodore. Would you-uns be like kin to them? Well, no, I guess not, because you-uns comes over the waters. Whaur did you-uns come from? Are you married? So am I. Well, well! My wife went over to Linville to pick galax for a week. If she was here I'd have ye lodge with us. That's my house. No, thata one, thar. Them's my fields, way up to the yan side of thata wood and then yan ways down the creek. Hit's a right pretty piece.

"And how old did you-uns say you-uns is? Why, and jes kinda hikin' round? That's what ol' man Alison did. He came over the waters too. He jes went sportin' roun' peddlin'. I hain't seed the like o' thata one. He was an Irishman. He jes went snoopin' aroun' like you-uns, peddlin' things, toting 'em on his back, and gettin' folk to take him in o' nights. He sure was the workingest man I ever seed. He used to tell us about Canady and Jerusalem. Sight in the world o' peddlers comes thisa way and they all says what Alison says: 'Thar hain't better water nor the mountain water in the world.' Hit's plumb pure."

On the air was the odor of fallen apples. On the highest ranges of the mountains drawn back in gray austerity white clouds were curtaining. A blue gauze of thundercloud shone in a low gap. The sky, burdened for hours, and tiring of its pulling sacks of vapor, seemed to pause, look around helplessly. Unable to hold out, it released those blue sacks and the white hail grain streamed and channeled down. And dull balls of thunder bumped over the gap and rolled cannoning down the creek.

"That sure is a pretty sight," shouted Mr. Pearcy as we ran. "Hit's fallin' right hard."

Mr. Pearcy's sister, Mrs. Ayres, lived in a shack of two small rooms, each containing two wide beds. The walls and roof had slits of open air between the cracks in the beams and boards. There was no ceiling. The walls were partly papered by tailors' catalogues and newspapers. There was a fireless iron stove in the middle of the room. Mrs. Ayres had a pale earthen countenance, and a chin which levered forth her words resonantly.

But Mr. Pearcy's gusty eloquence silenced all by its heartiness. He picked up a newspaper three months old and began reading about Mustafa Kemal. "That's what ol' man Alison used to say. He waur the travelingest man I know'd. Hit's dangerous, he told me. If that thar Mustafa goes on a 'fiscatin' o' everything, that'll get the Greco-Japanese alliance plumb tore up. Was you-uns ever in Jerusalem? No? Alison was. Thar hain't nowhaur Alison hain't bin."

Mrs. Ayres, allied with the smell of dinner, silenced her brother. As we took our places on the benches she shouted, "Now you-uns jes help your-selves, like hit was your own homes, and jes reach what you-uns wants. Here, Ned"—to her husband, sliding some chunks of salt-encrusted bacon to him off the dish. Then to us, explaining, "I help him first, like he was kind o' handier."

Everyone ate with great gesticulation, Mrs. Ayres standing on the bridge, as it were, commanding as the conversation continued scrappily.

"Have ye fed the hogs, Ned?"

"Zeb Vance says he's got pretty smart o' honey, this month."

"Thar's sights o' wagons on the pike goin' up and Tom McKinney's got his mules."

"If only this rain had fallen in the summer. When I seed them clouds fall-in' over the gap, I thought, Hit sure is goin' to rain at last. An' hit come, plumb hard."

"Hit's real mean haulin' water from the spring, because our'n dried up."

After a pause, a thin piping voice from the end of the table: "Whaur does you-uns 'spectation to end, like whaur is you-all goin'?"

I had scarcely noticed him before, Mrs. Ayres's husband. He had sat against the wall with his small flat head against a string of drying peppers. His skin was pink and fair, and was tightly stretched over his face making his eyes peer out in two small, hard balls, inquisitively, birdlike. As he sat there, his head barely above the table, he seemed ephemeral, like a slice of thun-dercloud with a pink sunset flush to it, which might melt into colored waters and disappear if the sun became too strong. He was but the cloud. His brother-in-law was the thunder.

After dinner a neighboring mountaineer and his wife stopped and came in, slowly and gravely, smiling appropriately like a diplomatic corps. The conversation of the men drifted strangely to the subject of courthouses and trials, and Mr. Pearcy expatiated on the rights of juries, and by a suspicious association of ideas began to talk freely about "hit," and how difficult it was to make "hit," but how, in spite of the "revenue," some assumed the risk.

I was surprised at these confidences, but an apologetic, quizzical expres-sion on the face of the grave neighbor led me to believe that Nat Pearcy, having found an audience, was remembering "with advantages." Talk waned to the subject of postage stamps, and then Nat Pearcy picked up the newspaper again and brought us back to Mustafa Kemal. Mr. Ayres, cloud pale, said shyly:

"Nat sure is the readingest man in the world."

But Nat demurred modestly:

"The readingest man and the travelingest man I ever know'd waur Gashry Alison. I hain't seed him for a right smart bit. Mebbe he has quit peddlin' and built him a house somewhaur."

The strangers went. Mr. and Mrs. Ayres and their three children blew out the lamp and got into the two beds, with all their clothes on. We were given the other bed. Through the wide cracks and holes in the walls and roof we could see the wet, vague hills and hear the shrill scissoring of the crickets. Once in the night, rain drummed down and splashed at us. The wide air pushed in. All night the room was loud with the squeaking, creaking and scampering of little feet on the floors and beds, and with the tearing of paper and the overturning of tins, in minute pandemonium. Gashry Alison— what a name, I thought. And he had slept under that very roof.

A Mountain Sheriff

Broken in to the mountains now, we assaulted new heights, took unknown trails and saw with little wonder the mounting contours and abrupt dropping of the ridges. The leaves of the rhododendrons were long, dew-weighted arcs. The massed and intricate undergrowth of the woods drooped with condensing vapors. Infinitesimal spheres of water lay in dim rind over bark and foliage. Early forms of mist floated like curled leaves in the pools of morning in the valleys.

Clouds were low like motionless surf, poised forever without falling. There were the wet odors of fallen and decaying leaves, of new-cut timber, of sodden fibrous soil, the green dankness of the woods, the rude smell of bruised leaves and of moss-grown tree wreckage, the tang of broken ramage of fir, balsam, spruce, of chestnut, hickory, walnut, oak and maple. The morning vapors sucked strong flavors from the earth, and the tepid gray of coming rain seemed to draw out of the mountain floor a bitter, green exhalation of sap.

We climbed over miles of mist-choked woodland, passing no one except an occasional black-hatted mountaineer with his gun, swinging out of the laurel and jumping onto the track, hiding his suspicions with a parrying "Howdy." Clay and ocher leaves were matted on the boots of these men, and moss stains were on their overalls, and their black hats were faded to lichen and verdigris.

Violet smoke spiraled cannily heavenward from dingles where women were boiling water and washing clothes near the springs. They boiled the clothes in huge brass caldrons. The greeting was always the smiling, "Howdy," masking a quick scrutiny. But the polite hospitality always shone through: "If you-uns is tired, get ye chairs up at t'house and rest up a spell, an' take some apples. The spring done dried up so I hauled the clothes down to thisa one and lit me a fire here to save fetchin' water to bile. Has thar bin no rain whaur you-uns come fro'? Wall they claim hit's the same in all the world."

The shacks were one- or two-roomed, with a bending porch and a barn, the timber charred and flaked with age, like warped black wafers. Trays of sliced apples would be drying on the roofs, strings of peppers hanging in the windows, and a drying sheepskin in the barn. Lines of rain were traveling down the creek toward us, a dense warp taut from the looms of cloud. Scarlet birds pitched out of the laurel with the tumbling flights of bats.

"Hit's clar over Cloudland," said a youth, gathering apples. "But them weather birds means rain."

Crossing the stepping-stones of a river we met in midstream an oldish man carrying a bag. He was gentler than the usual mountaineer. He wore a frayed but neat black suit, and a newish black hat with a crown unsullied by defiant bulge or hollow. He wore no collar. His eyes were pale as watery sunlight and the lineaments of his face were penciled with a natural irony and obstinacy. He spoke in reedy falsetto. He twinkled half gayly, half superciliously before us and said:

"Howdy. Pretty day! Yessir! What's your name? Where do you all come from? Waal. That your wife? Where are ye going? My name's Sam Robinson. I am a preacher. I go everywhere. I belong to no one. No one belongs to me. I belong to myself. Kinda strange to think of a man not belonging to himself! Mighty glad to know ye and if you're over the Tennessee side ye'll find my folk on the hills. They've got farms, and cows and hogs and sheep. Sam Robinson, and remember I don't belong to no one."

Leaving it at that he left us abruptly, jumped to the next stone in the river and turned up the mountain; and the woof of haze rising in the rain's warp wove him into the gray-green blur of wet.

We entered the trees again and still climbing, we heard the rain clattering on the roof of the forest and leaking in crackling channels and spouts. We went for miles up the green forest caverns, and the close, spindling tree trunks, distancing to a blur of silver, seemed to pour like cold and noiseless torrents from the sky. Gashry Alison must have taken that trail a score of times, we imagined, silently trudging, absorbing from the still air of the solitary acres of woodland, new currents of eloquence.

At a break in the trail we hit a creek and there was a high barnlike store there propped up high on a platform. Posters of sales, wanted men, and advertisements were pasted on the planks, and were tearing limply from them. The storekeeper was sitting at the door reading a large Bible. His gun stood beside him. It turned out he was the sheriff, and from his conversation and girth we perceived he played a gigantic part in the scattered community of ten farms and a white church tiptoed on a knoll.

A yellow beard, like a corn shuck, spouted from the sheriff's chin. His voice had the nasal pitch of the village dialectician. He denounced Darwin partly as a nincompoop, partly as an ill-equipped emissary from Avernus. He told us of the theological disputes of the creek, the public debates about the Scriptures, in which he had downed many an opponent amid the applause of one side and the groans of the other.

"The last time waur wan I defended ol' Sam Robinson. Does you-uns know him? Waal, he hain't no debater and waur kinda 'fused like by a feller from Roarin' Creek. He allowed he waur a right smart feller, but he looked a purty mean sort o' popskull wan I'd finished. 'I suspicioned hit all 'long,' I said opening the Bible. 'Ye can't 'scape Holy Writ. Ye hain't even got your tex' c'rrect!'"

For days afterward I confess I was merely amused by this muscular Christian, who the next moment was describing how he had repulsed a "shootin' up fray" from over the state line, roped his prisoners to chairs, and read the New Testament to them. But a mountaineer took me to task and showed me that men like the sheriff had done a lot, after their fashion, to destroy much of the superstition and emotionalism to be found in the creeks.

"Sky's gettin' clar," said the sheriff as we walked to the door. I asked if he had ever heard of Gashry Alison, the peddler.

"Why, reckon I did. He used to come in here, peddlin' things—clothes, spectacles, brooches. He tol' me he was born in Jerusalem. That's in Turkey. Waal, pretty smart o' peddlers and sich comes thisa way. But thar hain't one like ol' Gash Alison. He's bin sportin' 'roun' the whole of Americky on foot. He's a quare man. He's got a quare furrin name too. He tol' me, 'I'm the only Gash in the world. My mother said wan I was born—'"

A horseman jumping down at the door looked in, up, about and around, and stopped when he saw us. He then picked up a sack of flour and laid it behind the saddle. Mounting, he leaned over and smiled at the sheriff, and called:

"Doc says the apples is all picked and the firs' waggon is way up on the yan side o' Ripshin Ridge."

"Jinks," exclaimed the sheriff. "Must be plumb on the Pike."

And locking up the store, he walked off lankily with his gun and his Bible.

What the Voice Said

He looked at us tolerantly. He turned and pointed up the creek, saying: "I disremember 'xackly, but mebbe hit's ten miles an' terrible rough. Does you-uns 'spectation to get to the top? Waal, it sure is a wunnerful place. They say ye can see—"

"It's burning. Keep a-stirrin' it," threw in his wife, a dry, cane-colored woman, crisp and lined like a corn shuck. His little rapture fell like a cut stalk. He turned to the steam and the smoke and went on stirring the apple butter in the huge black caldron. He was stirring with a heavy wooden pole six feet long.

The caldron was standing on a stick fire in the field, and at a distance from

318

the heat of it his barefooted wife and his barefooted daughters were slicing apples and throwing them into the caldron. The eyes of this family seen through the keen haze of cobalt smoke had a wildness in them. This might have been the witch scene in *Macbeth*.

"Hit's awful mean stirrin', stirrin'—" apologized the man.

The range we were to cross against his advice was nearly seven thousand feet high. It was forest-covered from base to summit, and a rocky trail, once used by ox wagons in fetching lumber but now altogether disused, tackled the slope abruptly and looped the contours.

When the trail reached the high gap it fizzled out into a wide "bald," a bare dome of mountain where the gales had cleared away the trees and cropped the turf almost to the roots. The skeleton gray stumps of cut or uprooted trees stared oddly, vacantly, like forgotten milestones. The earth was windstripped and seemed to be lighted only by the gaze of the fog as it moved over.

It is simple thus in a few lines to indicate hours of struggle, for comparatively low as the range was, it takes large effort to haul oneself up such slopes. The filtering underworld gloom of the forest is something to fight through. After plodding and hard breathing without any apparent gain, we would see through a gap in the trees that already we were head and shoulders out of the lower valley ocean where the choppy hillocks swirled minutely and crumbled into green surf.

Then we would turn and dive again into the submarine forest verdure and feel its fluid air. The spindling gray trunks of millions of trees packed like threads of water into a blurred torrent of distance, poured and splashed down in immense silence about us. We had the sensation of walking in flooded vaults of touchless sap-distilled water.

The earth drew the noise out of our feet as we strode from silence to silence, while the multitudinous forest waited. In cities silence is negative, is the absence of sound. But on that vast shield of mountain forest the silence was positive. One felt its presence, breathed it in tangible, inaudible drafts.

At times we felt there was no air; only this greenish, glassy quiet in which the falling of the crisp body of a leaf hit distinctly, deliberately, with the ring of event.

For hours we pushed, pushed, pushed back the air, pressed back the trees, stamped the earth, toed the rocks, shouldered all our forces to the ascent. After the first ridge I vowed I would never climb a mountain again. But which is worse, to climb a mountain or to be in a valley wanting to climb one?

The thought of Gashry Alison comforted me. It was the constant mention of him among the mountaineers, and the spur which the unknown gives to the imagination, that made this lonely and unknown figure a companion. His pack must have been heavier than mine, what with his clothes, spectacles and peddling staff.

How did he find the ascent? Did this quiet solidify against him? Seize him like deep pervading water? Or did his warm nature melt and release the mountain forces, till leaves fell from the trees like the crash of cymbals, and springs sang out, and partridges rattled up from cover like country people cluttering out of church, and till winds mounted and swelled a manifold diapason through the forest's mighty register of pipes?

How was it with Alison? Did he sing? Did he muse? Did he tire? Did he rush his hills? Or did he sink back into his own pace and lug his body up glumly, while the forest, always ahead and standing in thin, silver battalions, ordered him up and up, in its inescapable routine?

Perhaps traveling is a mundane thing. All our giants are windmills, all our armies are sheep, if we go forth with the rhetorical expectations of Don Quixote. Gashry Alison must have had something the Spanish gentleman missed.

It takes more than a pair of legs to make a man climb mountains and live on salt bacon and pastry among strangers in order to peddle brooches, clothes and spectacles. I believe all Alison's windmills must have been giants.

There was always some news of Alison to be got at a mountaineer's hut. Sitting on the porch while leading the lanky, genial but suspicious "Doc" or "Pete" onto the subject, one would eventually hear something like this:

"Thar hain't no one the like o' Gash Alison. He's the travelin'est man I ever seed. Seemed like as though he waur always footin' it over the worl'. 'Wan will I build me a house an' settle?' he says, the last night he waur here. 'Boys,' he says, 'I fit in three wars and seen a sight o' frays and places, and guess I'll jes be shacklin' 'round till I'm as ol' as you-uns is, grandf'er.'"

Before dusk we reached the "bald" and were as high as we ever climbed in our wanderings. Over the gale-cropped dome of the "bald," the gritty gray clouds passed low like enormous buzzards. Scarves of cloud moved down from the banks, and looking below them as through a half-covered window, we could see the sun-honeycombed forest cast distantly away into the ultimate hollows of the world.

The clouds rolled like a surge over the spruce and balsam, smudging the indigo masses with fog. But westward we could see the tidal summits of an ocean of hills; varying, pellucid ranges over which passed squalls of green, ultramarine and gray. The long fields swept up obliquely to where the summits broke or rolled over, throwing up calls of spray to the inaccessible sky.

This was crisis. Alison must have stood where we were standing, many a time, a wind-dark speck pausing on the dome of the "bald." Now I should find him, hear all about him. Or this would be the end.

But life and mountains do not have our dramatic sense. I heard of Alison again that night and again the day following, when, like a falling star, his golden course burned suddenly out halfway up in the heavens, unfinished. But this night we slept in a shack in the upper branch. The grandfather, father, mother, daughter and son of the house slept in one room and we in the other. The mountaineers will give anything up for a stranger, do anything for them. In fact, the conversation turned that way as we sat before the fire.

"We-uns niver turns away no one wan they asks for shelter an' a meal's victuals. Thar's always someone comin' through the gap, peddlers and sich. Gash Alison uster come reg'lar."

The father broke in with high-up voice:

"Does you-uns know Gash Alison? Waal, he were a furriner and him comin' over the waters. He 'llows he's the only Gash in the worl'. He says the day he waur born his mother didn't know how to call him till one night, like it would be ol' man Alison had a dream, and a v'ice said, plumb loud, so hit woke him, 'Gashry!!' That's a right quare name. 'How d'ye spell it?' I asks. 'I couldn't rightly denote,' says Gash. 'Like the v'ice kinda didn't say nathiong more'n that.'"

The Woman Who Smiled

I sat on the porch of the shack of the woman who smiled.

Everyone on the creek was related to everyone else. There had been intensive intermarriage for generations. The wit who said a man might be his own grandmother and not know it, erred more in lack of tact than he erred in exaggeration. The Ayreses, the Ingrams and the Vances brooded in their lofty hollows far from call of man or beast from the plains.

The blue smoke of the caldrons scratched the air, the bare, damp feet of the women and children were marked by the basket patterning of the field grass. These earth-held families raised corn, sliced apples, made honey, shot in the woods, and brought sacks of flour on horseback to their shacks.

The Ayreses, the Ingrams and the Vances brooded and fattened turkeys, and nothing ever happened except a great gale or a spell of drought. The boys tried the settlement school for a while, grew up and felt their legs getting too long for them, took guns and went up into the woods alone to live, till inclement weather or weariness of excitement drove them down to the creek again.

The wind is clever, the rain is sharp, and earth clings to boots and body; and something of the wind, the rain and the clay, something careless, dynamic, stolid, entered the ways of these boys, these Ulstermen, these Scotsmen, these English whom the mountains held.

These boys had never seen the sea, or cities, or Negroes. One of them told me he first saw a Negro when he was eighteen, and that he ran home frightened, shouting, "I've seen the boogeyman!" Horace Kephart, in his book on the mountains, tells almost the same tale.

Skies are fair today, but tomorrow gray gullies of water may spurt down, or winds hiss arrowing through the air. So one night Ed Ingram—I naturally never give the real names of these mountaineers—who was eighteen, ran off with Rose Vance, who was fourteen. It was not exactly an elopement because nearly everyone knew about it.

The couple ran over into Tennessee, where the marriage laws are easier; and the magistrate in one of the creeks married them. The ceremony was brief. Mountain ceremonies always are brief. A tale is current that one magistrate boasted his marriage ceremony to be only four words: "Stand up. Jine. Hitched." I understand it is longer nowadays.

At news of the elopement the parents were scandalized, having done exactly the same themselves; then resigned; then relieved. As old McCoy Vance said, "Wan a woman takes an idee into her head hit hain't no good obstructioning. I've got twelve daughters and seven sons, an' I know summat about it."

THE APPALACHIAN MOUNTAINS

Ed Ingram worked a bit, loafed a bit and went for days and days on end shooting in the woods. He could never resist the cool, lengthy woods, free and clear to him as spring water. He didn't harm anyone. He didn't interfere with anyone. The mountains are wide as the wind. Why should anyone want to interfere with him? Isn't there room enough and to spare for all in the mountains?

It is good enough to enjoy one's own happiness. It is bad enough to suffer one's own wretchedness. What business is it all of strangers, of educators, of-ficers, of the monotonous, organized people of the plains, where the water is so poor and warm with lying in lead pipes that the townspeople have to put ice in it! Fancy putting ice in water!

Rose Ingram may have five, ten, fifteen children by now. Besides there are turkeys to fatten, fruit to preserve, food to cook, and that man to wait on hand and foot; and water to carry from the springs, and clothes to mend, taxes to pay, and apples to sell.

Once in a while she washes clothes, not often, though; and complains of the clouds of flies that fill her bedroom-cum-kitchen-cum-parlor. If she and Ed were to read this they would probably resent the implication of poverty, for a mountaineer will admit himself to be everything except poor.

"Wan has you-uns ever lacked a meal's victuals or a bed in the moun-tains?" I can hear them asking. But it is not that kind of poverty. If hospital-ity is riches, then the mountaineers are the richest people in the world. I re-member the rebuke I received from a man whom I had offered to pay for a service:

"Pore folks haster work. But we don't hafter work. We hain't pore."

All this I thought while sitting on the porch of the hut of the woman who smiled. Gray parallelograms of rain shadowed the creek, and soaking scarves of white cloud surf flew from the wet blue and madder mountains. The water haze was over the creek, a web of flat vapor. The sky was hoofed and rutted with botched cloud traveling and thrown up in heavy clods.

Runnels of bright clay water were richly pouring with the note of clear cattle bells, and a stocky rain tapped like drumsticks on the roof of the hut. Escaping from the collapse of rain, we rushed to the porch of the woman's house. It was little more than a shed propped up high on four piles of rock.

A semicircle of beehives made of pipes and tin cans with rocks for lids

323

stood in the clearing before the house. A lambskin was stretched over the wall to dry.

The woman was sitting on the floor in the doorway of the hut. She was scantily clothed in a coarse dress, and her legs and feet were bare. Her straw-colored hair was drawn from her forehead and fell in limp tails down her back. Ten ragged and contented children were crawling over her as she nursed a young baby, and sat curled on the floor like a gentle animal, uncomplainingly.

She was as pale as water, pale as sap, pale as a cane of rye, and her faint, narrow eyes shone with an idling light. She looked at us dreamily; and her lips, weirdly thin and colorless (from wind and rain and not from poverty, we felt), construed a little changeless smile. It was always there. She seemed to look at us and smile at us through water from another world. It was the smile of Mona Lisa.

Questions dawdled from between her lifted lips:

"Whar does you-uns come from? What did you-uns say you-uns was called? Is you-all man and wife? Uh, huh. How old are ye? An' you-uns comes over the waters? That'd be a scandalous long ways, yander, I reckon. Would you-all like some apples? If you-uns wants any, jes get ye them. Thar's more apples this y'ar nor any y'ar I ever seed."

This reads absurdly, for every sentence loafed between linked pauses in that drooping intonation which is of the soil. She said she had been married when she was fifteen and was now twenty-nine. She said she had eight children, and had three sisters younger than her own eldest daughter. She herself had been one of a family of twenty-one.

She smiled continuously her faint pearl smile.

"Las' night the moon was travelin' north," she said. "Hit'll rain a right smart piece more and get cold. I mind the time wan our spring friz plumb up on the first of September."

I laughed at this and she looked at the feathering rain. And her lips lifted and her constant smiles moved lightly like a single ripple of water.

A break in the thicket showed two men coming to the house. Lanky figures with hands in pockets, and a gun apiece laid horizontally between their arms behind their backs. They stopped when they saw us, then jumped onto the porch and smiled a doubtful "Howdy" and scanned the dimly greeting lips of the woman for information about us.

They went inside the house and studied us from behind the curtains, evidently very suspicious. "I know whar ye've bin, daddy," cried out one of the children, but the father came out genially and clapped his hand over the child's mouth. He introduced himself: "I'm Tom McKinney, yours truly. I didn't catch yourn?"

He went inside and fell to whispering with his companion. A lot of mysterious operations went on inside the room. We noticed signaling with fingers, chins and lips. Turning sharply, I caught the woman scrutinizing us closely with awakened clear eyes, but when she saw me turn they fell back subtly to the underwater idling gaze.

The man walked up and down impatiently inside the house, and, muttering, stepped to the window to peer at us. We were obviously not wanted, and they were all greatly relieved when we rose to go, although they pressed us politely to stay. I remember seeing the lifted lips of the woman. A pale, queer smile has been dawdling after me ever since.

In the Smokies

It was the last house in the creek, and we stayed the night there. Beyond was a heaped wall of enmeshing forest, and mountains, retreating ridge by ridge and outflanking valley by valley into Tennessee: virgin forest, pathless, uninhabited except by shy bears and other wild animals. The last house, after that nothing, smudges of dull green, cold, dark.

The house was a half-roofless shack hidden by a palisade of tall corn. There were two bedrooms with sacks nailed over the windows for lack of glass. And a kitchen with only three walls, the fourth being the forest. Another room and the kitchen were roofless.

It was vague blue dark when we asked for shelter, but the tall shrill woman of the house took us in pleasantly enough, but in an impersonal way as though we entered by the right of nature, like the wind and the rain.

She intoned her welcome in a voice that was neither melancholy nor joyful, but like a bodyless voice, a thing soughing from the trees or talking over the soil.

We groped in by the yellow light of the lamp, sat, and so fixed our shadows on the walls; and talked with the family. There were a man, the woman, her daughter and her son, and an older woman who must have been the boy's grandmother.

They asked us the usual questions. They had always lived in the mountains until two years before when they migrated to South Carolina to work in the cotton mills. But owing to the changes in trade the family had returned to the mountains, and were now ten miles away from the nearest store, five miles away from a wagon road, with two rivers to ford and steep land, steep as clouds, to till. Well may they speak of a man falling out of his field.

As we talked, bats flew into the room and dodged around. Bars of heavy blue night lay solidly between the rafters. All we could get to eat was cold pastry and molasses; but the white stars, like drooping small wells of white water, hung closely above us. There was not a flake of moon.

The shrill woman lamented her inhospitality: "I hain't handy at all with me stove all tore up from jolting in the wagon."

Conversation dropped, and there were stark silences. There were glances, and the grandmother said, "I'm a going to bed now," and climbed into bed with all her clothes on. The girl shouted to her brother, "Get ye to your pallet."

We sorted ourselves out. The father slept in our room in the other bed, snored all night and talked to himself, while the wind blew at the sacking nailed over the window, and the crickets scissored their monody of high notes.

Early in the morning, while it was still empty and dark and all sound but the creeping of water in the stream had stopped, the man got out of bed and tapped on the wall. He was answered, and later met his wife in the kitchen where they began to prepare breakfast. It seemed to us it could hardly be much past midnight, and we dragged ourselves dismally to a meal of hot pastry, salt bacon, blackberries and buttermilk; with the shrill woman urging, arguing and persuading all the time. She said it was six o'clock.

Came a thump and scuffling from the other room and in ran the grandmother shouting, "Does you-uns know what the time is? Waal, hit's three o'clock!" Protests were in vain. It was only three o'clock. I had felt it in my bones. It turned out the man had only guessed the time when he knocked on the wall, and that his wife had looked at her clock without lighting a match, and had thought it was half past five!

We all stood there, gray and vacant forms, with a yellow film of lamplight cast limply without enthusiasm upon us. At last when the shrill debate had ended the woman said, "Waal, reckon I'll hafter make an extry meal today to make up. And you-uns will be able to get the bursted chestnuts before the squirr'ls gets them."

But we went back to bed.

The man set off on foot—he had no horse—down the creek on his ten-mile journey to the nearest store, to bring back a sack of flour.

Later that morning we discovered where the woman had bought her molasses of the night before. A man was standing in a field supervising the crushing of rye cane between two revolving rollers set in a frame to which was attached a pole ten feet long. A mule was harnessed to the pole and as he walked round and round, the rollers turned, the cane was crushed and the syrup oozed down a gully pipe and was strained through sacking into a tub.

"Today's 'll be a right smart piece cl'arer than what you-uns had las' night," said the man.

His son, a sinewy fellow, was chopping at a stump of tree: "I'm hewin' me a block for my corn mill," he said. He had already built a large wooden wheel, and a race propped high in the air on stilts. All the grinding in the mountains is done by these old watermills and the corn is crushed between two enormous millstones.

After miles and miles of climbing we prepared to assault one of the flanking ridges and so descend into a far creek, where there was a lumber camp. The distance was varyingly given as between two and ten miles. It turned out to be over fifteen miles, and the hardest fifteen, the roughest and the steepest, I have ever done. Eight miles of it was done in heavy rain and cloud. We took a mountain youth to guide us to the top of the ridge.

He was as silent and as expressionless as a leaf. He had carved blue eyes. He strode easily where we struggled. And the more I tried to get conversation out of him, the more laconic and defensive he became, replying "Uh huh" to nearly everything I said. We went on something like this:

"Hot," I said, feeling very blown.

"Warm," he replied.

"You're used to it"—from me.

"Uh huh."

"Do you often go this way?"

"Uh huh."

"Is it far?"

"Uh huh."

"Have you always lived in that creek?"

"Uh huh."

The only time he became eloquent was when we passed a deserted farm lying in a boulder-strewn clearing in the mountain forest.

"Beaumont Starr's farm," he drawled. "He left las' spring. Hit was too hard. Siles gone old and wore out, an' nothin' 'll grow in that thar."

Tremendous chestnut trees shot like isolated gray columns out of the green ruin of thickets. Beaumont Starr had lived there with his brother, and their ancestors before them, tilling granite.

We climbed for three hours through steep woods of pine, balsam, chestnut and hickory; of bellwood, maple, walnut and oak—a struggle in green monotone. On the summit, which seemed unattainable, we finally flung ourselves down on the hard earth utterly exhausted; with a faint ocean of blue ranges palely washing and lapping in noiseless surge and foam of cloud-capped summits, below us.

The air was still. Not a sound. Not even the motion of one leaf touching another. It seemed that the world had stopped: that we lay supine at a point beyond all sound and effort, that we lay closely beneath the flawless and level ceiling of the world.

We saw sturdy and extraordinary foreshortened clouds and ethereal territories of mountains, range after range, merging into a haze of moth silver. The mountains were strips of water modeled by the air. Ranks of solidifying ether. Anything but mountains. Anything.

From our "Necket" we could see our ridge slung like a firm hammock of green from knob to knob, a blue-green causeway crossing the water of sky, or broad and churned with green and choppy light like the wake of a steamer. Distantly was Clingman's Dome, with the other gray hosts, while a wide surf cloud lay fixedly, mazedly upon them. From their highest elevation bannered a stilly chrome wash of startled light.

We descended alone. Rain collapsed on the roof of the trees and spouted through. We shattered the forest silence as a rod splits emerald ice. We hurtled down, deeper at every jump, into the high and bare cold cavern of frigid trees. A shot suddenly was fired somewhere before us and below, and its staccato echoes ricocheted on the polished walls of green. Were we at last mistaken for revenue officers as had been prophesied? But life lacks our sense of the dramatic. We soon came upon three hunters standing in a ditch and they smiled ironically at our little excitement.

When at last we came out under the open sky it was torn into rags of mist and vapors which drifted, a soaking tatterdemalion, across the knobs and creeks; and entering a valley, whose form was quite smudged out by rain and night, we splashed through sodden miles of clay, eight miles to the lumber camp, and found bed there.

Sitting in a Mountain Town

In the morning I crossed the river and walked into the town. It had a railway station, four churches, a bank, a main street, two side turnings and no "movie," among other things, for the distraction of its eight hundred or more inhabitants.

An automobile road looping through the mountains from the center of North Carolina was just nearing completion, and during the day one might occasionally see gangs of colored men throbbing by on trucks to the excavations and quarries, and an odd white-bearded mountaineer of the old school riding horseback and sidling and prancing about as though he were conducting a daring military operation.

The main street of the town was shaded by an avenue of maples, and poplars with dull green and silver leaves. The wide almost motionless river was rust yellow and cloudy dense with clay flood water, on which lay the heavy cobalt and sepia shadows of trees.

In the street the sunlight opened in grotesque and formless gapes between rare shadows. Men in blue overalls and monstrous black hats were sitting on walls, fences and benches in the sun.

These men were spare, long and springy as whips. Some walked with guns behind their backs, or sat with their long ungainly legs propped up or pulled out across the pavement. They had lengthy, calculating noses, and judicious deprecatory chins. They rarely moved. But they saw everything.

One knew this by the sensitive jerking of the crowns of their hats, if a Ford car clattered by or if a cannonade of blasting pealed on the new road, or if a stranger crossed brazenly into the sun, and had his boots cleaned. Wind blew in casually, as everything else did.

The only thing to do in the town was to find a foot of unoccupied bench and sit on it. I sat. I sat for hours and watched better men than I—also sitting.

I sat on the wall of the bridge first of all, and soon another sitter there began to edge toward me. We inspected each other from under the brims of our hats. Our eyes reconnoitered. We tried to give our inevitable, approaching acquaintanceship a strategic casualness, as though it were an accident and not a matter of passionate curiosity.

The man was an Indian half-caste. His eyes were thick, cloudy and red hot. He pulled at his yellow, twiggy mustache and stared at the river. He said ultimately: "Thar's right smart o' fish in th' river. Catfish. Yellow catfish and blue uns. An' a redfeller—red horse like we call him."

The sun wheeling like a white stream filled in the hollow of broken silence, leveled it up and flowed over as though nothing had happened. The half-caste pulled in his belt and let his length of leg dangle forward, and so stepped away as it were on tiptoe, like a marionette.

"Reckon I'll turn aroun' and seek arter a bit o' grub," he said. And he went to the barber's doorstep and sat there in the shade.

The mountains lay in masterful elevation around the town and descended into it. Their ardent slopes, green-pored and filigreed, rose to every touch of sun. There were cool smoky blue forms of shadows modeled into the body of the ranges. A bare heat, like the look in an animal's eyes, and a prolific coarseness and toughness, as of a bullock's hide, were in the mountains. They stood like herds of green bison. The little town seemed within the casual print of a great mountain hoof.

I climbed up a stairway into the shade, and shortly a man came up and sat on the stair below me. He was oldish, agile, with stringy red skin, and a fistful of mustache stuffed under his nose like straw. He wore one brown boot and one black boot. We fell into conversation.

He had lived in the mountains all his life and knew every creek of them. He was very scornful of the "ol' fellers" of the previous generation, and especially of their queer ways, speech and customs. And he fed his scorn on the constant reading of a book describing the amusing life of the mountaineers. He referred to them as "ol' crackters."

"Wan he came hyur and writ thata book he writ the truth. Hit's jes the way the ol' fellers uster speak. They was a quare c'llection. He's a right smart boy, and the travelin'est man I knowed. He's seed the whole worl' except two states and now he jes stays foolin' aroun' writin'."

His reference was to that noted writer on the mountains, Horace Kephart.

I led him gently to reminiscence.

"I've bin four times over Clingman's Dome. Thar hain't no trail, but twen'y y'ars ago a feller cut a wagon trail, figgerin' he waur going to haul lumber along the top. But I reckon that'd be covered plumb up with laurel an' trees, the way nobody wouldn't never know it.

"I've done purty smart o' b'ar huntin', sometimes with the snow that high. B'ars is harmless an' is jes as afeered of you as you is o' them. Thar hain't no real reason fer huntin' up so, either. Rattlesnakes is the same. Reckon all animals is like that. Don't harm them an' they won't touch ye.

"Waal, hit's mighty dense up thar and terrible rough. If ye get up on top of the Dome and shins up a tree a man could see everywhars in the worl' almos' till—till his eyes was a-tired o' lookin', an' he come down an' go away. But ye hafter climb. The Dome's too coveredly wi' trees to see without.

"Yeh, I've had many experiments with b'ars," he continued. "Pete Hughes was the real boy fer b'ars, though. He fell into a b'ar wallow on the Dome one day an' lit plum' on top o' the greates' ol' b'ar he'd ever seed, and kinda got into a reg'lar spat with him. Reckon that's in the book, too. Wane'er the ol' boy heered summat good like that he made a note of it so's not to disremember.

"Nat'rally thar's a sight o' things bin writ that hain't never occurred. Like ol' Uncle Durham uster say that every time a story crossed water it doubled itself.

"Did you-uns ever hear o' Phil Morris's defeat? That's a true un. Phil, like the rest o' us, was in a kinda o' mixed-up business. Hit'd be hard to say what kinda business it'd be with one thing an' another an' nothin' reg'lar.

"Waal, we was up in the woods and thar was snow on the ground and the country 'most friz up. We lit a fire and Phil sits him down and offs with his boots to kinda rest up his feet like.

"Waal, durin' the night one of them boots gets pushed into the fire and burned up. An' in the mornin' Phil sent up a great hollerin', and had to make him moccasins out of his leggins and walk back sixteen miles in 'em. And ever since they have called that place Phil Morris's defeat."

A rending explosion of dynamite on the new road shook the town, and there was a short brushing of wind in the trees and the tossing up of a few birds.

"That's the deefeninest n'ise," said the man. "Muster bin like that in France. Was you-uns ever in France? Uh huh. French is heathians."

"It's hot in the sun," I said.

"Waal now, I'll tell ye, I hain't bin out in the sun yet today. Reckon I'll be broguin' round a bit."

And he backed obliquely down the stairs, brown boot first.

[1925]

Design by David Bullen
Typeset in Mergenthaler Granjon
with Bulmer display
by Wilsted & Taylor
Printed by Maple-Vail
on acid-free paper